D0948349

THE FIRM DIVIDED

The Firm Divided

MANAGER–SHAREHOLDER CONFLICT AND THE FIGHT
FOR CONTROL OF THE MODERN CORPORATION

Graeme Guthrie

OXFORD
UNIVERSITY PRESS

OXFORD
UNIVERSITY PRESS

Oxford University Press is a department of the University of Oxford. It furthers
the University's objective of excellence in research, scholarship, and education
by publishing worldwide. Oxford is a registered trade mark of Oxford University
Press in the UK and certain other countries.

Published in the United States of America by Oxford University Press
198 Madison Avenue, New York, NY 10016, United States of America.

© Oxford University Press 2017

CIP data is on file at the Library of Congress
ISBN 978–0–19–064118–4

9 8 7 6 5 4 3 2 1

Printed by Sheridan Books, Inc., United States of America

Contents

PART FIVE | THE RULES OF THE GAME MATTER AS WELL

14. Caught in the middle: Reforming the legal and regulatory environment 241

Preface

SHAREHOLDERS AT AMERICA'S best-known firms are revolting. In 2015, shareholders at Macy's wanted the department store's real estate assets sold and the proceeds paid out as a dividend.[1] At Yahoo, they wanted a cash stockpile paid out to shareholders to stop it being spent on more wasteful acquisitions.[2] Dole Foods' former shareholders were saying, "We told you so." A Delaware judge had just ruled that the firm's chief executive officer (CEO) had deliberately driven down the share price so that he could buy the company back from shareholders more cheaply.[3] Shareholders at eBay and FedEx demanded a greater say in their firms' affairs.[4] At Ford and Google, they just wanted their shares to have the same voting rights as those owned by the firms' founders.[5] Shareholders at Starbucks and Target tried to strip the CEO of some of his power.[6] At mattress maker Tempur Sealy, they just wanted him fired.[7]

The surveys of CEO pay that appear in the business press each year add fuel to the fire. In the *Wall Street Journal*'s 2015 survey, the highest paid CEO received $112m; according to the *New York Times*, a different CEO was paid more, $156m; *Bloomberg* gave top prize to someone else, with $285m.[8] Each outlet has its own ranking, which just serves to sow confusion in the minds of shareholders. However, the underlying message sent to shareholders is consistent: CEO pay is high, probably too high, getting higher, and not closely linked to firm performance. At some firms, shareholders appear powerless to do anything about it. The tech firm Oracle is a good example. Every year for four years, more than half of the votes cast at Oracle's annual shareholder meeting rejected the firm's executive compensation policies.[9] The votes were not binding on Oracle's board, so executives got their pay. However, the votes reveal shareholder opposition to the firm's pay practices and their inability to do anything about it.

Shareholders get angry when executives do not seem to have their best interests at heart. They get angrier when they believe executives are being paid excessively and angrier still when they feel powerless to do anything about it. Shareholders' power is limited because they do not appoint the CEO directly. Instead they elect the firm's board of directors, which does have the power to fire the CEO. However, even board power is limited. It does not help that boards are chaired by the firm's CEO at 84% of large corporations.[10] Making matters worse, shareholders are offered the same number of candidates as there are vacancies at most annual board elections—and the candidates are chosen by the board itself! Unsurprisingly, they are reelected almost every time.[11] To many shareholders, CEOs seem untouchable.

If there is one thing that makes shareholders even angrier it is the fact that most of the behavior they dislike is legal. In fact, all of the behavior described in this book is entirely legal. There are no accounting scandals in the pages that follow; there is no insider trading. Instead, there is a collection of individuals operating within the rules and structures that directors, politicians, regulators, and shareholders have put in place.

The ultimate source of shareholder anger is a conflict within the modern corporation. Manager–shareholder conflict has been around for as long as there have been public corporations. Scholars have studied its consequences since the early 1930s, when Adolf Berle and Gardiner Means published *The Modern Corporation and Private Property*.[12] Berle and Means showed how control of the largest U.S. corporations had become separated from their ownership and raised the awkward question of whether corporations were being run for the benefit of owners or managers. This question is at least as relevant now as it was in the early 1930s. Indeed, with corporations growing ever larger and control seeming to be held in fewer hands, the question is even more relevant now.[13]

Financial and legal scholars have spent the decades since Berle and Means published their book investigating corporate governance, which is the term they use to describe the arrangements that are supposed to better align the interests of managers and shareholders. In this book I describe the causes and consequences of manager–shareholder conflict, and the governance arrangements that have evolved in response to this conflict. I do it by telling the stories of some of the firms that make up corporate America and of some of the individuals that make those firms operate in the way they do. Along the way we will follow the antics of a septuagenarian shareholder who traveled the country tormenting CEOs, learn how an activist hedge fund was able to dislodge one CEO in just a few weeks after buying only 1.3% of a firm's shares, and see how a self-made man once described by a U.S. federal judge as a "snake in sheep's clothing" managed to seize control of the world's most valuable sports team.

There are many partial solutions to manager–shareholder conflict, but none of them work perfectly. In fact, even when they are all combined, the outcome is far from perfect.

However, they all make a contribution to reducing the conflict between a firm's executives and its shareholders. This book works its way through these solutions, one by one. In some solutions, shareholders and directors play a hands-on role, taking responsibility themselves for keeping managers in line. In short, they *monitor*. Shareholders do some monitoring themselves; the rest they leave to a board of directors, which they elect—but everyone is involved in managing the managers. Directors play more of a hands-off role in the next set of solutions. They set a few ground rules that executives must follow, create a few incentives, and then step back and allow events to unfold. That is, they *motivate*. However, directors cannot do everything themselves, so in the third set of solutions they enlist outside parties to do some of the monitoring and motivating on their behalf. They *delegate*. These outsiders have their own selfish reasons for getting involved, but their presence can still benefit shareholders. As a last resort, and the last time that shareholders are even indirectly involved in the game, shareholders can *sell*, or threaten to sell, their shares to another firm. Selling is the ultimate hands-off policy. All of these approaches to corporate governance occur in a world of rules and regulations. That is why there is a final solution to manager–shareholder conflict, of which shareholders are entirely passive beneficiaries: the fight to change the *rules of the game*. These are the key steps to effective corporate governance: monitor, motivate, delegate, sell. The rules of the game matter as well.

We start our journey at the epicenter of manager–shareholder conflict, the annual shareholders' meeting where executives and shareholders eyeball each other. Each new solution to manager–shareholder conflict takes us slightly further afield, first to the boardroom, where directors are supposed to work on shareholders' behalf, doing some eyeballing of their own, and then to the executive labor markets, where executives are matched with firms. Our next steps take us further away still, to the capital markets where those firms try to raise the funds they need to survive and prosper, and then to the market for corporate control that puts fear into executives' hearts. We will finish our journey in Washington, DC, in congressional committee rooms and at hearings of the Securities and Exchange Commission (SEC). It is about as far away from the annual shareholders' meeting as possible, but decisions made in Washington profoundly influence what happens at shareholder meetings across the country.

Before we begin, a note about the role of economics. This is a book about corporations and what economists think about how they are run. Economists look at individuals operating within a set of rules and try to understand the behavior they observe. They try to understand what drives that behavior and to predict the behavioral changes that would occur if the rules were changed. Mainstream economists do this by assuming that, at every turn, individuals act in ways that advance their own best interests. That is the economic framework adopted in this book. We try to understand individuals' decisions by imagining what they would do if they were interested only in looking after number one. It is not an assertion of what motivates the particular individuals we will meet in these pages. It is simply the tool that economists use to try to understand the world. We are going to start by using that tool to try to understand why most shareholders sit back and take no part in a firm's affairs: we are going to start at the annual shareholders' meeting.

1   Monitor

I have quite a bit of influence. Don't ever underestimate Evelyn Y. Davis.[1]

EVELYN Y. DAVIS (2007)

1 A gadfly in the ointment
THE CONSEQUENCES OF SEPARATING OWNERSHIP AND CONTROL

THE ANNUAL SHAREHOLDERS' meeting should be the showpiece of shareholder democracy. It is where shareholders hold executives to account and where the big decisions are made. It is where the weighty issues are discussed, as well as some less weighty ones. Sometimes events are just plain bizarre. That is usually the case when Evelyn Y. Davis, just 5'1" tall and with the thickest of thick Dutch accents, is in attendance. Perhaps the lowlight in a career spanning decades was her challenge to the chairman of a medical-equipment manufacturer about the performance of his firm's thermometers. Why, she demanded to know, was the oral thermometer she had purchased so inaccurate when the rectal one worked fine? The chairman was nonplussed, but a quick-thinking executive came to his rescue: "Well, Mrs. Davis, I can understand why you would get an accurate reading with a thermometer used rectally. But, unfortunately, for a thermometer used orally to register properly, one must be able to keep one's mouth shut." It brought the house down.[2]

A handful of shareholders dominate annual meetings. Whether it is a craving for the limelight or possession of an axe to grind, they are the ones who take center stage. They bring with them a mixed bag of inaccurate thermometers, out-of-control egos, and (sometimes) serious proposals to keep managers in line. In short, they are like Davis, who dominated annual shareholders' meetings for five decades. Some things changed over that time, her clothes mainly. In the early 1970s she wore a bathing suit to a General Motors meeting and a hard hat and riding britches to an AT&T meeting.[3] By the mid-2000s, the outlandish clothes had been replaced by designer suits, but Davis made sure they were still the center of attention. She quizzed a succession of Federated Department Stores

CEOs to see whether they could identify the designer of the clothes she was wearing (they could), informed her fellow Fannie Mae shareholders one year that she never paid retail for new clothes, and told Morgan Stanley shareholders that, although she had once been to Walmart, "I will never set foot in there again."[4] Remember, this is supposed to be the showpiece of shareholder democracy.

In many ways, 2005 was like any other year in Davis's five-decade-long career. The 75-year-old was fighting with other shareholders at the Morgan Stanley meeting: "You're just a local person. I am the nationally known queen of the corporate jungle."[5] She was attacking female executives at the Bristol-Myers Squibb meeting: "[H]er only motivation is just personal jealousy of me, because I am a famous and glamorous woman unlike herself."[6] And she was flirting with the CEO at Delta Air Lines' meeting: "Jerry, you don't need to re-attract me, you've always attracted me."[7] However, annoying though they may be, grandstanders like Davis are not all bad news for shareholders. Alongside the nonsense is a consistent challenge to firms' management. In 2005 alone, Davis sponsored proposals that were put to the vote at 41 firms. Thanks to that "queen of the corporate jungle," Morgan Stanley shareholders were able to vote on whether the board of directors would have to stand for reelection every year, or continue the past practice of having directors serve staggered three-year terms; Bristol-Myers Squibb shareholders were able to vote on whether or not the firm should have to disclose its political donations; and Delta Air Lines shareholders were able to vote on the rules the firm used to elect directors each year.[8] Such shareholder votes are not usually binding on firms' management, but Davis's efforts ensured that shareholders had a say.

Why do the vast majority of shareholders sit back and leave the likes of Davis to hog the limelight? Anyone who has seen Davis in action can testify to the danger associated with trying to wrest control away from her. However, even if she were not present, few shareholders would step up to the microphone. The explanation for why shareholders are ordinarily so passive can ultimately be found in the way that modern corporations separate ownership and control.

Benefits of separation

Typical modern corporations are so large that few individual investors can afford to own an entire firm themselves. For example, the shares of each of the firms targeted by Davis in 2005 were worth $70b on average at the time of their annual meetings.[9] Investors pool their funds and jointly share ownership of each firm. When a firm is set up, they jointly contribute the funds it needs to operate. Once the firm is established they jointly receive some of the firm's profits in the form of dividends and jointly sacrifice the rest of the firm's profits so that it may continue to invest and grow.

Shares in these firms are traded on organized stock exchanges, so that shareholders who do not want to own a part of a firm can sell their stake to investors who do want to, all without disrupting the firm's operations. As well as allocating the ownership of firms across individuals, stock markets allocate the risks associated with this ownership. Some investors will choose to invest all their money in a single firm. They may opt for the pharmaceutical sector and hold all their savings in Bristol-Myers Squibb shares, or favor the airline sector and put all their savings in Delta shares; some may prefer the financial services sector and pour their money into Morgan Stanley. In any given year, they may do very well or very badly. Other investors—the sensible ones—will spread their savings over a large number of different firms in different industries. All of those individual investors can choose portfolios that contain some Bristol-Myers Squibb shares, some Delta shares, and some in Morgan Stanley. In any given year, some companies will do well and some will do poorly, but the winners and losers average out to some extent, so that the risk of each investor's portfolio will be reduced. However, there are many industries, and many firms, so for investors to hold diversified portfolios they have to spread their savings quite thinly. The result is what we see at the firms in Davis's portfolio: a very large number of individual shareholders, each owning a very small fraction of the firm.

With such a large number of owners, it is impractical for shareholders to make the day-to-day decisions needed to run a modern corporation. Instead, they hire a CEO to focus solely on running the firm. The owners bring the capital needed to finance the firm's operations. The CEO brings his—or hers, but even now a large firm's CEO is most likely to be male—expertise in the industry to the task of controlling those operations.[10] CEOs are usually much wealthier than their shareholders, but not usually so rich that they can afford to own a large stake of their firms themselves. At the firms targeted by Davis in 2005, the CEOs owned just 0.2% of their firms' shares on average. The rest of the senior executives owned a combined stake of 0.2% on average, and the non-executive directors—that is, people on the firms' boards of directors who were not employees—owned a combined stake of 0.3%. The other shareholders owned the remaining 99.3%.[11] Such low levels of managerial ownership are typical at U.S. corporations.[12]

Matching managers and firms

The result of investors' desire to hold diversified portfolios and executives' limited wealth is the separation of ownership and control that we see at a typical modern corporation. Shareholders own most of the firm, but have little control. Executives have control of the firm, but have relatively low ownership. If it all works well, shareholders benefit from the executives' skills and executives benefit from the shareholders' capital. However, it works well only if executives have the attributes and skills that benefit shareholders.

Executives typically have attributes that make them well suited to managing firms. For example, CEOs are typically more optimistic and risk-tolerant than the rest of the population.[13] They also spend the early part of their careers acquiring the general management skills needed to run firms. For example, the Morgan Stanley CEO who sparred with Davis in 2005 started his career with an MBA and a job as a management consultant. Bristol-Myers Squibb's CEO that year had used his MBA to land a marketing job at General Foods.[14] Successful firms tend to be led by CEOs with better general management ability, with execution skills being more important than softer communication and interpersonal skills.[15] Even though general management ability is becoming increasingly important, industry experience is still valuable.[16] For example, Delta Air Lines' CEO had previously headed firms in the transport sector. Bristol-Myers Squibb's CEO worked for the firm for 13 years before getting the top job. Morgan Stanley's CEO had launched the Discover credit card for Dean Witter 20 years earlier and had been CEO of the firm, in its various manifestations, ever since.[17]

A firm's shareholders benefit most if the CEO has attributes that best meet the firm's needs—and budget.[18] That is possibly why firms that undertake more mergers and acquisitions tend to employ CEOs who are more risk-tolerant.[19] Those that adopt relatively conservative policies (including low levels of investment and low debt) are more likely to employ CEOs with military experience.[20] On the other hand, firms that have high debt levels tend to employ CEOs with backgrounds in accounting or finance, greater tolerance of risk, and more personal debt.[21] Firms that invest more in innovation tend to employ overconfident CEOs.[22]

Competition in the executive labor market matches the best CEOs to the firms where they can add the most value. Of course, all firms would like to employ the best CEO, but it is the firms where a good CEO can add the most value that can afford to hire the best CEOs. The magic of a competitive market, if it works properly, results in a match between managers and firms that leaves each firm unwilling to change its manager.[23] Even if a firm could attract a more skilled CEO than its current one, the resulting increase in the firm's value would not be large enough to justify the increase in CEO pay needed to snatch such a CEO away from another firm. Likewise, no firm is willing to incur the loss of value that would result from cutting pay and hiring a less able CEO.

The actions CEOs take and the policies they adopt can affect an entire firm, which explains why a good CEO can usually add more value to a big firm than to an otherwise similar small firm. This is why the highest paid CEOs tend to be the ones managing the largest firms: large firms can afford to hire the best, and most expensive, CEOs because it is at these firms that the CEOs can add the most value. It is also why small differences in talent can be associated with large differences in pay: a slightly better CEO gets to apply his skills at a larger—sometimes a much larger—firm.[24]

A well-oiled machine: Governance in principle

The modern corporation is a hive of activity, much of it revolving around the many decisions made throughout the organization. How much should a firm spend on its

CEO's pet project? Should a firm sell its assets to a more successful rival or continue to soldier on alone? Should the firm bank its profits for a rainy day, pay them out to shareholders as dividends, or use them to pay off some of its debt? (And that is just the next three chapters.) Ultimately what matters to shareholders is the firm's bottom line, but the size of the number in that bottom line—and whether it is printed in black or red ink—depends on the decisions made throughout the firm.

It is impractical for the firm's joint owners to make all of the firm's decisions. The cost of coordinating such decision-making could be substantial even in a small partnership. However, there can be millions of individual owners of a corporation with its shares traded on a major stock exchange, rendering collective decision-making impossible. That is why corporations typically have the hierarchical structure shown in Figure 1.1. Shareholders sit on top, being actively involved only at the annual meetings, when they vote on the biggest decisions and elect the board of directors. Shareholders delegate responsibility for the rest of the firm's decisions to the board of directors, whose performance they monitor and consider when they decide whether to reelect board members at future annual meetings.

The board meets every month or so and is responsible for the decisions delegated to it by shareholders. It typically contains a mix of current and retired executives from other firms, often with experience in relevant industries, as well as accounting and legal professionals. On average, the boards of large U.S. corporations have 2.2 directors who are employees of the firm and 8.1 outsiders, but these averages mask substantial variation. Firms that are complex, large, old, or that have an old CEO tend to have large boards. Large firms and old firms tend to have boards with a small percentage of directors who are employees, whereas firms with old CEOs tend to have a high percentage of inside directors.[25] Eighty-four percent of boards are chaired by the firm's CEO, 36% have a majority of directors who sit on the boards of two or more other firms, 11% of directors are at least 70 years of age, and 42% have family, financial, or social ties to the CEO.[26]

Directors make only the most important decisions themselves and delegate the rest to a CEO who the board itself appoints. The board monitors the CEO's performance relating to the delegated tasks and also plays an advisory role. The process of delegation does not

FIGURE 1.1 Corporate governance structure

stop there. The CEO is ultimately responsible for making the decisions delegated by the board, but will make only some of these decisions himself and delegate the rest to senior managers who he appoints. Senior managers delegate to middle managers, who delegate to junior managers, and on it goes.

Many corporations look like this, but other forms occur as well. In some corporations the CEO holds a much larger ownership stake. For example, the CEOs of two of the 45 firms targeted by Davis in 2005 owned 10% stakes.[27] When managers own large numbers of shares, they start to look like shareholders, so that the separation between ownership and control is relatively small. Some corporations have highly concentrated ownership. There may still be many small shareholders, but these firms also have some large shareholders, so large that they can use their influence to obtain a seat around the boardroom table. If we broaden the notion of management to include directors alongside the CEO, then once more the separation of ownership and control is relatively small.

Most firms—as well as our well-oiled machine above—are structured according to the principle that one share gets one vote. Thus, if an individual wants to exert some degree of control over a firm's decision-making—which requires holding a large number of votes—then that individual needs to acquire a large number of shares. However, some firms divide ownership up into more than one class of share, with all shares receiving equal proportions of the firm's dividends but some shares giving their owners more votes than others. For example, two of Davis's targets, Ford and Comcast, had dual-class ownership structures. The owners of the super shares at Ford owned 3.9% of the firm but controlled 40% of the votes. At Comcast, the owners of a 0.4% stake controlled 33% of the votes.[28]

Using multiple classes of shares like this allows founders to retain control even after they start selling shares to the general public. This often results in families controlling the firms, with multiple members of the same family being involved as shareholders or executives. In many cases, this control passes from one generation to the next. At Ford, the founder's great-grandson was CEO in 2005; at Comcast, the CEO was the founder's son.[29] Individual shareholders like Davis can invest in family firms that have shares traded on public exchanges, but they have to accept that the family will retain control.

All of the firms we have seen so far have shares traded on public stock exchanges, but there are other corporations with shares so tightly held by their owners that they are not traded on stock exchanges. You or I (or Davis) might want to own a small stake in these firms, but ownership is by invitation only. These are the so-called private equity firms. They typically borrow much more than similar firms that trade their shares on public share markets, which makes it easier to find a small number of investors wealthy enough to put up the rest of the funds needed to carry out business. Thus, private equity firms tend to have a small number of shareholders, each owning a very large number of shares and having a seat on the board of directors, in contrast to our well-oiled machine, which is owned by a large number of shareholders who each own relatively few shares and will never get anywhere near the company boardroom.

However, these various corporate forms all have one thing in common: they employ a manager and delegate much of the running of the firm to that individual. Managers of different types of firm will behave differently, but—at least to some extent—these managers all want much the same thing. The differences in behavior are largely due to the different corporate environments that they operate in.

What can shareholders do?

The main opportunity for shareholders with small ownership stakes to directly influence management's behavior occurs at a firm's annual meeting. The board's chairman, and often some of the firm's senior executives, will make speeches. Shareholders will elect a new board of directors and be given an opportunity to ask questions of the firm's management. They will also vote on proposals offered by either the firm's board or its shareholders. A few shareholders will go to the meeting and vote in person, but the vast majority will vote electronically or by mailing in a proxy card, which instructs the firm how to vote on their behalf. Few shareholders attend these meetings. Of those who do, some go to participate in shareholder democracy, some for the experience, some for the food and gift packs, some to meet a celebrity-CEO, and some to make a nuisance of themselves.

Davis may have been a nuisance, but she also made a more substantive contribution to most of the meetings she attended by sponsoring proposals that were put to the vote. Any shareholder whose stake in the firm was worth at least $2,000 throughout the year prior to the meeting can initiate a proposal of their own, and these proposals appear in the proxy statements sent out to all shareholders before the meeting.[30] Few shareholders do so, but those who do make up for the rest: Davis, active since the early 1960s, sponsored proposals at approximately 40 firms each year.[31]

Shareholder proposals are not allowed to relate to a firm's day-to-day business operations. Firms have used this to restrict the scope of proposals presented at annual meetings, even though the proposals that are allowed are not binding on the firm. Like most proposals sponsored by individual shareholders, Davis's 2005 proposals attempted to weaken the firms' defenses against hostile takeovers, change the firms' voting rules, and limit executive compensation.[32]

Davis liked to claim that she was influential, but how influential was she? After one meeting she boasted to a reporter, "I run the meeting. You know that, don't you?"[33] She was right; she dominated the annual meetings she attended. However, beyond those set pieces her influence was limited. On average, her proposals in the late 1980s and early 1990s attracted support from just 16% of the votes cast. Even in one of her most successful years, 2005, they attracted just 25% of the votes cast. Only 15% of those proposals won majority support and just half of the successful ones were adopted by firms.[34]

Proposals sponsored by other individual shareholders were not much more successful than Davis's. Just 2.9% of such proposals in the late 1980s attracted majority support and boards ignored most of the proposals that did pass.[35] Voting support has increased over the years: 8.3% of proposals sponsored by individuals in the late 1990s won majority support, and 32% in the early 2000s. This increased support for shareholder proposals, combined with greater pressure on boards to be more responsive to shareholders' demands, has resulted in more of the successful proposals being implemented by firms: just 10% of successful proposals in the late 1990s were implemented, rising to 33% in the early 2000s.[36]

What made 2005 so special for Davis, and so unusual, was that several firms set about implementing one particular proposal that had won support the previous year. Shareholders at seven firms in 2004 had voted in favor of Davis's proposal to force all directors to seek reelection each year, rather than have staggered three-year terms. Six of those firms had got the message and put the change to a binding vote of their shareholders in 2005. Every one passed, allowing Davis to run an extended victory lap. However, it had been a long time coming. For example, she had presented the same proposal to one of the firms each year since 1988, winning a majority of the votes cast each year since 2000, before the board finally adopted the proposal as its own. Shareholders of another firm had voted on the proposal each year since 1991. Their counterparts at a third firm had voted in favor of the change in each of the three previous years before the board adopted the proposed change.[37] Why did these boards suddenly change their minds in 2005? It is difficult to believe that Davis's persistence was instrumental in the change. A more likely explanation is that the boards were succumbing to peer pressure as an increasing number of firms abandoned staggered board elections in favor of the annual elections advocated by Davis. Still, it was shareholders like Davis who had kept the issue on annual meetings' agendas for so long.

What *will* shareholders do?

Perhaps the most startling thing is that shareholders are so passive. Shareholders at only 27 of the 41 firms targeted by Davis in 2005 sponsored proposals related to how firms were managed; on average, there were just 1.7 such proposals voted on at each annual meeting, excluding the ones sponsored by Davis.[38]

To see why shareholders are so disengaged, we need to put ourselves in the shoes of a shareholder who is considering sponsoring a proposal at a firm's forthcoming annual meeting. First we need to familiarize ourselves with the process of getting a proposal before the annual meeting. We have seen the proposals in the proxy statements that have been sent to us in the past, we might even have heard about some of the activists, so we know what is possible. We need to decide exactly what we want in our proposal, and then write a supporting statement no longer than 500 words and send it to the firm.[39] Lastly, we need to attend the annual meeting or the proposal will not be put to the vote. Formulating the proposal is probably the most costly step, because we need to invest some time in following management's actions and identifying courses of action that we think would improve the way the firm is run. If we go ahead and sponsor a proposal then we, and we alone, bear these costs. If someone else sponsors it, they bear the costs. The benefits, however, are shared by all shareholders regardless of who put the proposal on the meeting's agenda. If the proposal wins majority support, is adopted by the firm's management, and makes the firm more valuable, then the value of *all* shares will increase equally, even those owned by shareholders who did not incur any of the costs.

The fact that individual shareholders bear the cost of their monitoring activities but have to share any benefits they create means not enough monitoring takes place. To help understand the problem, suppose we owned the same portfolio as Davis. The average firm in her portfolio was worth $70b and the average value of her stake in a firm was $22,000.[40] Suppose that if our proposal was adopted, that average firm's value would increase by 1%. That is an increase in the value of the firm of $700m, but our portfolio would have increased in value by only $220. If the cost to us of sponsoring the proposal was more than $220 then we should not do it: the benefit *to us* of sponsoring the proposal would be less than the cost of doing so.[41] We should not sponsor the proposal, even though doing so would increase the firm's value by $700m. Even if it would cost us just $221 to increase the value of the firm by $700m, we should not do it. We cannot shift even a dollar of that cost onto the other shareholders, and we cannot increase our share of the gains, so we do not sponsor the proposal. It is this arithmetic that creates a lot of lost opportunities for individual shareholders to increase a firm's value.

Every other shareholder makes the same calculation. Proposals have to be submitted at least four months before the firm is scheduled to send out its proxy statement, so individual shareholders must decide whether or not to submit a proposal without knowing what other shareholders have decided.[42] Economists analyze situations like this by assuming that each shareholder randomly decides whether or not to submit a proposal.[43] Because each individual shareholder's decision is random, the overall outcome is random as well. Sometimes there will be no proposals sponsored, other times there will be several, but there will be too few proposals sponsored overall. The problem would be less severe if the shareholders who do act could somehow pass some of the costs of acting onto those who do not act, or if they could keep the lion's share of the gains for themselves. However, they cannot share the costs and they must share the benefits. The result is that some actions that would benefit shareholders collectively do not take place because they do not benefit shareholders individually. Economists call this the free-rider problem. It gets its name from the notion that individual shareholders sit back in order to get a free ride from other shareholders—and while everyone is sitting back, nothing gets done.

The most disappointing aspect of all of this is that the problem becomes worse—that is, the probability that nobody submits a proposal becomes larger—the more people own shares in a firm.[44] For the theoretical ideal ownership structure, where firms are owned by large numbers of small shareholders, there will be little monitoring of management by shareholders. Unless something else disciplines managers' behavior, they will have a free hand to build empires, consume perks, hire family members, negotiate excessive compensation packages for themselves, or just enjoy a quiet life.

Gadflies

Davis and the other members of the band of shareholders moving from one annual meeting to the next, creating havoc for chairmen and drawing the ire of other shareholders, have attracted the label "gadfly investors." Gadflies are insects that bite or annoy livestock. Smaller and weaker than the livestock that they irritate, they occasionally provoke a disproportionate response due to sheer persistence—much like Evelyn Davis did in 1996 when a red-faced Ted Turner threatened to personally evict her from Turner Broadcasting's annual meeting.[45]

The life of a gadfly has never been easy. Davis was thrown out of the 1965 Consolidated Edison Co. meeting—"the women literally threw me on the sidewalk"—action that drew loud applause from many shareholders there that day.[46] At the 1977 meeting of Eastern Airlines, Davis so incensed a fellow shareholder that he lunged at her, causing her to fall against a metal flowerpot and cut her ear. (Davis sued Eastern, settling out of court for $7,500 in damages.)[47] Eastern should have followed the example of IBM, which provided Davis with a bodyguard in 1963 to protect her from fellow shareholders, one of whom threatened to throw her out of the meeting.[48]

Typical shareholders compare the cost of monitoring management with the effect monitoring will have on the value of their own portfolio, and decide to stay on the sidelines. Gadflies compare the same costs and benefits and then add in the personal benefits, the ones they do not have to share with other shareholders. These benefits include the satisfaction they derive from calling the powerful to account, as well as the publicity. Do not underestimate the role of publicity. It was Davis who spent time at the 1984 meeting of the Washington Post Co. criticizing the newspaper's coverage of other firms' annual meetings—because she was not named in the stories.[49] The strongest motivation for many gadflies is, as Davis admitted, the power that their time in front of the microphone brings them: "The power—that's really what life is all about. It's all how you use it. It's better than being a nonentity. I couldn't stand being a nonentity."[50]

As one CEO said, Davis's "most lethal weapon is the fact that she does not care what anyone else thinks of her, so she's prepared to be rude, to interrupt, to be domineering and to do essentially whatever it takes to command attention."[51] That underlying threat of creating bedlam at an annual meeting generated other benefits for Davis. CEOs would return her phone calls; some would contact her themselves prior to their firm's annual meeting.[52] Ford's CEO went so far as to personally deliver the new car she had purchased, and then issued a press release to mark the occasion.[53] Many CEOs ensured that their firms subscribed to Davis's annual newsletter, *Highlights and Lowlights*. As well as colorful accounts of the year's shareholder meetings, it offered the busy executive helpful advice:

"When in Europe there are many cities with VERY similar names, sometimes in the SAME country. Be sure YOU go to the one you intend to go to."[54] There was a letters to the editor section as well: "Dear Evelyn: We missed YOU at OUR annual meeting," signed "SEVERAL CEO'S!!!."[55] Davis charged $600 an issue for material like this and encouraged CEOs to buy multiple copies. Many paid her $5,000 or more annually for the benefit of her wisdom.[56] Some complained (usually anonymously) that they were being blackmailed into their subscriptions by the threat of disruptions to their annual meetings, but they paid up all the same.[57] It is benefits like these, which do not have to be shared with other shareholders, that motivate gadflies to act while other shareholders sit back.

This is the point in our journey where shareholders take their hands off the wheel and hand responsibility for monitoring management over to a board of directors. The board's job is to monitor and advise the CEO and make the firm's big, strategic decisions, putting shareholders' interests first the whole time. Some shareholders, such as Davis, hang around as back-seat drivers, heckling directors and management indiscriminately, but with little effect. The free-rider problem means that the rest, who make up the vast majority of a firm's shareholders, quickly fade into the distance.

If the court was a stockholder of Occidental, it might vote for new directors;
if it was on the board, it might vote for new management ... [b]ut its options
are limited ... to applying [the] law ...[1]
JUDGE MAURICE HARTNETT (1990)

2 Whose side are you on?
THE ROLE OF THE BOARD OF DIRECTORS

WHEN THE LOS ANGELES-BASED oil firm Occidental Petroleum sent out its proxy
statement to shareholders in March 2010, all the usual information was there. It contained
the shareholder proposals to be voted on at the upcoming annual meeting, the list of
nominees for the forthcoming board elections, and information about the CEO's pay.
Shareholders read that the board had approved yet another outsized pay package for the
CEO, Ray Irani. He had been paid $530m during the previous decade and there was no
sign of this changing anytime soon.[2] Although Irani was past the board's compulsory
retirement age of 75, the board did not appear to be working very hard on a succession
plan.[3] Indeed, during the year it had granted him an incentive award that would pay out
based on the firm's performance over the next four years.[4] Irani was going nowhere. And
it was not just the CEO who was being paid generously: the proxy statement revealed that
directors received $450,000 each, on average, for their work the year before.[5]

Oxy's shareholders, especially the ones with long memories, must have been concerned, because Oxy had a history of boards allowing the firm's CEO to run riot. Irani's
predecessor as CEO, Armand Hammer, had been in charge of the firm for 33 years. For
much of that time, Hammer seemed to use Oxy as a personal expense account to fund
his hobbies. That is how Oxy acquired a stake in the firm that made "Arm & Hammer"
baking soda.[6] (Say it quickly.) It set up a film subsidiary, Armand Hammer Productions,
that made films showing Hammer in a favorable light.[7] And it established an Arabian
horse subsidiary, Oxy Arabians, whose chief buyer seems to have been Hammer himself.[8]
Oxy's directors had allowed all of this to happen.

At the time shareholders were absorbing the information in Oxy's proxy statement, Irani seemed as unpopular as Hammer had been two decades earlier. Some shareholders alleged that the board charged with monitoring Irani was as ineffective as the one that had failed to control Hammer. A few of the more vocal shareholders complained about the apparent lack of a succession plan and called for an "orderly transition to the next CEO."[9] They demanded that the board enforce the retirement-age rule that would rid the firm of Irani.[10] However, the free-rider problem afflicting shareholders meant that it was up to the board to do something about it. Unfortunately for shareholders who wanted a change, it would take three more years before Irani was finally ejected from Oxy's headquarters.

A framework for analyzing board–CEO interactions

A firm's board of directors has three main roles: making decisions delegated to it by shareholders, advising the CEO, and monitoring the CEO's performance. In each of these roles, the board interacts with the CEO. Economists interpret these interactions as so-called bargaining games. Sometimes the bargaining is explicit, as when Oxy's board negotiated with representatives of Hammer's favorite charity over the size of Oxy's donation. Years later, explicit bargaining was involved when the board negotiated the tortuous departure of Hammer's replacement, Irani, from the CEO's suite. Other times the bargaining is implicit, such as when one side makes a decision subject to a tacit understanding about the options that can be chosen. This happened at Oxy when membership of Oxy's board evolved during Irani's tenure as CEO.

Whether the bargaining is explicit or implicit, both sides can be made better off if an agreement is reached, but the details of that agreement will determine how much better off each side will be. In a very simple example of a bargaining game, you and I can have $100 to share amongst ourselves *provided that we both agree* about how to share it. I want as much of the $100 as possible, but so do you. However, if we cannot agree on who gets what, then neither of us gets anything. There are few set rules for deciding the outcome of situations such as this. Whatever arrangement is reached, all participants must agree to it; no participant can impose a solution on any other. However, one side may have more bargaining power than the other, so that the prize need not be allocated equally.[11]

Each party involved in a bargaining game wants as many of the benefits from reaching agreement as possible, but needs to offer enough to the other party to ensure that an agreement is reached. The resulting wide range of allowable outcomes means that if we are to understand the outcome of negotiations then we need to understand the motivations of the negotiating parties and the strengths of their bargaining positions. There is no better place to start than the Hammer Museum in the Westwood neighborhood of Los Angeles.

The Hammer Museum: It's a bargain

Our story begins in 1989, when Armand Hammer was Oxy's CEO. The firm's board was deciding how much of the firm's resources to contribute to a museum about to be built next to Oxy's headquarters, a museum designed to house Hammer's art collection. He contributed nothing to the cost of the new building, the land underneath it, or the museum's running costs. These were paid for by Oxy's shareholders.[12] As for the art collection itself, the magnitude of Hammer's personal generosity is difficult to judge. The charity that owned most of it—the Armand Hammer Foundation—was funded from various sources, including large donations from Oxy.[13] Some pieces that had been exhibited as part of Hammer's personal collection were actually owned by Oxy.[14] One high-profile item, a series of sketches by Leonardo da Vinci, had been publicized as a personal gift from Hammer to the charitable foundation, when the $5m price had actually been paid by Oxy.[15]

Every dollar contributed to the museum project was a dollar that could have been paid to shareholders as dividends, so the board was ultimately deciding how much of shareholders' equity in the firm would be given away. Some would go to the museum, the rest to Oxy's shareholders. Hammer himself would have wanted the donation to be large, but the goals of Oxy's other directors are not quite so obvious. Shareholders would have wanted the smallest possible donation, and in an ideal world this is what directors would have wanted as well. However, two of those directors sat with Hammer on the board of the Armand Hammer Foundation, which was the charitable organization that would contribute much of the art collection to be housed in the proposed museum. They had a duty to get the best deal possible for the charitable foundation when wearing their "foundation hats" and a duty to get the best deal possible for Oxy when wearing their "Oxy hats." Because of this hopeless conflict of interest, they did not participate in the donation decision-making. Six other directors—including Irani—were Oxy employees, and so answerable to Hammer. They also stepped aside due to the obvious conflict of interest their employment status created.

This left eight directors without an obvious conflict of interest, who formed a special committee to make the museum decision. The committee was selected, met on its own, and approved the proposed funding arrangement at one of the regularly scheduled board meetings in 1989. Oxy would construct the new museum building, renovate portions of its own headquarters next door for use by the museum, and construct a parking garage, costing $50m in total. Oxy would lease the new building and parts of its own headquarters to the museum, rent-free, for 30 years. Oxy would pay the property taxes. Oxy would put aside $36m to fund the museum's operations during its initial years. Oxy would grant the museum an option to buy the new building, and Oxy's headquarters, in 30 years for its current value of $55m. Oxy would do all this, but the museum would be named after Hammer![16]

As this example illustrates, almost anything goes in board–CEO bargaining games. When some Oxy shareholders tried to limit the museum donation by taking the firm to court, the judge was critical of Oxy's donation, writing in his decision that "[i]f the court was a stockholder of Occidental, it might vote for new directors; if it was on the board, it might vote for new management, and if it was a member of the special committee, it might vote against the museum project."[17] However, he reluctantly approved a settlement of the case that allowed the donation to proceed, partly because he believed that the so-called business judgment rule would have protected Oxy's directors if the original case had gone to trial.[18]

Directors have a fiduciary duty to shareholders. That duty has two components.[19] The duty of loyalty to the firm's shareholders means directors are legally required to put shareholders' interests ahead of their own personal interests. The duty of care means that, in addition, they have to exercise good judgment and act in a way that a reasonably prudent person would act. As long as the directors on Oxy's special committee had no obvious conflict of interest, they would be deemed to have satisfied their duty of loyalty. As long as they followed a reasonable decision-making process, they would be deemed to have satisfied their duty of care: the courts will not second-guess a board's judgment when it comes to business matters. Shareholders have to prove that directors did not act in good faith, and that is exceedingly hard to do. The lesson is clear: the courts impose few restrictions on the outcome of negotiations involving boards of directors and executives.

How independent are independent directors?

Oxy's board had been careful to delegate the donation decision to a committee of directors deemed to have no conflict of interest. Most firms will do this when faced with controversial decisions. However, the extent to which such committees are independent of the CEO is often called into question. For example, in the legal challenges that followed the decision to approve the museum project, disgruntled shareholders complained that two members of the special committee had ongoing business ties with Oxy that created a potential conflict of interest. These directors were associated with a law firm that was subsequently reported to earn a third of its revenue from Oxy and, according to one report on the firm's prospects, "the firm's heavy reliance on [Oxy] has some people edgy."[20] One of the directors was Hammer's lawyer when he faced federal prosecution in the 1970s for making illegal campaign contributions to President Richard Nixon; the other had written in support of Hammer during the trial, urging leniency.[21] Questions were also raised concerning the independence of two directors who had past business relationships with Oxy. One, the special committee's chairman, was a former U.S. senator who had been employed by Oxy shortly after losing a reelection bid and who went on to work as a senior executive for 11 years.[22] The other had a history of doing deals with Hammer, first in 1966 when he sold the firm he founded to Oxy and again in 1982 when he was on the board of another firm acquired by Oxy.[23]

The four remaining directors on the special committee all had strong social ties with Hammer. One had been described as a "long-term friend" in 1980, and another represented a Saudi investor described as having a "longstanding friendship" with Hammer.[24] Of another director, Hammer had once said "I was deeply touched when he once told me he wished he was my son."[25] Even a casual glance at the society pages of the *Los Angeles Times* during the 1980s reveals the social ties between Hammer and the tenth director.[26]

In addition to these specific concerns, there was a general feeling that the special committee was too closely linked to Hammer to be truly independent. On average, members of the special committee had sat on Oxy's board for nine years, long enough to form a close relationship with Hammer. Three members of the special committee sat on the board of the Armand Hammer United World College of the American West (a college in New Mexico that was funded mainly by Oxy and various Hammer charities). Four of the "conflicted" Oxy directors, including Hammer himself, also sat on the college board.[27] It was all very cosy.

If the two sides could reach an agreement, then Hammer would get the benefit of seeing his museum legacy realized in his lifetime and the special committee would get to avoid all of the costs of a breakdown in their personal and professional relationship with Hammer. Do not underestimate those costs: Hammer had removed uncooperative directors from Oxy's board in the past, so directors must have wondered if there was a risk they would lose their own jobs if a deal with the foundation was not made.[28] The source of the gains from reaching agreement—called the surplus—is the value that Hammer attached to seeing the museum completed and the value the special committee attached to not falling out with Hammer. The size of the donation that the two parties agreed to determined how much of this surplus was allocated to Hammer and how much to directors. The bigger the donation, the grander the museum, and the happier Hammer would be. Of course, the bigger the donation, the greater the cost to shareholders, and the unhappier directors would (or should) be.

Sources of bargaining power

Exactly how the surplus from reaching agreement is divided up in a bargaining game depends on the two sides' bargaining power. The special committee of Oxy's directors might have been able to reduce the firm's contribution to the museum if it had gone back to Hammer with a counteroffer. For example, it might have suggested building a smaller museum, or perhaps funding only a fraction of the one proposed. However, this benefit would have been offset by some costs, even if an agreement was eventually reached. More meetings would be required to formulate the counter proposal and directors would have to deal with a disappointed Hammer. The committee had to weigh these costs against the benefits to shareholders from prolonging negotiations. Hammer faced a similar problem. At any point during the negotiations, he could have accepted the committee's offer or made a counteroffer of his own. At each such point, he had to weigh his costs from prolonging negotiations against the benefits he might receive.

With each side considering its own tradeoff, the side with the higher cost of continuing to bargain was in the weaker position. It had less bargaining power, and both sides knew it. The other side could use this to its advantage, asking for a relatively large share of the surplus—and getting it, so keen was the high-cost side to avoid prolonged negotiations. Unfortunately for Oxy's shareholders, the special committee would have found prolonged bargaining especially costly. Three of its eight members were aged in their 80s; another three were in their 70s. When disgruntled shareholders subsequently took Oxy to court, it emerged that the special committee's chairman had found the going so difficult that he did not seem to understand who would own the museum, the deal's tax consequences, or even the approximate value of the collection it would contain.[29] The representatives from the Hammer foundation could use this to their advantage by asking for a relatively large donation.

Many other factors contribute to a high cost of continuing bargaining. Directors who are busy—perhaps they sit on boards at many firms or are themselves CEOs at other firms—find prolonged negotiations costly. Anyone who has served on a committee will know how much more effort can be required to reach decisions when the committee grows in size. If directors have strong ties to the CEO then the longer negotiations last, the greater the cost to directors. Family ties might be strained, financial ties might be jeopardized. All these factors—busy directors, large boards, and strong ties to the CEO—weaken a board's bargaining position and help explain the generosity of Oxy's donation to Hammer's museum project.

Changing the guard

It is difficult to believe that the museum deal was a good one for Oxy's shareholders. What were directors thinking? The bargaining-game framework suggests one explanation: they agreed to it because they were too close to the CEO. However, this immediately generates another question: How is it possible for boards—which are supposed to represent shareholders' interests and are elected by the shareholders themselves—to become so close to CEOs? The bargaining-game framework has an explanation for that as well.[30] To see what it is, we take a look at how Oxy's board evolved after Hammer's death.

Hammer died two weeks after the museum opened in November 1990. While shareholders celebrated—the announcement of his death was associated with a 9.6% increase in Oxy's share price—his position as CEO was filled by Ray Irani.[31] Within a few weeks of Hammer's death, Irani had sold Oxy's stake in the Arm & Hammer manufacturer.[32] By the end of the year, Oxy had written off its investments in its film subsidiary and its

Arabian horse breeding business.[33] In the future, Oxy would concentrate on its chemicals and energy businesses. It largely left the risk associated with exploring for new oil and gas reserves to its competitors and focused instead on squeezing more out of mature fields. Oxy sold some of its existing fields and acquired others that, after adopting state-of-the-art technologies, were cheaper to operate.[34]

It was not just Oxy's business operations that were shaken up. Its board was rejuvenated as well. During Irani's first decade as CEO, most of the measures of board bargaining power moved in shareholders' favor. For example, the board became smaller, more independent, younger, and less entrenched. However, many of these trends were reversed in his second decade, when the board became bigger, older, and more entrenched again.[35] And all the time the ties between CEO and board grew stronger: of the 11 outside directors who joined the board prior to the 2010 meeting, at least seven had previously worked alongside Irani in some capacity. One, the ex-president of the Colombian national oil company, worked with him on an oil exploration joint venture in the 1980s.[36] Another, the CEO of an investment bank, had helped Oxy sell its meat-packing firm in the early 1990s.[37] Two had spent several years sitting alongside Irani on the boards of other firms.[38] Another had been chief financial officer at one of those firms.[39] A former Energy Secretary had appointed Irani to his advisory board three years before being invited onto Oxy's board.[40] The seventh had been the managing partner of Oxy's auditors for Irani's first 12 years as CEO.[41] By the time of the 2010 annual meeting, just two independent directors had been on the board since before Irani became CEO.[42]

The fact that so many of the new directors had previously worked with Irani does not mean that they intended to shirk their directorial responsibilities. However, the new directors' biographies do not look like those of candidates that Oxy's shareholders would have chosen themselves if they wanted effective monitors of the CEO. That is not surprising, because shareholders did not get to choose the new directors. Instead, they got to vote for the candidates chosen by the board itself. In practice, the board delegates the task of selecting the slate of candidates to a committee made up of several of the firm's current independent directors.[43]

Existing directors seeking reelection and new candidates seeking to join the board for the first time are elected by shareholders at the annual meeting. The owner of each share can vote "yes" or "no," or abstain from voting, for each candidate. At many public corporations, directors are elected by plurality voting. Under this scheme, if the board is to have ten directors, then the ten candidates with the largest number of "yes" votes are elected. If there are as many candidates as there are vacancies, which is usually the case, then all a candidate needs to be elected is a single "yes" vote (which may be their own!). Other corporations elect their boards by majority voting, especially when the number of candidates equals the number of vacancies. Under majority voting, only those candidates who receive more "yes" votes than "no" votes are elected. This is the system that Oxy uses now, but in 2010 its board was elected by plurality voting—although any candidate who had attracted more "no" votes than "yes" votes would have been elected to the board only if the nominating committee decided to appoint the candidate anyway.[44]

Regardless of whether plurality or majority voting is used, board candidates are almost always elected. For example, 99.8% of the candidates nominated for board seats at the 3,000 largest U.S. corporations in 2011 were proposed by the incumbent directors; 99.9% of them were elected.[45] The key challenge for any budding director is therefore not to get elected, but to get nominated. If a firm's CEO dominates the directors on the nominating committee, then he can exert considerable influence on the board's composition—and, with it, the outcome of future bargaining games involving himself and the board. This is consistent with the empirical evidence that boards tend to be less independent at firms where the CEO has more influence, whether that influence is due to a high CEO ownership stake, the CEO having been in the job for a long time, directors having small ownership stakes, or the firm having strong defenses against hostile takeovers.[46]

The nomination process can itself be interpreted using the bargaining game framework, with a firm's CEO and its nominating committee negotiating over what the board will look like in the future. If one of the current directors is retiring, will the position be left empty (which will, by making the board smaller, increase the board's future bargaining power)? If the two sides agree that the departing director be replaced, will his replacement have close ties to the CEO? Will his replacement be so busy working as a CEO or serving on other firms' boards that he will find it difficult to be an effective monitor? Although the negotiations may focus on specific details such as these, what the two sides are effectively bargaining over is the relative importance that directors will attach to their advisory, decision-making, and monitoring roles in the future. This is the key issue, because the board's monitoring effectiveness will determine how many perks the CEO can consume, how many donations the firm will make to his pet charities, and so much more.

The CEO and the independent directors are again bargaining over how to divide up the firm's resources, but now they are doing so indirectly (by bargaining over the type of board the firm will have) rather than directly (by bargaining over payments to the CEO's pet charity). If the two sides agree to a board that is small and without especially close ties to the CEO, then shareholders will get a larger portion of the surplus from reaching agreement in future bargaining games. If, instead, they agree to a large board dominated by insiders and friends of the CEO, or directors who are busy sitting on multiple boards or being the CEO at their own firm, then shareholders can expect to receive a much smaller portion of that surplus.

This bargaining process offers one explanation for what happened at Oxy during Irani's second decade in charge. Oxy's adoption of new technology to squeeze more oil and gas out of old fields, coupled with booming energy prices, contributed to several years of exceptional stock returns.[47] An investor with $100 to spare at the time of the 1999 annual meeting could have turned it into $282 by investing in Oxy for the next five years, compared to $191 by investing in a portfolio of other firms in the same industry.[48] If the board believed that Irani's ability had contributed to these high returns, then he was in a strong bargaining position. Directors would not want to lose him by driving a hard bargain over the board's structure. Instead they would make sure that any new directors had strong ties to Irani and outside commitments that limited their monitoring ability. And the new directors would not replace any of Oxy's existing—and aging—board. Instead, the boardroom table would be expanded to make room for the new additions. A bigger, older, board, with closer ties to the CEO; that should keep him happy. And that is exactly what happened. Instead of retiring its elderly directors, several of whom were approaching the board's compulsory retirement age of 72, Oxy's board quietly raised the retirement age to 75. The change was hidden in the appendices of the proxy statement sent to shareholders.[49] Who can blame the old timers for hanging on? It was a win–win situation. The CEO won because his future bargaining power was strengthened. The elderly directors won because they got to keep collecting their directors' fees, which averaged $212,000 in 2005 alone.[50] Of course, it was not quite a win–win situation: shareholders who wanted closer monitoring of the CEO lost.

However, this is just one interpretation. Even if the directors are interested solely in obtaining the best outcome for shareholders, it may be best to keep the CEO happy by not monitoring his performance too closely.[51] If the board monitors the CEO so closely that he becomes disgruntled, he might reduce the flow of information to the board, making it more difficult for directors to perform their advisory (and, for that matter, monitoring) jobs. If the CEO becomes especially annoyed, he might even resign, leaving the firm without a permanent CEO while the board looks for a replacement. It is probably in shareholders' best interests for directors to give the CEO some leeway when they carry out their monitoring role. For the same reason, evidence of close ties between the CEO and directors is not necessarily a bad thing for shareholders. They want the relationship between board and CEO to be functional and close ties will help ensure this.

In for the long haul

As we have just seen, the procedures for electing directors allow strong CEOs to influence the board's composition, stacking it with insiders, notionally independent outsiders with close ties to the CEO, and directors who are too busy to monitor the CEO closely. This would not be such a problem if the effects were short lived, if the procedure could be reversed when the pendulum swings away from the CEO towards the board. However, corporate governance does not work that way. What happens instead is that CEOs can use the board election process to transform temporary strength into enduring strength, short-term bargaining power into long-term bargaining power. If a CEO can achieve this, then even when the pendulum swings back towards the board, which it eventually will, he will still be dominant. His power can be locked in for long periods of time, so that extremely poor performance will be needed in the future before his position is threatened. In short, he will be entrenched.

Irani's tenure as Oxy's CEO provides the perfect example of the behavior that corporate-governance theories based on bargaining games try to explain. According to this interpretation, the boom years allowed Irani to build a board that shareholders, at least, regarded as overly friendly and overly generous: Irani had been paid $530m during the period 2000–2009 for his work as CEO, most of that in the last five years, when he had averaged annual pay of $81m.[52] At a time when generous executive pay packages were causing outrage, Irani was getting the wrong sort of attention, being labeled an "insanely overpaid . . . excessive-pay hall-of-famer" who received a "cash-delivery program, rather than an incentive plan" in the business press.[53]

At the board elections from 2000 to 2008, Irani had averaged 97% "yes" votes, but his support slipped to 72% "yes" votes at the 2009 meeting. Shareholders had watched their investments fall in value by 29% the previous year. Although the share price bounced back, Irani's support did not: he received just 76% "yes" votes at the 2010 meeting.[54] That level of support would be overwhelming in a political setting, but in the context of board elections it was a clear signal that shareholders were ready for a change of CEO.

As the clock started counting down to the next year's meeting, open rebellion broke out amongst shareholders. Two of the firm's largest shareholders—a huge public pension fund and one of the activist hedge funds we will meet in Chapter 10—had Irani in their sights. They were complaining about his pay, the board's failure to enforce its own retirement age, and the apparent lack of a succession plan. They wanted Irani out.[55]

In an average year, 3.8% of the CEOs of large corporations are fired.[56] A CEO is more likely to be fired if his firm's performance is worse than the industry average, but even then weak boards rarely get rid of the CEO. For example, a CEO's chances of being fired are less closely linked to firm performance when the board is large or dominated by a firm's executives, when the majority of directors sit on at least two other boards, and when the majority of directors have family, financial, or social ties to the CEO.[57] Unfortunately for those Oxy shareholders who wanted a change in leadership, their board fit these criteria. It was large and, as we have already seen, many directors had close ties to the CEO.

Irani had one other valuable card to play, which strengthened his bargaining position immeasurably: 29% of Oxy's production of oil and natural gas was in the Middle East and North Africa, where Irani had built strong personal ties with the main players.[58] He was even reported to have given Persian Gulf oil ministers his home telephone number so they could reach him day or night to discuss projects.[59] These ties were valuable to Oxy's shareholders, so the board had to be careful not to alienate Irani and lose the benefit of his contacts in the region.

The key issue facing Irani and the board in what is our final example of a bargaining game was the extent of the CEO's continuing involvement in the firm.[60] Would he stay as CEO? Perhaps instead he could be a full-time executive chairman of the board, handing day-to-day control of the firm over to another executive? How about keeping him on as board chairman, but not as one of the firm's executives? Would he accept staying on as a director, but not chairman? What about some sort of consulting contract? It had worked at other firms, but would Irani agree?

Irani's importance to Oxy's Middle East operations enabled him to retain a substantial role at the firm when he retired as CEO at the next annual meeting. He was replaced as CEO by the firm's president and chief operating officer, Steve Chazen. However, Irani was appointed to a new position, executive chairman, that allowed him to continue to hold sway over Oxy. In his new job, he concentrated on corporate strategy, Middle East operations, and international business development. Although Chazen was the CEO, several of Oxy's business units continued to report to Irani.[61] This outcome reflected Irani's strong bargaining position. However, his position was not strong enough to stop the board becoming more independent. Two elderly directors with ties to Irani did not stand for reelection at the next annual meeting and were replaced by directors without such ties.[62] A stronger board might have been able to further diminish Irani's power, but Oxy's board of 2010 had only limited success.

There are lessons here for CEOs who want to improve their position in future negotiations with their boards of directors, and for directors who want to prevent this happening. If a CEO can prevent a potential replacement from becoming established in the firm, then his own bargaining position will be strengthened.[63] Hammer was alleged to have managed just that: the joke doing the rounds in 1990 was that the president's office at Oxy had so many occupants—four in the last ten years of Hammer's tenure—that it needed a revolving door.[64] If a CEO can shape his firm's strategy in ways that make the firm more reliant on him, then his position will be strengthened as well. That is not necessarily what happened at Oxy—the firm did very well out of its involvement in the Middle East—but it must be tempting for CEOs to do something similar. Directors need to be on the lookout for executives trying to make themselves indispensable. It will not end well.

Cleaning house

Like many CEOs, Irani did not leave the firm entirely when he retired. Approximately half of all CEOs are appointed to their firm's board after they step down as CEO.[65] Whether or not a CEO is able to continue to influence the firm in this way depends on his bargaining power at the time of his departure. The data reveals that CEOs are more likely to stay on the board for several years at firms with boards chaired by the CEO, fewer independent directors, more directors who were appointed during the departing CEO's tenure, and stock returns that were strong when the CEO was still in charge.[66] Oxy ticked most of these boxes. This, and Irani's strong bargaining position in 2010—originating in Oxy's exposure to the Middle East and North Africa—means it is not surprising that he retained a place on Oxy's board.

However, Irani was no ordinary director. He was executive chairman, a full-time job in which he continued to be responsible for setting Oxy's overall strategy in consultation with the board. He also retained responsibility for international business development and Oxy's Middle East operations. The new CEO, Chazen, picked up responsibility for implementing Oxy's overall strategy.[67] Irani may have retired as CEO, but he still dominated the firm. This was reflected in the executive compensation figures reported to shareholders: in 2012, the first fiscal year after Irani's retirement, his reported pay was 60% higher than the new CEO's.[68]

From shareholders' point of view, there are advantages and disadvantages to appointing former CEOs to the board. We have already mentioned the advisory and networking assets that Irani provided to Oxy's board, but these are potentially offset by the difficulty a new CEO may have in undertaking any restructuring that is seen as a criticism of the way the former CEO ran the firm. In the case of Oxy, press reports suggested that Chazen wanted Oxy to concentrate on its North American operations, and had been focusing on boosting production in Texas and California, whereas Irani opposed reducing the role of Oxy's operations in the Middle East and North Africa.[69]

The empirical evidence suggests that the outcome for shareholders of keeping a former CEO on the board is related to the strength of the board. On average, firms with a former CEO on their board have better operating performance. However, digging a little deeper into the data shows that of the firms that appoint their former CEO to the board, the firms with more independent boards have higher subsequent performance.[70] This suggests that former CEOs who are appointed to the board are more valuable if the appointment was driven by a strong board wanting continued access to a former CEO's expertise, rather than by a powerful former CEO wanting to retain influence.

Even with—or perhaps because of—Irani's continued presence on the board, Oxy's early performance under Chazen was poor. An investor who spent $100 on Oxy shares shortly after Chazen was appointed CEO, and reinvested all dividends in more Oxy shares, held shares worth just $74 at the end of 2012. If she had invested $100 in a portfolio of other firms in the same industry, that portfolio would have been worth $87.[71] Early in 2013, the board announced that it had decided to seek a replacement for its CEO. Chazen took the news graciously, admitting publicly that he "did not ask to leave at this time" and promising to stay on until a new CEO was appointed.[72] Perhaps the news did not come as a surprise. Certainly the existing empirical evidence shows that the probability that a CEO is fired following poor share-price performance is much greater at firms where the former CEO sits on the board.[73]

One possible explanation for CEOs' vulnerability at firms with the former CEO on the board is that firing the new CEO is easier; his predecessor is still involved in the firm's affairs and so can return to the top job. Directors might be more reluctant to fire an under-performing new CEO if the potential replacements are outsiders, whose ability—and perhaps even identity—the board is unsure about. However, we should not rule out explanations that are not so good for shareholders. After all, there are real people involved, with all the associated conflicts and jealousies, and leaving the former CEO on the board gives him the opportunity to undermine his successor. In the case of Oxy, press reports suggested that Irani was behind Chazen's dumping and had proposed replacing him with a former Oxy executive who had worked with Irani for more than 20 years, going back to the period before Irani joined Oxy.[74] It was even suggested that Irani was motivated partly by resentment at Chazen's perceived lack of support during the rebellion in 2010.[75]

Clearly worried by these reports, the board announced that the decision to replace Chazen had the unanimous support of the independent directors and that Irani had played no role in the decision. The board went further, confirming that Irani would retire at the end of 2014, as scheduled.[76] However, the news was greeted with skepticism.[77] Seven of the board's nine independent directors had been appointed before Chazen became CEO, so the board appeared more closely aligned with Irani than his successor.[78] There was even speculation that Irani wanted to return as CEO.[79] Some of Oxy's largest shareholders were publicly supporting the CEO and calling for Irani to go altogether; others were being encouraged to vote against Irani and the longest-serving independent director at the upcoming annual meeting.[80]

At the end of April, Oxy announced a set of concessions: two new independent directors would be appointed; in the future, the board would be chaired by an independent director and retired CEOs would not be allowed to become directors.[81] The press release was notably vague about whether the new rules would apply to Irani. Still he held on. At the same time, the board announced that Chazen would remain as CEO until the end of 2014 and had taken responsibility for all of Oxy operations, including the international operations that had previously reported to Irani. These concessions were not enough to pacify shareholders. At the 2013 annual meeting, held four days later, Irani received less than 24% "yes" votes, the lowest of any director.[82] He resigned from the board immediately and was replaced as chairman by one of the reelected independent directors. Chazen, who received 99% "yes" votes, more than any other director, was still gracious. He told the meeting after announcing Irani's departure, "I'm not going to say that every day was a trip to Disneyland [but] every day I learned something."[83]

When Irani had been appointed Oxy's CEO in 1990, he quickly set about purging the firm of Armand Hammer's influence. Much the same thing happened when Irani finally left the firm more than 22 years later. Less than six months afterwards, Oxy announced plans to sell a minority stake in its Middle East and North Africa operations.[84] Just four months after that, Oxy announced it was moving its headquarters to Houston and spinning off its Californian operation as a separate firm. Rubbing salt in Irani's wounds, at the same time Chazen's term as CEO was extended by two years.[85] Irani was gone, but getting rid of him had not been easy.

Shareholders know that the free-rider problem means they will not adequately monitor their firm's senior managers themselves. That is why they elect a board and give directors the job of monitoring management. Directors are supposed to work in shareholders' best interests, but the events at Oxy suggest that directors' ability to do this might be limited by the CEO's bargaining power.

There is another problem facing shareholders, one which was not obvious in the events at Oxy. No matter how carefully a board monitors management, that monitoring will never be perfect. It will always be the case that the CEO knows more than directors about what the CEO is doing. Economists call it asymmetry of information and it can have far-reaching implications. Nobody knew that better than the directors at Yahoo when Microsoft's Steve Ballmer came shopping in 2008. Like their counterparts at Oxy, they had the hands-on task of monitoring the firm's management. As we are about to see, that is difficult when you do not know what is going on.

They had their chance. [If it] made business sense, why didn't they do it sooner?[1]

---

3 Overseeing the unseeable
THE CONFLICT BETWEEN MANAGERS AND SHAREHOLDERS

IN 1995, DAVID FILO and Jerry Yang were barefoot graduate students working in their trailer parked on the Stanford University campus. In 2008, they were billionaires sitting in Yang's private jet parked on the tarmac at Seattle. On both occasions they fielded offers from tech companies wanting to buy Yahoo, the company they created in that trailer. In 1995, AOL offered $2m.[2] In 2008, Microsoft offered $45b.[3] However, it was not just their surroundings and the prices they were being offered that distinguished the two events. In 1995, Filo and Yang owned 100% of the firm they were being asked to sell. In 2008, they owned less than 10%.[4]

Filo and Yang rejected AOL's offer in 1995. They soon accepted funding from a venture capitalist that allowed Yahoo to remain independent, and Yahoo quickly became a darling of the dot-com era. In contrast, Microsoft's campaign to acquire Yahoo in 2008 was long and bitter. After three months of acrimony, Filo and Yang finally flew to Seattle one Saturday morning to talk terms with Microsoft's CEO. Their asking price was too high and Microsoft walked away. Again Yahoo remained independent, but when the markets opened the following Monday morning, its shares were worth $14b less than Microsoft had been offering to pay.[5]

The weekend had been a disaster for Yahoo's shareholders. They directed their anger at Yang, who was Yahoo's CEO at the time. Shareholders did not know what happened inside the private jet at Seattle that day, or what had happened in Yahoo's boardroom previously. In fact, they could not know. Still, they directed their fury at Yang. Some of the firm's largest shareholders were openly critical of his role in resisting Microsoft's bid for the company; some publicly challenged Yahoo's claims of shareholder support.[6] At the next board election, Yang received only 66% "yes" votes, down drastically from the 97% he had averaged over the previous three years.[7] Yang was just one of many people involved in the whole fiasco, so why did he attract so much of the blame?

Decision-making made easy

Yahoo was conceived during 1994 in a cramped trailer parked on the Stanford University campus. With blinds drawn in broad daylight, it was filled with dirty laundry, empty pizza cartons, and golf clubs. One visitor called it "every mother's idea of the bedroom that she wishes her sons never had."[8] David Filo and Jerry Yang, doctoral students who should have been working on their electrical engineering dissertations, were inside compiling a list of their favorite internet sites. They posted "Jerry's Guide to the World Wide Web" on their own website and word of mouth did the rest.[9] Within a few months 20,000 people were visiting their website each day and university officials were asking them to take it (and the crippling traffic it was generating) off-campus.[10]

A swarm of potential investors visited Filo and Yang in their trailer, starting in November 1994. One hopeful soul offered them $5,000.[11] Many, much more generous, offers followed from some of the leading online providers of the day.[12] Many of those potential investors wanted to buy Yahoo outright, merge it into their existing firms, and hire Filo and Yang to continue operating it. However, the two founders wanted to build a firm that would outlive them, not work for somebody else.[13]

If Filo and Yang were to retain Yahoo's independence, they would have to forego those offers and wait for the right investor to come along. The more conditions they imposed, the fewer the potential investors and the lower the price that investors would be willing to pay for a stake in the firm. Filo and Yang had some tough decisions to make. They would have to weigh the benefit they received from retaining Yahoo's independence against the lower price investors would be willing to pay. The managers (Filo and Yang) received all of the benefit and the owners (Filo and Yang again) bore all of the costs, so at least there would be no manager–shareholder conflict. There could be none: the managers *were* the shareholders.

In the end, independence won out over price: Filo and Yang turned down purchase offers from the period's leading tech companies and financing from a venture capitalist that would have required Yahoo to be merged with another internet search engine.[14] Instead, after six weeks of negotiations they sold a minority ownership stake to a venture capitalist who was willing to act "as an eye from 30,000 feet above sea level."[15] Within a few months, the trailer had been left behind and the workforce had grown to 16 employees.[16] Yahoo was still independent.

Filo and Yang brought in executives to run the business side of things and gave themselves the titles of "Chief Yahoo." Filo retreated to his cubicle with its "Microsoft must die" sticker on the wall, from where he played the role of technology guru.[17] Yang stayed out front, carving out a unique role that was part strategist, part corporate spokesman, and part lobbyist.[18] He was the public face of Yahoo, which sold shares to the public for the first time in 1996. Less than four years later, the firm was worth $132b.[19]

(Just like) starting over

The glory days did not last forever. After the dot-com bubble burst, the value of Yahoo's shares fell to just $4.6b.[20] However, unlike so many of its counterparts, Yahoo survived. It even prospered, thanks to early efforts to streamline its operations; a boom in broadband usage by consumers helped.[21] By early 2006, the value of its shares was back up to $62b.[22] However, the emergence of Google as the dominant player in online search brought Yahoo's resurgence to an end.[23] Yahoo returned to its old habits, earning criticism for trying to do so many different things that it did them all poorly. It lost out to Google in the race to buy YouTube; its social network, Yahoo 360, failed to take off; and its advertising business stalled as crucial new software experienced delays of more than a year.[24] As Yahoo's problems mounted, the value of its shares fell: by mid-2007, they were worth just $37b.[25]

After more than a decade watching other people fill the role of CEO, Yang took the helm in 2007.[26] With Filo, he had built Yahoo from nothing in the 1990s. He had helped rebuild it after the carnage of the dot-com bust. In 2007, he planned to rebuild it again. Hundred-day strategic reviews were promised and "big bets" were announced, but still the share price languished.[27] After seven months with Yang as CEO, Yahoo's shares were worth even less than when he had started, just $25b.[28]

Then the phone rang. It was Microsoft's CEO, Steve Ballmer. He was proposing to buy Yahoo and merge it with Microsoft's own operations. If the deal went ahead, Microsoft would issue new shares and give them, plus some cash, to Yahoo's shareholders in exchange for their Yahoo shares. Once these exchanges were made, Yahoo would be rolled into Microsoft and a single merged firm would be born.

Shareholders must have been excited when they heard about that phone call. Their shares had been worth $19 each immediately before the phone rang; here was someone offering to exchange them for a package of cash and Microsoft shares worth $31. What about Yang? We do not know how he reacted, but we can put ourselves in his shoes and imagine how we would have reacted. Our firm, which we created from nothing and hoped would outlive us, was on the brink of being swallowed up by Microsoft. Yes, Microsoft. Our plans for rebuilding our firm were at risk of being abandoned before they had a chance to work. Our chance to prove ourself as a CEO would be lost. There would be no place for a Chief Yahoo (or two) if the merger went ahead, so if we wanted to prove ourselves, we would have to start again from scratch. Many of our employees, our friends, who helped create the firm stood to lose their jobs if it became just another business unit of Microsoft. That had not been the case back in the trailer, when Yahoo had just two employees, Filo and Yang; in 2008 there were 14,300 employees to worry about.[29] If Yang was filled with dread when he realized what that phone call was about, he would only have been human.

These different responses to a simple phone call—shareholders excited and a CEO filled with dread—sum up the conflict between managers and shareholders in a nutshell. Unfortunately for shareholders, a founder's desire to maintain his creation's independence is just one example of the conflict of interest that can arise between managers and shareholders. CEOs divide their time between working for their firm and improving their golf handicap. They divide the firm's spare cash between paying dividends to shareholders and investing in projects that will enhance their own prestige. When employing new executives, they weigh up the benefits of employing the best people for the job against the personal benefits of employing family members. The common theme underlying all of these sources of conflict is the opportunities that managers' positions give them to benefit themselves at the expense of shareholders.

Like the rest of Yahoo's directors and senior executives, Yang had a fiduciary duty to shareholders.[30] The duty of loyalty meant that even if Yang was filled with dread when Microsoft's offer arrived, he was legally required to put shareholders' interests ahead of his own personal interests. The duty of care meant that, in addition, he had to exercise good judgment and act in a way that a reasonably prudent person would act. In the context of Microsoft's offer to buy Yahoo, Yang's duty to shareholders was to get the highest offer possible from Microsoft. As long as Microsoft was paying more than Yahoo would have been worth if it remained independent, Yang's job was to ensure the deal took place. Yang's subsequent accusers implied that he was actually putting his own interests ahead of shareholders. Some shareholders were quite explicit about it, with one major shareholder complaining that "I don't believe that Jerry Yang as a founder, as someone who is emotionally attached to the company, was really looking out for my interest as a shareholder."[31]

Motive

One of the most influential academic articles in financial economics, written by Michael Jensen and William Meckling in the 1970s, looks at situations just like the one involving Yahoo in 2008.[32] According to their theory, shareholders have a set of very clear demands—do what is required to make the firm's shares as valuable as possible—but executives have other considerations. If Yang was behaving like one of Jensen and Meckling's CEOs, he would have been interested only in how he was personally affected by the proposed merger. If the deal went ahead he would no longer be able to walk down Yahoo's halls as the "revered founder."[33] That is bad. On the other hand, if the deal went ahead, it would avert shareholder outrage and a hostile annual meeting. That is good. Of course, if the deal went ahead, it would also increase his wealth dramatically. Yang owned almost 4% of Yahoo's shares and Microsoft was offering him the same deal that it was offering every other shareholder.[34] Completion of the proposed merger would have given Yang a combination of cash and Microsoft shares worth $1,777m.[35] The day after Microsoft abandoned its bid, Yang's Yahoo stake was worth just $1,240m.[36] However, perhaps the "lost" $537m was not as bad as we might think. After all, just a few years earlier it had been Yang who said "I lived on $19,000 a year as a grad student and I could live on $19,000 today. It's nice to know that your family is provided for, but the money isn't that important."[37]

When one of Jensen and Meckling's CEOs is confronted with a situation like this, he weighs up the good and the bad. If the non-financial cost associated with an event (the equivalent of Yang's loss of prestige) exactly matches the non-financial benefit (the equivalent of Yang's relief at avoiding hostile shareholders), then the CEO will want the event to occur provided that the financial benefit is positive. The CEO wants the event to occur if and only if he makes money out of it, and that happens if and only if shareholders make money out of it. There is no conflict between manager and shareholders because they want the same thing. Problems arise, however, when the non-financial cost of an event differs from the non-financial benefit. For example, suppose the cost outweighs the benefit, which is what some of Yahoo's shareholders were worried about. Then—from the CEO's point of view—it is not enough for the event to make money for shareholders: it has to make so much money for shareholders that the financial benefit to the CEO compensates him for the non-financial net loss. Jensen and Meckling's CEOs will oppose actions that are good for their shareholders if the actions are not good enough to overcome the CEOs' non-financial costs. They will even support actions that are bad for their shareholders provided the actions are not bad enough to outweigh their own non-financial benefits.

This had not been a problem in 1995 because back then the decision-makers—Filo and Yang—had owned the whole firm. Yahoo's owners would agree with every decision the managers made because Yahoo's owners *were* the managers. However, Yang's stake had fallen to approximately 4% by 2008, so there was potential for disagreement between the firm's owners and managers. Suppose, just for example, that Yang needed $1m of personal financial benefits to overcome his personal non-financial net costs. Yang would be personally better off doing anything that would give Yahoo's shareholders financial benefits of at least $25m, because his 4% stake would give him at least $1m in financial benefits. That is enough to offset the non-financial net costs he would incur. What if Yang could make Yahoo's shareholders just $20m better off? Not good enough, because Yang's share of the financial benefits would be just $0.8m, not enough to offset his personal non-financial net costs. Yang's 4% ownership stake means that in this hypothetical example there is a wide range of payoffs that make shareholders better off—in many cases, much better off—but leave him worse off.

It would have been an even bigger problem if Yang had owned fewer Yahoo shares. Suppose Yang—Jensen and Meckling's version, again—had owned only one-tenth as many shares, approximately the same number as the company president, and typical for the CEO of a large corporation.[38] Staying with our example in which Yang needed $1m of financial benefits to overcome his non-financial net costs, he would now be personally worse off doing anything that would give Yahoo's shareholders financial benefits of less than $250m, because a 0.4% stake would generate financial benefits of less than $1m. That is not enough to offset Yang's non-financial net costs. Compared to the actual case, a 0.4% ownership stake would have meant that there was an even wider range of payoffs that would make shareholders better off but would leave him worse off. Just imagine what would have happened if he had owned one-hundredth as many shares (approximately as many as the firm's general counsel owned).[39] Any deal that made shareholders less than $2.5b better off would have made Yang worse off. The lesson is clear: the smaller the CEO's ownership stake, the larger the total benefit for shareholders needed to win the CEO's support—and the more good deals opposed by one of Jensen and Meckling's CEOs.

The shareholders who accused Yang of working against shareholders' best interests were making a very serious accusation. Any CEO who did what these shareholders were alleging would not just be breaching an ethical convention: the CEO would be breaching his fiduciary duty to shareholders.[40] However, even an executive who has no intention of doing such a thing might still subconsciously take personal costs and benefits into account when making decisions that affect shareholders. For example, a founder might be overly confident about the value of the firm if it stays independent. This would only be human. And that is perhaps the main point: executives are only human. Even if they try to evaluate a strategy objectively, even if they are determined to put shareholders first, they may not be able to be truly objective. If they owned 100% of the firm then there would be no conflict as they alone would bear any losses caused by their overconfidence. However, when there is a separation of ownership and control, some of the cost of that reluctance to face reality is borne by shareholders.

Means

In 1995, Yahoo's potential purchasers had approached the shareholders, Filo and Yang, directly. Microsoft could not approach shareholders directly in 2008 because there were too many of them and their identities were not known to outsiders. Besides, even though Yahoo's shareholders would ultimately have to vote to decide whether a negotiated deal went ahead, it was not feasible for them to vote on every decision needed during the negotiation process. Instead, responsibility was delegated to Yahoo's board of directors. It was the board that Microsoft approached in the first instance.

When an offer like Microsoft's arrives, the target's board has to ensure the bid is evaluated rigorously. Yahoo's directors were too busy to do the entire job themselves. The board's chairman also chaired Northwest Airlines' board, which was in the process of negotiating a merger with Delta Air Lines.[41] One director was CEO of Activision (maker of the *Call of Duty* video game franchise) and busy trying to complete the merger of his firm with a French conglomerate.[42] Another, the head of Hewlett-Packard's printer division, was struggling with declining consumer printer sales and a CEO who was "not real happy about it."[43] Even if Yahoo's directors had been able to find the time to manage negotiations themselves, they did not have the firm-specific knowledge. To make matters worse, the board's chairman had been in his position for just 15 minutes when Microsoft's offer arrived![44] Yahoo's directors had little choice other than to delegate much of the work to the firm's executives.[45] The CEO's involvement in a firm's day-to-day operations, and the intimate knowledge of the firm that this generates, makes him the obvious choice to handle much of the offer-related work.

Economists have a name for relationships like the one between Yahoo's board of directors and its CEO: they call them principal–agent relationships. The principal (in this case, Yahoo's board) delegates responsibility for carrying out a task to the agent (in this case, Yahoo's CEO). The first formal board meeting after Microsoft's offer arrived provides an ideal setting for exploring principal–agent relationships.[46] A week had already passed and the board needed to make a decision about how to respond to Microsoft's offer. There were three options on the table. One was for the board to accept Microsoft's offer, thrash out the details of the deal, and refer it to shareholders for a final vote. Another was for the board to enter into negotiations with Microsoft in an attempt to get a better deal for Yahoo's shareholders. The board's third option was to reject the offer out of hand and see if Microsoft returned offering a higher price. Yang's job during that first week had been to gather the information the board needed in order to choose the best option for shareholders.

Directors needed to understand Yahoo's prospects if the merger did not go ahead: what would Yahoo do if it remained independent and how much would it be worth? Everything was shrouded in secrecy, but if the press reports are correct then Yang had been busy investigating some of these alternatives. He had eaten dinner with News Corp. chairman Rupert Murdoch, where they discussed the possibility that News Corp. might sell its MySpace social networking site to Yahoo in return for Yahoo shares.[47] He had called Time Warner to discuss the possibility of a deal involving its AOL unit.[48] And he had talked to Google's CEO when Eric Schmidt called to offer his company's help in fending off the Microsoft bid.[49] One possibility, perhaps Yahoo's best hope of staying out of Microsoft's clutches, was to outsource its search-related advertising business to Google. Yang reported all of this back to the board. According to press reports, he advised the board that an independent Yahoo was worth more than what Microsoft had offered.[50]

Shareholders were skeptical when they heard about the outsourcing option. "They had their chance," said one shareholder, adding that if it "made business sense, why didn't they do it sooner?"[51] It was a legitimate question. Yang could have been pursuing these options during the seven months he had been CEO, but he had waited until Microsoft launched its bid to buy the firm. If these options were good for Yahoo's shareholders—and Yang had been working solely in shareholders' best interests—then he should have pursued them previously. If they were not good for shareholders, then he should not have been pursuing them now. Was he doing so simply to avoid losing control of Yahoo to Microsoft?

The board decided to reject Microsoft's initial bid without making a counteroffer of its own. It was already clear that Yang, despite being the agent in this principal–agent relationship, was influential. He continued to play an influential role as Microsoft pushed ahead with its bid to buy Yahoo. Yang's accusers alleged that he used that influence to benefit himself at shareholders' expense. Like any self-interested agent in a principal–agent relationship, there are two ways that Yang could have done this. He might have affected the outcome directly by his own actions and indirectly by controlling the flow of information available to the principal in a way that influenced the principal's actions.

When the cat's away, the mice *can* play

Yahoo's board rejected Microsoft's first offer out of hand, but the two firms' representatives still met several times afterwards to discuss the prospects of a merger. Yahoo's board sent Yang. These meetings provided the CEO with an opportunity to get a higher price for shareholders. He might have been able to persuade Microsoft that Yahoo was in better shape than they realized. He might also have been able to gather intelligence regarding Microsoft's willingness to pay a higher price, which would have been useful to the board if it eventually made a counteroffer. Unfortunately for Yahoo's shareholders, he might also have been able to sabotage the deal.

Directors faced a problem common to most principals: as they were not present at these meetings, they could not observe the agent's actions. Economists are a cynical bunch, so when they look at a situation like this they assume that the agent will work in his own best interests. The problem—economists call it moral hazard—is that what is best for the agent may not be what is best for the principal. Unfortunately for the principal, what it can observe is at best only a noisy indicator of the agent's intentions, and this uncertainty gives the agent cover to act in its own best interests. The principal may suspect the agent did a poor job, but cannot prove it. The agent knows this, and therefore acts in its own interests. That, at least, is how economists view situations like this.

At first glance, it might seem that the mere occurrence of these meetings proves that Yahoo's executives were *not* acting in their own interests. However, it is not quite that simple. Executives might have been deemed to have breached their fiduciary duty to shareholders if they had not made an effort to extract a better offer from Microsoft. Were Yahoo's executives trying to get a better offer out of Microsoft, or were they trying to be seen to try and get a better offer out of Microsoft? The problem facing directors, who were not present at these meetings, was the principal's old enemy: there was no way for directors to know for certain exactly what the executives did at the series of meetings. To make the board's problem even more difficult, Yahoo's investment bankers were reported to have been excluded from the early meetings between the two firms' executives: directors could not even rely on the bankers for an independent view of how negotiations were going.[52]

The most important issue for shareholders, and directors working in shareholders' best interests, was the price that Microsoft was willing to pay for each Yahoo share. However, according to later press reports, Yahoo's executives seemed more interested in learning about how a merger would affect them than in achieving a high price for shareholders. Apparently price was not even discussed at the first meeting between the two firms' executives, which focused on job losses and other non-price matters.[53] In a meeting one month later, Yang was still not willing to talk about a purchase price. According to press reports, Microsoft's general counsel called it "one of the strangest meetings that we've ever had."[54]

Did Yahoo's shareholders really need their firm's executives negotiating with Microsoft about what Microsoft would do with Yahoo once it owned the company? That is like trying to sell our home and negotiating with potential purchasers over the colors they will use when they repaint the kitchen. What they plan to do with the kitchen is their business. We just need to know what price they are willing to pay. Likewise, all that mattered to Yahoo's shareholders was the price that Microsoft was willing to pay. At first glance, it looked like Yahoo's executives succumbing to a conflict of interest, negotiating their own futures rather than negotiating shareholders' payout.

Executives' refusal to negotiate over price was not the only aspect of their behavior of concern to shareholders. Less than two weeks after Microsoft launched its bid, the compensation committee of Yahoo's board approved changes in the severance plans that covered all of Yahoo's full-time employees, including the firm's senior executives. It was Yahoo's directors who approved the changes, but disgruntled shareholders singled out Yang as the driving force.[55] Under the revised plans, if an employee left the firm under certain (very broad) circumstances within two years of Yahoo being acquired by another firm, they would be entitled to up to two years of severance pay, thousands of dollars in reimbursement for outplacement services, and favorable treatment of any shares and other Yahoo securities they had been granted previously.[56] If the merger had gone ahead, the introduction of this severance plan would have reduced the amount that Microsoft was willing to pay—if it did not sink the deal altogether. That is, ultimately, it would have been Yahoo's shareholders who paid for the plan. The more generous the plan, the better the news for Yahoo's executives and the lower the payout for Yahoo's shareholders. At first glance, this looked like a case of Yang sacrificing shareholders' interests in order to keep his creation independent.

However, the reality was not quite so simple. Even if Yahoo's shareholders voted in favor of a merger, there was a risk that it would never be completed. Any deal might be prohibited by regulators, who might take a year or more to decide. If that happened—and employees worried about their future under Microsoft management fled Yahoo in the meantime—then shareholders would be left owning a firm that was a shell of its former self. That is why it was important even to Yahoo's shareholders that the firm retained key staff. Even shareholders should have wanted executives to spend *some* time negotiating staffing arrangements with Microsoft; even shareholders should have wanted Yahoo to make *some* effort to retain staff until Microsoft's bid was resolved one way or the other.

There is an important general point to note here. Sometimes a conflict between managers and shareholders is easy to spot. Shareholders want managers to work hard; managers want to play golf. However, in many situations, perhaps most of them, conflict is more subtle. Executives have multiple tasks to complete and shareholders will often want executives to put some effort into all of them. The conflict is over how much effort to allocate to each task. When it came to discussing Yahoo's future under Microsoft management, even Yahoo's shareholders should have wanted the two sides to discuss organizational plans. However, executives and shareholders differed in the importance they attached to those discussions—and the effort that should be committed to them. The problem for shareholders was not that executives spent effort and scarce bargaining time negotiating future employment matters, but that they might have spent *too much* time negotiating them.

Controlling the flow of information

Three months passed after Microsoft made its offer before Yahoo's board decided it was time to make a counteroffer. According to press reports, talks between the two firms had intensified and Microsoft had indicated that it was willing to raise its offer price.[57] Yahoo's board met on the first Friday in May to choose an asking price.

Directors had a fiduciary duty to get the best deal possible for Yahoo's shareholders. That needed a good prediction of what Microsoft was willing to pay. If they had asked for a price that was too low, Yahoo's shareholders would have missed out on a higher payout. If they had set it too high, Microsoft might have walked away altogether. Yang and the other Yahoo executives present at the meetings with Microsoft had the best information. As at previous stages of the process, this gave them considerable influence over the outcome.

Yahoo's directors faced a problem common to all principals. Like the problem discussed in the preceding section, this one was due to differences in the information available to the principal and the agent. When the agent possesses relevant information that is not available to the principal, the agent can choose whether, or how, to communicate that information to the principal. If the agent is self-interested, then he can choose to communicate the information in ways that benefit himself. Merger negotiations provide just one example of the potential conflict this creates between managers and shareholders. Perhaps a CEO wants a deal to go ahead because the acquiring firm has offered him a lucrative employment arrangement. If so, then he might try to induce the board to set a low asking price. That would be harmful to shareholders, but good for the CEO. Alternatively—and this would have been the fear of Yahoo's directors—the CEO might want a deal to fail and try to achieve that end by inducing the board to set a high asking price.

As the principal in the principal–agent relationship, Yahoo's directors actually wanted Yang to filter information when reporting back to the board. The alternative was that the executive negotiating team brought the board a record of every conversation and every document, together with an account of every twitch and every facial expression of the Microsoft executives. This would have reduced the information asymmetry between the board and CEO, but in doing so it would have defeated the purpose of delegating responsibility to the CEO in the first place.

In short, delegation comes with benefits and costs. If directors want the benefits (experts involved in the negotiations) then they need to incur some costs (experts who have the means and motive to act in their own interest). When Yahoo's directors decided to step back from negotiations with Microsoft, they weighed the benefits against the costs. Ultimately, however, Yahoo's directors needed to make a crucial decision: what price would they ask for? Press reports suggested Yang wanted $38 per share but that the board eventually decided to notify Microsoft that it would sell the firm—well, recommend to shareholders that they sell the firm—for $37 per share.[58]

Bad behavior or bad luck?

Filo and Yang flew to Seattle early on Saturday morning, to meet with Ballmer. Microsoft's executives were on standby: they would have to work through the weekend if a deal was reached. After several hours of discussions, Ballmer raised Microsoft's offer to $33 per share. Yang and Filo revealed the Yahoo board's $37 asking price and flew home to await Microsoft's response. They did not have to wait long for an answer. Ballmer phoned again: "We're done." Microsoft was walking away.[59]

There would be no merger, no cash payment to Yahoo's shareholders, and no stake in Microsoft for them either. Shareholders got nothing in return. There was no deal with News Corp. involving MySpace and no deal with Time Warner involving AOL. There was not even a lasting deal with Google, because the outsourcing arrangement was abandoned when the Department of Justice threatened to file an antitrust lawsuit to block its implementation.[60]

The cost to Yahoo's shareholders of the failed takeover bid was enormous. Microsoft had been willing to pay $45b for Yahoo's shares, but when the share market opened after Microsoft's withdrawal was announced, they were worth just $32b. Six months later, with all hope of the deal being resurrected having died, the value of Yahoo's shares fell to $12b.[61] It would take five long years before Yahoo's share price reached the $33 that Microsoft had been willing to pay.[62]

Was what happened at Yahoo an example of a CEO acting in ways that benefited himself at the expense of shareholders, as some disgruntled shareholders alleged in the aftermath of the deal's collapse? Some Microsoft insiders certainly believed the pair had obstructed the deal "having long reviled Microsoft and its culture."[63] A member of the *Wall Street Journal* editorial board went so far as to suggest that Yang had effectively sabotaged the deal in order to "fulfill his dream of having an independent Yahoo whose halls he [could] continue to walk as the revered 'founder.'"[64] These suspicions were fueled by the central role that Yang, and not Yahoo's board of directors, seemed to play in the negotiations.[65] It cannot have helped matters when the *New York Times* reported that Yang and his team had exchanged high fives when they learnt that Microsoft was walking away, a report swiftly denied by the man himself.[66] Alternatively, was it, as Yang's defenders suggested, a case of Microsoft getting cold feet and using Yahoo's rejection of Microsoft's initial bid as an excuse to avoid what it saw as a costly mistake?[67] In short, was it bad behavior or bad luck?

The point of this chapter is not to judge Yang's intentions. In fact, one of the most important lessons from this chapter is that we *cannot* judge a CEO's intentions. Nobody apart from the individuals themselves knows exactly why they took the decisions they did. That is the most important feature of manager–shareholder conflict. If manager–shareholder conflict was observable, if shareholders could detect it with a degree of certainty that would stand up in court, then it would be relatively easy to prevent. Contracts could be written to prevent it happening; the threat of future lawsuits would act as a deterrent. However, because executives' intentions cannot be known with this level of certainty, neither contracts nor lawsuits can eliminate bad behavior.

The bad news for shareholders is that principal–agent relationships pop up everywhere in a firm. Even a deal as big as Microsoft's attempt to acquire Yahoo—with billions of dollars at stake—had to have crucial tasks delegated to executives by the board. For the more mundane matters associated with running a corporation day after day, week after week, delegation to executives is ubiquitous. And wherever there is a principal–agent relationship, there is bound to be asymmetric information. Directors' inability to observe everything executives do gives those executives the means to undertake actions that benefit themselves at the expense of shareholders. It also gives them the means to influence the information that they convey to directors. Lastly, and crucially, the separation of ownership and control gives executives a motive to exploit these opportunities.

Hands-on monitoring can achieve only so much: a board cannot stop what it cannot see. However, shareholders need not despair, because monitoring is just one of the responses to manager–shareholder conflict. There are other responses, which are less susceptible to the problems posed by asymmetric information. Even if boards cannot always prevent executives from acting in ways that harm shareholders, they can arrange things so that executives do not want to behave that way. With less desire to act in ways that harm shareholders, it does not matter (as much) that directors cannot observe the bad behavior. It is not done with mind control, but with motivation—and not pep talks from motivational speakers, but arrangements that put cold hard cash in executives' pockets if they behave well. Directors are still involved, and they should still be working in shareholders' best interests, but their hands-on role stops once the incentive structures have been put in place. After that, directors take a back seat and let managers manage, which is just what happened at the next firm we meet.

2 Motivate

$28b worth of debt creates a different kind of stress.[1]

JACK BOVENDER (2008)

···

4 Narrowing the gap
THE INCENTIVES GENERATED BY MANAGERIAL OWNERSHIP

THE POTENTIAL FOR manager–shareholder conflict at Yahoo was high because its CEO, Jerry Yang, owned just 4% of the firm's shares. However, Yahoo's shareholders were fortunate, because Yang's ownership stake was large by the standards of most firms. His stake was large because he co-founded the firm.[2] At one stage Yang owned 50%, but this diminished as he and co-founder David Filo sold parts of the firm to raise capital. Still, such a big initial stake meant that Yang had a relatively large ownership stake even many years after Yahoo was founded.

At firms without a founder in the top job, one of the very first things a board will try to do when it appoints a new CEO is find ways to boost his ownership stake. That was what happened at Hospital Corporation of America (HCA) when Jack Bovender was appointed CEO. Bovender had worked at the for-profit hospital operator for almost a quarter century; his ownership stake had been built up from scratch over that period.[3] HCA's sheer scale—it was worth $28b when he got the top job—meant that even after working in senior executive positions for many years, Bovender owned just 0.02% of its shares at the time of his appointment. Boosting the new CEO's ownership stake would give him a stronger incentive to increase the value of the firm, taking some of the pressure off the board to monitor the CEO.

Ownership stakes as low as Bovender's create enormous potential for manager–shareholder conflict. An easy solution is to just give the new CEO shares in the firm. Easy, but expensive. The challenge directors face is to create the same incentive benefits as share ownership but at lower cost. It was a challenge that HCA's board met head on. During

Bovender's first five years as CEO, the board did give him shares, but it also gave him options to buy many more shares. In total, Bovender received shares and options worth $33m. The board used almost every trick in the book to keep the cost down. Without those tricks, it would have needed to spend $82m to generate comparable incentives.[4]

In the sixth year of Bovender's term, HCA's board took things to a new level when it approved what at the time was the biggest ever deal of its type. It would have been breathtaking in any industry, but this was the normally staid for-profit hospital sector. It was a deal that—depending on your point of view—either made shareholders more than $3b or cost them almost $13b. Like so many of the board's actions during Bovender's term, a key element was the way in which the deal narrowed the separation of ownership and control.

A culinary detour

Before we see how HCA's board did such a good job of boosting Bovender's incentives, we need to make an investment in one more conceptual framework. Like the bargaining-game framework we met in Chapter 2, this one will help us understand the economic forces at work behind the scenes. The framework we are about to meet helps explain how HCA's board was able to lower the cost of boosting Bovender's ownership-generated incentives. It will also—in later chapters—help us understand how boards can use debt to keep executives in line and how hostile raiders can use debt to help overcome a firm's takeover defenses.

The basis of this new framework is a very stylized model of the firm. Well, not so much a model, as a cake. When we bake a cake, we mix the ingredients together in a bowl, transfer the mixture to a cake pan, put the pan in a heated oven, and wait. If all goes well, after a short time we can take the baked cake out of the oven, cut it into slices, and eat it. If all does not go well—perhaps the cake fails to rise—then what we take out of the oven will not be quite what we had hoped for. Our corporate cake works in much the same way, except that the ingredients are the assets that the firm uses to generate its profits; selecting and mixing the ingredients is the job of the firm's management. The baked cake is the firm in the future, once the performance of the assets is known. Just as the size of the cake emerging from our oven can be unpredictable, so the future value of our corporate cake is unpredictable.

The cash that a firm like HCA generates is paid out to different classes of investors. Bondholders get interest payments and repayments of principal, shareholders get dividends, and executive option-holders get the right to buy shares (and the dividends that they generate) at a fixed price. Bondholders have the highest priority when cash is paid out, so if the available resources are less than the amount they are owed, bondholders take everything and shareholders and option-holders get nothing. However, if the firm's available resources are greater than the amount owed to bondholders, they are paid in full and what is left over is available for shareholders and option-holders.

When executives exercise their options, they pay the specified purchase price to the firm, which immediately issues new shares to the executives. That is why option-holders will allow their options to expire without being exercised if the share price stays below the specified purchase price. If this happens, the option-holders receive nothing. However, if the share price rises above the specified purchase price, they will exercise their options and *become* shareholders. This forces shareholders to share the firm's cash flows with option-holders.

The cake that comes out of our oven can be divided up the same way. The individuals with the highest priority (the bondholders) might be entitled to the bottom two inches of cake. If the cake does not rise this far while it is baking, the high-priority individuals get the whole cake, and everybody else goes hungry. However, if the cake rises above this point, then the high-priority individuals get their full two-inch entitlement and everyone else can share the excess. The individuals with the second-highest priority (the shareholders) might be entitled to the next inch of cake. If the cake does not rise this far while it is baking, the individuals with the second-highest priority get all of the cake above the bottom two inches, and everybody left gets nothing. However, if the cake rises above this point, then they will get their full one-inch entitlement, and share what is left with the lowest priority individuals (the option-holders).

Figure 4.1 shows a cake representing HCA in January 2001, when Bovender became CEO. The dark-gray layer at the bottom of the cake is the portion allocated to the firm's bondholders, the light-gray layer above it is the portion allocated to the firm's shareholders, and the white band around the top of the cake is the portion allocated to the options awarded to the firm's executives.[5] The option band starts a fixed distance above the debt slice, with the distance being greater when the price that option-holders have to pay for the shares they acquire is higher, and the band being thicker when executives have been granted more options. It extends all the way to the top of the cake pan.

Imagine we are watching the cake slowly rising as it bakes. The highlighted slices in the light-gray and white portions of the cake in Figure 4.1 represent the shares and options, respectively, owned by Bovender. He owned 0.02% of HCA's shares, so for each additional $100 that ends up in the light-gray portion of the cake, he receives just an additional 2c. As long as the cake ends up below the bottom of the white band then his options will pay nothing, but as the cake rises above this point, so does his payoff. In the region above the

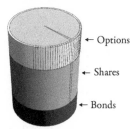

← Options

← Shares

← Bonds

FIGURE 4.1 Cutting the company cake into bonds, shares, and options

option band, for every additional $100 of cake, Bovender receives an additional 19c, with 2c coming from his shares and 17c from his options.

Measuring ownership

At first glance, measuring the size of an executive's ownership stake seems as easy as dividing the number of shares the executive owns by the total number of the firm's shares. According to that measure, Bovender's ownership stake was just 0.02% when he was appointed CEO. That would be the correct approach if we were interested in his voting power. However, we are interested in the incentives generated by Bovender's portfolio of HCA securities, and these incentives are determined by his economic ownership, which involves option ownership as well as share ownership.

What matters for incentives is the reward that an executive receives from making a firm more valuable, so that is what we try to calculate. We do it by conducting a thought experiment that involves making the firm more valuable and asking how much of the increase in value is received by the executive. Take Bovender for example. Increasing the value of HCA's cake is like putting extra ingredients into the cake pan before it goes into the oven. Provided the bond portion is not too big to begin with, the pre-baked value of the bond portion does not change much, as bondholders were previously confident they would get all of their promised slice and adding more ingredients does not change that. However, the news is much better for shareholders and option-holders as it means their slices will probably be larger when the cake comes out of the oven. They get everything above the fixed height of the bond portion, so the extra ingredients make their portions more valuable as well. On the other hand, if the debt portion is large enough that there is some possibility that the cake will not rise up far enough to pay out the bonds in full, news of more ingredients makes the bonds more valuable: the firm is more likely to repay its debt in full. The increase in value of the bonds means a smaller increase in the value of shares and options, but shareholders and option-holders still benefit from the added ingredients.

In the case of HCA at the time Bovender was appointed CEO, almost all of that extra value would go to shareholders and option-holders. How much would go to Bovender? Suppose the increase in value drove the share price up by $1; that is an increase in the cake's total value of approximately $543m, or $1 per share. Bovender owned 113,000 shares, so his share portfolio would have become $113,000 more valuable. He also owned options to buy 921,000 additional shares. Each option would have become more valuable as well, because the price he would have had to pay for a share if he exercised the option would not have changed, but the value of what he would get would have increased by $1. However, because he might not have exercised the options for several years, the current value of the options would have risen by less than $921,000. In fact, if this change in share price had happened at the time Bovender became CEO, his options would have increased in value by $770,000.[6] Once the shares are added in, his portfolio would have been $883,000 more valuable, or 0.16% of the total increase in the cake's value. That is why we say that Bovender's *effective* ownership stake was 0.16%, even though his *actual* ownership stake was just 0.02%.[7]

Even with the effect of his options included, Bovender's effective ownership stake was low in comparison with other CEOs. In the for-profit hospital sector, effective CEO ownership was 4.2% on average.[8] However, the range was wide, from 1.6% (another recently appointed CEO) to 16.8% (a company founder).[9] Across all large U.S. corporations, effective CEO ownership is 1.4% on average.[10]

Size matters, at least for incentives

An executive's effective ownership stake tells us what fraction of any increase in firm value he will receive. However, if we are to really understand the incentives generated by ownership, we need to understand the effect of firm size. Sometimes a small ownership stake in a big firm can generate stronger incentives than a big ownership stake in a small one. For example, where were the incentives likely to be stronger: at HCA, where the CEO had a 0.16% effective ownership stake in a business with 196 hospitals and 164,000 employees, or at LifePoint Hospitals, Inc., where the CEO had a 1.6% effective ownership stake in a business with 21 hospitals and 6,450 employees?[11]

In some situations, such as perk consumption, firm size does not matter much. For example, if the CEO delays renovating his office, the firm saves the same amount of money regardless of the firm's size. To calculate the CEO's personal benefit from delaying the renovations (and hence the strength of his incentive to do so), we simply multiply the increase in the cake's value by the CEO's effective ownership stake. If delaying the hypothetical renovation saves a firm $100,000, then Bovender would have gained $160 by delaying renovations when he was appointed CEO; his counterpart at LifePoint would have gained $1,600 by doing the same thing. At least as far as perk consumption was concerned, neither CEO's ownership stake was large enough to provide much discouragement, but Bovender had the weaker incentive to delay those renovations.

Perk consumption makes good headlines and can incite shareholder anger, but it is relatively unimportant for many firms, especially big ones. At such firms, shareholder value is more dependent on managers' actions that affect an entire firm, such as restructuring the firm, evaluating its expansion plans, or deciding on strategy when negotiating with suppliers. Where these "scaleable" actions are concerned, a CEO would have more impact on the market value of a large firm than if he exerted exactly the same effort at a small firm. A reasonable approximation is that the percentage impact on a firm's market value will be independent of the firm's size. That is, the same CEO exerting the same effort would increase any firm's market value by the same percentage. Of course, this is just an approximation, but it can be a useful one.[12]

Scaleable actions such as these will not have much effect on the value of the firm's cash stockpile, but they will affect the value of the firm's other assets. That is why when we assess incentives we focus on a firm's so-called enterprise value, which is the value of the firm's assets, minus the amount of cash that it holds. This is the value of the corporate cake, minus any cash contained in its list of ingredients.

HCA's enterprise value when Bovender became CEO was $28b; LifePoint's was just $1.5b.[13] If Bovender had managed a restructuring program that increased HCA's enterprise value by 1%, or $280m, he would have been $448,000 better off. That is 0.16% of $280m, his share of the increase in HCA's enterprise value. If, by exerting the same effort, LifePoint's CEO had been able to increase his firm's enterprise value by 1%, or $15m, his 1.6% effective ownership stake would have yielded him just $240,000. Bovender may have had a much smaller effective ownership stake, but HCA's sheer scale meant that he received a much bigger financial reward from achieving such "percentage gains" in enterprise value.

There is one more wrinkle. Economists assume that executives derive satisfaction (they call it "utility") from the money they are paid and having the time available to enjoy what it can buy. Working harder may give executives more money to spend, but it also means they have less time to spend it—and the higher their overall level of pay, the greater the cost of missing out on that enjoyment. That is why some economists argue that we should not measure the strength of executives' incentives by the increase in their wealth that comes from working harder. Instead, we should express this increase in wealth as a percentage of the executive's annual pay.[14] For example, by exerting the effort needed to increase HCA's enterprise value by 1%, Bovender could have increased his personal wealth by $448,000, but that was just 6.7% of his pay in the year he became CEO. In contrast, if LifePoint's CEO had been able to increase his firm's enterprise value by the same percentage, the $240,000 increase in his personal wealth amounted to 20% of his annual pay that year. According to this measure, at least, ownership-generated incentives were stronger at LifePoint than at HCA.[15]

Boards can strengthen executives' incentives ...

Boards are able to influence the size of their executives' ownership stakes. They can grant executives shares and options as part of their pay packages. Boards can even force executives to hold some minimum level of their wealth in the firm's securities: Bovender had to own shares worth at least five times his base salary.[16] Boards appear to use such arrangements to stop ownership stakes moving too far away from target levels. For example, firms grant lower than average quantities of shares and options when the effective ownership stakes of their CEOs are high relative to typical ownership stakes for firms with similar characteristics. When the CEOs' effective ownership stakes are relatively low, firms tend to grant higher than average quantities.[17]

This is what HCA's board did when Bovender was appointed CEO. It needed to, because his incentives were weak. His ownership stake, low by industry standards, had been built up only in the previous three years, when he had returned to HCA after a brief retirement.[18] During Bovender's first five years as CEO, HCA's board awarded him shares and options that generated comparable incentives to those generated by a portfolio of 1.2m shares.[19]

It was not cheap: Bovender's share grants during that period cost HCA's shareholders $9m and the options cost them a further $24m. However, it would have been even more expensive to create the same incentives without options. Take Bovender's first option grant as CEO for example. If HCA's share price increased by $1, the value of the 400,000 options would have increased by $252,000, so the options generated comparable incentives to 252,000 shares. That many shares would have cost HCA's shareholders $9.4m to give to Bovender; the options cost them just $6.3m. It was a similar story for his other option grants. In total, it would have cost shareholders $43m to achieve with share grants what the board was able to achieve with option grants costing $24m.[20]

Executive stock options get a bad press because of the enormous payoffs that some CEOs have received, but Bovender's example shows their main benefit: they are a relatively cheap source of ownership-generated incentives. Bovender's view of the cake in Figure 4.1 reveals the source of the cost saving. Provided the baked cake rose as far as his options, each additional dollar of cake was shared by Bovender and shareholders in just the same way as if he owned shares. However, because Bovender received no payoff if the cake fell short of the point in the pan where his options began, the options were less valuable than the same number of shares. Options provide low-cost incentives by exposing executives to the upper, and most risky, part of the corporate cake. Shares, in contrast, extend deep down into the relatively safe part of the cake in Figure 4.1. There are not many incentives down there, so why give that part of the cake to the firm's executives? Options give more (incentive) bangs for shareholders' buck.

Firms can engineer a similar outcome by raising the height of the debt layer of cake so that the equity slices do not go down so far. The process is known as a share buyback, and it works like this. The firm sells new bonds to investors and uses the cash this raises to buy back shares from shareholders who wish to sell them. Such buyback programs do not directly affect the firm's productive assets—the ingredients of the cake do not change—but the debt layer of cake becomes larger and the equity layer becomes smaller. As the number of shares owned by shareholders has fallen, the equity layer of the cake is resliced into a smaller number of shares. Each remaining share corresponds to a larger slice of a smaller portion of cake, meaning that executives end up with a larger percentage ownership stake.

This is exactly what HCA was doing. During Bovender's first five years as CEO, HCA spent $7.9b repurchasing shares.[21] Bovender owned shares and options generating comparable incentives to 0.9m shares when he was appointed CEO—out of 543m shares in total. Five years later, his much bigger portfolio generated incentives comparable to

1.9m shares—out of 418m shares in total. The bigger numerator and smaller denominator meant that his effective ownership stake increased from 0.16% to 0.46% over this period, significantly strengthening his incentives: a 1% increase in HCA's enterprise value would have made Bovender $448,000 better off if it occurred immediately after he was appointed CEO and $1.4m better off at the end of his fifth year in the job. If the board had tried to achieve the buyback-induced strengthening of incentives by awarding shares, HCA would have had to give Bovender shares worth $30m.[22] The buyback did not cost shareholders a dime.

The process does not go on indefinitely. Eventually a board will decide that executives' ownership stakes have reached a desirable level: increasing them any further would incur costs that are bigger than the benefits that come with the greater ownership. The firms with the greatest need for motivated managers—and therefore the most to gain from boosting ownership—tend to be the ones with the highest ownership stakes. For example, managerial ownership tends to be high at firms with high investment and R&D spending (where executives need to be motivated to make the effort to evaluate these growth opportunities) and the greatest opportunities for discretionary spending (where executives need to be motivated to restrict consumption of perks). However, shareholders find it costly to increase executives' ownership stake. There is the direct cost of handing over an ownership stake in the firm, whether it is done by granting shares or options, or (as is usually the case) both. There is also the indirect cost of forcing the CEO to hold an undiversified portfolio and having to boost his pay to compensate for the risk that exposes him to. This might explain the relatively low levels of managerial ownership at firms with very volatile share prices, as these firms' executives incur relatively high costs from holding undiversified share portfolios.[23]

... and executives can weaken them

HCA's shareholders spent $33m to boost Bovender's effective ownership stake in the firm, $9m on shares and $24m on options. They might have expected that ownership stake to generate strong incentives for him to increase shareholder wealth for many years to come. Instead, Bovender unwound many of those incentives at exactly the time shareholders needed him to have strong incentives. There is a lesson here for the shareholders of any firm: ownership-generated incentives provided at great cost to shareholders can be undone rapidly by executives selling their shares.

Executives may need to work for a firm for several years before they are allowed to sell their shares, but eventually they will be able to do so.[24] When they sell shares, their ownership stake falls, the separation of ownership and control widens, and their incentives are weakened. They will also eventually be allowed to exercise their options. Executives usually quickly sell the shares they receive when they exercise options, which also separates ownership and control and weakens their incentives.[25] For example,

Bovender exercised 500,000 options in February 2005, paying $13m for shares that he sold the same day for $22m. The strength of Bovender's ownership-generated incentives, built up over several years, fell by almost a quarter in a single day.[26] The lesson? Incentives can be unwound very easily.

Unfortunately for shareholders, that was not the only lesson. Such share sales can weaken incentives at exactly the time when shareholders need those incentives to be strongest, which is what happened at HCA in 2005. Bovender was not the only executive who reduced his effective ownership stake that year. During a seven-week period, the company president, the chief financial officer, and one of HCA's group presidents all exercised options and then immediately sold the shares. In each case, the executive exercised approximately a quarter of the options in his portfolio at the time. These executives exercised more options in the first half of 2005 than they had in the previous seven years combined.[27]

A month after the last of these options were exercised, HCA released poor earnings news that triggered a 9% drop in the firm's share price.[28] It was a fortunate coincidence for the executives, who would have received smaller payoffs if they had exercised their options in the second half of the year. It was an unfortunate coincidence for shareholders, who found that the firm's management had weaker incentives to increase the share price at precisely the time when the firm was struggling.

Shareholders need to be aware of other ways that executives can unwind their incentives. Some executives enter into so-called hedge contracts with investment banks to pay each other amounts in the future that depend on their firm's share price. Typically, the executive pays cash to the bank when the share price rises and receives cash from the bank when the share price falls. From the point of view of an executive who holds shares and options in his firm, if the firm does well, then his shares and options increase in value, but he has to share some of the gains with the investment bank. On the other hand, if the firm does poorly, his shares and options will fall in value, but the blow will be softened by the payment he receives from the investment bank. It is effectively an insurance scheme that makes the executive's future wealth less risky. However, by making his wealth less sensitive to the share price, it has weakened his incentive to increase the share price, which is bad for shareholders. To make matters worse, although such arrangements have to be reported to the SEC, the disclosure rules are sufficiently vague that hedges enable executives to unwind incentives in ways that attract relatively little investor scrutiny.[29]

Reslicing the corporate cake

HCA's buyback program had narrowed the gap between ownership and control by raising the CEO's effective ownership stake. In 2006, HCA did something that narrowed this gap even further. That something was a leveraged buyout, said at the time to be the biggest buyout that financial markets had ever seen.[30] Buyouts, like buybacks, involve issuing debt to fund the purchase of a firm's shares. However, the shares are not purchased by the firm itself as in a buyback. Instead they are purchased by a different firm, usually a shell company set up especially for this purpose. At HCA the shell company was formed by three private equity funds and HCA's founder, Tommy Frist.

The owners of the shell company contributed $3.8b in cash; Frist contributed HCA shares worth $0.9b. The shell company borrowed the rest of the money it needed to purchase all of HCA's remaining shares, spending $20b in total.[31] When the deal was done, the shell company owned all of HCA's assets and had taken responsibility for all of HCA's existing debt; HCA shares no longer traded on the New York Stock Exchange (NYSE). Although the corporate cake's ingredients did not change, the way in which the cake was sliced changed dramatically. The situations before and after the buyout are illustrated in Figure 4.2. Immediately before the buyout, HCA had debt of $12b (the dark gray slice at the bottom of the left-hand cake) and equity worth $21b (the light gray slice at the top of the cake). Immediately after the buyout, its debt comprised the old HCA loans plus the new shell-company loans, more than $28b in total, and it had equity of almost $5b.[32] Such huge changes in debt levels are fairly typical for leveraged buyouts. For example, for a typical buyout during the period from 1990 to 2006, debt comprised 24% of the cake before the buyout and 70% afterwards.[33]

The new venture had another group of investors: HCA's executives contributed HCA shares and options worth $0.1b.[34] Bovender sold some of his shares during the buyout and also exercised some of his options, immediately selling the shares he acquired by doing so. This netted him $24m cash in total. However, he converted his remaining shares and options into shares and options in the shell company. Other executives negotiated similar arrangements. Although the actual value of Bovender's stake fell, HCA's extremely high debt level after the buyout meant that his effective ownership stake increased by almost a half.[35] Bovender was able to simultaneously reduce the amount of his wealth invested in HCA and increase his effective ownership stake. A quick look at Figure 4.2 reveals how. The left-hand cake shows that before the buyout Bovender owned an equity slice that started close to the bottom of the cake pan, far below where the baked cake was likely to reach. This slice provided only weak incentives, but at relatively high cost. In

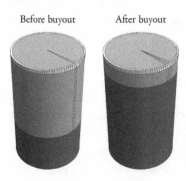

Before buyout   After buyout

FIGURE 4.2 HCA's leveraged buyout and Bovender's ownership stake

the right-hand (post-buyout) cake, the equity slice starts much higher up the pan but, as shareholders own fewer shares in total, Bovender's slice is thicker than before. Thicker, and generating stronger incentives as a result: a 1% increase in HCA's enterprise value would have made Bovender $1.7m better off if it occurred immediately before the buyout and $2.3m better off if it occurred immediately afterwards.[36]

The changes in ownership of the equity layer of the corporate cake also led to a fundamental change in board makeup. Before the buyout, HCA's shareholder base comprised many investors, most of them with just a small stake in the firm. This was reflected in the board's composition. At the last annual meeting before the buyout, HCA's board comprised Bovender, his second-in-charge Richard Bracken, and 12 other directors. One of them was Frist, one of the company's largest shareholders, with a 5.8% effective ownership stake. The rest were independent directors, each with an average 0.01% effective ownership stake.[37] After the buyout, 95% of HCA was owned by the three private equity funds and the Frist family. With new owners came a new board. Bovender, Bracken, and Frist were still there, but the other directors had gone, replaced by a Frist family member and nine independent directors, three from each of the private equity firms that had participated in the buyout. Frist's effective ownership stake had increased to 20%, and the other non-executive directors represented funds with a combined 75% ownership stake.[38] The separation of ownership and control was now only the width of the boardroom table.

Narrow the gap, improve performance

As is the case for most management-led buyouts, HCA's senior executives had much larger effective ownership stakes after the buyout than before and its board of directors was made up solely of large shareholders (or their representatives).[39] All parties involved in the firm's key decision-making, senior executives and directors, therefore had a much stronger incentive to increase the value of the firm. If ownership-generated incentives matter, then the firm's performance should have improved after the management-led buyout.

That is what happened. Compared to their local competitors, HCA hospitals reduced capital investment, expenses, and staff numbers after the buyout.[40] HCA's operating profitability was higher after the buyout, but, because the extra debt meant higher (tax-deductible) interest payments, it paid less tax.[41] These changes happen more generally as well. On average, investment and employment falls following management-led buyouts and sales to private equity funds.[42] After firms are acquired by private equity funds, they tend to close low-productivity plants and open new high-productivity plants more aggressively than firms that have not been taken private. Wages per worker fall on average.[43]

Plenty of CEOs use their firms' profits to build empires, fund their own pet projects, and generally benefit themselves at the expense of investors. This could have happened at

HCA, except that the decision-makers there had a strong incentive to pay cash flow out to investors rather than keeping it within the firm—the decision-makers *were* the investors. Indeed, HCA paid out more cash to investors during the four years that its shares were held privately than it did during the previous 12 years combined.[44] A series of dividend payments totaling $4.4b was made in 2010 alone.[45]

All of these events occurred after the buyout, so would seem to benefit HCA's new owners. Fortunately for the pre-buyout owners, they were able to share in some of the spoils by extracting them up front, at the time of the buyout. A month before the buyout proposal was announced, HCA's share price was just $42.75, but the buyout partners paid $51 for each share they bought, a 19% premium.[46] (The premium for a typical buyout is approximately 29%.)[47] In total, shareholders received $3.4b more for their shares than they were worth a month before the buyout offer was announced.

At the time the buyout occurred, for each one-dollar increase in the purchase price, the pre-buyout shareholders would have been $400m better off and the buyout investors $400m worse off. If we are to understand how the benefits from a leveraged buyout are to be allocated, then we need to understand how the purchase price is determined. We need to know how such deals are done and we need to appreciate the potential for conflicts of interest involving the key players. That potential is always present. We saw a similar situation in Chapter 3, when Microsoft tried to acquire Yahoo. There the allegations were made by shareholders afraid that the target firm's CEO might be opposed to a deal at any price. That was not a problem at HCA, where the CEO, together with a very powerful director, was supportive of the deal. The potential problem at HCA was that the firm's insiders did not just support the deal, they wanted to be part of it—on the buy side!

Between a rock and a hard place

The private equity funds' objective was obvious: acquire HCA for the lowest price possible. HCA's rank-and-file shareholders wanted the purchase price to be as high as possible. Their ownership of HCA gave them bargaining power, and the buyout group needed to share some of the anticipated gains if it was to get access to the goose about to lay the golden eggs. However, as we saw in Chapter 3, despite having so much at stake, shareholders have to stand on the sidelines in such situations. HCA's rank-and-file shareholders delegated the task of negotiating with the buyout partners to the board of directors; the board delegated it to a special committee of independent directors.

The board was dominated by Frist, who was HCA's largest individual shareholder.[48] Together with his father, Frist had founded Nashville-headquartered HCA in 1968. He had been there as it grew into the country's biggest hospital chain and he had been there to rebuild it in the late 1990s after its ill-fated merger with Columbia Healthcare Corp.[49] At the time of the buyout, Frist had a foot in both camps. He was part of the buyout group, but he was a shareholder too. As Frist was rolling his shares over to the shell company, he would not be directly affected by the purchase price. However, if the price was high, the private equity funds would have to contribute more of their own cash. If the price was too high, they might walk away from the deal. Even if this did not happen, their larger contribution would mean that they would demand a larger percentage of the shares in the new firm, which would mean fewer shares for Frist. Unlike HCA's other shareholders, Frist benefited from a low price, not a high one, and that is why he was not a part of the special committee that bargained with the buyout group.

That left the directors on the special committee. One of their biggest challenges was the information available to the committee. The board's usual financial advisor, Merrill Lynch, was now unavailable because one of the participating private equity funds was its private equity affiliate, Merrill Lynch Global Private Equity. The two replacement financial advisors engaged by the committee (Credit Suisse and Morgan Stanley) had not been involved with HCA for several years, and so were playing catch-up in their own analysis.[50] All parties—the special committee and its two new advisors—were to some extent relying on financial projections prepared by Bovender and other executives who would be participating in the buyout as investors, and who therefore had their own conflict of interest. The best the board could do was engage its own advisors and hope that they would be able to provide accurate information in the limited time available.

The special committee was in an unenviable position. On the one hand, the directors' job was to get the best possible deal for shareholders; they were shareholders themselves, so they had a direct, though relatively small, financial interest in the outcome of negotiations. On the other hand, as one observer said, "in Nashville . . . there are three ways to do things: the right way, the wrong way, and the Frist way." If the press reports are to be believed, Frist did not like losing. Ten years previously, supposedly after it became clear that Frist would not be appointed chairman of Vanderbilt University, he quit the university's board of trustees and donated $25m to Princeton. More recently, his alma mater, Montgomery Bell Academy, had refused to go co-ed in return for a $100m donation from Frist. He did not just withdraw the offer. He quit the school board and financed the creation of a co-ed rival school across town.[51] Directors could reasonably anticipate some unpleasant future board meetings if they blocked the deal—that is if they kept their jobs as directors.

Another factor contributing to the committee's difficulties was the paucity of outside options. The committee negotiated a "go-shop period," during which HCA could solicit competing buyout offers, and engaged Credit Suisse and Morgan Stanley to go out and look for competing bidders.[52] In order to boost the number of potential bidders, HCA's board tried to level the playing field. One potential lender to the buyout group was allowed to conduct due diligence only on the condition that it did not enter into an exclusive arrangement with the three private equity funds. HCA executives were not permitted to negotiate the terms of their involvement until after the offer price was agreed. Frist was not allowed to enter into an exclusive arrangement with the three funds.[53] Despite these restrictions, no competing proposals were received during the go-shop period. Perhaps this is not surprising. What rival bidder would want to buy the firm when its largest individual shareholder (Frist), its current CEO (Bovender), and other senior executives were already linked with a rival consortium? The inevitable, and understandable, hostility from HCA's management would lower the price that any rival bidder would be willing to pay. To further complicate matters, the buyout bid was a so-called club deal, with three separate private equity funds part of the consortium. If only one had been involved, HCA could have sought competing bids from the other two, but that was not an option here.

A solution, or just another problem?

The buyout group had an information advantage, limited competition amongst potential bidders meant that it was the only bidder for the firm, and the involvement of the largest individual shareholder and the firm's senior executives put pressure on the board to ensure the deal went ahead. Despite this, HCA's board was able to negotiate a purchase price of $51 per share, a 19% premium on HCA's share price a month before the buyout proposal was announced. Alternatively, as some shareholders alleged, because of this, HCA's board was able to negotiate a purchase price of *only* $51 per share.[54]

Subsequent events gave an indication of how the benefits from the buyout were allocated between HCA's pre-buyout and post-buyout owners. A series of dividend payments totaling $4.4b was made in 2010 alone.[55] One year later, HCA issued new shares to outside investors, used the proceeds to repay some debt, and allowed its shares to trade on the NYSE once more. The buyout investors took the opportunity to collect $1.7b by selling some of their own shares at the same time. Including the dividends, that is a total of $6.1b in just over four years, and they still owned 72% of the firm—a stake worth $11b—even after these events. Not bad for an investment of $4.8b, and equivalent to earning a 37% annual rate of return throughout the period from the buyout until the shares were traded publicly again. The S&P 500 index, in contrast, had earned an annual rate of return of *minus* 1.8% over the same period. Adding everything up, the total gain resulting from the buyout—measured from one month before the merger announcement in July 2006 until just after the firm went public again in March 2011—was $16b. HCA's pre-buyout shareholders received just over a fifth of this and the buyout investors received the rest.[56]

Two interpretations of this outcome are possible. One is that the huge debt levels exposed HCA's post-buyout owners to enormous risk and that their large share of the $16b gains was compensation for bearing that risk. According to this interpretation, HCA's board did a good job for the firm's pre-buyout shareholders; leveraged buyouts are an effective way for firms to narrow the gap between ownership and control, and to pass some of the benefits of this narrowing onto shareholders. The other interpretation is that the firm's management could have achieved the post-buyout performance improvements while working for the pre-buyout owners, but waited until they stood to receive a larger percentage of any value gains they created before lifting their performance. According to this interpretation, HCA's board failed the firm's pre-buyout shareholders in two ways: first, by not extracting these performance improvements earlier; second, by not negotiating a higher price once the buyout plan was hatched. If this interpretation is correct, then leveraged buyouts are not a solution to manager–shareholder conflict, but just another way for executives and other firm insiders to transfer shareholders' wealth into their own pockets.

One thing is clear, however. Whether a leveraged buyout is good or bad for a firm's shareholders depends on the board's performance. It is up to a firm's board to pressure its CEO to make performance improvements under the firm's pre-buyout ownership, and if he waits to take the firm private before making these improvements then the board needs to negotiate a purchase price that reflects the expected post-buyout improvements. The board is the absolutely crucial piece of the puzzle. We will see it again and again throughout this book: tools that can reduce manager–shareholder conflict when used by effective boards can worsen it when used by ineffective ones.

Before and—especially—after the buyout, HCA's board monitored executives closely. Events at HCA show another way in which directors can influence executives' performance: boost executives' effective ownership stakes and then leave them to do what they are hopefully good at, which is to manage the firm. The bigger ownership stakes mean the executives have stronger incentives to increase the firm's market value; the stronger incentives mean there is less manager–shareholder conflict and less need for the board to monitor management closely.

Increased executive ownership stakes do not come cheap. Even with the cost-cutting techniques described in this chapter, generating incentives this way can cost shareholders tens of millions of dollars. That is money that ultimately finds its way into executives' pockets, which is why the issue of managerial ownership is intrinsically connected to the most controversial topic in corporate governance today and the one we look at next: executive pay.

I always felt, up until the somewhat difficult ending, that I was the owner.[1]

MICHAEL EISNER (2008)

5 A primer on pay
EXECUTIVE COMPENSATION AND EFFICIENT CONTRACTING

MICHAEL EISNER, DISNEY'S CEO for 21 years, was never far from the limelight. There were feuds with the founders of DreamWorks Studios and Pixar. High-profile court cases washed Disney's dirty linen in public. An especially nasty public battle involved the last remaining Disney executive with family ties to Walt himself.[2] However, the limelight shone brightest on Eisner's pay, especially in 1999. That was the year when he topped *BusinessWeek*'s rankings of CEO pay with $576m in pay for a year's work.[3] That was more than Disney's shareholders received in dividends that year and it was paid against a backdrop of falling profitability and poor stock returns.[4]

Eisner's $576m pay packet was not actually compensation just for his work in a single year. It was the consequence of a grant of stock options negotiated almost a decade earlier. Eisner got his massive payout because Disney's share price grew from $17 when the options were granted to $95 when he exercised them. If the share price had gone up further, his payoff would have been even greater; if it had fallen below the initial $17, his payoff would have been zero. Basing pay on firm performance like this allows boards to motivate executives to make personal sacrifices. These sacrifices can take many different forms—working harder, restricting perk consumption, resisting the temptation to build an empire—but they all benefit shareholders. Executives make these sacrifices because doing so improves the firm's performance, which increases their pay. From executives' point of view, benefiting shareholders is a mere byproduct. From shareholders' point of view, it is the only possible justification for such high pay levels.

But what sort of performance was Eisner being rewarded for? Although Disney's share price had grown rapidly since Eisner's options were granted, the overall stock market had done well too. In fact, if Disney had done only as well as the overall market, Eisner's entry in *BusinessWeek*'s 1999 rankings would still have been $295m.[5] Think about that for a moment. Even if Disney had only done as well as the market as a whole—if Eisner had been an "average" CEO—he would still have been in line for a payout of $295m.

It can seem hard to believe now, but early in Eisner's tenure, his pay arrangements were regarded as good for Disney's shareholders.[6] Later on, Eisner's pay arrangements were condemned.[7] How did it all go wrong? The answer involves an architect, an attorney, and an elementary school principal.

The limitations of performance-based pay

The bargaining-game framework introduced in Chapter 2 can be used to understand the negotiations involved in setting executives' pay. However, we need to consider one extra feature. In Chapter 2, the two sides (the CEO and the board) negotiated only over how to allocate the surplus from reaching agreement. Here the two sides also have to negotiate over how big to make the surplus in the first place. Of course, it is not phrased in those terms. What they really negotiate over is how strong to make the CEO's incentives to work hard. Will the CEO be motivated to work the long hours needed to properly evaluate projects? Will he sacrifice friendships for the good of the firm? Will he resist the temptation to build a legacy at shareholders' expense? These are just some of the issues that concern shareholders. The common theme is whether or not the CEO will make some personal sacrifice that benefits shareholders. Carefully designed compensation schemes can motivate a CEO to make such a sacrifice, even if he is entirely self-interested.

The two sides in pay negotiations need to overcome a serious problem: pay-for-sacrifice is not feasible because the board cannot observe the CEO's sacrifice. It is our old friend from Chapter 3, information asymmetry, back again. For example, when Eisner started work at Disney, two of his most important tasks were to oversee the development of the new theme park planned for the outskirts of Paris and to revive its hotel business. The board wanted him to put effort into evaluating and improving the Euro Disney plans, but it could never know exactly how much effort he devoted to the task. The board also wanted to discourage Eisner from making self-serving decisions when expanding the firm's hotel business. Directors soon realized that Eisner wanted to be a patron of architecture, but when he brought famous architects in to design the new hotels Disney was planning, directors could not tell whether he was advancing his own interests or lifting quality to benefit shareholders.[8] The board could not measure the sacrifice to a standard that would stand up in court, so it could not base Eisner's pay on his sacrifice.

The only feasible approach is to base the CEO's pay on what can be observed. For example, Disney's board could not observe the effort Eisner put into developing Euro Disney, but it could observe the new park's profitability. It would never know why Eisner promoted the use of famous architects for the new hotels, but it could observe the profitability of those hotels. If Eisner's pay was based, even indirectly, on the profitability of Euro Disney or the new hotels, then he would have some incentive to make a personal sacrifice to improve that profitability. The more personal benefits he was willing to sacrifice, the greater the profitability, and the greater his pay. The more sensitive his pay was to their profitability, the greater Eisner's reward from making the sacrifice, and so the more sacrifice he would be willing to make.

The development of overseas theme parks and new hotels was just a part of Eisner's job. Disney was in trouble when he joined. He also had to reinvigorate the film studio, increase the value generated by its film library, and improve the profitability of the existing theme parks, to name just three further challenges. Any effort he put into one task was effort he could not put into the others. If he behaved the way that economists assume people behave, he would have exerted the most effort on those tasks that generated the greatest personal benefit—in this case, the highest pay. If some tasks did not affect his pay, then he would exert no effort on them. The danger for shareholders is that a well-intentioned incentive scheme can backfire by encouraging the CEO to exert too much effort on some tasks and not enough on others. A common response is to base the CEO's pay on company-wide measures of performance, such as profits and the share price. After all, Disney's shareholders did not (or should not) care about the hotels any more or less than they cared about the film studio. What mattered was the performance of the firm as a whole, so that is what was used to set Eisner's pay.

The costs of performance-based pay

Making pay more sensitive to performance will motivate a CEO to make bigger sacrifices in an effort to boost firm performance—and to boost his pay. However, this comes at a cost. Two costs, actually, and they are both shared by the CEO and the firm's shareholders.

The first, and most obvious, cost reflects the fact that the CEO is doing things that he would not otherwise want to do. That is why we call them sacrifices. Putting effort into evaluating the plans for Euro Disney or passing up the opportunity to become an architecture patron would have made Eisner worse off. More effort meant less leisure; cheaper architects meant less prestige. The board boosted his pay in partial compensation, but this did not reduce the cost: it just shifted some of it onto shareholders.

The second cost is more subtle. Paying Eisner on the basis of Disney's performance shifted some of the risk of Disney-specific events from shareholders onto the CEO. For example, when cost overruns occurred at the new Euro Disney project, the low company profit meant that Eisner's pay fell. Although he came from a wealthy family and had enjoyed a successful career prior to joining Disney, the bulk of his wealth was tied up in Disney because Disney offered Eisner the possibility of many years of multi-million-dollar pay packages. If Disney performed poorly then Eisner's wealth would suffer. Exposure to risk like this is costly—that is why people buy insurance—and the increased exposure to risk is the source of the second cost of performance-based pay.

Basing Eisner's pay on Disney's performance meant shareholders were less exposed to Disney's firm-specific risk. For example, instead of incurring all of the consequences of those cost overruns, shareholders shared them with Eisner. However, there was a big difference between Eisner and the shareholders. Many of the latter owned diversified portfolios, perhaps through their investments in managed funds. For such investors, the prospect of unexpected cost overruns at Euro Disney faded into insignificance. Sure, Disney's share price would suffer if costs got out of control, but none of the other firms in their portfolios would be affected. If the shareholders had spread their wealth over enough firms and industries, then the effect of the drop in Disney's share price would be small because holding a diversified portfolio largely eliminates firm-specific risk. Executives do not have this luxury because they cannot diversify this risk away.

It is this different attitude to risk that generates the second cost of performance-based pay. As pay becomes more sensitive to a firm's performance, more firm-specific risk is shifted from shareholders to the CEO. Shareholders could have diversified this risk away, so they derive little benefit from reducing their exposure to it. However, the CEO cannot diversify this risk away, so the cost to him of the increased exposure to risk is much greater. The board can boost the CEO's pay to compensate for some of this extra risk, but, as for the first cost, this merely shifts some of the cost onto shareholders.

Eisner's first employment agreement

When Eisner's lawyer, Irwin Russell, and Disney's board chairman, Ray Watson, sat down in 1984 to negotiate the new CEO's first employment agreement, they were faced with two key questions. First, how sensitive would Eisner's compensation be to Disney's performance? Second, how valuable would the overall pay package be? The answer to the first question would determine the sacrifice the CEO would make for the firm's shareholders, and therefore the size of the surplus from reaching an agreement, which includes the extra value of Disney that comes from having performance-based pay, less the costs we met in the previous section. Economic theory suggests that the two sides would agree on a level of pay–performance sensitivity that makes this surplus as large as possible.[9] The answer to the second question would determine how this surplus would be shared. From what we saw in Chapter 2, the answer to the second question should depend on the relative bargaining power of Eisner and Disney's board.

Unfortunately for Eisner, the circumstances leading up to his appointment left him in a weak bargaining position. The previous CEO, Walt Disney's son-in-law Ron Miller, had frantically tried to recruit Eisner as his deputy. At the same time, Watson had wooed Eisner by saying he would recommend to the board that Eisner got Miller's job. For his part, Eisner had told his boss at Paramount, where he was company president, that he was about to be offered the Disney CEO job.[10] What could possibly go wrong? Plenty. For a start, when the board fired Miller, it opened up a competitive search for a new CEO rather than following its chairman's recommendation to offer the job to Eisner. Media speculation was rife, with suggested candidates including three current and former executives at rival film studios, in addition to Eisner.[11] For Eisner, worse news was to come: he learnt, via the *Wall Street Journal*, that he was about to be fired from Paramount.[12] He preempted his own dismissal and resigned. Eisner found himself in the unenviable position of competing for a new job with at least three other experienced executives. Although Disney soon offered Eisner the job, he was in a weak bargaining position: if pay negotiations broke down, Disney had other CEO candidates waiting in the wings; Eisner did not have another job to go to.

Russell and Watson agreed on a contract that would determine Eisner's compensation for the next six years. Its key components were an annual salary of $750,000 and rules for determining future performance-based payments, which would come to dwarf Eisner's salary. Those payments came in two forms: an annual bonus and a grant of options to buy Disney shares in the future.[13]

The size of Eisner's annual bonus depended on Disney's profitability. Each year, he received 2% of any "economic profit" that Disney earned. Economic profit is different from the profit firms report in their financial statements. In addition to the usual costs used to calculate profit—such as the firm's operating expenses, interest that has to be paid on its loans, and taxes—economic profit recognizes the cost that shareholders incur by investing in the firm's shares instead of some other investment. For example, Disney's shareholders could have invested their savings in some other asset, maybe a bank deposit, and earned a return. They missed out on that return because they had invested in Disney's shares instead. It is this cost—economists call it an opportunity cost, accountants call it a capital charge—that was subtracted from Disney's profit to obtain the economic profit that determined Eisner's annual bonus.

The options Eisner was granted in his first employment agreement expired ten years after he joined Disney and gave him the right to buy a 1.5% stake in the firm for $29m, which was the market value of such a stake when he joined. If the value of the firm increased over the next ten years, then so would the value of the 1.5% stake that he had the right to buy, but the purchase price would be fixed at $29m. This option would end up worthless if the value of the stake fell below $29m and stayed there for ten years.

Combating short-termism

Pay arrangements like Eisner's generate strong incentives to increase a firm's profitability. If an executive is able to make a firm more profitable, then reported profits will rise, and so will the executive's bonus. The share price should also rise—once investors realize the firm has become more profitable—which makes the executive's shares, as well as all his options to buy those shares, more valuable.

Unfortunately, pay arrangements like Eisner's also give the executive a strong incentive to "manage" the firm's earnings, taking them away from periods when they do not contribute much to the executive's bonus and adding them to periods when they will boost pay. For example, if the firm's profits are currently so low that no bonus will be paid or so high that this year's bonus cannot get any bigger, then a CEO might try to shift profits forward into the future. He might have the firm defer revenue until the next fiscal year or even prepay some of next year's costs this year. On the other hand, if boosting this year's profits would increase the CEO's bonus, he has an incentive to bring forward reported revenue and defer costs.

Shifting earnings across time like this has little effect on long-run profits, so the main cost to shareholders is the higher CEO pay. However, bonus arrangements can also create an incentive to reduce actual profits in the long run in order to increase reported profits in the short-run. This short-term focus is much more costly to shareholders. For example, Eisner could have cut back on Disney's maintenance spending and its investment in theme parks. In the long run, patrons would have realized that the quality of the theme-park experience had fallen and might have gone elsewhere, but in the short run revenues would have held up. The result? Higher short-run profits and a bigger CEO bonus.

Short-termism takes many forms. For example, executives may favor projects with high short-term cash flows but bad long-term prospects. Alternatively, they might put their effort into tasks that have immediate observable rewards (such as completing a major acquisition) and divert effort away from tasks that are at least as important, but with outcomes that will not be observed for years (such as doing the proper assessment needed to ensure that only acquisitions that benefit shareholders are undertaken). The common factor is that profitability and the CEO's bonus increase in the short run. They will fall in the long run, but that affects the CEO only if he is still around. It is a real concern for shareholders, because average CEO tenures are about six years.[14] A bonus scheme might even create the incentive for a CEO to leave early, after pumping up the bonus, of course.

In principle, boards can reduce the severity of these unwelcome incentives by paying part of an executive's compensation in shares or, as in Eisner's case, options. A firm's share price will suffer if executives chase high short-run reported profits at the expense of lower long-run actual profits. We saw in Chapter 4 that ownership of shares or options gives an executive an incentive to act in ways that increase a firm's share price, and a disincentive to act in ways that reduce its share price. The cost of pumping up short-term profits to boost a bonus may therefore be too high to be worthwhile if an executive owns enough shares and options. Disney's board made sure that Eisner had plenty.

However, it is not quite so simple in practice. Investors use a firm's current profitability to forecast future profitability, and these forecasts influence how much they are willing to pay for a firm's shares. This gives executives whose wealth depends on their firm's share price an incentive to pump up profits in the short term—which increases investors' forecasts of profits in the long term—even if this means reducing the firm's actual profits in the long term. The more sensitive the CEO's wealth is to his firm's share price, the greater the incentive to chase short-term profits in this way.[15]

In the cases we have seen so far, the problem is that short-term pay gains are not reversed in the long term if those short-term gains are found to have come at the expense of long-term performance. High bonuses are not paid back; an executive's windfall from selling shares when prices are artificially high is not passed onto shareholders if the share price subsequently falls; pay rises negotiated when times look good are difficult to reverse.[16]

One response is for firms to hold onto short-term pay for long enough that unwarranted pay in the short term can be clawed back in the long term. Bonuses can be calculated based on performance over periods spanning several years. Portions of bonuses can be held back in a so-called bonus bank, and paid out to executives in future years if particular targets are met. Executives can also be motivated to focus on long-term performance by making them wait for long periods of time before they take ownership of shares and options granted to them as part of their pay packages. These so-called vesting periods can last for many years. For example, 20% of the options Eisner was granted in his first employment agreement vested each year for the first five years after he started work.

Unfortunately, even these responses can create problems of their own. For example, executives who lose their jobs following poor firm performance might lose all their unvested shares and options, so long vesting periods give CEOs a strong incentive to avoid being fired. What is a good way to avoid being fired? Boost the firm's short-term profitability, of course, and hope that the board mistakes that for improved long-term performance.[17] The lesson is clear: boards have delicate balancing acts to carry out when designing executive pay packages if they are to avoid the traps of short-termism.

The role of managerial wealth

Four years after Russell and Watson negotiated Eisner's first employment agreement, they sat down to negotiate a new one. They needed to reach agreement on the same two key questions as in 1984. First, how sensitive would Eisner's pay be to Disney's performance? The answer would determine the strength of Eisner's financial incentive to make personal sacrifices that benefited Disney's shareholders. Second, how would the surplus from reaching agreement be divided? The questions were the same as in 1984, but the circumstances surrounding the negotiations were quite different. How Disney's board and CEO responded to the changed circumstances reveals a great deal about the first question in pay negotiations: how sensitive should pay be to performance?

The highest profile change at Disney during the first four years of Eisner's tenure was the turnaround in performance of Disney's motion picture business. It released only 12 films in 1988, but three of them—*Who Framed Roger Rabbit?*, *Good Morning Vietnam*, and *Three Men and a Baby*—were amongst the industry's six highest grossing films of the year. Disney had the largest market share of any film studio, 19%, up from a miserable 3% in 1984.[18] However, the main sources of improvement in the company's profitability were less exciting: higher admission prices at theme parks; expansion of Disney-owned hotels; and home-video sales of classic animated films from Disney's back catalog.[19]

The improved performance was reflected in Disney's bottom line. Profit was more than five times larger in 1988 than it had been in the year before Eisner joined.[20] This profit was what determined Eisner's annual bonus. With higher profits came a higher share price. $100 invested in Disney shares the day before the board approved Eisner's appointment in 1984 would have grown to $447 by the time his new employment contract was signed early in 1989, an annual rate of return of 42%.[21] As Disney's share price grew, so did the value of the options that Eisner had been awarded in his first employment agreement.

When Eisner instructed his lawyer to negotiate the new employment contract at the end of 1988, Eisner had already been paid $83m for his first four years of employment.[22] Disney was proving to be quite a magical kingdom for Eisner. His increased wealth affected the choice of pay–performance sensitivity in two different ways. First, just as shareholders incurred an opportunity cost when they invested in Disney shares, Eisner incurred an opportunity cost when he put effort into his job as CEO. For example, rather than working an extra weekend in 1989, he could spend the time at his new 16,000 square foot "log cabin" in Aspen, designed for him by a leading architect, Robert Stern.[23] (Remember that name.) If Eisner was to be motivated to work that extra weekend, he needed to be compensated—via his pay for the resulting improved performance of Disney—for the lost opportunity to do something else. The required compensation would be greater in 1989 than it was in 1984. After all, Aspen beckoned.[24] Disney's increased size meant that the value Eisner could add to the firm by working that extra weekend had increased as well. Economists looking at a situation like this predict that Eisner's pay would be made more sensitive to Disney's performance; if it was not, he would have slackened off too much.

Eisner's increased wealth affected the agreed sensitivity of pay to performance in a second way. A common view amongst economists is that as individuals become wealthier, the compensation they need for taking on a given amount of risk falls.[25] Thus, a billionaire may need no compensation to gamble $1,000 on the toss of a coin, but the rest of us would need some sort of inducement to take part. Similarly, the 1989 version of Eisner would have needed less compensation than his 1984 counterpart for having a given amount of his pay at risk. As the cost of shifting risk from the shareholders to the CEO had fallen, so the cost of providing the CEO with incentives had fallen. This would have encouraged both sides to agree to make the CEO's pay more sensitive to performance.

Consistent with these predictions, Eisner's new contract tied his pay even more closely to Disney's performance than the previous contract. Eisner's annual bonus remained set at

2% of Disney's economic profit, but his exposure to Disney's share price increased due to the granting of options to buy another 1.5% of the firm, this time for $142m.[26] At the time Eisner signed his initial employment agreement, if Disney's enterprise value had increased by 1%, the value of the options to be granted during the life of the contract would have increased by just $0.2m. In contrast, at the time he signed his second contract, the value of the options to be granted during that contract's term would increase by $0.7m if Disney's enterprise value increased by 1%. However, this captures just a part of Eisner's new pay–performance sensitivity: the shares and unexercised options remaining from his first contract would increase in value by $1.2m.[27] In total, the value of his shares and options from the two contracts would increase by $1.9m for each 1% increase in Disney's enterprise value, an almost ten-fold increase from 1984.

Eisner was even wealthier in 1996, when he signed his third employment agreement. Under his third contract, the sensitivity of his wealth to Disney's enterprise value increased by a factor of almost six. If Disney's enterprise value rose by 1%, Eisner's existing portfolio of Disney shares and options would increase in value by $8.7m, and the additional options that Eisner would receive under his third contract would increase in value by $2.4m. Eisner said that he felt like the owner of Disney during his time as CEO.[28] Now we have some idea why: his personal wealth was very closely tied to Disney's enterprise value.

Competing for managerial talent

Disney and Eisner were operating on different sides of a competitive market for managerial talent. The competitive process in any talent market works like some sort of matchmaker. This matchmaker lines executives up from the most capable to the least capable. Then it arranges firms in a separate queue, with the firms where executives can add the most value at the front and those where executives can add the least value at the back. Finally, it pairs them up, with the top ranked executive being partnered with the firm where executive talent adds the most value, the second-ranked executive being partnered with the firm where executive talent can add the second-most value, and so on. Executive pay is highest at the front of the queue, and it falls as we work our way towards the back.

When Eisner's first employment agreement was negotiated, he was a long way from the front of the line of executives queuing up in the market for managerial talent. By the time Eisner's second agreement was negotiated, Disney's strong financial performance under his leadership meant that he was much nearer the front. The man who had resigned from Paramount just as he was about to be fired was being described on the front cover of *Time* magazine as the man who transformed Disney.[29] By 1996, when his third employment agreement was negotiated, he was even closer to the front of the queue. As Eisner moved towards the front of the queue, competition in the managerial talent market meant that he could expect to be paired off with a higher-ranked firm. As Eisner's outside opportunities improved, the amount that Disney's board had to pay him to keep him from moving to another firm increased.

Something else happened during that period: Disney grew much larger. In fact, its enterprise value increased by a factor of almost 20 during the terms of Eisner's first two employment agreements.[30] A talented CEO could add much more value to Disney in 1996 than the same CEO would have been able to add in 1984. A poor CEO could destroy much more value as well. Competition between firms for good executives must have contributed to the increase in the amount that Disney was willing to pay for its CEO. No matter who Disney employed as its CEO in 1996, we should expect that CEO to be paid more than they would have been paid in 1984. That is how competitive talent markets work and it is one of the reasons why Eisner's pay grew so much during his tenure at Disney.

There is a more general point to make here as well. As the size of firms has increased, so has the value created by talented CEOs, and therefore so has their pay. It is not just the size of the CEO's own firm that matters here, but also the size of other firms in the economy, because if firms on the whole are growing larger then the gains from employing the best CEOs grow as well, and so—thanks to competition for CEOs—will the average level of CEO pay.[31] And firms are growing larger: the average market value of the 500 largest U.S. firms increased by a factor of five between 1980 and 2011.[32] That is why many economists believe that the increased size of corporations provides part of the explanation for extremely high levels of executive compensation. However, it is a controversial topic. Exactly how much of the increase it explains is a matter of hot debate.[33]

The role of bargaining power

Eisner's growing reputation, and the outside employment opportunities that it reflected, boosted his bargaining power in his pay negotiations with Disney's board. By 1996, when his third employment agreement was negotiated, he was in an even stronger position, thanks to his influence over board appointments in the previous decade. The outcome of those negotiations illustrates how CEO power affects the second question in pay negotiations: how much pay does a CEO receive.

Eisner had failed spectacularly to groom a successor, or, perhaps, succeeded spectacularly in *not* grooming a successor. Frank Wells, Eisner's No. 2 since they had both joined Disney in 1984, had died in a helicopter crash in April 1994. Jeffrey Katzenberg, who Eisner had brought with him from Paramount to head Walt Disney Studios, left Disney in September 1994 after Eisner had refused to appoint him to Wells' old position as company president.[34] Michael Ovitz was hired as president in October 1995, but left 14 months later.[35] Disney's latest chief financial officer had lasted nine months in the job before quitting.[36] If Disney could not agree the terms of Eisner's new employment contract, it was not obvious who could replace him as CEO.

This entrenchment helped Eisner in his negotiations with the board. When the second contract was negotiated, there had been several potential internal candidates to replace Eisner if a deal could not be reached, including Wells and Katzenberg. In 1996, there was only Ovitz, but he was about to be fired, not promoted. If a deal with Eisner had not been reached, Disney would have had to go outside and search for a replacement. This restricted Disney's outside options and increased the amount that Eisner achieved from the negotiations.

Further strengthening his position, Eisner had closer personal ties to directors than in the past. Indeed, by the time of Eisner's third employment contract, eight of the ten independent directors had been appointed to the board since his arrival.[37] One of those new directors was Robert Stern, the architect who designed his parents' Manhattan apartment in the 1970s and his Aspen holiday home in the 1980s.[38] Prior to joining the board in 1992, Stern had designed two hotels for Disney in Florida, and another two in France. The work continued after he became a director: the Feature Animation Building at Burbank, a hotel in Japan, and more projects in Florida.[39] Another new director, the principal of the elementary school that Eisner's children had attended, joined the board in 1993.[40] The president of Georgetown University, where Eisner had sat on the board for several years, joined shortly before Eisner's new contract was approved.[41] The discussion in Chapter 2 suggests that these changes in board composition increased Eisner's bargaining power, meaning he would receive a larger share of the surplus from reaching agreement over the terms of his third contract than he did from the first two.

Another board appointment made Eisner's position even stronger. Less than three years after Eisner arrived at Disney, Irwin Russell joined the board. Russell, who would be a Disney director until 2001, had been Eisner's personal lawyer since the mid-1970s and had represented Eisner in the pay negotiations when Eisner joined Disney.[42] He was the trustee of the trust that was buying land in Malibu in 1996 for Eisner's new home, to be designed by Robert Stern. (Yes, the same Robert Stern.) Russell's office address was even listed as the mailing address for Eisner's primary residence.[43]

Despite their very close personal ties, Russell chaired Disney's compensation committee at the time of Eisner's pay negotiations. The compensation committee is responsible for determining the compensation of the firm's CEO and other senior executives. As the committee's chairman, Russell played a key role in determining compensation at Disney. Surely this put Russell in an awkward position when negotiating with Eisner, on Disney's behalf, over pay? Apparently not, because Russell did not negotiate with Eisner. He negotiated *for* Eisner. He temporarily stepped down from the compensation committee and Watson temporarily stepped up to represent Disney.[44]

Russell was wearing two hats. When he sat around the boardroom table wearing his Disney director hat, his job was to advance the best interests of Disney shareholders, and if that meant conflict with Eisner, then so be it—he was working for the shareholders. When Russell sat down to negotiate the terms of Eisner's third employment contract, this time wearing his I'm-Eisner's-personal-lawyer hat, he was working to advance the best interests of Eisner, just as he had worked to advance Eisner's interests when he helped negotiate the latter's first two contracts. When Russell chaired compensation committee meetings that set the pay for the firm's senior executives below the CEO level, he again was working for Disney's shareholders. His goals: make the Disney cake as large as possible and get as much of it as possible for shareholders. The difficulty he faced was that Eisner's pay would be set relative to other executives' pay, so the more successful he was when wearing his I-work-for-shareholders hat, the less successful he would be when he was wearing his I'm-Eisner's-personal-lawyer hat. If Russell could not resolve this conflict, then the balance of bargaining power would shift in Eisner's favor.

Offsetting these influences, and weakening Eisner's strong bargaining position, were directors' fears of shareholder outrage if Eisner received an excessively generous pay package. Eisner's third contract was negotiated a few months before the next annual shareholders' meeting. Shareholders were already angry about executive pay at Disney. In fact, some institutional investors would promote a campaign to withhold votes from the five directors who were standing for reelection to the board. Thirteen percent of votes were withheld: not enough to kick any directors off the board, but large by historical standards and large enough to send a clear message.[45] Later that year, Disney's was named the "worst board" in America by *BusinessWeek* magazine.[46] Directors who were concerned for their own future on Disney's board, or for seats on other firms' boards, and anticipated such reactions, would bargain harder to limit Eisner's pay in the negotiations.

The contract that Eisner and Disney signed left his annual salary unchanged, but modified the formula used to calculate his annual bonus. It also granted him options to buy another 1.2% of the firm, vesting over the lifetime of the contract.[47] Eisner's bargaining power had increased across the three employment agreements; unsurprisingly, so did the level of pay that he was able to negotiate. Measured at the time the options were granted, Eisner's option grants were worth $12m for the first (six year) contract, $40m for the second (ten year) contract, and $108m for the third (ten year) contract.[48]

With friends like these...

Eisner's power peaked in the mid-1990s, when he set out to recruit his close friend Michael Ovitz to replace the late Frank Wells as company president. Eisner and Ovitz had taken vacations together; Ovitz had been at Eisner's bedside for days after the latter's quadruple heart bypass; now, or so Ovitz thought, they would run Disney as partners.[49] Disney's board had little involvement in the process. Instead, Irwin Russell, Eisner's personal attorney and chair of the compensation committee, ran the negotiations over Ovitz's pay (and subsequently collected a $250,000 fee for his trouble).[50] The first time that the compensation committee met to discuss the terms of Ovitz's employment contract was six weeks *after* Eisner and Ovitz had signed the agreement that outlined the basic terms of his appointment. That is also how long Disney's board waited before it met to approve Ovitz's appointment.[51]

Within a few months of starting work, Ovitz's "elitist" behavior was rubbing Disney's employees up the wrong way. Eisner was complaining to directors that Ovitz was failing to adapt to the company culture. Concerns were growing about Ovitz's alleged extravagant spending.[52] Other executives complained that he was wasting time on a string of marginal projects.[53]

Less than a year after Ovitz started work, Eisner sent an emissary to suggest that his friend start looking for a graceful exit. Ovitz resisted the overture at first, tried and failed to get a job elsewhere, and then told Eisner he was staying put.[54] Eisner had little choice: the only way to get rid of Ovitz was to fire him. It took another emissary, but Ovitz's employment was eventually terminated.[55] The press release said he had left "by mutual agreement."[56] Those three words ensured that Ovitz received the severance pay specified in his employment agreement, including a $39m cash payout and stock options worth $89m.[57] It was a massive payout for 14 months' work. The blame was laid squarely at Eisner's feet.

Some shareholders, outraged at the scale of Ovitz's severance package, tried to challenge the arrangement in the courts.[58] They alleged that Disney's directors breached their fiduciary duty to shareholders. First, the shareholders claimed, the board should have had greater involvement in the hiring and pay-setting processes. Second, Ovitz's performance was so poor that the board could and should have fired him "for cause," which would have allowed Disney to avoid making the large severance payout. It took ten years and six individual court decisions, but the case was eventually resolved in directors' favor.[59] Eisner and the other directors did not engage in any self-dealing, so they fulfilled their duty of loyalty to shareholders. Thanks to the all-powerful business judgment rule, their duty of care was fulfilled as well. Eisner and his fellow directors did not emerge unscathed however. According to the judge who wrote the key decision, Eisner was "Machiavellian" and "imperial," and had "stacked his (and I intentionally write 'his' as opposed to 'the company's') board of directors with friends and other acquaintances . . ."[60] Yet, despite this rebuke for the CEO, the business judgment rule left the judge powerless to intervene.

The Ovitz case shows that the courts will not try to implement good corporate governance for shareholders. In fact, the judge made this point explicitly: the law "cannot hold fiduciaries liable for a failure to comply with the aspirational ideal of best practices."[61] Shareholders need not waste their time looking to the courts for help enforcing good governance. It is a firm's board, and not the courts, that must prevent a powerful CEO from dominating the pay-setting process.

Measuring pay

As Eisner's employment agreements illustrate, executive pay comes in many different forms. Events at Disney show that pay delivered in some of these forms can be especially difficult to measure. That is a pity, because accurately measuring pay is crucial for good corporate governance. A clear picture of a CEO's pay gives shareholders more information when they decide how to vote at the annual meeting. It gives directors a better idea of whether the CEO's pay is justified by his performance and helps activist investors decide whether or not to involve themselves in a firm's affairs.

How much was Eisner paid? His annual salary is easily dealt with: just count the salary actually paid during that year. Dealing with Eisner's annual bonus is a little more difficult, because although the rule used to calculate his bonus was written into his multi-year employment contract, the amount actually paid varied from year to year according to Disney's profitability. However, what matters to shareholders in any particular year is the amount the firm has actually paid its CEO in that year. It is reported in the proxy statement released annually.

This leaves options and other stock-based forms of pay, which are the ones that cause all the problems. Press coverage often focusses on executives' profits from option exercises. That is not surprising, because this approach can make for some spectacular headlines. For example, in its survey of executive pay for 1993, *BusinessWeek* magazine ranked Eisner as the highest paid CEO, with total compensation of $203m; the second place-getter was paid "just" $53m.[62] In a precursor to what would happen with Eisner's even bigger payday five years later, almost all of Eisner's total can be tracked down to a single day, when he exercised approximately two-thirds of the options he had been awarded. He paid Disney $20m for shares worth $222m.[63] *BusinessWeek* counted the resulting profit of $202m towards his compensation that year. This is hardly an accurate measure of Eisner's pay in 1992. He earned those options in the 1980s, not at the end of 1992.

If we used this standard, Eisner's reported option-based compensation during his first decade at Disney would have been the net payoff of $33m in 1988 from exercising approximately a third of the options granted under the terms of his first contract, $202m in 1993 from exercising the other two thirds, and zero in the other eight years. Another approach, which the SEC has required firms to use when reporting compensation since 2010, is to report an estimate of the market value of options at the time they are granted. Although pricing options is often described as "rocket science," the numbers these calculations produce are only estimates, and often not very precise estimates. NASA would never have made it to the moon if its calculations were as imprecise as the ones used to value executives' stock options. Nevertheless, if this reporting standard had been applied in the past, the size of Eisner's reported option-based compensation during his first decade at Disney would have been the estimated market value of the first combined option grant, $12m, in 1984; the estimated market value of the second combined option grant, $40m, in 1989; and zero in the other eight years. Different valuation models would have given different estimates, but the timing would have been the same.

Both approaches can give a misleading impression of pay levels. What is needed is a measure of pay that better captures the compensation that Eisner received from his options in each year that he worked at Disney. The approach that is introduced here, and which is used throughout this book, is a variant of one that has been advocated by leading scholars in accounting, economics, and finance.[64] It spreads the compensation from option grants out over time. The component of compensation from options in any given year is the extra wealth the CEO received from his past and present option grants by working that year.

The simplest way to explain how this works involves a couple of "What if?" questions. Start with the first year. What if Eisner had worked for just the first year and then quit? He did not receive the options granted in his first contract all at once. Instead, each year, for five years, 20% of the options vested. That meant that if Eisner left Disney at the end of the first year, he would have received only the 20% of the options that had vested, and he would have had to exercise them as soon as he left the firm. The vested options would have been worth $3.3m to him.[65] We count this as the option-component of his first year of pay.

What if, instead, Eisner had worked for the second year as well and then quit? He would have been able to extend the lifetime of the first 20% of his options until the end of the second year and would also have received the second 20% batch. However, he would have had to exercise both batches soon after he left. Extending the lifetime of the first batch by a year would have been worth $0.2m to Eisner and receiving the second batch would have been worth $12.8m. In total, the option-component of his second year of pay comes to $13m.[66]

We could continue to do this for every year that Eisner worked at Disney, calculating the value of extending the lifetimes of the options that had already vested (out to their maximum lifetime of ten years), and adding this to the value of the options that were scheduled to vest during the year. Figure 5.1 shows Eisner's pay at Disney, with option-based pay reported this way. For example, option-based pay amounts to $13m in 1986 (even though no options were granted or exercised that year) and $22m in 1993 (even though that year Eisner received $202m from exercising options that had vested in previous years). This approach—reporting pay as it is earned—smooths out option-based

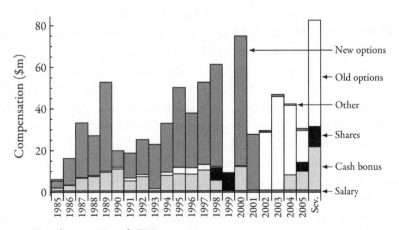

FIGURE 5.1 Eisner's pay as Disney's CEO

pay relative to the other two reporting standards and is used throughout this book for the purposes of reporting compensation levels. It gives a more accurate measure of CEO pay than approaches that recognize compensation only when options are exercised or granted—and shows that Eisner was paid $802m for 21 years' work.

Just what sort of performance is being rewarded?

Less than a year after his third contract was finalized, Eisner exercised all of the options granted in 1989 that had vested up until then. He paid Disney $130m in return for shares worth $700m, giving him a net payoff of $570m.[67] At first glance, this payoff was Eisner's reward for Disney's strong financial performance during his time as CEO. However, look a little closer and it raises serious questions about the desirability of motivating CEOs using options, questions such as what sort of performance is rewarded.

Eisner's jaw-dropping payoff reflected Disney's strong share-price performance during the period: if shareholders had bought Disney shares when Eisner's options were granted and held them, reinvesting all dividends, until the last options vested, their portfolio would have earned an average annual rate of return of 16%. That return was undoubtedly high, especially as it was maintained over a decade, but industry-wide returns were high in Disney's main lines of business as well. For example, if shareholders had invested in a portfolio of non-Disney film and television businesses over the same period, their average annual rate of return would also have been 16%. For non-Disney hotel operators, the average annual rate of return was 12%; for non-Disney toy manufacturers, it was 24%.[68] The value of Eisner's stock options appears to have grown largely because the industries in which Disney operated were performing very well.

The close relationship between Eisner's pay and industry-wide performance indicates a misallocation of risk between Disney's shareholders and its CEO. Eisner was being rewarded for his sacrifices that helped increase Disney's share price, but he was also exposed to the risk of events outside his control also affecting the share price. It would have been much cheaper for Disney's shareholders to have borne some of this risk themselves rather than compensating Eisner for bearing it instead. An optimal employment contract would have shifted as much of this risk as possible onto shareholders. It could have done this by filtering out the effects of all shocks that were observable, outside of Eisner's control, and which Eisner found more costly to bear than shareholders.[69]

It sounds simple, but in practice, shifting specific risks onto shareholders like this can be difficult. Some of the underlying factors affecting Disney's share price are easy to identify, such as adverse weather events that reduce visitor numbers in Florida and a weak dollar that boosts overseas-visitor numbers. However, the extent of their effect on Disney's performance will not be known precisely, making it difficult to adjust pay without opening up yet another round of bargaining games involving the CEO and the board. Other underlying factors may be unknown.

There is a simple, practical approach to improving the allocation of risk that boards can use. This approach, relative performance evaluation, sets the CEO's pay on the basis of how the firm performs relative to firms operating in similar industries. A CEO will not be rewarded just because his firm performs well—it will have to perform better than other firms in the industry. The superficial motivation for relative performance evaluation is that it is fair: shareholders should pay only for above-average performance. However, the contribution it can make to shareholder value is actually more subtle. It motivates executives to make sacrifices that affect something they can influence, which is the firm's performance relative to the industry, without exposing them to risk that could be more easily diversified by shareholders, which is the performance of the industry as a whole. There is little to be gained by making pay sensitive to industry-wide performance. All that does is force shareholders to compensate the executive for bearing risk that generates no offsetting incentive benefits.

A subtle source of manager–shareholder conflict

Executives can have a significant effect on the risks facing their firms' shareholders. Eisner did when he engineered Disney's acquisition of Capital Cities/ABC in 1996, acquiring a firm that had an enterprise value more than half as big as Disney's in a deal that involved Disney borrowing $8.8b.[70] Executives find it much more difficult than shareholders to diversify away risks such as these. That is why executives tend to dislike risk more than shareholders. If executives are left to their own devices, they will have the firm take too little risk for shareholders' liking. If boards want executives to take on an appropriate level of risk then something has to be done to overcome the effects of executives' difficulties in diversifying risk.

One way that boards address this problem is to pay executives using options. This motivates executives to take on more risk. If the firm's performance is good and its share price climbs, then the executives' options can become very valuable. However, if the results are poor and the firm's share price falls, all that happens is that the executives are left holding options that are worthless. Greater risk increases the upside potential, but has no effect on the downside. When executives own options, risk is not something to be feared: it is a source of value. The danger is that boards get it wrong and grant too many options. If that happens, executives may take much more risk than shareholders would like.

Another approach, also used by Disney's board, is the use of long-term employment agreements. Almost half of large corporations use explicit agreements when employing CEOs.[71] A typical agreement covers a three-year term and is 13 pages long, but the details vary from firm to firm. For example, Ray Irani's original contract at Occidental Petroleum had a seven-year term that was automatically extended each day.[72] Employment agreements typically specify the CEO's responsibilities and any additional jobs titles, such as board chairman or company president.[73] They will specify crucial aspects of the executive's pay package, as well as the precise descriptions of the types of employment termination that guarantee the executive receives severance pay. For example, if Eisner was ever stripped of his chairmanship of Disney's board then he could resign as CEO for "good reason" and collect that severance pay.[74]

Just like stock options, long-term employment agreements limit the downside risk of executives' pay without restricting the upside risk. Often they stop pay from decreasing if a firm performs poorly by including explicit clauses that prevent reductions in the executive's pay during the term of the agreement. Even if such a clause is omitted, carefully specified severance pay arrangements will make it costly for a firm to fire an executive or induce him to resign. (Just look at Ovitz.) That is why long-term employment agreements give executives greater protection against dismissal. This protection makes it easier for an executive to resist pressure to renegotiate a lower level of pay during periods of poor firm performance. Despite this downside protection, long-term employment agreements do not prevent pay increases during periods of good firm performance. The ability to renegotiate an agreement means that if a firm's short-term performance is good enough that an executive's outside options improve, then the board may have to agree to a boost in pay to keep the executive.

The downward rigidity in pay, without offsetting upward rigidity, is why long-term employment agreements make risk more attractive to an executive. It means that he still gets the benefit of better-than-expected outcomes, while getting some protection against worse-than-expected outcomes. It is almost like the executive has an option, but this one is on his human capital rather than the firm's shares. The effect is similar. Longer-term agreements give greater protection and so create stronger incentives for risk taking.[75]

Not every firm needs to use long-term employment agreements. However, any firm that would find it relatively easy to fire an executive who has fallen out of favor is prone to executives being excessively risk averse. Perhaps the cost of firing an executive is low, which tends to be the case for executives who are hired from outside the firm and so start off with relatively weak personal ties to directors. Perhaps it is relatively easy to replace fired executives, as is the case when firms operate in industries for which executives need generic management skills rather than firm- or industry-specific ones. These are the types of firms that use long-term employment agreements in practice.[76] However, employment agreements are less important for older executives. Their longer track records mean that their career prospects are less sensitive to the short-term performance of their current firms, giving them less to fear from short-term bad news. This might explain why older executives are less likely to have explicit severance agreements than their younger colleagues.[77]

As well as reducing manager–shareholder conflict over risk, long-term employment agreements help reduce the severity of short-termism by reducing CEOs' reluctance to take on projects that are good for their firm in the long run but look bad in the short run. The resulting downward pay rigidity reduces the likelihood that the CEO's pay will be revised downwards in the short term, while still allowing the CEO to benefit when the good long-term performance is revealed. Unfortunately for shareholders, long-term employment agreements do not completely eliminate short-termism. They will not stop a CEO from wanting to artificially boost short-term profits. In fact, they might even make things worse in the year or two before a contract runs out as the CEO seeks to lock in high pay when the agreement is renewed.

Making sure that pay promises are kept

Shares and options offer one way to motivate executives to focus on a firm's long-term performance. They have another important benefit as well: granting shares and options actually commits the firm to keep its promises to reward executives for the firm's long-run performance. Do not underestimate the importance of such commitment. Disney tried a different approach to rewarding one Disney executive for long-run performance and it did not work out well.

Jeffrey Katzenberg, an ex-Paramount executive like Eisner, followed his old boss to Disney. He was appointed chairman of Walt Disney Studios and given the task of turning around the poorly performing movie division. He decided to revive the animation operation. Output increased from a new animated feature film every four years to one a year; animation staff numbers increased from 170 to 600 during his first five years in charge; and scripts were used in film development, just like in live-action movies, rather than storyboards.[78] The effects of such decisions on Disney's profitability were long lasting. In the short run, production costs and ticket revenue were affected. In the long run, profits from merchandising, home video sales, and the Broadway musical versions of animated films were also affected.

Disney tried to reduce the prospect of short-termism by making Katzenberg's pay sensitive to the long-run consequences of his actions and decisions. It promised to pay him 2% of the profits each year from the films and television shows produced while he was running Walt Disney Studios. These payments were to continue even after he left Disney.[79] This arrangement gave Katzenberg a strong incentive to improve the long-term performance of the Disney studio. In addition, by homing in on the performance of his own projects, it shielded Katzenberg from the risk associated with parts of Disney's business that he had no influence over. For example, shareholders, not Katzenberg, carried the risk associated with the performance of Disney's theme parks and hotels, reducing the misallocation of risk that can so easily come with performance-based pay.

This seems fine in principle, but the promise to make performance-based payments even after an executive leaves a firm is not especially credible: as long as the executive is working for the firm, he cannot be short-changed without risking his resignation, but once he has gone, it is tempting to stop the checks. Katzenberg learnt that the hard way. When he resigned from Disney in 1994 after not being promoted to company president,

Eisner refused to pay out the bonuses, arguing that because he had resigned before the end of his contract, the bonus scheme did not apply. Katzenberg sued Disney for the money he claimed he was owed. The dispute was settled three years later, but not before much dirty linen had been aired in public. Disney agreed to pay Katzenberg a confidential sum, subsequently reported to be $280m.[80]

There is an important lesson here that applies to all firms, not just Disney. Executives offered compensation schemes like Katzenberg's will (at least, they should) anticipate payment difficulties upon leaving the firm. Even if, like Katzenberg, they ultimately win in court, they still incur costs in legal fees and time spent fighting for their pay. Once executives take these costs into account, their expected reward for good performance is reduced, which weakens the incentives generated by the pay scheme. There will be some sacrifices that would have been worth making if the promises regarding future bonuses were credible, but are not made because of the lower, more realistic, value the executive attaches to them. The only way for the firm to induce the executive to make these sacrifices is to give him higher short-term bonuses. Unfortunately for shareholders, this will have to happen year after year in order to keep the executive motivated, lowering the value of the firm to shareholders. Lower bonuses—meaning more money left over for shareholders—could have delivered the same sacrifice if the firm could credibly commit to paying bonuses after the executive's employment ends.

Awarding shares and options, rather than long-term bonuses, to managers offers one way to add credibility to promises to base pay on long-term performance. When a firm grants a share to an executive (or sells him one when he exercises an option) it is committing to pay that executive a stream of future cash flows equal to the dividends that it pays the holder of each and every share in the company. When the executive leaves the firm, the payments continue as long as he owns the share; if he sells the share, the sale price reflects the value of the stream of dividends that he would have received. The firm cannot stop paying the executive without stopping dividends to all shareholders, and that is just not going to happen.

Shares and options are not without their shortcomings. They measure long-run performance only if the share price accurately reflects the true value of the dividend stream that the share will generate. Whether that happens in practice is a topic of hot debate.[81] Even if the share price does this accurately, changes in the share price reflect company-wide performance. That was fine for Eisner, who was responsible for the performance of the firm as a whole. However, Katzenberg was responsible for only one, clearly defined, part of Disney. Although paying him with shares and options would credibly commit Disney to paying him for long-run performance, it would be pay for the performance of the hotels and theme parks as well, not just the film studio. When they negotiated his pay package, Katzenberg and Disney needed to weigh up the commitment benefits of paying in shares and options against the more sensible allocation of risk that resulted from paying long-term bonuses. They opted for the latter.

Leaving broken, but not broke

There is one other aspect of pay that is determined during pay negotiations: the payout an executive will get when he leaves a firm. The relative bargaining power of board and executive is crucial here as well. However, it is the bargaining power at the time the negotiations occur, not at the time the executive leaves. That is why executives who are hounded out of a firm—at times when their bargaining power can be very weak—often leave with substantial pay packages. Here, too, Eisner provides an excellent example.

Disney performed poorly during the first seven years of Eisner's third contract. Its attempt to develop an internet portal to rival Yahoo failed and its acquisitions of television networks struggled.[82] Eisner's clashes with Steve Jobs, CEO of Pixar, threatened the survival of the lucrative agreement that saw Disney marketing and distributing Pixar's films.[83] The exodus of senior executives from the company continued, including another chief financial officer, the chief strategic officer, Katzenberg's replacement at Disney's studios, successive chairmen of the parks and resorts division, and the general counsel.[84] These problems all contributed to Disney's disappointing share-price performance: Disney shareholders earned average annual rates of return that were four percentage points lower than those on the S&P 500 index in the first seven years after Eisner signed his third contract.[85]

By the time of the 2004 annual meeting, shareholders were fed up: 43% of the votes cast withheld support for Eisner. Later that day, Disney's board announced that, although Eisner would stay on as CEO, he would be replaced as board chairman by one of the other directors.[86] After 19 months of this humiliation, Eisner retired as CEO, one year before the end of his contract and 21 years after he joined Disney. However, thanks to his strong bargaining position in 1996, Eisner's contract allowed him to leave early if he was not retained as CEO and chairman, and to walk away with a generous golden handshake. He received his fixed salary of $1m for the year remaining in his contract, as well as annual bonuses of $7.5m for that year and the two years after that. Eisner was allowed to hold onto the options he had been granted back when the contract was signed for up to five more years.[87] In total, Eisner's golden handshake was worth $83m.[88] It was a generous payout—because of his strong position in 1996 and despite his weak position in 2005.

Eisner had been Disney's CEO for 21 extremely well paid years. It is the level of pay, $802m in total, that grabs people's attention, but there is so much more to Eisner's story than that. It shows how CEO pay-setting can be understood as a series of negotiations between a CEO and his board, with the CEO trying to secure pay arrangements that are in his best interest and directors trying to secure ones that benefit shareholders. Two things emerge out of these negotiations: a relationship between pay and firm performance that tries to create strong incentives without piling too much risk onto executives, and an overall level of pay that reflects the sides' bargaining power. Most of the time, what constrains the CEO's pay is the requirement that the board has to agree to his compensation scheme. However, as many firms have found, the CEO's bargaining position can become so strong that it is shareholders, not directors, who limit pay. That opens up a whole new can of worms, one that we investigate in the next chapter.

A trained monkey could have run a publicly traded home builder over the past three years and done pretty well.[1]

DIRECTOR OF CORPORATE AFFAIRS, UNITED BROTHERHOOD OF CARPENTERS (2006)

....

6 Hiding high pay
EXECUTIVE COMPENSATION AND MANAGERIAL POWER

ONE DAY IN 2005, two old hands of the homebuilding industry, with over 50 years' CEO experience between them, took part in a panel discussion on the future of real estate.[2] Bruce Karatz of KB Home and Larry Mizel of MDC Holdings had seen housing booms end badly before. This time, they told the audience, would be different. There was a "supply-and-demand balance that [would] stay good for many years" according to Karatz. Mizel was just as bullish: "We're in a market with real depth and real legs on it."[3] The two firms' share prices peaked just three months later, on the day the chairman of the Federal Reserve warned of the risk of a housing bubble.[4] The next few years were ugly: both firms' annual revenue fell by more than 80%; KB Home's share price fell by 85%, MDC's by 64%.[5] So much for that "supply-and-demand balance." So much for that "market with real depth."

Predictions like these left Karatz and Mizel looking foolish, but this did not stop them—and their counterparts at other homebuilding firms—from being among the highest paid CEOs in the U.S. Karatz was paid $160m during the five-year period leading up to his departure from KB Home at the end of 2006; Mizel was paid $117m over the same period.[6] Shareholders did well too: a shareholder who invested $100 in KB Home five years before the peak would have seen her investment grow to $891; for MDC, $783. Nobody seemed to mind that KB Home and MDC were not doing all that well relative to other firms in the homebuilding industry: they were ranked just seventh and eighth, respectively, on the basis of shareholder returns.[7] Karatz and Mizel did not receive high pay because KB Home and MDC were outperforming their competitors. Their pay was high because they were operating in an industry that was booming. They were in the right place at the right time.

This all changed when the housing boom turned into a bust. Profits turned into losses, share prices plummeted, and boards started taking industry conditions into account when setting bonuses. KB Home used increased customer satisfaction levels to help justify paying its CEO a $6.0m bonus.[8] MDC claimed that its awful performance was not so bad when compared with its competitors' awful performances, and then paid its CEO a $4.3m bonus made up of cash and shares in the company.[9] Then it changed its bonus formula to make earning a bonus even easier than it had been in the past.[10]

Pay practices in the homebuilding industry cannot be explained by directors acting like they did in Chapter 5. There is no reason for them to have changed compensation approaches so dramatically at the peak of the market. Something else was going on. Many economics and legal scholars believe that this change in behavior can occur at times when CEOs are so powerful that directors do not matter much. According to this theory, directors become so ineffective at limiting executive pay that it is left to shareholders to stop things getting out of hand.[11] Shareholders have taken a back seat in the last few chapters as they left governance of the corporation to the board. They will not play much of a direct role in this chapter either, but their presence in the background—and the possibility that they will not stay in the background—is the key to explaining pay practices when CEOs get too powerful.

Superstar CEOs

During the housing boom, Karatz's status soared with house prices. He was a frequent guest on CNBC and was named "Best Chairman" at the American Business Awards in 2005, the year after KB Home was named "Best Overall Company."[12] As interest in Karatz-the-CEO continued, interest in Karatz-the-man grew: *Forbes* profiled the "biking builder," *Fortune* discussed his Harley-Davidson V-Rod.[13] Karatz was a superstar.

A CEO has many more opportunities to do things that he enjoys once he attains superstar status. The cost of making sacrifices that benefit shareholders goes up, because making these sacrifices means giving up more attractive outside opportunities than before. Karatz, in particular, was enjoying the highlife: cycling with Lance Armstrong, holidaying with Sean ("P. Diddy") Combs on a chartered yacht in the Mediterranean, and appearing as a featured business mentor on CNN's reality show, *The TurnAround*.[14] We saw something similar happen with Michael Eisner in Chapter 5, when we predicted the effects of his increased wealth. Our story went something like this. Before the CEO became a superstar (in Eisner's case, before he built that luxurious log cabin in Aspen), his pay–performance sensitivity was set at the level that motivated him to make only those sacrifices that cost the CEO less than they benefited shareholders—who ultimately are the ones paying for the sacrifice. Once the CEO has become a superstar, and the opportunity cost of those sacrifices has increased, it is not worth shareholders paying him to make some of those sacrifices. Furthermore, the CEO will need to be paid more to motivate him to make the remaining sacrifices, which *do* benefit shareholders. The end result: pay will need to be more sensitive to performance than before, but the superstar CEO will still make fewer sacrifices than before he attained superstar status.

One difficulty in testing this prediction is that we cannot observe the extent of the sacrifices that CEOs make. However, there are telltale signs of a slackening of CEO effort. For example, CEOs who win business awards subsequently write more books and have lower golf handicaps, signs that they spend more time on leisure activities. After winning an award, a CEO's equity-based pay increases, consistent with the prediction that superstar status is accompanied by an increase in pay–performance sensitivity. The apparent reduction in effort, like the increase in equity-based pay, is strongest in firms that have the characteristics of weak governance.[15]

Something similar happened at KB Home. We will never know whether Karatz exerted less effort as the firm's share price soared, but we do know that his golf handicap improved. When *Golf Digest* ranked the top golfing CEOs in 2002, Karatz was in 128th place, with a handicap of 14.2. Two years later, he was ranked 46th, with a handicap of 9.6. By the time of the 2006 survey, his handicap had fallen to 9.1.[16] We also know that as Karatz's golf handicap improved, his use of the company plane for personal travel increased: KB Home provided him with personal travel perks worth $113,000 in 2004, $248,000 in 2005, and $558,000 in 2006.[17] Does this mean that Karatz started to take things easy as the housing market boomed? No, it does not. It means his golf handicap improved and he spent much more company money on personal travel. And his pay went through the roof.

Meet the pay-setters

As we saw in Chapters 2 and 5, another consequence of attaining superstar status is that a CEO is in a very strong bargaining position when interacting with his board of directors. Over time, that seems to result in changes in board composition that further strengthen the CEO's position. This is reflected in the makeup of the board's compensation committee, which is the group of directors responsible for setting the pay of a firm's most senior executives.

If we want to understand the determinants of executive compensation and to identify firms where there are likely to be problems, we need to understand the workings of these committees. Consider KB Home's committee when Karatz's pay was at its peak. The committee had negotiated Karatz's series of employment agreements. His last one, signed in 2001, was intended to cover his employment until the end of 2008. It fixed some elements of his pay, such as his annual bonus, which would equal a percentage of KB Home's pre-tax profit, with the precise percentage calculated according to a formula specified in the agreement. The committee retained some flexibility to choose other elements of his pay. For example, although the agreement specified the level of his 2001 salary, the committee was able to raise his salary in future years. However, the details of the most valuable component of his pay—the annual option grants—were not specified in the agreement, being left entirely to the committee's future discretion.[18]

The committee that met in 2005 to exercise this discretion had six members. We met the chairman in Chapter 2: Ray Irani, CEO of Occidental Petroleum. Three other members were current, former, or soon-to-be CEOs of public corporations: Terrence Lanni, CEO of casino operator MGM Mirage; James Johnson, retired CEO of Fannie Mae; and Leslie Moonves, about to become CEO of CBS. All six members had been appointed to the board since Karatz became CEO in 1986. Four had been appointed since he became board chairman in 1993, none owned more than 0.08% of the firm's shares, and all were busy.[19] Irani was meeting Muammar Qaddafi as Oxy tried to resume operations in Libya after a 19-year absence, fighting efforts to have Oxy kicked out of its operations in Ecuador, and, back in the U.S., plotting the $3.7b acquisition of a competitor.[20] Lanni was completing the $7.8b acquisition of a rival casino operator as well as working on a $7.0b real-estate development in Las Vegas.[21] Johnson sat on the boards of five other public corporations, including Goldman Sachs Group and Target, and chaired the compensation committees at all five firms.[22] Moonves was busy spinning off Viacom's CBS division as a separate corporation.[23]

KB Home's committee members were not strangers to high levels of CEO pay. Irani received total compensation from Oxy in 2005 worth $72m. In the same year—his last before becoming CEO of CBS—Moonves received compensation from Viacom worth $31m. Lanni's 2005 compensation package from MGM Mirage came in at $23m.[24] Another committee member, Barry Munitz, CEO of the J. Paul Getty Trust, was spending so much of the trust's money on lavish perks that the California Attorney General launched an investigation. By the time the investigation was completed in 2006, Munitz had resigned from the trust and forfeited a severance package worth more than $2m.[25] This was the team tasked with getting the best possible pay deal for KB Home's shareholders.

We can think of pay-setting at KB Home as another bargaining game and analyze it using the framework we first met in Chapter 2. Four factors suggest that the committee had relatively little bargaining power. First, most committee members had time-consuming outside obligations, so their ability to participate in a lengthy pay-setting process was limited. Second, the committee's members had low ownership stakes and, third, they had long working relationships with Karatz, so the private reward from prolonging bargaining was relatively low and the interpersonal cost relatively high. Fourth, the majority of committee members were, or had been, highly paid CEOs themselves, so they were likely to be sympathetic to the view that high pay was needed to attract and motivate high-quality executives. These factors all combined to give Karatz substantial bargaining power. The bargaining framework we met in Chapter 2 and applied in Chapter 5 predicts that he would benefit by taking home a large proportion of the total surplus from any agreement the two sides might reach.

What they don't know won't hurt me

According to one theory proposed by economists, CEOs can get into such strong bargaining positions that it is not the board that restricts their pay, but their desire to avoid provoking shareholder outrage.[26] If such CEOs bargained hard, they would be able to get their boards to agree to pay packages so excessive that even normally passive shareholders would act. Irani's two forced retirements at Oxy (Chapter 2) and Eisner's ouster at Disney (Chapter 5) give an indication of the possible consequences for executives when shareholders get riled up. In fact, during the period from 1997 to 2007, activist investors targeted their pay-related shareholder proposals and vote-no campaigns mainly at firms with higher pay levels. Shareholder proposals gained greater support at firms where pay appeared to be more excessive and approximately one third of pay-related proposals that gained majority support were implemented. Pay at firms targeted by vote-no campaigns fell by 38% on average.[27] Executives who want to protect their current pay arrangements should not push for pay levels that will generate such investor activism.

The disciplinary effect of possible shareholder outrage varies according to how well the firm is doing. For example, while KB Home's share price was surging, criticism of Karatz's pay was muted. The critical press coverage that did occur usually presented Karatz's pay in the context of pay levels across all companies. During the housing boom there was little shareholder outrage. For example, no shareholder proposals related to executive compensation were voted on at KB Home's annual meetings between 1995 and 2006, and the firm's directors were overwhelmingly reelected during this period. On average, directors seeking reelection during this period received over 96% "yes" votes.[28]

This changed when the housing boom ended and press coverage started to focus on Karatz's pay and the compensation committee's role.[29] Pension funds, which had sponsored pay-related proposals at other firms during the boom, also turned their attention to KB Home.[30] Shareholders voted on nine pay-related proposals in the next four years. Three of them—related to severance-payments and the rules surrounding when shares and options awarded to executives should vest—won majority support. Even for the losing proposals, on average almost a third of the votes cast supported the proposals. At the same time, support for directors seeking reelection fell. All directors up for reelection in 2007 received less than 85% "yes" votes; the following year, two of the three directors up for reelection received just 71% "yes" votes.[31]

However, shareholders cannot be outraged by pay they are not aware of. That might be why executives and compensation committees bargain over *how* to pay as well as over *how much* to pay. Executives gain from being paid in ways that do not attract shareholder attention because each dollar of hidden pay gives them the same benefit as a dollar of public pay, but without any shareholder outrage. A compensation committee that works in shareholders' best interests will try to make executive pay as transparent as possible, but its ability to do so will be limited by its bargaining power. If a firm's CEO is as strong as Karatz was at KB Home in 2005, then—according to the theory described in this chapter—we should expect the firm to make greater use of hidden forms of executive pay.

Peering into the proxy statements

Before we look at pay that is hidden from shareholders, we need to take a look at how pay—some of it, anyway—is reported to shareholders in the proxy statements that firms send to their shareholders prior to their annual meetings.

Firms are required to disclose information about the compensation paid to their CEO, chief financial officer, and the three highest-paid of their other executives. The SEC requires firms to include summary information in a table in the proxy statements they send to shareholders prior to their annual meetings, with the table having to follow a specific format. It is this summary table that grabs the attention of investors and analysts alike. However, more detailed information is provided as well. Patience, and a search of paperwork filed with the SEC when shares and options are issued to executives, can result in what appears to be a detailed picture of executive pay.[32]

Karatz's pay arrangements provide a good example. In 2005, which was Karatz's best year, his salary was $1.1m and his annual cash bonus—calculated from the firm's pre-tax profit according to a formula in his employment agreement—was $5.0m. The firm's profitability also partly determined the size of the multi-year bonus he received at the end of the year, another $3.5m. By working for KB Home in 2005, he was able to extend the lives of his vested options as well as adding to his portfolio of vested options and shares (another $33m).[33] Figure 6.1 shows Karatz's pay from 1995 until he left the firm at the end of 2006. Like the CEOs of other homebuilders, Karatz's pay was affected by the housing boom, especially in 2005 and 2006. However, it displays the characteristics of executive pay across the whole corporate sector: pay increasing rapidly in the years leading up to 2001 and stabilizing at historically high levels afterwards, with options (and later shares) being big contributors to the increase.[34]

In the short run, the level of Karatz's pay depended on KB Home's profitability and its share-price performance. In the long run, it was also affected by the compensation committee's decisions regarding future bonus rules and option grants. A stronger board should achieve a bargaining outcome that gives executives a smaller proportion of any surplus from reaching agreement with the board. Of course, board strength will not be the only factor that is associated with pay, so if we want to check this prediction then we need to filter out the effect of factors such as firm size and profitability. Once this is done, it appears that executive compensation is indeed lower for firms that have signs of stronger

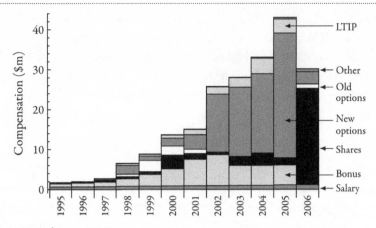

FIGURE 6.1 Karatz's pay at KB Home

corporate governance. For example, firms with small boards of directors who are not too busy, and firms with boards that are not chaired by the CEO, tend to have relatively low levels of CEO pay. Firms where the board has weak social ties with the CEO or where the CEO appointed few of the independent directors are also associated with low CEO pay. Lastly, firms in which the compensation committee members own more shares are associated with lower CEO pay, as are firms with a larger proportion of shares owned by a small number of institutional investors.[35]

Camouflaging pay as perks

There are many ways to camouflage high pay. The most notorious involves paying executives in the form of perquisites (or "perks"). Some perks we know about, because the SEC requires firms to include in their proxy statements the cost of providing perks for each of the executives appearing in the summary compensation table. Individual perks above a particular threshold have to be singled out.[36] This is how we know that in 2006 KB Home provided Karatz with financial planning and tax preparation services, an automobile and gasoline allowance, tickets to sporting events, personal gifts, personal meal and lodging expenses, and club membership fees. It is also how we know that KB Home incurred costs of $558,000 related to his personal use of company-owned aircraft.[37]

However, firms provide executives with many other things that you and I might regard as perks, but which do not have to be disclosed because the SEC regards them as being "directly related to the performance of the executive's duties."[38] To make matters worse, firms do not need to disclose the additional costs of providing gold-plated items if they are "directly related to the performance of the executive's duties." For example, booking the CEO into the Presidential Suite of a hotel when he is on a business trip does not count as a perk, even if less luxurious accommodation is available.

There is no need for a firm to provide an executive with perks. It could instead boost his salary and leave him to spend the money as he chooses. If he wants to upgrade to the Presidential Suite next time he travels on business then he can choose to do so—and pay for it himself. Of course, in some circumstances it can be better for shareholders to provide the perk. For example, if hotel upgrades cost the firm less than it would cost the CEO, providing the perk is just as good as a salary boost from the CEO's perspective, but costs shareholders less. However, shareholders know about the increased salary, whereas they do not know about the hotel upgrade, so paying in perks rather than in cash reduces the threat of shareholder outrage.

Camouflaging pay by backdating option grants

There is another perk: CEOs can influence when jobs are done, jobs like granting options. Consider the 600,000 options that Karatz was awarded by KB Home's compensation committee when it met early in October 2001. Each option would give him the right to buy one share for a fixed price equal to the share price on the day when the options were granted. The SEC alleged that Karatz, working with KB Home's executive vice president of human resources, chose the day. The options could have been granted immediately after the board approved the deal, in which case Karatz would have had to pay $29.72 per share when he eventually exercised them.[39] Instead, the SEC alleged, the pair waited until the end of the financial year on November 30, and then backdated the option grant to October 30, when the share price had been just $27.90—the lowest price between the committee meeting and the end of the financial year.[40] By working backwards and locking in a day when the share price was low, they were able to ensure that when Karatz eventually exercised his options he would have to pay just $27.90 per share, rather than $29.72.

Anybody reading KB Home's proxy statement would have seen the firm granted the CEO options to buy KB Home shares at a price of $27.90 at a time when shares were worth $27.90. If shareholders had been keen, they could have used standard option pricing models to estimate the value of the options Karatz had been granted, $7.4m. However, if the proxy statement had accurately reported that the firm granted the CEO options to buy KB Home shares at a price of $27.90 at a time when shares were worth $29.72, those same models would have produced a more accurate value, $9.8m. One effect of the alleged backdating of the option grant was to hide future compensation worth $2.4m.[41]

According to the SEC, this was not the first time it had happened. In 1999, Karatz had also waited until the end of the financial year and then backdated his option grant to a date in October, which meant that options actually worth $4.5m when they were granted appeared to be worth $3.2m. He allegedly backdated his 2000 grant as well, making a grant worth $7.1m look like it was worth $5.2m.[42] In each case, the SEC said that he chose the day with the lowest share price between the committee meeting and the end of the financial year. The Sarbanes-Oxley Act (SOX) made behavior like this more difficult when it was enacted in 2002. Previously, option grants had to be reported only within 45 days of the end of the fiscal year.[43] However, SOX requires that they are reported by the end of the second business day after the options have been granted. This still allows a firm to report an official grant date up to two days prior to the grant actually being implemented. For example, at least according to the SEC, in 2003 Karatz waited until October 28, a Tuesday, and then backdated the option grant to the previous Friday. This had the effect of making a grant actually worth $7.5m look like one worth $7.3m.[44] The option grants in 2004 and 2005 were allegedly backdated this way as well.

Before SOX, and to a lesser extent even now, backdating option grants has the effect of camouflaging executive compensation.[45] Shareholders know exactly what options have been granted, and at what price, but they do not necessarily know when the decision to grant the options was made. If the grants are being backdated, then the information provided to shareholders will lead them to underestimate the true value of the options granted to the firm's executive.

Allegations of option backdating were not confined to KB Home. Estimates of the frequency of option backdating vary, but most studies agree that the practice was widespread in the period leading up to passage of SOX. One study estimated that more than 30% of firms backdated options sometime during the period 1996–2002.[46] Backdating caught the public's attention with the publication of the results of a *Wall Street Journal* investigation in 2006.[47] The SEC began investigating backdating shortly afterwards, launching probes into more than 100 firms in 2006 alone.[48] These investigations revealed clear evidence of the motivations behind backdating at some firms. In other cases, all we have are suspicious coincidences, with grants just happening to occur on low-price days. This is where the large-scale empirical investigations that academic researchers specialize in come to the fore. Unlike the SEC's searches of companies' email servers, these cannot identify specific instances of deliberate backdating. However, they reveal patterns of behavior that suggest backdating is more likely when corporate governance is weak. For example, during the decade prior to backdating being revealed, option grants were more likely to occur on low-price days at firms where the CEO had been in the job for a long time, the CEO chaired the board, the majority of directors were firm employees, more of the outside directors had been appointed by the current CEO, or there was no large shareholder on the compensation committee.[49] In short, backdating seems to have been more prevalent at firms with powerful CEOs.

Twelve weeks after KB Home revealed that the SEC was investigating its option grants, and on the same day that the firm announced the results of its own inquiry, Karatz retired, effective immediately.[50] The exercise prices of Karatz's outstanding options were reset and he agreed to repay KB Home the excess profits he had earned from exercising backdated options.[51] Dozens of CEOs resigned or were fired after option backdating was discovered, but Karatz was one of the few to be prosecuted. Backdating options is not illegal, provided that the practice is reported accurately. However, secret backdating can lead firms to misstate their compensation expenses, leading to charges of making false statements to the

SEC and of underreporting tax liabilities.[52] In April 2010, Karatz was found guilty of mail fraud and making false statements, but was acquitted of other charges, including securities fraud. He was fined $1.0m, ordered to complete 2,000 hours of community service, and sentenced to eight months of home detention.[53] KB Home's executive vice president of human resources settled with the SEC, repaying the excess profits to KB Home and paying a $50,000 fine.[54]

Pay me when nobody is watching

Karatz's departure from KB Home shone a bright light on another way that high pay can be hidden from view—shifting some of the CEO's pay forward in time so that it is paid out only once he retires. Such was the urgency surrounding Karatz's departure that the exact nature of his termination was not resolved before he was fired. Was he dismissed "for cause," in which case he was not entitled to a severance package, or was he dismissed "without cause"? If it was the latter, then he would walk away with an extremely lucrative payout. This would include a lump-sum severance payment equal to the combined total of the salary and bonus he had received over the previous three years: value $62m. All outstanding restricted shares would vest immediately: value $72m. All unvested options, many of them rendered worthless by the recent collapse of the share price, would vest immediately: value $1.2m. KB Home's Retirement Plan would pay him an agreed sum each year for 20 years: value $14m. The Supplemental Executive Retirement Plan (SERP) specified in his employment agreement would pay out his average salary over the last three years, each year for the next 25 years: value $15m. In total, Karatz might take away $165m. And that is before we add in the post-retirement perks: medical and dental benefits for Karatz and his partner for the rest of his life, as well as provision of an office and administrative support "commensurate with [his] former status" as CEO.[55]

When the dust (and the shareholder lawsuits) had settled, Karatz kept his retirement plan and the SERP, as well as restricted shares that had been worth $7.0m when he retired. He surrendered the remaining unvested shares and options, the lump-sum severance payment, and the post-retirement perks. Karatz also paid KB Home $8.5m in cash to compensate it for the costs associated with option backdating.[56] However, if we want to understand how high pay can be camouflaged, what matters is how much Karatz *could have* received, and that is the full $165m payout resulting from the employment agreement he negotiated back in 2001.

KB Home was not the only homebuilder to lose its CEO. Although homebuilders struggled in the aftermath of the housing bust, they were still able to give departing executives generous severance packages. When Ryland Group's CEO retired, its board awarded him a lump-sum cash payment of $2.0m.[57] When Standard Pacific's CEO left his job, he received a severance payment, kept unvested shares and options, and the terms of his vested options were altered; the package was worth $3.2m.[58] When Pulte

Homes' founder resigned, he was paid $3.3m in cash and entered into a $3.0m consulting arrangement that would see him work no more than 600 hours over the next two years.[59] Lastly, when Beazer Homes' board fired its CEO just three months after he agreed to repay $6.5m in cash and return shares as part of a settlement with the SEC involving allegedly fraudulent financial statements, he received severance pay and unvested shares worth $5.8m.[60]

The SEC's rules at the time for disclosing executive pay meant that Karatz's two retirement plans did not appear in the summary compensation table in KB Home's proxy statements. The specific arrangements were written into his employment contracts, so the details did find their way into the proxy statements (and the contracts themselves were filed with the SEC).[61] However, shifting pay forward in time like this meant that its full extent did not appear in the all-important summary compensation table. By the time many shareholders realized what had happened, it was too late.

If we were a CEO in a strong bargaining position, how might we boost our pay without attracting too much attention? First up, we could ask the compensation committee to add a few post-retirement perks into our employment agreement when it is renegotiated. Perhaps the committee could throw in lifetime medical and dental benefits, and promise us an office and administrative support after we retire. That is what happened when Karatz's 1995 employment agreement was renegotiated by Irani and the rest of the compensation committee in 2001.[62] Then we could ask the committee to increase the benefits promised by our SERP. Perhaps the committee could increase the promised annual payment from $0.5m to the level of our salary, and then increase our salary so that it cannot fall below $0.9m. That change was buried in Karatz's 2001 employment agreement as well.[63] If we are really serious, we could ask for higher severance pay in the event we are dismissed without cause. Perhaps instead of promising to pay us a lump sum equal to two times our annual salary and bonus the committee could promise to pay us a lump sum equal to three times this amount. This change also appeared in Karatz's 2001 agreement.[64] Adding up the numbers, even ignoring the post-retirement perks, these changes increased the amount that Karatz could have received when he was dismissed in 2006 by $29m—and few shareholders would have noticed at the time because none of these changes appeared in the summary compensation tables in KB Home's proxy statements.[65]

Retirement pay is not all bad. After all, it gives the CEO an incentive to ensure that the firm is still in business after he retires so that it can pay him all he is owed. If it is disclosed properly, then its ability to camouflage high pay can be reduced. Since 2006, firms have had to report the arrangements made regarding their top five executives' post-employment pay in more detail. The main change to the summary compensation table is that firms now have to report changes in the estimated market value of retirement plans that have defined benefits, such as Karatz's two schemes.[66] If the level of post-employment payout is raised, as it was when Karatz's employment agreement was amended in 2001, then the market value rises, and this would now show up in the summary compensation table.

The times they are a-changin'

Everything changed when the housing boom turned to a bust. KB Home went from selling 37,000 homes in 2005 to just 24,000 in 2007. The $842m profit in 2005 turned into a $929m loss in 2007.[67] The value of its shares fell from their peak of $8.1b in 2005 to $1.9b by the end of 2007.[68] KB Home's new CEO, Jeffrey Mezger, was entitled to a fixed percentage of the firm's pre-tax pre-bonus profit, just like Karatz had been during the boom. However, there was no profit in the 2007 fiscal year, just a $929m loss, so Mezger was looking at a year with no bonus. Fortunately for him, the compensation committee exercised its discretion and awarded him a bonus anyway. Sure, the shares had lost almost 60% of their value during the last year, but the committee still seemed pleased with Mezger's performance: KB Home's customer satisfaction levels had increased; staffing levels were down by 39%; and the firm's French operations had been sold with the proceeds used to reduce outstanding debt. For this, Mezger was paid a $6.0m bonus.[69]

Boards risk provoking shareholder outrage if they ignore their own rules when setting executives' bonuses. High pay is less likely to trigger shareholder outrage if it is accompanied by good firm performance. That is why boards that agree to camouflage high pay can do so by artificially boosting reported performance. One way to do this is to change the rules when the going gets tough.

We do not know why firms in the homebuilding industry changed their rules for pay-setting during the housing bust, but we do know what the changes were. KB Home's compensation committee changed its bonus formula: in light of the poor market conditions, the new formula would give Mezger a bonus as long as KB Home did no worse than make a $300m *loss*.[70] Stop and think about that for a moment. When the housing market was booming, the compensation committee did not raise the performance threshold so that the CEO would receive a bonus only if the firm made an especially large profit. However, once the housing market was in the doldrums, it lowered the performance threshold so that the CEO could receive a bonus even if the firm made a loss.

It was not just KB Home. Compensation committees at many homebuilders were scrambling to change the rules. Take Larry Mizel's MDC Holdings, for example. Its bonus scheme had been in place since 1994. MDC made a loss in 2007, so the CEO and president were set to receive zero bonuses that year. However, the compensation committee (chaired by a director who had been on the board since Mizel founded the company in 1972) exercised its discretion, ignored its own formula, and paid the CEO and president each a bonus worth $4.3m.[71] Apparently, not awarding a bonus would have been "unfair and inappropriate" given "the superior performance of the executive officers ... in the face of the extraordinary break-down in the homebuilding industry."[72] To make sure this did not have to happen again, the compensation committee changed the bonus formula before the end of the next fiscal year by creating a back-up bonus as an insurance policy, which would pay out if the profit-based bonus was not high enough. Each year, the compensation committee would establish targets and if these targets were met, the CEO and president would each be eligible for a bonus made up of $2.5m in cash and 60,000 shares.[73] The back-up bonus was needed, because without it the CEO and president would not have each received cash and shares worth $4.5m in 2008.[74]

MDC's compensation committee made another change, which is buried in the detail of the 2008 proxy statement.[75] If MDC's pre-tax profit exceeded a capital charge then the CEO and president each received additional bonuses equal to 1.5% of the difference between the pre-tax profit and the capital charge. Anything that made the capital charge smaller would make their bonuses bigger. Each year since 1994, the capital charge had been set equal to 10% of the average of something called the "book value" of shareholders' investment at the firm, where the average was calculated over the four previous years.[76] However, from 2008 onwards, it would be set equal to 10% of the book value at the end of the most recent year: there would be no more averaging.

This may seem like a trivial change, but look at Figure 6.2, which plots the two different levels of the capital charge, with the pre-2008 rule used to draw the dashed curve and the post-2008 rule used to draw the solid one. During the housing boom, MDC's high profits meant that the book value was growing every year, so basing the capital charge on the average book value over the last four years resulted in a relatively small capital charge and a relatively big bonus. However, once the housing market collapsed and the book value started to fall, it was using just the most recent book value that led to a relatively small capital charge. The change in bonus rules occurred at just the right time to keep the capital charge lower, the profit target easier to achieve, and the additional bonus larger. It was a small change to the rules for calculating bonuses, but the effect could be substantial: if the new rule had been applied in 2005, the CEO's bonus would have been $0.7m smaller.[77]

MDC claimed that when the compensation committee was setting bonuses for 2007, it was "confronted with the realization" that the bonus formula approved by shareholders in 1994 was "based solely on the Company's Adjusted Pre-Tax Return on Average Stockholders' Equity and failed to take into consideration the achievements of the senior executive officers in preserving the financial integrity of the Company in view of current

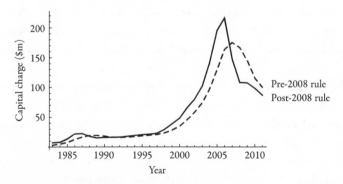

FIGURE 6.2 Changing the capital charge at MDC Holdings

market conditions."[78] Really? It took 14 years for MDC's directors to realize that the bonus scheme made no adjustment for overall market conditions? They did not realize this, not even during the housing boom when MDC's CEO was awarded enormous bonuses largely because of industry-wide conditions? Apparently it took a housing bust for the committee to realize how sensitive the bonus formula was to industry-wide conditions.

Other homebuilders' explanations were not much more convincing. For example, when Pennsylvania-based Toll Brothers proposed changing its bonus formula from one based on the firm's profit and share-price performance to one based on profit and a discretionary component, the CEO said that it was being done so that the bonus plan was "easier to follow" and had fewer "bells or whistles."[79] One of those "bells or whistles" tied the amount of the CEO's bonus to the firm's share-price performance. It boosted his bonus during the housing boom, but would have restricted his bonus if it had been kept in place during the housing bust.[80]

Camouflaging pay using friendly performance measures

There is a pattern here: while the industry (and hence the firm) is booming, measure the firm's performance in isolation; once the industry (and hence the firm) is struggling, measure the firm's performance relative to the industry as a whole. It must be tempting for a CEO to push for just such a choice of performance measures. If he can persuade his compensation committee to switch to a favorable performance measure, he might be able to increase his pay for the year without provoking shareholder outrage.

Can a powerful CEO influence discretionary pay by influencing the choice of performance measure? Given everything we have seen so far, we should be suspicious when firms change from measures showing poor performance to different measures that suggest better performance. Unless the authorities peek into the firm's email servers (like they did when investigating option backdating at KB Home), we will never know what actually motivated committee members at any individual firm. However, empirical research involving large numbers of firms reveals that the sensitivity of CEO pay to accounting performance is higher when accounting performance is better than share-price performance, and the sensitivity of CEO pay to share-price performance is higher when share-price performance is better than accounting performance. That is, the sensitivity of pay to either performance measure is higher when that performance measure paints a better picture of the firm's—and hence the CEO's—performance. This behavior is most noticeable in firms where the CEO has no obvious successor, the board is chaired by the CEO, or the board is dominated by directors who are either employees of the firm or were appointed to the board during the CEO's tenure.[81] This is consistent with CEOs in strong bargaining positions putting pressure on compensation committees to base pay on more favorable performance measures.

Compensation committees can also boost apparent performance by making selective allowance for industry-wide conditions, as appeared to happen in the homebuilding industry. From Chapter 5, performance-based pay schemes should transfer as much diversifiable risk as possible from executives to shareholders. It is cheaper for shareholders to bear this risk—they can diversify it away—than for them to compensate executives for bearing it instead. If pay is based on specific performance measures, then those performance measures should have the effects of as much diversifiable risk filtered out of them as possible. This filtering can be done explicitly, by basing executive compensation on a firm's performance relative to the rest of the industry. It can also be done implicitly. For example, if a firm appears to be doing well in absolute terms, but is lagging other firms in the same industry, the compensation committee can lower the number of options granted or reduce the size of other discretionary grants.

That is what should happen, but there is not much sign it did happen in the homebuilding industry. Instead, homebuilders' CEOs seemed to be rewarded for their firms' good absolute performance during the boom, even when their relative performance was poor, but to be buffered from the effects of their firms' poor absolute performance during the bust. It looks like they were being rewarded for good luck, but not punished for bad luck. According to one study that looked at firms in many different industries, this is precisely what happens at many firms. Good luck, which would increase pay, tends to be kept in the performance measures used to calculate pay; bad luck, which would reduce pay, is filtered out. Pay is buffered against bad luck much more at firms with weak corporate governance than it is at firms with strong corporate governance.[82] This is consistent with our story that powerful CEOs are able to use good luck, when it occurs, to justify high pay, and bad luck, when it occurs, as an excuse to prevent low pay. Heads, the CEO wins; tails, shareholders lose.

Choose your peers carefully

We have seen how CEOs and weak compensation committees can hide high pay by making the firm's performance look better than it really is. Another possibility is that they can make the "fair" pay level look higher than it really is. This involves manipulating the benchmarking exercises that many compensation committees carry out, in which executives' pay packages are compared with the pay they would receive if they worked at comparable firms.

In principle, the committee identifies a group of firms with which it competes for executive talent. The average peer group of a large publicly traded company comprises 20 firms, of which 44% are from the firm's own industry and 54% have annual sales that are at least half, and no more than twice, as large as the firm's.[83] The committee includes the amounts these firms pay their own executives amongst the information it uses when setting pay. If the peer group is chosen properly, the committee cannot set pay much below the level at these firms without running the risk that the firm's executives go and work for them. It does not need to set pay much above the level at these firms because if the firm's executives get upset and leave then the committee should be able to attract replacements from firms in the peer group.

A strong compensation committee can use peer groups to bolster its bargaining position and deliver a better outcome for shareholders. ("Sorry, we just can't pay you that much—and here's the evidence.") At least, that is the theory. In practice, however, there is the potential for disagreement over the identity of a firm's competitors for executive talent. Some firms in the same industry will be too large to be genuine competitors for executive talent—but how large is too large? Some firms of comparable size will operate in industries that are too different to be genuine competitors—but how different is too different? A weak compensation committee may agree to use this ambiguity to choose peer groups that camouflage high pay. It can include high-pay firms and exclude low-pay firms, making the amount that true competitors for executive talent pay their executives seem larger than it really is.

After filtering out the effects of other firm characteristics, CEOs of larger firms receive higher pay on average.[84] Therefore, if directors want to boost a CEO's pay without outraging shareholders, they can start by stacking the peer group with large firms (where the pay is probably relatively high). This is why shareholders should look very closely at the composition of their firm's peer group, which has had to be reported in the proxy statement since late 2006.[85] Take Mizel's MDC Holdings as an example, and the peer group it used to evaluate executive pay in 2010. The group comprised the 12 largest U.S. homebuilders.[86] Eleven of those firms had more revenue than MDC in 2009. Six of them had more than twice MDC's revenue. Four of them had more than three times MDC's revenue.[87] Were these firms, especially the four largest, really competing with MDC for executives? Many of MDC's shareholders did not seem to think so, as a majority of them voted against MDC's pay arrangements at the 2011 annual meeting. One of the reasons given for the shareholder revolt was the firm's choice of an inappropriate peer group.[88]

Manipulating peer groups may seem too conspiratorial to be credible. However, the peer group data disclosed since late 2006 reveals that, even after controlling for factors such as industry, size, and CEO characteristics, firms with high-pay CEOs are more likely to be included in peer groups than firms with low-pay CEOs. This result is stronger in firms where the CEO is the chairman of the board of directors, the CEO has longer tenure, directors are busier serving on multiple boards, or there are few large shareholders.[89] The circumstantial evidence that weak boards hide high pay is mounting.

There is one more trick involving peer groups that weak compensation committees can play on shareholders. If firms benchmark their pay against peers, the compensation committee must pick a point within the range of peer-group pay to use as the benchmark. According to one study, 32% of large publicly traded firms that specified a peer group in 2006 targeted a level somewhere in the top half of their group. A typical firm targeted a level such that 56% of its peers paid less than this target. Every firm that does this is trying to say that its executives are so sought after that they might be headhunted by the highest payers in the firm's peer group: that is how good the firm's management is and that is why pay has to be higher than average. That is fine, but when too many firms start saying the same thing, it all starts to look like Lake Wobegon, where all the children (CEOs in this case) are above average. Firms with large numbers of directors appointed during the current CEO's tenure tended to choose peer groups made up of relatively large firms and to then choose a target level somewhere in the top half of their group.[90] This is consistent with weak boards using peer groups to justify excessive executive pay.

Appeal to the experts

Events in the homebuilding sector have illustrated how high pay can be camouflaged by paying some of it in the form of perks, backdating option grants to days when the options awarded do not appear to be so valuable, delaying some pay until after an executive leaves the firm, switching performance measures in ways that make high pay appear to be justified, and selecting peer groups that make high pay seem necessary to attract and retain executive talent. There is one final tactic that can reduce shareholder outrage: appeal to the experts. In this case the experts are the compensation consultants that committees turn to for advice regarding executive pay packages.

In 2006, 86% of large public corporations used compensation consultants, with a handful of large consulting firms getting most of the work.[91] Consultants contribute their expertise regarding compensation practices and legal requirements, and access to detailed proprietary information on compensation practices that can help in benchmarking exercises. In an ideal world, consultants providing objective expert advice help CEOs and compensation committees agree on an appropriate degree of pay–performance sensitivity, as well as strengthening the committee's bargaining position when it comes to allocating the surplus between shareholders and the CEO.

However, it is not this simple in the real world. One study found that 58% of the firms using compensation consultants choose consultants that also provide services unrelated to executive compensation.[92] These services include auditing pension plans and advising firms about pay for mid-level managers. Although consultants are typically selected by the compensation committee, the CEO is ultimately responsible for selecting firms that provide other services to the firm, which puts those consultants also seeking to provide such services in a difficult position. Should they tailor their advice to the committee so that the CEO's pay is boosted, and possibly increase their chances of getting lucrative deals to provide other services? Should they tailor advice to match what they think the committee wants to hear, and possibly increase their chances of being rehired next year? Or should they give objective advice and maintain a reputation as an honest broker? There is potential, at least, for CEOs and compensation committees to use conflicted consultants to, in effect, certify high pay as being reasonable, dampening shareholder outrage.

Since the end of 2006, firms must disclose their use of compensation consultants in their proxy statements.[93] Researchers are digging into the data this has generated, but the early evidence is mixed. Total CEO pay is higher, on average, at firms that employ consultants than at firms that do not employ them. Among the firms that do employ consultants, it is higher, on average, for consultants who are conflicted than for those who are not. However, this may be due to firms with weaker corporate governance being more likely to employ consultants, in which case the high pay may be due to governance shortcomings rather than the use of a consultant.[94] At this stage, we do not have a clear picture of the effect, if any, of the conflict of interest.

What we do know is that, like many of the other possible solutions to manager–shareholder conflict, the use of compensation consultants can be a two-edged sword. At firms with strong boards, genuinely independent compensation consultants can be selected and their advice used to strengthen the compensation committee's bargaining power. However, at firms with weak boards, the opposite can happen. A high-pay consultant can be appointed and their recommendation used to mollify shareholders. The strength of the board of directors is crucial.

Taking stock

In 2005, the year that Karatz and Mizel both received their highest compensation, they were paid $43m and $33m, respectively.[95] Figures like these fueled widespread condemnation of executive pay. The problem is not just that firms with weak boards might overpay their executives, but that firms with strong boards end up overpaying their executives as well. They have to, otherwise they will be unable to attract and retain talented executives. The widespread use of compensation peer groups accentuates the problem. One study estimated that if only 10% of firms attempt to pay twice as much as their competitors, then all CEOs' pay doubles.[96] Another study analyzed CEO pay in the wake of changes in Delaware case law in the 1990s that weakened corporate governance by increasing firms' protection against hostile takeovers. Firms directly affected by the new law tended to pay their CEOs more after the law change, *as did their competitors*.[97] The contagion effect is strong.

Extremely high levels of executive compensation have prompted changes in financial reporting rules that have made it harder (but not impossible) for firms to hide high pay. The threat of shareholder outrage should therefore be more effective at restricting excessive pay than it has been in the past. However, focusing on the level of executive compensation runs the risk of missing a much more important point. Yes, the sums paid to many CEOs are enormous, but their magnitude appears more modest when viewed from the perspective of the firms' owners. If Karatz and Mizel had worked for free in 2005, the saving per share would have been just 0.6% and 1.3% of the end-of-year share price, respectively, for their two firms.[98] Of more relevance to shareholders is whether performance-based pay is providing the right incentives for managers to make sacrifices on their behalf. Based on what we have seen so far in this book, it looks like performance-based pay schemes may not always be designed with this goal in mind, especially at firms with weak corporate governance. The very firms that would most benefit from well-designed compensation schemes seem to be the ones that do not get them. When viewed from this perspective, excessive pay is important, but mainly as an indicator of poor corporate governance and as an easily identifiable symptom of deeper, underlying problems in a firm.

The last three chapters have shown various ways in which a board can arrange incentives for the firm's senior executives and then step back and let managers manage. In Chapter 4, these incentives came from owning part of the corporate cake. Unless the CEO was a company founder, the typical way of acquiring such an ownership stake was to receive it as part of a pay package. These incentives were created by past pay. Chapters 5 and 6 covered the incentives generated by current pay. Next up, in the spirit of Ebenezer Scrooge, we look at the incentives generated by the ghost of pay yet to come.

[M]y role has changed, and it no longer matches my aspirations.[1]

CARL YANKOWSKI (2001)

I still have it within me to run a major organization.[2]

CARL YANKOWSKI (2003)

I'm contemplating whether I want to be the CEO of a medium or large company, or start something new.[3]

CARL YANKOWSKI (2009)

---

7 Separating the wheat from the chaff
INCENTIVES GENERATED BY EXECUTIVES' CAREER CONCERNS

TEN YEARS IS a long time, just ask Carl Yankowski. In March 2000 he was CEO of Palm Inc., maker of the PalmPilot and a pioneer in the field of handheld computing devices. Investors valued the firm at $53b when the firm's shares traded publicly on the NASDAQ exchange for the first time.[4] He celebrated by wearing a suit with pinstripes made of pure gold.[5] Twenty months later, investors who had bought shares from the company had lost 94% of their investment.[6] Yankowski resigned; according to the chairman, his departure was by "mutual agreement" with the board.[7] A few years passed before Yankowski resurfaced as the CEO of a video game publisher. It was a much smaller firm than Palm, valued at just $225m when he joined. After only ten months, shareholders had lost 82% of their investment.[8] Yankowski resigned, once again leaving by "mutual agreement."[9] By the time the ten-year anniversary of that golden day at Palm arrived, Yankowski had started and finished another CEO job, this one heading a startup with a staff of ten. One of its flagship products was a weather-forecasting umbrella: the handle lit up when rain was imminent. His time there had been brief as well. One of the firm's directors was reported as describing Yankowski's departure as "very much a mutual situation."[10]

With each apparent failure, Yankowski's career options dwindled. We have seen in the last two chapters that executive compensation schemes make an executive's pay sensitive to his firm's performance, but something different was happening to Yankowski. His *future* pay seemed to be sensitive to his firm's *current* performance. At first glance, that makes little sense. It is not the job of an executive's future employers to reward or punish him for his current performance. That is the job of his current employers; future employers care about future performance.

Despite the apparent irrationality of this behavior, economists have an explanation. As we should probably expect, the origins of that explanation can be found in the competition that occurs in markets of every flavor. What might be unexpected is that the economists' explanation shows that competition in the executive labor market creates incentives for executives similar to those generated by well-designed pay schemes. Best of all, unlike performance-based pay, these incentives do not cost shareholders a dime.

The view from the boardroom

When Yankowski joined Palm after five years at Sony and 15 months at Reebok, Palm was merely one division of a larger firm.[11] It was famous for the PalmPilot, precursor of today's smartphones and tablets, and plans were well advanced to spin the division off as a separate corporation. Just 11 weeks after Yankowski's arrival, Palm's shares were trading on the NASDAQ exchange and Yankowski found himself CEO of a public corporation for the first time, reporting to the new firm's board of directors.[12]

One of a board's most important jobs is to quickly and accurately evaluate key executives' abilities. High-ability executives will boost a firm's value, so boards need to do what they can to retain the services of such executives. Low-ability executives can do enormous harm, the more harm the longer they stay in their jobs, so shareholders look to boards to identify such executives and get rid of them. However, firm performance is determined only partly by executives' innate ability. It is also affected by the sacrifices that executives are willing to make and by luck: events that are completely outside executives' control can have a significant effect on firm performance. Even if directors can observe such random events (and in many cases they cannot), there will always be a degree of uncertainty around exactly what effect those events had on the firm's performance.

Executive ability comes in many flavors, but one of the most important is the ability to make sound strategic decisions. Indeed, Yankowski described his role as "chief evangelist of the Palm brand and architect of the overarching Palm vision."[13] One of the biggest long-term challenges facing Palm when Yankowski arrived was boosting corporate sales, which was where the big profit margins lay. Microsoft's dominance of the corporate marketplace thanks to its Windows operating system and Office software gave it an advantage over Palm if only it could develop its own handheld computing solution. That is just what Microsoft was doing with its new PocketPC software. Microsoft was starting to win business users away from Palm and securities analysts were starting to talk up the Microsoft threat.[14] It was Yankowski's job to help come up with a response.

Yankowski's plans revolved around Palm's proposed merger with a firm producing software that allowed users of mobile devices like the PalmPilot to tap into corporate networks, giving easier access to the databases, printers, and other resources that mobile users needed.[15] However, in the middle of 2001—and just before the merger was due to be completed—Palm's share price collapsed, falling 63% in ten weeks.[16] The merger was called off and Palm was left scrambling to find a different strategy.[17] Palm's directors must have been asking themselves several questions as they watched this unfold. Was it bad luck or a bad strategy? If it was a bad strategy, was that because Yankowski did not put enough effort into its development? Was he not up to the job? Lots of questions, but no easy answers.

Maybe we cannot let Yankowski off the hook because of a plunging share price. That fall in share price was due, at least in part, to Palm's management botching the rollout of a crucial new product earlier that year. This brings us to another skill boards look for in executives: the ability to make good operational decisions. Early in 2001, Palm had responded to the first signs of slowing sales by announcing the imminent release of two new models. Sales of existing models fell when customers decided to wait for the new lineup. That would not have been a problem if the new models had been launched on schedule, two weeks later, but they were not. Instead, it took six weeks for the new product lineup to hit the market, and the prolonged lull in sales led to an inventory buildup and price war.[18] What must Palm's directors have been asking themselves? It might have been bad luck. After all, new products can be delayed through no fault of a firm's senior management. However, could bad luck alone explain a two-week period of fine-tuning turning into a six-week wait, or was management asleep at the wheel?

Perhaps the new-product rollout would not have been botched if Yankowski had spent more time on monitoring these operational matters. Palm had been massively underestimating demand as far back as Yankowski's arrival at the firm and the resulting component shortages hurt profitability the following year.[19] However, soon after Palm ramped up production, it was "blindsided" by falling sales.[20] During this crucial period, Yankowski seemed to have little involvement in Palm's operational workings. He admitted as much, telling a reporter "I was externally focused before and now I'm internally focused."[21] One of the skills boards look for in executives is the ability to judge how to allocate their time, so the botched rollout raised more questions for Palm's directors. Was Yankowski correct to be so "externally focused"? And, if he was not, was this a misjudgment or simply a case of the CEO spending his time on the parts of the job that he enjoyed the most. In other words, was it low ability, insufficient sacrifice, or just bad luck?

Yankowski's hands-off approach was fine in principle, but if it was to work in practice he needed to select the right people and monitor their performance properly. Here, again, the outcome is a mixture of skill, sacrifice, and luck. Yankowski had created an "operations council" of senior executives to oversee Palm's operations, but he attended meetings infrequently. Continuing to live in Massachusetts and commuting to California cannot have helped. Instead, Yankowski relied on regular briefings from Palm's chief financial officer.[22] If this delegation was failing—and Palm's poor operational performance suggests it might have been—the board needed to identify the cause. Perhaps Yankowski did not have good delegation skills. There was not much the board could do about that except look for a new CEO. Perhaps the problem was his absenteeism. If so, then the answer might be to persuade him to make the sacrifice of moving his home to California. Or perhaps it was simply bad luck: even great delegation skills and incredible effort can be overcome by bad luck.

Sometimes an executive cannot delegate; sometimes he needs to get his hands dirty. That is what happened to Yankowski in 2001 when he began to involve himself more in Palm's operational council. As with the other dimensions of executive skill, the board cannot observe the ability to master a firm's operational details. Instead, it can look at the firm's operating performance and try to figure out how much of that performance is due to an executive's ability, how much to the effort that he puts in, and how much to luck. At Palm it appears that the board decided that at least some of the firm's poor operating performance was due to Yankowski's weaknesses, because as 2001 progressed, Palm's directors took an increasingly active role in managing the firm.[23]

Wheat that might be chaff; chaff that might be wheat

Effective boards try to discern executives' ability, especially early in their careers. Shareholders benefit if the board can separate the executive wheat from the chaff, retaining the wheat and dismissing the chaff. However, as we have just seen, separating the two can be difficult. To see how difficult, look at things from the perspective of Palm's outside directors, who were looking for the answers to many questions. Was Yankowski able to make sound strategic decisions? Could he make good operational ones? Did he know how to allocate his time? Could he select and monitor subordinates? Could he get to grips with the firm's operational details?

Palm's directors must have had confidence in Yankowski's ability when he joined the firm, otherwise they would not have offered him the CEO job. However, they could not have been *certain* about that ability. There was always the possibility that what they thought was wheat was actually chaff. He had never been the CEO of a firm before and, as some industry players reminded them, Yankowski was new to the industry.[24] Compounding the board's uncertainty, when Yankowski left Reebok, reports emerged suggesting he had asked the Reebok head to help in his management of Reebok Brand in the months prior to his departure.[25]

Six months after Yankowski's arrival, the bad results started to come in. If his ability really was high and he had worked as hard as the board expected, then he must have been extremely unlucky for the firm's performance to be so poor. The alternative was that his ability was actually low, but then much of the strong performance in his past must have been due to good luck. Palm's directors had a conundrum: either he was lucky before he joined Palm or he was unlucky since he arrived. If the directors followed the laws of probability that economists hold dear, then adding the information in the firm's recent performance to his strong past performance would have caused them to revise their beliefs downwards.[26] However likely they thought it was that Yankowski had high ability when he arrived, they would have been a little less confident six months later; however unlikely they thought it was that he had low ability, after six months they would have been a little more pessimistic.

One other thing had changed: the board would have been less uncertain about Yankowski's ability after those first six months. When he started work as Palm's CEO, directors had not seen him in action before. They had seen Reebok's performance during the 15 months that he headed up the Reebok division and must have tried to learn what they could about his performance there. They had also seen Sony's performance during Yankowski's four years there. Six months after he arrived at Palm, however, directors had much more information with which to assess his ability: Palm's performance under his leadership, as well as all the information they had gleaned from board meetings and their access to the other executives within the firm.

We will keep wearing our director's shoes and fast forward another six months, to the end of 2000. By that stage, more bad results had come in, triggering a similar evaluation process to the one the board had gone through previously. The results must have been worse than directors expected, given what they believed Yankowski's ability to be—even after they revised those beliefs downwards six months previously. Directors had the same conundrum as before: either he was lucky before joining Palm or he was unlucky since. However, there was a subtle difference from the situation six months earlier. This time, directors were starting their evaluation with less uncertainty and therefore more confidence in their assessment of the CEO's ability. Thus, when new information arrived—the latest poor performance figures—they would trust their prior assessment a little bit more than previously and trust the latest information a little bit less. Directors would still add the new information to what they had previously and they would still revise their beliefs downwards, but not by as much as before. First impressions count; second impressions count as well, but not as much.

Fast-forward another six months, to mid-2001, and yet more bad news had arrived. If Palm's performance was worse than the directors had expected—even after the previous downward revisions of their beliefs regarding Yankowski's ability—then they would have revised those beliefs downwards still further. However, as the information accumulated, so did the board's confidence in its beliefs about Yankowski's ability, and as the board's confidence grew, the impact of each piece of additional news shrank. In short, Palm's directors were starting to make up their minds.

Consistent with this learning process, the probability of a CEO being dismissed is much more sensitive to firm performance early in the CEO's tenure compared to later on.[27] That is, for an early-tenure CEO, the board will, correctly or incorrectly, infer a great deal from firm performance. If that performance is bad, then the board will significantly lower its assessment of the CEO's ability. However, for a long-tenure CEO, the board would not infer as much information from similar firm performance. Even if that performance is bad, it will not affect the board's assessment much at all, so it will have little effect on the probability that the CEO is fired.

By mid-2001, Palm's board had decided that Yankowski needed some help. Todd Bradley, who had until recently been a senior executive at the computer manufacturer Gateway Inc., was employed to run Palm's hardware unit. Two months later, Palm appointed David Nagel, AT&T's chief technology officer and a former Apple executive, to run the unit responsible for the operating system that ran Palm's devices.[28] As Bradley built up the management team of the hardware unit, Nagel began getting the software unit ready for spinning off as a separate business. Yankowski was being sidelined and he seemed to know his career at Palm might not last much longer.[29]

The board has decided you will resign

If Yankowski was worried about his career prospects, he would not be the only executive to do so. There are four different ways in which executives suffer if the labor market believes they have low ability. In each one executives tend to suffer after a string of poor performances, but they also prosper after a string of good ones.

An executive's first career concern is that his career may end earlier than he had hoped. According to press reports, and in a repeat of what happened at Reebok, Palm's board took an increasingly active role in managing the firm in the second half of 2001.[30] By November, events had reached a head and the firm announced Yankowski's resignation. The official line from Yankowski was that "[w]ith Palm's transition into two individual businesses almost complete, my role has changed, and it no longer matches my aspirations."[31] However, signs that Yankowski might have been dismissed soon emerged. His resignation took effect immediately, with the chairman of the board taking over as interim CEO, and the severance agreement saw him leave with a cash payout of over $1.4m and most of his unvested options, in line with the formula in his employment agreement that applied to dismissals.[32] The next day the chairman revealed that Yankowski's departure had been by "mutual agreement" with the board.[33]

In situations like Yankowski's departure from Palm, the question is often asked: did the CEO resign or was he fired? Boards do not make it easy for us. In fact, they often seem to go out of their way to obscure the reasons for an executive's departure. Rather than risk both sides washing their dirty laundry in public, the board and the departing executive will agree on the precise—and uninformative—wording to be used to describe the departure.[34]

Typical executive employment agreements allow for four forms of departure. First, the executive might be dismissed "for cause," meaning that he has committed a sackable offense and the board has chosen to fire him. Although such departures are involuntary, they are not (directly, anyway) performance-based. Second, the executive might have resigned without "good reason," meaning that he has decided to simply walk away from the job. He might have accepted a better job elsewhere; perhaps he has simply had enough. In these two cases, the executive will usually not receive any severance pay. Third, the executive might be dismissed "without cause," meaning that the board has decided to get rid of the executive despite him not having committed a sackable offense. Fourth, the executive might have resigned "for good reason," which usually means that his role has been greatly diminished due to changes in the way the firm is structured. Typical employment agreements guarantee the executive substantial severance pay in the third and fourth cases because in both cases the executive's departure is largely involuntary. In one, the board has decided to dismiss the CEO; in the other, the board has decided to change the structure of the firm in such a way that the executive's resignation could be anticipated.

Whether Yankowski resigned voluntarily or not, directors had obviously decided by November 2001 that he was underperforming. This raises two questions. Why did Palm's board not move earlier to sideline Yankowski? Should it have waited longer? The board's decision is not an easy one to make. No matter how much information is gathered, and how carefully they evaluate it, directors can never entirely eliminate their uncertainty about an executive's ability. There will always be a possibility that an executive written off as having low ability is actually a very unlucky high-ability CEO, just as there will always be a possibility that an executive hailed as having high ability is actually a very lucky low-ability CEO. If the board acts too soon it might lose a good (but unlucky) CEO: once a CEO is fired, he is not coming back. On the other hand, if the board waits too long to fire a poor CEO then the firm will suffer from prolonged poor management. The board needs to weigh the cost of acting too soon against the cost of waiting too long.

The board will also be uncertain about the ability of a replacement CEO. Nothing will be gained by replacing an underperforming CEO with someone who performs just as poorly, so incumbent CEOs are more vulnerable when either the board believes there are talented outsiders available or, as at Palm, there are strong inside candidates for the top job. Palm's board was fortunate because it had two inside candidates, Bradley and Nagel, lined up to replace Yankowski. By delaying Yankowski's firing—if that is what it was—the board could learn more about the abilities of the inside candidates to replace him. Waiting like this is costly for the firm if it prolongs a poor incumbent's tenure, but these costs must be weighed against the risk of acting too soon and having to fire his replacement as well. To paraphrase Oscar Wilde—to lose one CEO may be regarded as a misfortune; to lose two looks like carelessness.[35]

Early in an executive's tenure, there can be so much uncertainty about his actual ability that the best outcome for shareholders is for the board to wait and learn more about his ability.[36] Executives need to perform extremely poorly for an early dismissal to be good for shareholders. Boards should be especially tolerant when evaluating executives hired from outside the firm as these are the executives about whom they know the least. Conversely, an executive who has been in the job for many years has—hopefully—convinced the board he has high ability by producing a long sequence of strong performances; a few quarters of poor performance will have little effect on the board's perceptions of his ability, so the firm's short-term performance needs to be extremely poor for dismissal to be good for shareholders here as well. Consistent with this theory, the empirical evidence shows that CEOs are least vulnerable to dismissal very early in their tenure (when the board is presumably still learning about their ability) and after ten years in the job (by which time the board has presumably made up its mind).[37]

Individual members of a CEO's management team suffer as well if the firm performs poorly, but mainly as part of team replacement. For example, by the middle of 2002, the general manager of Palm's software unit had left; there was a new head of human resources; the chief marketing officer had resigned; the general counsel had gone; so had the chief internet officer.[38] And, of course, the CEO had gone. The empirical evidence suggests that non-CEOs are dismissed as frequently as CEOs, but non-CEOs are much more likely to leave a firm during years when a CEO departs than in other years. New CEOs who are appointed from outside a firm tend to bring their own executive teams with them and, if things do not work out, the team tends to leave together. After the effect of the CEO leaving has been filtered out, non-CEO turnover is fairly insensitive to the firm's share-price performance.[39] Put all this evidence together and it looks as though a firm's senior executives are evaluated, in part, as a group.

Bradley and Nagel were not really a part of Yankowski's management team: they had been brought into the firm when the board started to sideline the CEO. Sure enough, Bradley kept his job as chief operating officer of the hardware unit after Yankowski left, gradually assuming more responsibility, and Nagel ran the software unit.[40] Palm's board chairman filled the role of interim CEO for the next two years, until Palm formally split into two separate corporations, each with their own shares trading on the NASDAQ. Bradley was promoted to CEO of the hardware firm, called PalmOne; Nagel became CEO of the software firm, called PalmSource.[41]

What a board (thinks it) needs can change over time, as is illustrated by Bradley's subsequent experience as PalmOne's CEO. He was a good fit for the first few years, when product innovation was still strong and operational performance needed improving. However, by the time 2005 arrived, PalmOne's operational problems appeared to have been resolved. Unfortunately for Bradley, strategic concerns were mounting. In an interview two years later, the board chairman at the time of Bradley's departure was reported as saying that "several board members felt he did not have the vision required to lead the company into the future ..."[42] Nobody was questioning Bradley's ability to execute a strategy, but some were apparently questioning his ability to formulate that strategy in the first place. Bradley resigned, leaving with a severance package worth $4.6m.[43] "I feel the time is right," Bradley said when the news was announced, "for me to move on to another challenge."[44] The severance package suggests that his departure was not entirely voluntary.

Dusting off the résumé

Some CEOs get lucky and make it all the way to retirement, but many others will be dismissed along the way. When that happens, they are confronted with the second of the four career concerns we consider: what happens next?

Most CEOs who leave a firm without retiring or having another job lined up struggle to find new executive appointments. One study found that less than 5% of dismissed CEOs find jobs as senior executives at public corporations within the next four years.[45] Job prospects are more attractive for non-CEOs: 39% of dismissed non-CEO executives under the age of 50 obtain new executive jobs, but typically the new jobs are inferior to the ones they have lost.[46]

Consistent with this evidence, Yankowski had some lean years after leaving Palm. He was only 53 years old and not ready to retire. Publicly he was saying that with Palm's software business operating independently and a new COO taking care of the hardware business, the CEO role at Palm no longer matched his aspirations. Perhaps he was saving face—many departing CEOs would say something similar—but his comment suggests a desire to be CEO of another large firm. He was still looking almost two years later, telling his hometown newspaper "I still have it within me to run a major organization, both the skill set and the attitude." Yankowski, forever the optimist, said he was "exploring a number of avenues."[47]

One of those avenues was home to a small, privately-held Finnish software firm with aspirations to list its shares on the NASDAQ. The NASDAQ dream did not eventuate, despite Yankowski serving as interim CEO for a few months.[48] It was not until 2004, almost three years after leaving Palm, that Yankowski landed another CEO gig at a public corporation.[49] The video game publisher Majesco Holdings Inc. had carved out a niche at the value end of the market, but was attempting to break into the big-budget console-game marketplace. The firm's shares had been trading publicly for the previous eight months, but only on the over-the-counter market where brokers trade directly with each other rather than on a stock exchange.[50] Majesco's founder, who still controlled the firm, had big plans that included listing its shares on the NASDAQ. However, even with this ambition, Majesco was no Palm. When Yankowski joined Majesco, PalmOne had nine times the market value of his new firm, nine times as many employees, and eight times the annual revenue.[51] Still, it had been three lean years since Yankowski left Palm and Majesco was the perfect place to prove his ability once and for all.

The early signs were encouraging. Majesco's shares started trading on the NASDAQ five months after Yankowski arrived. It started shipping the much-hyped *Advent Rising* video game at the end of May. In June it was predicting annual revenue would be 50% higher than in the previous year.[52] Behind the scenes, however, things were starting to go wrong. The new head of sales and marketing resigned after less than five months in the job. *Advent Rising* was plagued by technical problems and sales quickly tapered off. Customers held off buying games in anticipation of upcoming changes in video game platforms.[53] It would all have felt quite familiar to investors who remembered Palm. The outcome for Yankowski was familiar as well: he resigned at the end of the first week in July, with $375,000 in severance pay.[54] However, the news was not released until the following Tuesday, when Majesco shocked investors by also announcing that the expected revenue growth was not going to eventuate: it was predicting that annual revenue would be at about the same level as the previous year. The share price fell 48% in a single day.[55] (When the year was over, revenue actually turned out to be just *half* the 2004 value.)[56]

At the time Yankowski left Palm, the well-documented inventory problems and botched product launches had raised doubts about his operational management skills. When similar events occurred at Majesco, these doubts compounded. Yankowski might have been unlucky at Palm. He might even have been unlucky at Palm *and* Majesco, but perhaps he had not been unlucky at all. Perhaps he just lacked the skills required of a CEO. Ultimately nobody could tell which of these possibilities was the right one, but the evidence was mounting that Yankowski was not just unlucky.

Bradley was also on the job market in 2005, having announced his (possibly forced) resignation at PalmOne. However, his circumstances were quite different from those of his former boss. In the first few years after Yankowski left Palm, Bradley had continued working there and been paid $13m; Yankowski had worked as CEO of a public corporation for less than 11 months and been paid $0.9m.[57] When Bradley eventually resigned, his agreement with the board resulted in him carrying on as CEO for a few weeks and then as a consultant for three more months; Yankowski's agreement with Majesco's board had resulted in him leaving the company immediately.[58] PalmOne's share price increased by 59% during the 15 months that Bradley was CEO; Majesco's *fell* by 82% during the ten months that Yankowski was in charge.[59] There were few doubts about Bradley's operational management skills. Some PalmOne directors may have had concerns about his strategic planning, but he was widely regarded as being "detail-oriented and a stickler for efficiency."[60] And even if PalmOne's directors had effectively dismissed Bradley, they were still keen on him hanging around for a few months to help manage the transition.

The difference in performance and the likely resulting difference in labor-market assessments were reflected in the two CEOs' careers after their 2005 resignations. Bradley was offered the job running Hewlett-Packard's PC division while he was still working for PalmOne.[61] He would not be CEO, but he would be responsible for a division of HP with annual revenue of $27b; PalmOne's annual revenue at the time was just $1.3b.[62] (As demotions go, that is not bad.) In Bradley's first six years at HP he was paid approximately $67m.[63] In contrast, more than two years after leaving Majesco, Yankowski was appointed CEO of a tiny start-up (maker of the weather-forecasting umbrella), but he departed after approximately 18 months and his career as an executive seemed to be over.[64]

Economists have investigated the links between share-price performance and reemployment prospects. Consistent with the diverging career paths of Bradley and Yankowski, the empirical evidence suggests that weak financial performance worsens the labor-market prospects of a firm's senior executives. For example, dismissed CEOs are less likely to obtain a senior executive position at a public corporation if their previous employer is less profitable or has weaker share-price performance. When executives move from one firm to another, their new job is less likely to be as CEO if they move from firms with weaker recent stock returns.[65] The experiences of the two ex-Palm executives suggest there might also be a vicious circle at work: executives who come from firms with poor financial performance might find their future employment options restricted to relatively weak firms, where it will be even more difficult to shine.

Climbing the greasy pole

The third aspect of career concerns is the possibility of promotion (or demotion) within an executive's current firm. Executive vacancies arise in firms from time to time, perhaps replacing a departing CEO or other senior executive, or filling positions created when a firm reorganizes itself. Such changes create promotion opportunities for current executives. Sometimes reorganizations can eliminate or degrade positions as well, creating the threat of a demotion or, worse, a dismissal. Like the two aspects of career concerns we have already considered, a firm's financial performance seems to affect its executives' promotion prospects. Bradley's two non-CEO stints, first at Palm and then at HP, illustrate how executives can be affected.

Bradley was chief operating officer of Palm's hardware operation when Yankowski resigned. He was promoted to become its president six months later and its CEO shortly after that.[66] Throughout this period he was clearly in line to succeed Palm's CEO. The most obvious sign was salary: Bradley's salary was almost twice as high as the next highest paid executive, with the exception of Nagel, who was running the software operation and would go with it when Palm spun it off in 2003.[67] Empirical studies suggest that an anointed successor benefits if his firm's performance is strong as this makes appointment of an external candidate less likely.[68] Palm's share price increased by 123% in the year before the split occurred.[69] Sure enough, Bradley was promoted to CEO of the hardware firm, PalmOne.

Bradley's second non-CEO stint, at HP, illustrates a different approach to promotions. Senior executives at some firms compete amongst themselves to be promoted to better, and higher paid, jobs.[70] Firms will not usually be explicit about these contests, which economists have colorfully named tournaments, but we can often find signs of them in the distribution of executive pay that firms report in their proxy statements. For example, during most of Bradley's first five years at HP, he was one of three executive vice presidents receiving the same base salary, second only to the CEO's.[71] Here were three executives, with identical salaries and comparable seniority, in all likelihood competing with each other for promotion. In tournaments where the winner is an insider, managers at divisions with greater profitability are more likely to be promoted compared to managers at other divisions.[72]

That is what happened to Bradley. He arrived at HP in mid-2005 to lead the firm's PC division. Within two years HP had overtaken Dell as the world's number-one PC maker. Suddenly he was being profiled in glowing terms by the *Wall Street Journal* and feted as the "smartest tech executive" by *Fortune* magazine.[73] However, there were missteps along the way, most notably involving his old firm Palm. HP had missed the mobile-computing revolution, and in an attempt to play catchup it acquired Palm in 2010. A year later, HP launched its first Palm-designed tablet, the TouchPad, with much fanfare. Reviews were mixed and sales were poor. Just seven weeks later, HP announced it would stop manufacturing and selling the TouchPad and all other products using the operating system it had acquired as part of the Palm acquisition.[74] It was a humiliating end for a mobile-computing and smartphone pioneer.

The damage to Bradley's reputation cannot have been too great, because in March 2012, HP combined his division with the printer operation run by Vyomesh Joshi to form a single division with annual sales of $60b.[75] This is a perfect example of the tournaments that economists talk about: two business divisions, two executive vice presidents, but only one job and only one winner. During the period that Bradley had been at HP, his division's sales had increased by 48% and, despite the TouchPad glitch, its profits had increased by 258%; Joshi's division's sales were up by 2% and its profits by 16%.[76] Bradley got the job and Joshi retired.

Of course, tournaments are never really over. The failure of HP's Palm-based mobile strategy came home to roost when PC sales collapsed; 15 months after his promotion Bradley was replaced by one of his subordinates in what was described as "a lateral move" by HP and a demotion by everybody else. A year later Bradley resigned to become company president of a software maker.[77]

There is life in the old dog yet

Our story so far is littered with casualties. We have seen Yankowski depart Palm in 2001 and then Majesco in 2005, and Joshi leave HP in 2012. Nagel also lost his job, retiring as PalmSource's CEO shortly before the firm was acquired by a Japanese software company.[78] All three followed the traditional path of retired executives, serving time on boards of directors. The prospect of such post-retirement activity, and the opportunities for pay and prestige that it brings, is the last of the four aspects of career prospects that we consider.

There is demand for executives to sit on boards of directors, with one study reporting that approximately two-thirds of directors are current or retired executives.[79] Back in Chapter 2 we saw that directors have important monitoring and advisory roles. Executives' experience makes them effective monitors because it gives them insight into the problems to look for and the tricks that executives might play. It also makes them effective advisors by giving them insight into the sort of advice that can be useful to an executive. Directors who are executives can also bring fat Rolodexes with them and this ability to open doors at other firms can be especially valuable to young growing firms. The most successful CEOs will be most in demand as directors, and so will pick the best firms to join. However, passage of the Sarbanes–Oxley Act of 2002 increased the burden on directors. This in turn has increased the demand for retired executives to sit on boards, as they bring many of the same attributes as current executives, but have more time to work on board matters.[80]

Yankowski's career as a director at public corporations peaked at the same time as his career as an executive. While he was still at Reebok, he was elected to the board of a venture capital firm worth $2.2b; while he was Palm's CEO, he was elected to the board of Novell, a software maker worth $1.5b when he joined.[81] His career as an independent director was all downhill from there. He left both boards following his departure from Palm, but he was able to replace these directorships with seats at two smaller firms, another software maker (worth $555m) and a manufacturing firm (worth $66m).[82] He left one of these boards within a few months of the Majesco fiasco, replacing it with a directorship at a tech company (worth just $19m).[83] The days of board seats at billion-dollar companies were long gone.

We do not know why Yankowski left the boards of those firms after his employment ended at Palm and Majesco, or why he chose to subsequently join the boards that he did. We do not know what other opportunities he turned down either. However, it looks like his opportunities were drying up as nomination committees absorbed the lessons from the poor performance of Palm and Majesco during his time in charge. It would not be surprising if this were the case because outside observers, just like the directors at Palm and Majesco, would attribute part of that poor performance to Yankowski having lower ability than previously believed. Directors with relatively low ability as executives have less to offer as monitors and advisors: if Yankowski could not manage those two firms successfully, then would his advice on running any other firm be of any value? As for the doors that a current or retired executive might open, while Yankowski's Rolodex was very valuable back in the glory days when he was Palm's CEO, its value had probably fallen post-Majesco. And, while it sounds awfully uncharitable, what sort of a signal would inviting Yankowski to join a firm's board send to investors? Many would surely ask why the firm could not attract somebody who had been more successful. A firm's share price is in trouble once investors start asking that question.

If Palm and Majesco had performed better, Yankowski's portfolio of directorships might have looked quite different. How different? There is no point looking at Bradley; it is too soon to tell what opportunities his performance at Palm and HP will create when he retires. However, Yankowski's other former colleague, Nagel, left PalmSource in 2005 aged 60. Within a few weeks of announcing his retirement, he had joined the boards of a tech firm worth $1.9b and an educational entertainment company worth $0.7b.[84] After retiring from HP, Joshi joined the boards of an IT services company worth $28b and a telecommunications equipment manufacturer worth $6.9b.[85] The post-retirement activities of Nagel and Joshi are typical of executives who find their executive careers winding down. Indeed, almost two thirds of retired CEOs will sit on at least two boards as independent directors soon after they have retired.[86] Large-scale empirical studies suggest that the market for independent directors rewards executives if the firms they manage perform well and punishes them if the firms perform poorly. Prior to retirement, executives whose firms are more profitable and who serve as independent directors at other firms typically hold more board seats. Once they retire, executives are likely to sit on more boards if their firm was more profitable while they were in charge.[87]

Rewarding ability, motivating effort

Now that we have seen how careers can work out, we can take a fresh look at the start of our story. When Yankowski joined Palm he did not know he would be leaving 23 months later. He did not know he would subsequently join, and quickly leave, Majesco. Like the rest of us, he had probably never heard of a weather-forecasting umbrella. However, like all executives, he must have realized that the executive labor market likes success and dislikes failure. With that realization came an incentive to perform that works in much the same way as the immediate financial incentives that come from ownership (Chapter 4) and pay (Chapter 5).

Yankowski's immediate financial incentives when he joined Palm were already strong, including an annual bonus of up to $0.6m. In addition, even before Palm's shares started to trade publicly, he had been granted shares and options that gave him an effective ownership stake of 0.2%. If he could increase Palm's enterprise value by 1% then the value of his ownership stake would increase by $0.4m.[88] However, the incentives generated by these factors need to be judged in the context of his future income-earning potential. In the first few years after Yankowski resigned from Palm, the period when he was "exploring a number of avenues" and working briefly at Majesco, he received $0.9m from his work as CEO of a public corporation; if he had been able to emulate Bradley, he would have been paid $13m during the same period. If, during the next six years, Yankowski had been emulating Bradley rather than "contemplating whether . . . to be the CEO of a medium or large company, or start something new," he would have been paid another $67m.[89]

The stark differences in the career paths of Yankowski and his former lieutenant are relevant for incentives only if executives can influence the likelihood of the good and bad outcomes occurring. If they cannot—for example, if Yankowski's departure from Palm had absolutely nothing to do with his actions—then these future variations in outcomes are just risks that executives have to bear. Fortunately for shareholders, executives can affect their future prospects.

It is a neat mechanism. Here is how it works.[90] A board's assessment of an executive's ability is an important contributor to the outcome when the board is deciding whether or not to dismiss him, or promote him, or recruit him from another firm. We have already seen how perceptions of ability are based on a mixture of the executive's actual ability, the effort and other sacrifices he makes for shareholders, and luck. He cannot do anything about his intrinsic ability or luck, but he can choose the sacrifices he makes. The more effort he exerts, or other sacrifices he makes for shareholders, the better the firm's performance. Boards cannot always distinguish effort from intrinsic ability when they are deciding whether to dismiss an executive. Neither can hiring committees when they are evaluating potential new recruits. Some of the improved performance that is actually due to the executive's extra effort will therefore be attributed to him having higher than expected ability. That means that an executive who makes more sacrifices for shareholders is less likely to be dismissed by his current employer and more likely to be hired by a new one.

Exerting that effort, or making that sacrifice, may be costly to the executive, but he benefits from improved career prospects. However, he is not being rewarded for his effort directly. Rather, the effort is resulting in an improved assessment of his ability and it is the improvement in that assessed ability that is being rewarded. If an executive decides to not exert that effort, the boards and hiring committees will see the reduced firm performance and attribute some of the drop to the executive's ability being lower than they had previously thought. Suddenly, dismissal becomes more likely, being recruited by another firm less likely. The executive labor market is rewarding high perceived ability—and punishing low perceived ability—but in doing so it is actually motivating increased effort.

The mechanism is subtle, perhaps too subtle for some. In the *Seinfeld* episode "The Hot Tub," George Costanza gave some career advice: "I sit around pretending that I'm busy. . . . I always look annoyed. Yeah, when you look annoyed all the time, people think that you're busy."[91] As happened so often to George, he got this completely wrong. According to our theory, at least, future employment opportunities reflect the market's assessment of an individual's ability. Acting busy, while actually being lazy, led to relatively poor observed performance by George, which—because he seemed to be working so hard—was interpreted by the market as low ability. Perhaps that explains why George spent so many of *Seinfeld*'s nine seasons unemployed. A better approach would have been for him to work hard but act lazy. The market would then have observed good performance and, because of his apparent laziness, attributed it to very high ability. The job offers would have followed.

CEOs are not the only executives motivated by career concerns. We have seen that non-CEO executives tend to be evaluated as part of the executive management team and that they are more likely to be dismissed when the CEO is dismissed. These two features motivate non-CEO executives to exert effort in ways that make the CEO look good—and the best way to do that is to improve the firm's performance. However, such executives are also motivated by concerns about their own promotion prospects. The incentives are relatively weak for anointed successors because, just like Bradley at Palm, a small change in performance has a relatively small effect on their promotion chances. However, the incentives are much stronger when tournaments are used because even small changes in an executive's job performance can have a big effect on his ranking. For example, when Bradley was competing in HP's tournament, even a small drop in his division's performance might have dropped him to second place in the tournament. (Of course, there was no second prize in that tournament, just an early retirement.) Executives seem to respond most strongly to these incentives when a CEO nears retirement (so that the tournament is reaching its climax) and least strongly when a firm has a new CEO (so that the tournament is just in its very early stages).[92]

As in all the other partial solutions to manager–shareholder conflict that we have seen so far, career concerns need a strong board of directors in order to be effective. The board needs to be strong and independent enough for the threat of dismissal following poor performance to be credible. At firms with such boards, executives are motivated to make sacrifices that improve firm performance. However, career concerns will provide little motivation to a CEO who dominates the board of directors because the threat of dismissal if low executive effort leads to poor firm performance is not credible.

Things can go wrong even if the board is strong. The incentives created by career concerns may not be strong enough to affect the behavior of experienced CEOs. If they have been generously paid for several years then they may never need to work again. Even if career concerns are strong enough to motivate executives, they might be motivated to do things that are not in shareholders' best interests. For example, the poor prognosis for dismissed CEOs creates a strong and unwelcome incentive for a new CEO to give establishing dominance over the board a very high priority. Non-CEO executives, who do not have the same opportunity to entrench themselves by shaping the board's makeup, can still advance their own careers by covering up poor individual performances and taking undeserved credit for other executives' good performances. None of these actions benefit shareholders, but they are a perfectly rational response for executives who are concerned about their careers.

You are only young once

The incentives created by career concerns are stronger for younger executives than for their older counterparts. Palm provides a good example: Bradley was 42 years old when he arrived in 2001, Nagel was 56 when he started work there a few weeks later.[93] Based on typical retirement ages of CEOs, Bradley could expect to work in similar positions for another 20 years or longer, Nagel for less than ten.[94]

Putting ourselves in the shoes of someone like Bradley helps us understand the strong incentives created by the career concerns of young executives.[95] We need to look backwards, then forwards. His previous executive experience in the tech sector was as a member of the computer manufacturer Gateway's executive management team, a position he held for just over two years.[96] This relatively brief track record meant there was considerable uncertainty regarding his ability at the time he joined Palm, so any effort he exerted would lead to a relatively large increase in the market's assessment of his ability. (Remember: first impressions count; second impressions count as well, but not as much.)

Now look forwards. Bradley had many years left in the workforce, so any increase in the market's assessment of his ability would lead to pay increases lasting many years. Putting the two pieces of the jigsaw together, we see that it must have been relatively easy for Bradley to improve the market's perceptions of his ability and that he would have received a relatively large reward from doing so. The result: the incentives created by career concerns were strong.

Now step into the shoes of an executive like Nagel. Looking backwards, before Nagel joined Palm he had been on the executive management teams at Apple and then AT&T for almost nine years in total.[97] This lengthy track record meant there was much less uncertainty regarding his ability than there was regarding Bradley's, so any effort Nagel exerted would lead to a relatively small increase in the market's assessment of his ability: if he worked especially hard, the market would attribute much of the improved firm performance to luck, not ability. (Again, early impressions count; later ones not so much.) Looking forwards, Nagel's age meant that he did not have many years left in the workforce, and so any increase in the market's assessment of his ability would lead to pay increases lasting just a few years. Put the pieces together and it is clear that Nagel's career-based incentives were relatively weak: it would take considerable sacrifice to improve the labor market's assessment of his ability and even then the reward from the change would be relatively small.

It is not just the increase in future pay that motivates a CEO to act in ways that raise his perceived ability: there is also the increased bargaining power that it brings. If the labor market's assessment of a CEO's ability improves, so will his outside opportunities. There is nothing quite like the prospect of headhunters enticing away a high-ability CEO to focus a board's attention. This makes it easier for the CEO to influence the board's composition. A period of strong performance leads to an upward revision in the CEO's ability, which leads to greater outside opportunities, greater bargaining power, and the prospect of a more compliant board in the future. What about a period of poor performance? The CEO's outside opportunities will diminish. If he is lucky, the worst he will have to deal with is a board that uses its greater bargaining power to replace directors close to the CEO with more independent ones. If he is unlucky, he may be dismissed and have to take one of those relatively unattractive outside opportunities. As Yankowski discovered when he landed at Majesco, the CEO opportunities available to executives who have been dismissed (or are even just suspected to have been dismissed) from one job can be challenging. It is much better to avoid being dismissed in the first place. Young CEOs, in particular, have a strong incentive to make sacrifices that lift firm performance, as doing so can greatly strengthen their position at the firm. Unfortunately for shareholders, the same economic forces imply that young inexperienced executives have a relatively strong incentive to promote short-term projects that manipulate the board's assessment of their ability.[98]

Only Bradley and Nagel know how they responded to the incentives generated by their career concerns. However, based on the empirical evidence at a large sample of firms, we have a fairly clear idea of how typical executives respond to their own incentives. Younger CEOs are busier: the firms they manage are more likely to enter new lines of business and withdraw entirely from others.[99] Their firms also tend to invest more in R&D than firms run by older CEOs.[100] Perhaps those older CEOs would prefer to boost short-term profits—and their bonuses—by cutting R&D spending rather than investing in future profitability that may not occur until after they have left office. Not all the incentives favor appointing young CEOs, however. When a firm grows larger by acquiring other firms, the CEO's pay tends to permanently increase whether or not the acquisition is good for shareholders; young CEOs have more to gain because they have more pay checks ahead of them. Sure enough, young CEOs tend to make more—and worse—acquisitions than old CEOs.[101]

Boards can exploit executives' career concerns

Strong boards can exploit executives' career concerns in ways that benefit shareholders. As with any scheme to motivate executives, the key is to make executives' wealth sensitive to a firm's performance. It is a mistake to do what some critics of executive pay practices have done and focus on just the sensitivity of an executive's *current* pay to firm performance.[102] Incentives come from three distinct sources: past pay, which is the source of many executives' ownership of their firms' shares and options (Chapter 4); current pay (Chapters 5 and 6); and future pay, which is the basis of executives' career concerns (this chapter).

To gain a complete picture of the incentive structure for a firm's executives we need to assess their ownership of the firm's securities: count the shares, count the options, convert everything into share-equivalents, and calculate their effective ownership stakes. Then we move on to the incentives generated by the executives' current pay arrangements. How are their bonuses related to the firm's performance? What determines the number of new shares and options that will be granted? How soon do they vest? And then we need to dig deeper into the pay information provided by firms in their proxy statements to see if they are hiding high pay and if they are paying their executives for good performance or good luck. Finally, we need to evaluate the career concerns of the CEO and the executive management team. Check the ages of the CEO and the other senior executives. See if the firm has announced a succession plan and look at the distribution of pay amongst the non-CEO executives to see if there is any sign of a tournament being used to determine promotions.

What matters to shareholders is the overall sensitivity of an executive's wealth to the firm's performance, as this is what determines the executive's incentives and hence his willingness to make sacrifices that benefit shareholders. A young executive will have relatively strong incentives generated by career concerns, so a board working in shareholders' best interests will ensure he has relatively weak ownership- and pay-based incentives.[103] It will make his pay relatively insensitive to firm performance, which reduces the firm-specific risk borne by the executive, which in turn reduces the pay needed to compensate the executive for bearing this risk. In contrast, an old executive's career-based incentives are weak. A board working in shareholders' best interests will make sure he has strong ownership- and pay-based incentives, even if this requires a relatively high level of pay to compensate him for the extra risk he must bear.

Boards can use the succession and promotion processes to provide strong incentives to non-CEO executives, but these processes must be chosen in tandem with pay arrangements. Below the CEO level, the sensitivity of pay to firm performance should differ according to whether or not a firm determines promotion outcomes using tournaments. We saw above that tournaments provide non-CEO executives with relatively strong incentives to perform. That means the competing executives' pay does not need to be especially sensitive to performance: the board should leave the tournament to generate the incentives. However, natural successors have weaker career-based incentives, so need stronger pay-based ones. Boards seem to get it right on average, because in practice natural successors receive a higher proportion of their pay in equity than the competing candidates in firms that appear to use tournaments to determine promotions.[104]

At the CEO level, in firms where a natural successor is already in place, the CEO will realize that the threat of dismissal is relatively strong. It is relatively easy for a firm's board to dismiss its CEO if there is a potential replacement waiting in the wings who is already well known to directors. The board will find dismissing the CEO much more difficult if it has to roll the dice by going outside the firm and hiring a CEO about whom relatively little is known. (Just ask Yankowski about his last few months at Palm, with Bradley waiting in the wings.) This threat gives the CEO a relatively strong incentive to perform, so the sensitivity of his pay to the firm's performance can be relatively weak. However, if no natural successor is present, then pay may be the primary means of motivating the CEO.

This chapter marks a transition in our story. We have seen how the board motivates executives using the implicit threat of dismissal following poor performance and, for everyone other than the CEO, the promise of promotion following good performance. This is just an extension of the way boards have been able to motivate executives in earlier chapters. However, something was added to the mix in this chapter: executives were motivated by parties outside their firm. In particular, they were motivated by the boards of other firms, which might hire them if they are fired, entice them away from their current firm if they are not, and offer them post-retirement board seats. What is more, a firm's board could take advantage of these externally-generated incentives when choosing its own incentive schemes.

The boards that employed Yankowski were effectively delegating some of their own responsibilities to outside parties, in this case the boards of other firms. Boards do not have to stop there. Strong boards will also delegate some of their monitoring responsibilities to the investors who provide firms with the funds they need to operate. In a twist, a strong board can deliberately weaken a firm in order to make that external monitoring more effective. At the firm we meet next, it was a strategy that reaped shareholders rewards worth many hundreds of millions of dollars.

3 Delegate

I wouldn't believe it unless it was Cablevision.[1]

STOCK ANALYST (2005)

---

8 With one hand tied behind their back
DELEGATING MONITORING TO EXTERNAL CAPITAL MARKETS

TELEVISION RECEPTION WAS poor in early 1960s Manhattan. The problems were caused by skyscrapers, but when Chuck Dolan arrived in town, he brought with him a solution from rural America: cable television. In 1965, Dolan's company, Sterling Communications, Inc., started building the nation's first urban cable-television system in Lower Manhattan.[2] Growing firms need capital and growing cable television systems need lots of it. Sterling's early losses were large, so Dolan had no choice but to go outside the firm to raise the capital he needed to roll out his cable network. The new investor he found was a subsidiary of Time Inc. The losses continued to mount and, after a while, Time's patience ran out. Time used its controlling ownership stake to liquidate the firm, taking the assets it wanted—including Dolan's other brainchild, the cable-television channel Home Box Office—and selling off the rest.[3] Dolan had learnt a lesson he would never forget: there is a limit to the amount of capital that outside investors will provide.

However, Dolan was not going to be beaten, so he bought back Sterling's Long Island cable franchise and started over.[4] By the time of its 2009 annual meeting, his new firm, Cablevision Systems Corp., was the fifth-largest cable operator in the U.S. Three million customers generated $7.2b in annual revenue. Its scope expanded to include the AMC and Sundance cable channels, the *Newsday* newspaper, Madison Square Garden, the New York Knicks basketball team, and the New York Rangers hockey team. There was even a movie-theater chain.[5]

When Dolan set up Cablevision, he was so determined it would not suffer the same fate as Sterling that he structured the firm in such a way that he and his family would never lose control. Family firms make up 29% of America's largest corporations and in most cases multiple generations of the same family retain control.[6] Two approaches to ensuring a family stays in charge are common and Dolan used them both.[7] First, he adopted a dual-class share structure. Each of the Class A shares—the shares traded on the NYSE—came with one vote; each of the Class B shares came with ten votes. Dolan and his family kept the Class B shares for themselves, so that at the time of Cablevision's 2009 annual meeting they owned 20% of the firm's shares when both classes were combined, but held 70% of the votes.[8] To make certain that the Dolan family could not lose control, the owners of the Class B super-shares also had the right to appoint three-quarters of the firm's directors. As we should expect by now, the board that emerged from this arrangement was dominated by the Dolan family. It was chaired by 82-year-old Chuck and eight of the other 16 directors were family members: three of Chuck's sons, three daughters, and two sons-in-law. One of those sons, Jim, worked as the Cablevision CEO—when he was not running the New York Knicks or performing as lead singer in his band "JD and the Straight Shot" (yes, really).[9]

At the end of July 2009, Cablevision announced that its board had decided to spin off the entertainment venues and sports teams into a separate company.[10] All Cablevision shareholders would receive shares in the new company, called Madison Square Garden Co. It would have the same dual-class share structure as Cablevision, giving the Dolan family the same 20%/70% ownership structure. The family could also choose three quarters of the firm's board; they chose Chuck, four of his children, two of his children's spouses, and one grandchild.[11] Not much was going to change. However, the news was associated with an increase in Cablevision's share price of 6.9%, a gain to shareholders worth $323m.[12]

The same thing happened 16 months later when Cablevision announced that its board had agreed to explore a spin-off of its cable channels.[13] The new company, AMC Networks Inc., would have the same dual-class share structure and the same 20%/70% ownership for the Dolan family. The family could choose three quarters of the directors on this board as well. In addition to Chuck, the board contained four of his children and two of his children's spouses.[14] Not much was going to change here either, yet the news was associated with a share price rise of 5.9%. What was left of Cablevision after the first spin-off increased in value again, by $427m this time.[15]

All Cablevision was doing was slicing its cake into three pieces. The combined assets of the three firms after the spin-offs would be exactly the same as the assets of the single firm before the spin-offs, so why did investors think the firm would be so much more valuable? The three separate firms would be dominated by the Dolan family, just as the single firm was. The CEOs of the three firms had all been senior executives at Cablevision at the time of the spin-offs.[16] Surely the three pieces of cake could not be more valuable apart than they were together? Surely all the problems that were there before the announcements would still be there once the spin-offs actually happened?

Voom is doomed

The explanation for investors' positive reaction to Cablevision's spin-offs can be found in the firm's long history of loss-making investments. That history includes buying the electronics retailer Nobody Beats The Wiz out of bankruptcy for $101m in 1998 and shutting it down five years later, by which time The Wiz had run up losses exceeding $460m.[17] It also includes buying the *Newsday* newspaper in 2008 for $630m and writing down the value of the asset by over $400m just six months afterwards.[18] The most spectacular of them all—an aborted satellite television business—triggered an epic battle between father and son.

External observers were unsure about who exactly was in charge at Cablevision.[19] Was it the father, chairman of the board Chuck, or the son, CEO Jim? Both men were Cablevision employees and in 2005, the year the satellite venture crashed to earth, both received pay packages worth approximately $10m.[20] Outsiders may have been unsure, but Jim knew that Chuck was in charge: "When you want to go to the absolute, ultimate authority in the company, you walk by my office and go down to the end of the hall."[21]

It was Chuck who drove Cablevision to enter the satellite business; Jim was a reluctant passenger.[22] "Rainbow-1," Cablevision's $250m satellite, was launched from Cape Canaveral in the summer of 2003.[23] The company planned to use the satellite to broadcast high-definition television signals directly into the homes of subscribers. If Chuck's hunch was right, distributing this service by satellite would have the same transformative effect as his Manhattan cable venture. However, there was a crucial difference. In the 1960s, Chuck was spending his own money and the money of investors who had chosen to invest. Four decades later, he was spending his own money and the money of investors who had no say in how their money was invested.

Stock analysts were skeptical that there was room for a new entrant in the direct-broadcast satellite market dominated by DirecTV and EchoStar Communications. According to one analyst, the venture had "limited chance for success and high potential to turn into a capital black hole." Another one said he wanted Rainbow-1 to blow up on the launch pad.[24] A year after Rainbow-1 began beaming its signal into customers' homes, analysts' gloomy predictions were starting to look spot-on. Voom, as the venture was known, had just 26,000 activated customers and numbers were actually falling.[25] One in five customers signing up for the service subsequently cancelled their subscription.[26] In 2004, Voom's first full year of operation, it earned revenue of less than $15m and incurred operating costs of $387m.[27]

Jim burst out of his father's shadow 18 months after Rainbow-1's launch when he sided with a majority of Cablevision's directors and decided to shut the satellite venture down. Chuck, who had championed the venture, was unhappy. Shortly afterwards, Chuck and his son Tom—who would have filled the CEO's role at Voom—sent a memo to employees revealing that the business was up for sale and indicating that father and son were potential bidders.[28] The next day, a little more than two hours after *Bloomberg* published details of the leaked memo, EchoStar Communications Corp. announced that it was purchasing Voom's sole satellite for $200m in cash.[29] Still Chuck did not give up. Three weeks later, Cablevision reached preliminary agreement to sell those parts of Voom left over after the EchoStar sale to a new company set up by Chuck and Tom. The agreed purchase price was zero, but the new company, called VoomHD, would have to take on the liabilities Voom had built up. A definitive agreement would have to be reached by the end of the month.[30]

The deadline arrived, with no agreement reached, and then the temperature heated up. First, CEO Jim and chairman Chuck sent conflicting memos to staff discussing the fate of Voom. Jim said it was shutting down, Chuck said it was not.[31] Two days later, Chuck used his control of Cablevision's Class B shares to fire three directors and replace them with five new ones, all with close personal ties to him; one was Chuck's son-in-law. "It's very unusual," said one corporate governance expert, but "probably legal."[32] The independent directors were still there, and angry about a new website that had been set up (without the board's knowledge) to take on new Voom subscribers. So much for shutting down. "It is imperative," they wrote to Chuck, "that this expansion of the business stop immediately and that actions taken by the Board be respected and carried out by the company's officers."[33] When the reconfigured board met at the start of the next week, with its five new directors, it gave Chuck until the end of the month to arrange a deal. Voom continued to operate in the meantime, but Chuck had to pay any extra costs and deposit $10m in cash and shares for that purpose.[34]

In a final desperate attempt to keep Voom's precious satellite out of EchoStar's hands, Chuck complained to the Federal Communications Commission (FCC), asking it to block the sale on the grounds that it would inhibit competition between broadcast satellite providers. Even close observers of the firm were bemused at the spectacle of a board chairman taking his own company to the FCC. One securities analyst said he "wouldn't believe it unless it was Cablevision."[35] In the end, however, no deal was done. Chuck and Tom abandoned their plans to acquire what was left of Voom and, after several days of silence, Cablevision announced that it had gone ahead and closed its satellite service.[36] Voom was dead.

This was a high-stakes family squabble, but one with shareholders' money at risk. It illustrates the discipline that external capital markets can provide and the indiscipline that internal capital markets can allow. When VoomHD was proposed as a stand-alone venture, when Chuck had no choice but to go to outside investors for funds, he could not, or would not, keep Voom flying. However, when he had access to the capital of Cablevision's current shareholders, he was Voom's strongest supporter. The key difference, and one possible explanation for Chuck's change of mind, is that in the first case the only way money was going to be spent on Voom was if the ultimate providers of the capital agreed to it; in the second case, Cablevision's decision-makers could invest other people's money without needing to get their consent.

Raising capital the hard way

Stock analysts believed Voom would require as much as $1.5b of additional capital to see it through its growing pains.[37] Chuck and Tom needed to attract this funding if VoomHD was to succeed. We are going to temporarily step into Chuck's shoes when he was fighting so hard to keep Voom alive, and ask: what would we have done?

We do not know what VoomHD would have been worth if Chuck and Tom had followed through with their plan, but we will start on an optimistic note and suppose that it would have been worth $2.0b. In terms of Chapter 4's corporate cake, the ingredients cost $1.5b and ownership of the final product, fresh from the oven, is worth $2.0b. If we sell a portion of cake worth $1.5b to new investors then they will be willing to provide all the cash needed for the venture to succeed. Our portion of cake—everything left over—will be worth $0.5b. Not bad, considering we did not invest a dollar of our own money.

There are other possibilities. For example, we might sell a portion of cake worth just $0.5b to new investors. That will raise a third of the funds that VoomHD needs, but we will need to contribute the remaining $1.0b ourselves. We can sell our stake in Cablevision, worth approximately $1.0b, and use the proceeds from that. We would be left owning a bigger portion of the VoomHD cake than before—this one would be worth $1.5b—this time for an investment of just $1.0b. Whichever way we do it, we will make a gain of $0.5b on whatever investment we make in VoomHD. If we were Chuck and VoomHD was worth $2.0b, we would surely make the investment.

The fact that Chuck and Tom did not make the investment suggests that a mature VoomHD was not going to be worth more than the $1.5b needed for the venture to succeed, so we will be pessimistic and suppose that VoomHD would have been worth just $1.0b. The ingredients needed to bake the corporate cake still cost $1.5b, but now the rights to the baked cake are worth $1.0b. The most we can raise from selling a portion of the cake to new investors is $1.0b, and we can raise this much only if we sell them the entire cake. We will need to put the remaining $0.5b in ourselves. That is, we sell half of our stake in Cablevision, pour the proceeds into VoomHD, and then are left with no ownership of the baked VoomHD cake. What does this give us? Bragging rights for making VoomHD succeed—and, given the barrage of criticism directed our way over Voom, that would be satisfying—but those bragging rights would cost us $0.5b.

Is there a cheaper way? Maybe investors could be sold a portion of cake worth $0.8b instead, leaving us with one worth $0.2b. However, that would raise just $0.8b of the $1.5b that we need to get VoomHD off the ground. We will have to contribute the remaining $0.7b ourselves, so the bragging rights still cost us the difference between what we contribute and what we receive in return: in this case, $0.5b. No matter how the deal is arranged, we have to pay $0.5b more for our portion of cake than it would be worth in financial markets. There is no escaping the fact that the project costs more to build than it is worth. The external investors we are relying on to provide the capital we need will not be fooled, so if we want the project to go ahead, we have to incur the full cost of the shortfall ourselves. If we attach a value of more than $0.5b to the bragging rights and other private benefits that come from controlling VoomHD, then we make the investment. Chuck and Tom did not invest, so it is a good bet that whatever value they attached to the personal benefits from VoomHD going ahead was not enough to compensate for the financial loss they would incur from the transaction.

The thing to remember about capital markets is that there are an enormous number of investors looking for profitable investments. If a firm has a good project then there will be many new investors competing for a slice of the action, which gives all the bargaining power to the firm's current shareholders. They will get to keep the surplus for themselves and outside investors will break even. Shareholders will not need to share much of the surplus with outsiders because there will always be another outsider willing to take part if one gets too demanding. However, if a firm is trying to fund a bad project, then it will not be able to shift any of the deficit onto outside investors because the latter can, and will, simply walk away without making an investment. Shareholders have to bear the deficit themselves and outside investors once again break even. This means that the firm's shareholders receive all of the surplus if the project is good—that is, if the completed project is worth *more* than the cost of completing it—and bear all of the deficit if the project is bad—that is, if the completed project is worth *less* than the cost of completing it. Well functioning capital markets will not stop a good project going ahead. Bad projects can still go ahead, but the project's owners will have to incur the full deficit themselves. This is the discipline of external capital markets.

Raising capital the easy way

The discipline enforced by external capital markets does not fully protect shareholders. We can use our corporate cake from Chapter 4 to explain why, even in the pessimistic scenario above, Cablevision could have raised the funds needed to keep Voom alive had the board supported Chuck. Cablevision without Voom corresponds to the left-hand cake in Figure 8.1. When the cake comes out of the oven, bondholders are entitled to

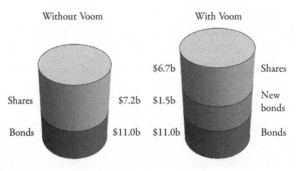

FIGURE 8.1 Cablevision considers keeping Voom alive

all of the cake up to the top of the dark gray layer; everything above that point goes to shareholders (and option-holders, but we keep things simple by ignoring them here). Without Voom, the entire Cablevision cake was worth approximately $18.2b. The firm had debts worth about $11.0b. What was left of the cake after the firm's lenders had taken their portion was owned by shareholders, and was therefore worth $7.2b.[38]

How would the picture have changed if Chuck had been able to convince the board to continue funding Voom? To make things as simple as possible, we will suppose that Cablevision raised the required $1.5b in the external capital markets and we will stick with the pessimistic scenario, in which Voom is worth $1.0b. In this case, Cablevision looks like the right-hand cake in Figure 8.1. Compared to the left-hand cake, this one is $1.0b bigger, reflecting the extra value provided by Voom. The firm's old bonds are still there, with their owners still entitled to the bottom $11.0b layer of the cake, but we must also consider the new bonds that were sold to raise the funds needed to keep Voom flying. As the firm raised $1.5b this way, the layer of cake allocated to the owners of new bonds—the second one from the bottom—must be worth $1.5b. If this layer is worth any less, these bondholders would not have invested $1.5b of their funds in Cablevision. This leaves Cablevision's shareholders, who are entitled to everything that remains. As the cake is worth $19.2b and the bondholders' two portions are worth $11.0b and $1.5b, the shareholders' portion must be worth $6.7b.

The shareholders' portion of cake is worth $7.2b without Voom and $6.7b with Voom. As was the case when Chuck and Tom were considering setting up their own firm to operate Voom, shareholders would have incurred the $0.5b loss caused by the ingredients being more expensive than the extra cake produced. As before, the bragging rights would have cost shareholders $0.5b. The discipline of external capital markets is holding: the project owners still bear the full cost of undertaking a bad project. However, when Chuck and Tom were trying to set up the stand-alone VoomHD themselves, they owned all of the shares and so would have had to bear the full $0.5b cost themselves. As long as Cablevision operated Voom, this cost would have been spread across all shareholders. As Chuck and Tom owned only 12% of Cablevision's shares, the cost to them would have been just 12% of the $0.5b total cost, which is $60m.[39] Acquiring the bragging rights from building Voom would still have been personally costly to them, but the cost would have been $60m rather than $0.5b. If we were in Chuck's shoes, and if we valued the bragging rights at more than $60m, then we would want Cablevision to keep Voom alive.

This example demonstrates that in some circumstances external capital markets will be willing to fund a bad project, but the project owners still bear the full cost. When this happens, managers may choose to undertake the project if their ownership stake is sufficiently small that their personal benefits from the project exceed their personal share of the costs. It is another incidence of the problem we found in Chapter 3, where executives weigh all of the personal non-financial costs and benefits of a decision against just a percentage—and often a very small percentage—of the financial costs and benefits, which are shared with the firm's other shareholders.

Free cash flow for sale

In the pessimistic scenario above, external capital markets would not have fully funded Voom if it was a stand-alone business, but would have done so if it was part of Cablevision. Why could VoomHD persuade external capital markets to provide only $1.0b in funding, whereas Cablevision could persuade them to provide $1.5b? The difference between the two situations is that if Chuck and Tom had gone to the external capital markets to raise the capital needed to fund VoomHD, all they would have had to offer was a claim to the VoomHD corporate cake. On the other hand, if Chuck had succeeded in persuading Cablevision's board to keep Voom alive, Cablevision would have gone to exactly the same external capital markets, but it would have been offering a claim to the combined Cablevision–Voom corporate cake. Any bonds issued by Cablevision would have given their new owners a claim against all of Cablevision's assets: not only the satellite operation, but also the profitable cable system, the cable channels, Madison Square Garden, the sport teams, and the cinema chain. Even if lenders did not like Voom, they might have liked Cablevision's other assets sufficiently that they would lend the firm the funds it wanted.

At first glance it appears that the new investors, the individuals who buy the new bonds issued by Cablevision, are the only ones who would have been contributing to funding the firm's expansion: Cablevision's existing shareholders would have contributed no cash. However, they would be contributing capital in their own way—by effectively putting up some of their portion of the Cablevision cake as collateral for the new bonds being issued. Put another way, new investors contribute cash immediately, whereas the firm's existing owners contribute the ownership right to future cash flows. There is a crucial difference between the two types of investors. The new investors are free to take their money and invest elsewhere, so they have to be offered a slice of cake worth at least as much as the amount of capital they invest or they will not participate. In contrast, the firm's existing owners do not get to choose whether to participate. The firm's board makes that decision when it decides whether or not to go to the external capital markets to raise the funds needed for expansion. It is this lack of choice that means the firm can extract a contribution from its own shareholders that is more valuable than the slice of cake they receive in return.

We have just seen some important results about firms' ability to raise capital. First, and most important, external capital markets push the surplus or deficit of a project back onto shareholders. Second, the only way that firms with few assets already in place can fund bad projects is for shareholders to *choose* to contribute more funds themselves. Third, firms with enough assets already in place can effectively offer those assets as collateral, allowing the firms to raise more funds from the external capital markets. However, the decision to use existing assets like this is delegated to the board: shareholders do not make it themselves. The separation of ownership and control makes it possible for boards of directors to use the firms' existing assets as collateral to fund projects that will actually cost more to complete than they will be worth once completed.

Economists say that a firm has "free cash flow" if its existing assets generate more cash flow than is needed to fund investment in "good" projects, the ones that are worth more finished than they cost to build. If a firm has run out of ways to profitably reinvest the cash that its assets generate, then this cash—the firm's free cash flow—should be paid out to bondholders and shareholders. If the CEO of a firm works in its owners' best interests, then the free cash flow generated by its assets will ultimately all be paid out to the firm's bondholders and shareholders. However, if he works in his own best interests then he will spend free cash flow in ways that advance those interests.[40]

We are meeting plenty of cases of managers spending free cash flow in this book, such as consumption of executive perks, empire building, and excessive pay. The challenge facing the owners of firms with high free cash flow is to make management pay free cash flow out to investors rather than keep it inside the firm where it can be used in ways that benefit managers rather than shareholders. The rest of this chapter looks at ways to achieve this.

Reslicing the corporate cake

The firms that find it easiest to raise capital are those that own cash cows, which are assets that generate loads of cash but have limited growth opportunities to spend it on. Cablevision had a cash cow: the cable system. The cash that these assets generate weakens the discipline provided by external capital markets because it means that firms can use these future cash flows as collateral to invest in completely unrelated projects. One way that the boards of such firms can preserve the disciplinary effects of external capital markets is to pre-commit the firm's free cash flow so that it cannot be wasted by management.[41]

This is what Cablevision's board did in 2006 when it borrowed $3.0b in order to pay shareholders a special dividend of $10 per share.[42] Transactions like this replace soft future payouts to shareholders with hard future payouts to bondholders. Why "soft" and "hard"? Payouts to shareholders are soft because they can be reduced reasonably easily. When times are difficult, dividends can be cut to preserve cash. When external capital needs to be raised, future dividends can be cut to pay the interest on new debt. Shareholders will be unhappy, and the share price may fall steeply, but the firm's management team will probably retain control of the firm. The board has much less flexibility in choosing the level of payments to bondholders. These payments are precisely specified in the bond contracts and if the payments are not made in full and on time, then ownership of the firm can switch to bondholders. If the firm defaults on its debt like this, its directors and executives will probably lose their jobs, being replaced by new ones appointed by the firm's new owners. This prospect makes directors and executives much less likely to reduce these payouts than they are to reduce payouts to shareholders. That is why we call payouts to bondholders hard.

Cablevision's $3.0b loan was designed so that the interest rate varied over time—like an adjustable rate mortgage—so we cannot calculate the exact amount that Cablevision would have to pay its lenders. However, if conditions did not change from those in place at the time the money was borrowed, Cablevision would have to pay out more than $0.2b of its free cash flow each year for the first six years, and approximately $3.0b in the seventh year.[43] Given Cablevision's past behavior—cinemas, The Wiz, Voom—only an optimist would have been confident that the firm would have paid that $0.2b out to *shareholders* each year, but the new debt meant it would have to pay that much out to its lenders.

This explains the difference between hard and soft payouts, but it does not explain how Cablevision's special dividend could benefit shareholders. The transaction had two components. Shareholders gave up future soft payouts in exchange for an up-front lump-sum payout of $3.0b; lenders contributed an up-front lump-sum payment of $3.0b in exchange for future hard payouts. Figure 8.2 explains everything using our corporate cake. The left-hand cake represents Cablevision in the event that the transaction had not occurred, with the dark layer at the bottom showing bondholders' portion. The middle cake shows what happens if the transaction occurs. The investors who lend Cablevision the $3.0b are awarded the middle layer of the cake. The money borrowed is immediately paid out to shareholders, so none is left over for investment in additional assets for the firm. In cake terms, this means the cake's ingredients remain the same. As the contents of the cake pan before it goes into the oven have not changed, the size of the cake that comes out of the oven is the same as it would have been if the debt-financed dividend had not been paid. However, because a new tier of debt has been introduced, the cake is divided up differently.

If that is all that happened—a reslicing of the cake—then the special dividend would not be of any benefit to shareholders. They would receive a $3.0b up-front payout, but the value of their shares would fall by the same amount. Overall, shareholders would be

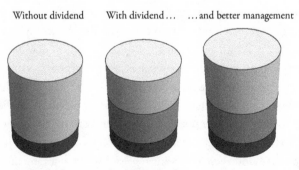

Without dividend   With dividend . . .   . . . and better management

FIGURE 8.2 Borrowing in order to pay a special dividend

no better or worse off than without the special dividend.[44] However, there is another, more subtle, change to the cake: the greater debt motivates the manager to work much harder to ensure the cake rises far enough to keep both sets of bondholders happy. Executives' career prospects suffer if the firms they manage are driven into bankruptcy, so the fear of such an outcome happening to them will affect their behavior. The higher the debt level the greater the fear, and the more sacrifices a manager will make to avoid bankruptcy. He will work harder to increase revenue and decrease operating expenditure. Perhaps he will downgrade the corporate jet. He might even lower his compensation demands when negotiating with the board. Plans for self-serving investments will be shelved. All of these actions, motivated by the high debt levels, will contribute to a larger corporate cake.

The manager of the left-hand firm in Figure 8.2 has a relatively easy job to avoid bankruptcy, because unless something disastrous happens while the cake is in the oven, the finished product will almost certainly fill the cake pan past the dark gray layer. The manager of the central firm will have to work much harder to ensure that the cake is high enough to fulfill all promised payments to bondholders. As a result of working this hard, the firm actually starts to look like the right-hand cake: the layers of debt are the same size, so all of the increase in the cake's size that has come from the improved management has passed to shareholders. That is, by replacing soft payments to shareholders with hard payments to bondholders, the debt-financed dividend will motivate the manager to make sure that more of the cake mixture goes into the pan. He will lick less off the spoon, resulting in a cake like the third cake in the figure. At the risk of pushing the cake metaphor one step (or possibly two steps) too far, the shareholders can have their cake and eat some of it too.

It is probably not being too unkind to suggest that a CEO such as Jim Dolan, a man whom *Fortune* magazine described as having "all the charm of a New York cabbie during rush hour," would be especially sensitive to debt levels.[45] If Cablevision defaulted on its loans under his stewardship, he was unlikely to get another CEO position in a firm unless it was controlled by his father. (Immediately after the Voom debacle, he might not have got the top job even if Chuck did control the firm!)

Debt as a commitment device

As long as a board has a strong bargaining position, it can ensure that much of the firm's free cash flow is paid out to shareholders in the form of dividends. However, even strong boards will worry that they will be in a weak position at some point in the future, unable to prevent a strong CEO from keeping free cash flow out of shareholders' pockets. Fortunately for shareholders, a strong board can use its firm's borrowing arrangements to make it harder for a CEO to waste the firm's free cash flow in the future, even during future periods when the board is in a weaker position. The board does this by having the firm issue more debt and pay the funds raised out to shareholders immediately, either by repurchasing some of the firm's shares from their owners or by paying a special dividend. This is what HCA did in Chapter 4 when it ran its share buyback campaign and what Cablevision did when it borrowed $3.0b in order to pay a special dividend of $10 per share. The Dolans may have had a different motivation for the special dividend—their large shareholding meant they would receive a payout of approximately $680m—but what they had done was to replace a series of soft future payouts (dividends) with a series of hard payouts (interest payments, plus repayments of principal).[46]

When a board approves a debt-funded share buyback or special dividend, it is committing itself to future good behavior. The board is taking an action when the board is strong that restricts its ability to take actions in the future that harm shareholders. The action considered here—increasing debt and paying the proceeds out to shareholders—will be difficult for even a strong CEO to reverse in the future. Doing so would involve going to external capital markets and asking investors to buy part of the corporate cake, exposing the CEO to the discipline that external capital markets provide. The board is effectively backing itself and its CEO into a corner.

Such strategies have been around for centuries. One of the best known examples occurred in the eighth century at the start of the Muslim invasion of the land that would one day become Spain. The commander of the invaders, Tariq ibn Ziyad, ordered his forces to burn the boats that brought them there. By destroying their only means of retreat, he committed his troops to fight to the death or to the point that victory was achieved. Tariq put it rather better than that: "Oh my warriors, whither would you flee? Behind you is the sea, before you, the enemy. You have left now only the hope of your courage and your constancy."[47] (They won.) That is almost exactly what Cablevision's board did in 2006. By borrowing so much money, the board committed itself to paying out free cash flow in the future. By replacing future soft payouts with hard payouts, it was burning its boats.

A greater proportion of debt, up to a point, will benefit shareholders by committing the board to paying out future free cash flow. However, there are costs, as well as benefits, from allocating part of the cake in the form of debt. If a firm has too much debt then relatively common events such as modest reductions in demand or increases in operating expenditure can lead to the firm being unable to pay its debts. Even if bankruptcy can be avoided, the actions a firm is forced to take to avoid bankruptcy can be very disruptive. Cablevision had its own cash crunch in 2002, triggered by underperforming non-core investments and an unsuccessful rollout of expensive Sony digital set-top boxes that threatened to leave the firm $1b short of the cash it needed to meet its operating expenses and debt repayments.[48] Cablevision's share price fell by 90% in the first eight months of the year.[49] It responded by cutting its workforce by 7%, cutting capital expenditure by $445m, and selling its majority stake in the successful cable channel Bravo for $1b.[50] This disruption could have been avoided if Cablevision had allocated more of the corporate cake to shareholders and less to bondholders.

Commitment on steroids

The amount of borrowing is just one of the decisions a firm's board has to make. Another is the term of the loans it takes out. The rich array of choices becomes clear when we delve into corporations' annual reports and discover the many different maturities of firms' debt. For example, at the time Cablevision's board was deciding to pay the special dividend, the firm had almost $10b in debt and, although some was relatively short-term bank debt, more than half was made up of various longer-term loans. Approximately 8% of these loans were for terms of five years, 13% were for terms of 20 years, and the remaining loans were for various terms between eight and 12 years.[51]

The maturity of a firm's debt affects the strength of its commitment to pay out future free cash flow.[52] If issuing debt ties one of the manager's hands behind his back, issuing short-term debt restricts the movement of his free hand. Consider the case of the loan Cablevision used to fund its special dividend in 2006. Cablevision might have tried to borrow the money for 20 years. If it had, then it would have had to pay out more than $0.2b of its free cash flow each year in interest for the first 19 years, and more—including repayment of the $3.0b principal—in the twentieth year. Alternatively, it could have borrowed $3.0b for just one year, and then rolled the debt over one year at a time. At the end of each year it would have had to pay lenders interest plus the outstanding principal, approximately $3.2b in total, but it could fund part of this by borrowing $3.0b for another year. The net payout of free cash flow would be $0.2b—the same as with the 20-year loan—but the crucial difference would be that Cablevision would have to go back to the external capital markets each year in order to roll over the loan.

Given Cablevision's history of unsuccessful investments, any investor who lent the firm $3.0b for a 20-year term would be concerned about the actions the Dolans may take during those 20 years and the effect those actions might have on the likelihood of the loan being repaid in full. However, provided that Cablevision made its $0.2b annual payments, there is little that the investor could do if it disapproved of the Dolans' decision-making early in the 20-year term. Short-term debt increases lenders' protection as the lenders are able to reevaluate their investment at more frequent intervals than the providers of long-term loans. The lenders know—and so would Cablevision's management—that poor investment decisions may jeopardize rolling over a large short-term loan, and therefore jeopardize the Dolan's continued control of Cablevision.

Short-term debt will not be appropriate for every firm. The boards of all firms must balance the disciplinary benefits of short-term debt against its liquidity costs. For example, firms with especially unpredictable cash flows should not issue as much debt as firms with more stable cash flows, and the debt they do issue should have a longer term. Looking back to Chapter 4, the leveraged buyout of HCA was feasible mainly because of the for-profit hospital chain's stable cash flows. Conglomerates also tend to have relatively stable cash flows: at any point in time, some divisions tend to perform better than expected and others perform worse than expected. This stability points to a generous helping of relatively short-term debt being appropriate. Cablevision's board settled on a seven-year term for its $3.0b dividend-financing loan.

The diversification discount

So far in this chapter we have seen, thanks to Cablevision, how cash cows can weaken the discipline imposed by external capital markets. We have also seen how issuing debt—especially relatively short-term debt—to pay special dividends and to buy back shares can strengthen that discipline by restricting executives' ability to access the free cash flow generated by cash cows. Now we consider another, much more disruptive, way to shrink that access even further.

We have already seen that the softening of the discipline imposed by external capital markets depends on the value of the collateral provided by a firm's existing assets. The value of that collateral depends on the nature of the firm's existing assets. If they are very closely related to the project being funded then the value of the collateral will be relatively low. After all, collateral is needed only when the project struggles, and if the other assets are struggling as well then they will not be much use in bailing out lenders. However, as the case of Cablevision illustrates, the discipline provided by external capital markets will be relatively weak for firms that operate in several unrelated industries.

Consider the renovation of Cablevision-owned Madison Square Garden, which was first mooted in 2004.[53] Initially estimated to cost $300m, the renovation eventually cost more than $1.0b.[54] If the Garden had been owned by a stand-alone firm, it would have been able to borrow the funds required only if the Garden's post-renovation profits were high enough to service the increased debt. At the time, the Garden was owned by a firm that also owned professional basketball and hockey teams based at the stadium (the Knicks and the Rangers). Those teams did not provide much collateral, because factors such as labor disputes that might affect the teams' profitability would also affect the venue's profitability. However, the Garden was owned by a firm that also owned a profitable cable system. This made it much easier to borrow the funds needed for the upgrade: those labor disputes would have less effect on the profitability of the cable system, which could ride to the lenders' rescue. That is why corporations like Cablevision, which was an amalgam of firms operating in several different industries, find it relatively easy to borrow the funds needed to undertake investment, even when the merits of the investments are questionable. Firms that are more diversified will find it even easier.

These diversified firms have an *internal* capital market that operates alongside the *external* capital markets we have been looking at so far in this chapter. The firms use their diversified portfolios of assets to raise capital from external capital markets and then allocate it amongst their various businesses. The capital-allocation decisions are made internally, not by external investors. That means they are made where discipline is weak, which is why firms like Cablevision are able to buy unprofitable electronics retail stores, struggling cinema chains, and overpriced newspapers. The resulting distortion of diversified firms' investment behavior seems to be severe enough for it to adversely affect their market values. Economists have found that the market values of diversified firms are significantly lower than what these firms are estimated to be worth if their various business segments were each operated as independent stand-alone firms. The difference between the actual value of a diversified firm and its hypothetical value as a collection of independent stand-alone firms is known as the diversification discount. Estimates vary, but diversification discounts of approximately 15% are typical.[55]

Cablevision had its own diversification discount: the wags on Wall Street called it the "Dolan discount."[56] Just before Cablevision's mid-2009 announcement that it planned to spin off Madison Square Garden and related assets, the firm's enterprise value was $17b. If the "Dolan discount" was 15%, then Cablevision's enterprise value would have been $20b if the cable television system, the cable channels, the entertainment venues, the newspapers, and the sports teams all operated independently. As bondholders take their portion of the corporate cake from the bottom, most of the $3b increase in enterprise value from splitting up Cablevision would have gone to shareholders, who own the top, risky portion of the corporate cake. Cablevision shares were worth approximately $6b in mid-2009, so raising their value by $3b would have lifted the share price by 50%.[57] It is no wonder the Dolans were unpopular with many Cablevision shareholders.

Spin-offs enhance the discipline of external capital markets

The existence of the diversification discount suggests there may be value inside diversified firms that is just waiting to be unlocked. One way to unlock that value is a spin-off, the type of transaction that we saw at the beginning of this chapter. When part of a firm is spun off, it is set up as a separate company and the assets of the original firm are allocated between the spin-off and what is left of the original firm. The owner of each share of the combined firm is given a fixed number of shares in the spin-off, so that an investor who owned 1% of the original firm will, immediately after the spin-off, own 1% of the spin-off and 1% of what is left of the parent.

The most important difference between the firm before the spin-off and the portfolio comprising the parent and its offspring after the spin-off is that a wall has been erected that stops the assets of one part of the original firm being used as collateral for the debt taken on by another part. The internal capital market has been broken up, making it more difficult for managers to fund poor investments. Consistent with this prediction, researchers have found that the investment activity of firms that spin off segments is more closely aligned to the quality of investment opportunities after the spin-offs than it was beforehand. Investment behavior improves the most when the parent and spin-off are in different industries, which is the situation with the greatest potential for cross-subsidization.[58] The disruption to the firm's internal capital market also prevents the spin-off using the parent's assets as collateral if it gets into financial trouble, which might explain why productivity typically improves after a spin-off.[59]

If a firm's internal discipline is weak, breaking up its internal capital market should make the firm more valuable: the whole is less than the sum of its parts. Indeed, researchers have found that the diversification discounts for firms that spin off a division tend to be large before the spin-off is announced and indistinguishable from zero one year after they occur. The diversification discount shrinks most when the parent and spin-off are least alike.[60]

This seems to be what happened when Cablevision spun off Madison Square Garden and AMC Networks. At the time the spin-offs were announced, Cablevision's recent history of poor investments was fresh in investors' minds. Whether it was The Wiz, Voom, or *Newsday*, they were all largely funded by the collateral provided by Cablevision's profitable cable system. Investors were also acutely aware of the prospect of more costly developments in the future, not the least of which was the $300m renovation of Madison Square Garden. Well, not $300m anymore. Shortly before the first spin-off announcement came news that the renovation would be more costly, and take longer, than had previously been announced. No figure was given, but a year later the cost was expected to be somewhere between $775m and $850m, and another year after that the figure of $980m was being suggested. The cost would eventually exceed $1.0b.[61]

As long as Madison Square Garden could draw on Cablevision's other assets as collateral, the limit on the project's cost was effectively the Dolan family's ambition. However, once Cablevision's internal capital market was disrupted, the Garden would have to stand on its own, which was good news for Cablevision's shareholders. The spin-offs did not directly improve Cablevision's internal governance: we have already seen the Dolan-dominated boards of the spun-off firms and investors should not have expected them to perform any better than the one that put Rainbow-1 into orbit. However, the internal capital market had been broken up, so Cablevision and its spin-offs would at least be subject to the greater discipline provided by external capital markets. Breaking up Cablevision's internal capital market would make the Dolans go to external capital markets to fund investment on a division-by-division basis. Investments by divisions with good prospects would find it easier to attract funding; investments by divisions with poor prospects would find it harder. By protecting the cash generated by Cablevision's cable system, the spin-offs would increase the amount of the cash cow's profits that would find their way into shareholders' dividend checks. The result: big increases in the value of Cablevision's shares as soon as investors heard the news of the pending spin-offs.

Making it happen

There is one last question we need to consider: Why did the Dolan family start breaking Cablevision into pieces in 2009 when it had spent most of the previous four decades acquiring the firm's eclectic portfolio of assets? After all, the lives of Chairman Chuck and CEO Jim must have been simpler with the firm's diversified asset portfolio buffering them from the discipline of external capital markets.

One reason might involve the Dolan family's substantial stake in the firm, which was 20% at the time of the first spin-off announcement. The wealth of the key players—Chuck and Jim—was closely tied to Cablevision's financial performance. We saw in Chapter 4 how ownership-generated incentives are determined by individuals' effective ownership stakes. If Cablevision's enterprise value increased by 1%, Chuck's portfolio of Cablevision securities would have increased in value by $15m; Jim's would have increased by $1.2m.[62] That was for a 1% increase in enterprise value. Breaking up the firm had the potential for a much bigger increase in value than that. Even if Chuck and Jim liked the freedom offered by an internal capital market, there were financial benefits they needed to consider.

However, the Dolans' role as shareholders was just one way in which they benefited from their involvement with Cablevision. Family members were also company directors and executives, and they were rewarded handsomely for their efforts. We know this because in 2006 the SEC tightened disclosure requirements relating to compensation paid to directors and to the immediate family members of executives and directors.[63] The proxy statements report that for the four-year period leading up to the first spin-off, Dolan family members received compensation for services rendered to Cablevision totaling $133m. Most of that went to Chuck ($54m) and Jim ($68m), but that still leaves $11m for other family members. The firm even paid Jim's mother-in-law $0.4m for her work as a "coordinator" for the firm.[64]

Splitting the firm into three parts created many more opportunities for family members to prosper. Executives usually remain involved in the parent firm and sell their shares in the spin-offs, but that is not what happened at Cablevision. Instead, Jim became executive chairman of Madison Square Garden, even though he remained Cablevision's CEO. Chuck became executive chairman of AMC Networks, even though he remained Cablevision's chairman. Of the nine Dolan family members on Cablevision's board at the time of the first spin-off, seven joined Madison Square Garden's board and six joined AMC Networks' board. The proxy statements report that during the first four years after the spin-offs began, family members received $25m for services rendered to Madison Square Garden and AMC Networks.[65] This was extra money, because even though Cablevision became a much smaller firm as a result of the spin-offs, the Dolan family was rewarded for services rendered just as generously as before: according to Cablevision's proxy statements, $134m in the first four years after the spin-offs began. Jim's mother-in-law was paid another $0.5m for her work as a "coordinator."[66] Splitting Cablevision up was good for the Dolans.

Of course, it is possible that the Dolans did not want to spin off the two divisions at all. Perhaps they were pressured into it by large shareholders. That would be consistent with evidence from the 1980s and 1990s, when spin-offs were typically preceded by the arrival of large shareholders.[67] It would also be consistent with the behavior of activist investors at Cablevision after mid-2008, when the share price had fallen 49% from its July 2007 peak.[68] One activist investor, who had owned 8.3% of the low-vote Class A shares for several years, was calling for Madison Square Garden to be spun off and was threatening a fight if it did not happen. Another acquired 8.1% of the Class A shares and wanted to share its views with the Dolans.[69] Due to the dual-class share structure, activist investors could not win a majority of seats on the board, but even a small number of hostile directors would have made life difficult for the Dolans. With 47% of the Class A shares owned by large shareholders at the time of the 2009 annual meeting (up from 39% the previous year), such a prospect seemed possible.[70] Two weeks before that meeting, Cablevision announced that it would investigate a spin-off of Madison Square Garden.[71]

Ultimately, the degree to which a firm diversifies and the level, and maturity structure, of its borrowing are determined by the ongoing interactions between the firm's management and its board of directors. If the board is in a weak bargaining position, then we might expect the firm's operations to be diversified and its debt level to be relatively low. That would relieve the dominant management from the discipline imposed by external capital markets. On the other hand, if the board is in a strong bargaining position—and its members work in shareholders' best interests—then we might expect the firm's operations to be focused and its debt level to be relatively high. This might happen directly, via the board forcing through a spin-off over the CEO's objections, or indirectly, by the board making the CEO's wealth sensitive to the firm's share price, and therefore making the CEO want the spin-off to occur. Fluctuations in the balance of power may have long-lasting effects if one side or the other uses a temporary improvement in their bargaining position to implement policies that lock in that strength. For example, a strong board may push through spin-offs, knowing that they will be difficult to reverse; it may raise debt to pay a special dividend, knowing that the higher debt will restrict management's behavior in the future.

External capital markets will impose effective discipline on a firm only if the investors in those markets can distinguish good and bad behavior by the firm's insiders. After all, corporate governance will not be enhanced if good decisions are punished and poor ones are rewarded. The difficulty facing investors is that the decision-makers—that is, the firm's directors and executives—have access to more information than they do. Outsiders may not like the decisions made by insiders, but are they bad decisions or are they actually good decisions using information not available to outsiders? Financial analysts have the job of reducing this asymmetry of information. If they do that job well, then delegating monitoring to the external capital markets will be more effective. There is another benefit as well: as we are about to see, if financial analysts do their job well, they can make effective delegated monitors themselves.

It's clear that things are much worse than even we expected...[1]

STOCK ANALYST (2004)

....

9 No skin in the game
DELEGATING MONITORING TO FINANCIAL ANALYSTS

JOHN BLYSTONE MOVED to the small Midwestern city of Muskegon in 1995 when he was appointed CEO of SPX Corp. He quickly set about dismantling the automotive-tool manufacturer and using its assets to construct his own empire. The company headquarters moved across the country, leaving the old headquarters on the shore of Lake Michigan to lie empty for a decade.[2] The Muskegon piston ring foundry, where SPX had begun business in 1911, was sold.[3] Other business units were shut down or sold. Thousands of workers were laid off. While this was happening, Blystone was engineering a series of mergers and acquisitions that saw SPX grow into a diversified manufacturer with its corporate fingers in many pies. By 2004, SPX's enterprise value had grown twelvefold.[4] However, its Muskegon days were over.

This expansion was good for Blystone, who was paid more than $195m during his nine years as CEO.[5] However, shareholders found it difficult to tell whether it was good for them as the continuing restructuring rendered historical comparisons of little value. Still, the information coming out of the firm was consistently upbeat. Even in February 2004, when SPX released its financial results for the previous year, the CEO had sounded pleased: "a strong fourth quarter"; "record free cash flow"; "excited about the company's prospects."[6] On the day the markets absorbed the good news, SPX's shares fell in value. Fell. In fact, SPX's share price fell further than every other share trading on the NYSE that day.[7] Those financial results wiped 21% off the value of SPX's shares.[8]

A launching pad in Muskegon

Its name may have changed over the years, but for almost a century after SPX Corp. was founded, its headquarters was in Muskegon, MI (population 40,000). First it was called the Piston Ring Company, then the Sealed Power Corporation. After initially making components used by car manufacturers, the firm diversified into the manufacture of the specialist tools used in vehicle maintenance and repair. The firm changed its name to SPX in 1988 to reflect its more diverse product range.[9] However, it was still heavily exposed to the U.S. auto industry, and the first few years after the name change were unhappy ones for shareholders. $100 invested in the firm's shares immediately before its name change, with all dividends reinvested, would have been worth $73 seven years later. That is an annual rate of return of *negative* 4.3%.[10]

SPX's CEO was fired in June 1995. One of the firm's directors, the founder's grandson, filled the role on an interim basis while the board sought a permanent replacement.[11] That replacement, John Blystone, joined the firm six months later as CEO, president, and chairman of the board.[12] Ambitious, restless, and just 42 years old, Blystone had already moved cities 15 times as an adult. He had spent the last year running General Electric's gas turbine business in Italy and he was not moving to Muskegon to retire.[13]

Soon after Blystone's arrival, SPX embarked on a rapid expansion program. Not content to stay focused on the automotive business, Blystone branched out into other industries. In his two biggest deals, SPX merged with diversified manufacturers with limited involvement in the automotive sector, General Signal in 1998 and United Dominion Industries in 2001. Once these deals were completed, SPX was manufacturing a wide range of products, from incubators to power transformers, from television antennas to road rollers.[14]

The portfolio of businesses managed by Blystone grew rapidly: in terms of annual revenue, almost fivefold in the first eight years.[15] The growth was ambitious and aggressive. For example, SPX had half the workforce of General Signal and half the revenue, but the merged firm still adopted the SPX name.[16] The General Signal headquarters in Stamford, CT, was shut down and the merged firm was run from Muskegon, with Blystone as CEO.[17] Only two of General Signal's eight directors kept their positions on the board of the merged firm.[18] General Signal's five highest paid executives, including the CEO, lost their jobs.[19] At least the CEO could walk away with the generous severance payment specified by his employment agreement.[20] He was lucky. United Dominion's CEO, who had run his firm for 14 years, lost his job—and the right to a similar payment—when negotiations to merge with SPX stalled.[21]

SPX was using a decision-making framework known as Economic Value Added (EVA). Rather than basing its decisions—and executives' pay—on the firm's accounting profit, allowance was also made for the return that investors could have earned investing elsewhere. Making a profit was not good enough. The profit had to be large enough for investors to earn a reasonable rate of return on their investment. When Blystone and the rest of SPX's management set about integrating the various businesses under their control, EVA was uppermost in their minds.[22] They shut down some operations and sold others. They even sold Sealed Power, the genesis of SPX, within the first year.[23] The remaining diverse business units were grouped into more streamlined divisions. That is how General Signal's television-antenna manufacturer Dielectric was wrapped into SPX's Broadcast and Communications Systems and Services (B&C) and how its laboratory-equipment manufacturer was reborn as SPX's Life Science Solutions business. Both became part of SPX's Technical Products and Systems segment. Valve manufacturers that had been part of General Signal and United Dominion were combined to form SPX Valves and Controls (V&C), part of the Flow Technology segment.[24] (If this all seems very confusing, spare a thought for those hardy SPX shareholders who were trying to keep track of the changes.)

While this was happening, SPX continued to expand. Dielectric embarked on a series of acquisitions, V&C bought more valve manufacturers, and Life Science Solutions spent $320m on another lab-equipment manufacturer, Kendro Laboratory Products.[25] SPX even branched out into new lines of business, including one that was an odd fit for a diversified manufacturing concern: security contracting. The new SPX Security and Investigations business grew out of a series of acquisitions of security providers. One of the first to be acquired had previously done work for SPX. Blystone must have liked the service so much that he bought the company![26]

The way Blystone was running SPX caught the imagination of investors and the business press. However, although Blystone got much of the credit, SPX had actually adopted EVA before he arrived on the scene. The firm's chief financial officer had persuaded Blystone's predecessor's predecessor to adopt EVA and the board had approved its adoption before appointing Blystone. It has even been reported that Blystone had only a passing familiarity with EVA before his arrival. Still, Blystone made his mark. Divisional executives needed to "think quantum," "stretch goals" were in vogue, and employees were "potential value change agents."[27] (No, I do not know what that means either.)

Something must have worked, because SPX's fortunes soared. When Blystone had arrived in Muskegon at the end of 1995, it was to manage a struggling firm with 8,300 employees, annual sales of $1.1b, and an enterprise value of $530m. Eight years later, ensconced in SPX's brand-new headquarters in North Carolina, Blystone was running a firm with 22,200 employees, annual sales of $5.1b, and an enterprise value of $6.3b.[28] He was the toast of Wall Street. One stock analyst could barely contain himself: "We continue to believe that Mr. Blystone and company need more assets to manage because [they are] far too talented a group to be running a relatively small company . . ."[29] There was even speculation that Blystone would be head-hunted away to run a rival conglomerate.[30] Such speculation has its rewards. In Blystone's case, those rewards included a one-off grant of shares in SPX worth $49m, which he could keep if he stayed at SPX for several more years.[31] SPX was proving to be a very effective vehicle for Blystone's career advancement.

Beware the empire builder

As the collection of assets that Blystone controlled grew in size, so did his pay. The year before the merger with General Signal, his total pay was $3.8m. The year after the merger with United Dominion, it was $87m.[32] Blystone's experience is an extreme example of what typically happens to CEOs at firms that grow via mergers. Pay usually increases, often substantially, and it does so even if shareholders are worse off as a result of the expansion. On average, CEO pay more than triples at firms that have acquisition programs lasting five years.[33] Blystone did better than that.

SPX was not growing by investing its profits in new ventures, but by merging with other firms. As the firm grew, the proportion that was owned by SPX's original shareholders shrank. After the General Signal merger, SPX's shareholders owned just 40% of the new firm, and after the subsequent United Dominion merger, they owned just 31%.[34] Figure 9.1 shows what was happening. The total height of each bar in the graph shows the market value of SPX's shares at the end of each year that Blystone was CEO. This value jumps up at the time of the mergers with General Signal in 1998 and United Dominion in 2001. The dark gray part of each bar shows the value of the shares originally owned by SPX shareholders when Blystone arrived. The fraction of the firm owned by these shareholders drops at the times of the two mergers. The other two parts of each bar show the values of the shares originally owned by General Signal (light gray) and United Dominion (white) shareholders.

Shareholders would benefit from the firm's expansion as long as the percentage of shares they owned did not fall too far. For example, if the merged firm was 2.5 times as valuable as the original one, shareholders needed to own at least 40% of the merged

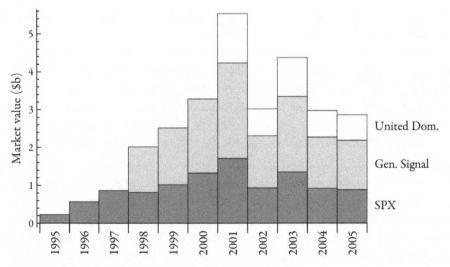

FIGURE 9.1 Blystone's empire grows

firm or the expansion made them worse off. This would happen only if the merger terms were satisfactory. The owners of the other firms (General Signal and United Dominion) would need to be offered an ownership stake in the combined firm that was large enough to entice them to agree to the merger, but small enough that SPX's current shareholders would not lose out. SPX's shareholders needed the CEO to get a good deal. The problem they faced was that, although the CEO of any rapidly growing firm shares the financial benefits of building a successful large firm with the firm's shareholders, he keeps all the personal benefits for himself. These benefits, such as the higher pay and greater prestige associated with running a larger firm, create an incentive for the CEO to give away too much in order to get the deal done.

Blystone's ambitious plans posed a problem for shareholders: was he using his position, and their assets, to maneuver himself into running a bigger, and hence more prestigious, firm? In short, was he empire-building? There were signs that shareholders were unhappy with the terms of the deals Blystone negotiated on their behalf.[35] When news of the merger with General Signal became public, SPX's shares *fell* in value by $56m (after adjusting for movements in the overall share market), but General Signal's shares increased in value by $247m. Over the course of ten days of negotiations between SPX and United Dominion, SPX's value barely changed but United Dominion's increased by $190m.[36] The market was saying that the deals Blystone was making were not good for SPX's shareholders.

The role of information asymmetry

When shareholders try to evaluate the performance of a firm's CEO, their main source of information is the financial data on the firm's performance that is released by the firm every three months. Early in 2004, SPX's shareholders were waiting for SPX to release the latest batch of data.

Firms' CEOs and chief financial officers are required to certify the accuracy of these financial reports.[37] The penalties for knowingly certifying inaccurate reports include large fines and imprisonment, so firms' executives have a strong incentive to make sure the information they release is accurate. However, "accurate" does not mean "complete" or "useful." Even the annual reports, which contain a great deal of information, offer only a partial picture of a firm's health. For example, consider the SPX shareholders early in 2004, trying to evaluate Blystone's performance. The most recent annual report, released early the previous year, was 125 pages long, but it was by no means complete. For instance, SPX had broken its results up into four segments, but the firm had 11 major business units at the time. The annual report would not have been much use to investors who wanted to evaluate the performance of a unit such as the television-antenna manufacturer Dielectric. Its financial results were lumped in with the lab-equipment manufacturer, the security contractor, the data network manufacturer, and the test-equipment manufacturer. The annual report did mention that Dielectric was "expected to realize single digit . . . revenue growth" in 2003, but that was about all.[38]

There is simply not enough information in an annual report to give outsiders a view of the firm's performance that is comparable to the view enjoyed by insiders. However, there is still more than enough information to confuse many investors and to deter others from digging too deeply into the annual and quarterly reports. Many investors (especially those without an accounting qualification) will stick to headline figures. Unfortunately, even if generally-accepted accounting principles are followed, those headline figures might paint an imperfect picture. A good example is the entry in the firm's income statement called "earnings from continuing operations," which measures the profits generated by the firm's ongoing operations. Profits (and losses) of parts of the firm that have been, or are going to be, disposed of are excluded. That sounds useful, especially for firms like SPX that are shedding parts of their business. However, the accounting rules are flexible enough that some one-off pieces of good news can be treated in ways that emphasize the good news, but de-emphasize the one-off part. It is legal and consistent with the accounting rules that firms' auditors abide by, but it means that investors who do not read past the headline figures are at a substantial informational disadvantage.

The challenge facing investors is especially difficult when a firm is undergoing substantial change. When Blystone arrived at SPX, investors knew the firm was performing poorly. Total revenue in 1995 was almost the same as in 1994, but a $14m profit in 1994 had turned into a $5m loss in 1995.[39] Clearly something was wrong at SPX. It was possible to compare the firm's performance at different times like this because the firm was relatively stable. SPX in 1995 looked like SPX in 1994, just not as profitable. However, by early 2004 the situation was much murkier. It was difficult to make meaningful comparisons with the firm's performance in previous years, because SPX in 2004 was quite different from SPX even as recently as 2001.

Despite their limitations, quarterly and annual reports provide investors with some insight into a firm's performance. However, they are backward-looking documents, providing an imperfect picture of how a firm has performed in the past. Firms often provide forward-looking information as well, notably in the form of profit forecasts. When SPX had released its most recent quarterly report, back in October 2003, it also announced that it expected earnings from continuing operations to be at least $3.40 per share for the 2003 fiscal year.[40] The firm confirmed this forecast on several subsequent occasions, including one more than two weeks after the end of the fiscal year.[41]

Lastly, much of the information that outsiders do not have access to cannot be quantified. In the case of SPX in early 2004, that information included the turmoil within parts of SPX as executives struggled to integrate the various businesses in the merged firm. Take the Technical Products and Systems segment, for example. It was home to Kendro Laboratory Products, the laboratory-equipment business, and Dielectric, the broadcasting and communications business. Several members of Kendro's top management lost their jobs during 2003.[42] So did Dielectric's president, fired after just 20 months on the job.[43] Perhaps his thinking was not sufficiently "quantum." The executive in charge of the whole Technical Products and Systems segment, which contributed 25% of SPX's revenue, left in January 2004.[44] The Flow Technology segment contributed another 19%.[45] One of its main units, the V&C valve business, lost its president in November 2003; he had been in the job for a year.[46] Had this information been widely known, and its significance appreciated, investors might have been more skeptical about those optimistic numbers coming out of SPX.

It is just not practical for firms to make all information like this available to outsiders. Indeed, it would not be desirable to do so even if it were possible. After all, the whole point of the separation of ownership and control that we first met in Chapter 1 is that shareholders delegate the management of their firm to managers who have the skill and time to manage it properly. What we are left with is the unavoidable reality that there is a substantial informational asymmetry between firm insiders (the CEO and other senior executives) and shareholders.

When is trading by insiders not insider trading?

Company insiders are not allowed to trade in their firm's shares when they possess material information that is not publicly available, even if they do not use that information to make their trading decisions. This creates problems for executives who want to sell shares for reasons unrelated to the firm's performance. They may be approaching retirement and want to convert shares into cash; they may need to raise cash to pay tax; there have even been cases where CEOs needed to raise cash as part of a divorce settlement. Selling shares in such circumstances would be regarded as insider trading if the sales occurred while the executive possessed inside information, even though the trading decision was not based on having that private information.

The SEC provides insiders with a workaround. Executives are allowed to sell shares using a preplanned schedule, as long as the trading plan's details are set while the executive is not in possession of material non-public information.[47] It is not insider trading because the executive had no inside information when the decision to trade was made. However, the plan (which does not need to be made public) cannot be altered in response to new information that might arrive before the preplanned sales have been completed. If it was altered in this way, that would be insider trading.

Blystone used one of these trading plans in 2004. During his first eight years at SPX, part of his pay had been in the form of stock options that he could use to buy shares from the firm at a fixed price written into the option contracts. Exercising the options—that is, buying the shares for the fixed price—was the easy part. Blystone's challenge was to sell the shares that he had bought without falling foul of the insider trading laws. He put in place a trading plan at the end of 2003 and then started to exercise his options, selling shares along the way.[48] In total, during the eight weeks leading up to the next release of

SPX's financial data, Blystone sold 0.8m shares at an average price of $57. As he had paid $26 per share, on average, thanks to the friendly terms of the options he was exercising, he made a net gain of $25m.[49]

The day after Blystone sold the last of the shares, SPX released its financial results for the final three months of 2003. The reported profit from SPX's continuing operations was $99m for the three-month period, in line with the company's own forecasts. However, the financial statements revealed that this was boosted by a one-off gain of $42m from the settlement of a patent infringement claim against Microsoft.[50] Unless there was the prospect of one of these settlements each three months—and there was not—then the actual performance of SPX's continuing operations was much poorer than investors had anticipated. To make matters worse, at the same time SPX predicted that it would be less profitable in 2004 than investors had been expecting. By the time investors had absorbed the news, SPX's share price had fallen by 21% and shareholders had lost $852m.[51]

If Blystone had sold those 0.8m shares immediately after the bad news became public, rather than before, his net payoff would have been just $13m, not the $25m he actually made.[52] Such good luck often happens when executives use prearranged trading plans to sell shares in their firms. When one researcher investigated a large sample of publicly disclosed plans, he found that insiders tended to adopt plans to sell shares after periods of rising prices and before periods of falling prices. In the majority of cases, the plans preceded clearly identifiable adverse news events, just like at SPX. On average, these adverse events triggered a 10% fall in the share price.[53]

A group of investors who had bought SPX shares during the period when Blystone was selling his shares subsequently alleged that his good luck was not luck at all. They accused him of using the prearranged trading plan as cover for insider trading. Their complaint hinged on two issues. First, did Blystone have material non-public information when he set up the plan? The plaintiffs said "yes," SPX said "no." Second, did SPX withhold material information while the plan was being implemented? The plaintiffs said "yes," SPX said "no." SPX settled the lawsuit without admitting any wrongdoing, but still paid the plaintiffs $10m.[54] Despite the publicity attracted by the lawsuit, the SEC did not investigate Blystone's share sales. However, as the use of these trading plans has increased, they have come under more scrutiny. In 2013, the SEC, the Federal Bureau of Investigation, and the Manhattan U.S. Attorney's office all investigated transactions similar to Blystone's at various companies, prompted by a series of articles in the *Wall Street Journal*.[55]

What contribution do stock analysts make?

The loudest response to SPX's February 2004 release of its financial data came from stock analysts. They gather, process, and distribute information about firms and, if everything works well, reduce the information asymmetry between firms' insiders and investors.

Everything did not work well leading up to February, but the analysts soon reasserted themselves.

Information gathering involves more than just reading firms' financial statements and analyzing their public statements. Analysts also conduct their own research into wider industry conditions and, usually, have the opportunity to communicate directly with firms by participating in the conference calls that most firms hold when they release their financial data. Usually, but not always: SPX stopped holding such calls in 2003, much to the annoyance of some analysts.[56]

Once they have gathered whatever information is available, analysts process what they have found and report it to their clients. They look backwards, sifting through records of the firm's recent performance for any signs that all is not what it seems. They look forwards, using what they have learnt about the firm and the industries in which it operates to forecast its future profitability. They even produce their own recommendations advising clients to buy, hold, or sell the firm's shares. This is exactly what Merrill Lynch's analyst had been busy doing during 2003. He had been digging through SPX's performance data and finding alarming signs that SPX's revenue was not growing as rapidly as outward appearances might suggest.[57] He was also calculating his own estimates of the firm's profitability. Shortly after SPX announced mid-year that it expected to make a profit of at least $3.40 per share, he released his own forecast of just $3.25.[58] As he gathered and processed more information, he refined his recommendations, switching from "hold" to "sell" in the middle of 2003, and back to "hold" again by the end of the year. His explanation for the reversal, which occurred as SPX was insisting that its earnings were still on track to finish above $3.40 per share? SPX had hit bottom. Oh dear.[59]

The only thing stopping SPX's shareholders gathering and processing information themselves was the free-rider problem. Analysts help overcome the free-rider problem by reducing the costs that shareholders face. Shareholders still compare their share of the benefits of monitoring management with the cost of doing so, but now what matters is the cost of keeping up with analysts rather than the much higher cost of doing the legwork themselves. And there are plenty of analysts to choose from: on average, if an analyst follows a firm, there will be 8.1 other analysts doing the same thing.[60] The bigger the firm, the greater the analyst coverage.[61]

Analysts reduce their own costs of information gathering by specializing in companies in particular industries. A typical analyst follows 15 firms in three industries and works for a firm employing 60 analysts.[62] What analysts learn about one firm in an industry will help them evaluate the performance of other firms in that industry. By lowering the cost of gathering information, this specialization increases the amount of information that is gathered. The existence of analysts allows specialization to occur where it is appropriate to do so. CEOs specialize and run their firms. Analysts specialize and monitor firms in particular industries. Investors *do not* specialize; they spread their wealth around and get the benefits of diversification.

The benefits of specialization were there for all to see when SPX released its financial data in late February 2004. Shareholders did not need to pore over the data themselves; they could follow their favorite analysts instead. Those analysts waded through the information released that day, all 122 pages of it, looking for the story behind the headline numbers. They were not pleased with what they found: an increased percentage of revenue was being eaten up by production costs; the Microsoft settlement was obscuring the firm's poor performance; and the president of the key Technical Products and Systems segment had resigned recently.[63] A common view, expressed by one analyst, was that "[i]t's clear that things are much worse than even we expected..."[64] Many analysts responded by recommending that investors sell SPX shares.[65] Investors seemed to follow the advice: 22% of the firm's shares changed hands in a single day—almost 20 times the daily average—and the share price plummeted.[66]

The events at SPX illustrate something that happens much more widely. Investors effectively delegate the monitoring of a firm's management to stock analysts and they take advantage of the information produced by those analysts when they decide whether to buy or sell the firm's shares. With more information available to investors, trading will be better informed and the share price will be a more accurate signal of executives' job performance.

That means boards will be able to use the share price to help them evaluate management, increasing board effectiveness (Chapter 2). Surely it is no coincidence that CEOs are more likely to be fired at firms that have attracted negative analyst recommendations. Indeed, if analysts' average recommendation changes from "hold" to "underperform," or from "underperform" to "sell," the probability that the CEO is fired increases by 1.8 percentage points.[67] Given the low overall probability of being fired, that is a big increase. Investors having access to better information also means the value of the executives' share and option portfolios will be tied more closely to their performance, so that managerial ownership provides stronger incentives for executives to work in shareholders' best interests (Chapter 4). The component of executives' pay that is tied to firm performance will be more closely tied to their *own* job performance, moving the trade-off between risk and incentives in shareholders' favor (Chapter 5). It is not just the firm's internal governance mechanisms that are made more effective if analysts follow the firm closely. The external mechanisms are more effective as well. For example, the executive labor market will get more information out of share-price performance, so career concerns will generate stronger incentives (Chapter 7). External capital markets will be better informed about firm performance, enabling them to wield their discipline more effectively (Chapter 8).

What motivates stock analysts?

It is not immediately obvious why stock analysts would exert the effort required to produce high-quality research. Many analysts' employers do not allow them to own shares in the firms that they follow. Even if they do own some shares, their stake may make up just a small part of their wealth. We cannot look to analysts' share ownership for a source of incentives.

The analysts we are most interested in are the "sell-side" analysts who work for financial-services firms. These firms provide research to their clients "for free," but the clients end up paying for it indirectly via higher commissions. The financial-services firms motivate their analysts to produce research that the firms' clients, and potential clients, find valuable by basing analysts' pay explicitly or implicitly on trading commissions.[68] This incentive component of analysts' total compensation can be substantial. In 2005, a typical analyst at one major investment bank was paid $647,500, with 70% coming in the form of an annual bonus. When markets are booming, the incentive component of pay can be much higher than this for the highest-paid analysts. At the same investment bank, the highest-paid analysts received annual compensation of more than $3m in the early 2000s.[69]

The highest-paid analysts tend to be the ones who rate highly in the annual rankings produced by the *Wall Street Journal* and *Institutional Investor* magazine. The "Best on the Street" rankings produced by the *Wall Street Journal* rank analysts according to the returns investors would earn by following their recommendations.[70] Pay is typically higher for analysts who the *Wall Street Journal* identifies as star stock-pickers, but the higher pay is related to the greater visibility that a high ranking brings, not the underlying stock-picking performance.[71] *Institutional Investor*'s annual list of "All-American" star analysts is quite different. Instead of being based on analysts' stock-picking performance, it is based on institutional investors' responses to surveys asking them to rank the analysts who had been most helpful during the previous 12 months. The top three vote winners in each industry win the All-Americans accolade.[72] These star analysts receive higher pay, on average, than their peers.[73] In other words, analysts who are highly regarded by institutional investors (and who therefore attract more business for their employers) are more highly paid. Even if analysts have no ownership stake—that is, no skin in the game—they still have strong incentives to perform.

Unfortunately, analysts also have the opportunity to shirk. Their employers' clients have a hard time distinguishing poor forecasting performance due to laziness from poor forecasting performance due to bad luck. After all, even the hardest working analyst can be caught out by unanticipated events or, as some analysts following SPX grumbled, by firms that do not keep them as well informed as they would like. This allows analysts to take the easy route—be lazy and blame bad luck if it all goes wrong.

The events at SPX in the lead-up to the February 2004 earnings report raise the question of how much effort analysts put into gathering information. Do they passively wait for firms to release their financial reports or do they go out and gather information themselves? For example, analysts complained that SPX had not told them about the departure of the president of the Technical Product and Systems segment until the firm's annual report was released at the end of February. There is just one problem: the trade magazine *Radio World* knew about it in January, shortly after it happened.[74] If the information was so important, why did the analysts with their seven-figure bonuses not find out as well?

As if the ability to shirk is not bad enough, analysts tend to move in herds. The case of SPX provides a good example. By the time the first cracks were appearing in 2003, SPX had enjoyed several years of extremely high returns. The consensus view, backed up by that history, was that SPX was a good investment. We should take a moment and step into the shoes of an analyst whose confidence in the firm was starting to waver. If we were absolutely confident in our view, we would have advised our clients to sell. However, if our analysis turned out to be wrong and the SPX share price had continued to grow, we would have been harshly criticized by any clients who followed our advice and missed out on the gains captured by everyone else. If, instead, we had kept silent and our analysis had turned out to be correct, any clients who had followed our "hold" advice would have lost money, but so would everyone else. We would not look any worse than any other analyst—so we might not be punished for our poor advice. The lesson is clear: stay with the herd.[75] We would not be the only analysts to do this. In fact, empirical research has found that the recommendations of individual analysts are influenced by consensus estimates, whether or not the consensus turns out to be correct; herding towards the consensus is especially strong when markets are booming.[76] Inexperienced analysts, who will be especially keen to avoid looking foolish, are the ones least likely to deviate from consensus forecasts.[77]

Reputation saves the day

It is not looking good for shareholders. Their delegated monitors—the stock analysts—can shirk and have a tendency to move in herds. Fortunately, there is an offsetting factor that can help out: analysts' desire to build and maintain a good reputation.

Although shirking makes an analyst's life easier in the short run, it also makes his forecasts less accurate. As soon as his forecasting performance becomes so consistently poor that his employer's clients suspect he is shirking, they will take their business elsewhere. It will not be long before his employer is reducing his bonus or getting rid of him altogether. Analysts have to weigh the short-term benefits of shirking against the long-term costs of reduced pay. If those costs are high enough then they will put in the work required to produce good research, giving shareholders their delegated monitor.

This trade-off illustrates the way that economists think about reputation and how it affects people's behavior. Economists do not bother with some abstract notion of reputation. They boil the problem down to costs and benefits. (Would they do anything else?) In economists' world-view, individuals making choices that affect their reputation are actually deciding whether or not to take advantage of opportunities to benefit themselves at the expense of others. The opportunities arise when individuals believe that they will not be caught until it is too late for the other parties to do anything about it. This time. It is the prospect of not being able to repeat this stunt indefinitely that causes the individuals to hesitate before exploiting such opportunities. When individuals do this, it looks like they are weighing up the consequences for their "reputation"; according to economists, they are actually weighing the short-term benefits of misbehavior against the long-term costs.

The economists' approach can be applied just as naturally to many interactions that we take for granted. When our car needs repairing, we will be willing to pay more if the mechanic doing the repairs has a reputation for not carrying out (and billing clients for) unnecessary repairs. When a pipe bursts, we will be willing to pay more if the repairs are carried out by a plumber with a reputation for doing the job properly. When we need a new pair of shoes, we will be willing to pay more for a brand with a reputation for being hard wearing. In all of these examples, we cannot observe some crucial information. Unless we are a mechanic, we will not know whether all of the work done on the car was necessary. Unless we are a plumber, we will not know if the mended pipes will hold together. And unless we saw the shoes being made, we will not know whether corners have been cut in their manufacture. This gives the other side in the interaction—the mechanic, the plumber, or the shoe manufacturer—the ability to shirk. However, provided the long-run costs of shirking are higher than the short-run benefits—that is, if reputation matters—then they have no incentive to do so.

Concerns about reputation work best in situations involving repeated interactions. Our mechanic values a good reputation because our car will probably need repairing in the future and if he treats us well this time he is more likely to get the job next time. The plumber realizes that he can make more money by doing the current job well and being called back in the future than he possibly could by ripping us off now and not being invited back. Even the shoe manufacturer weighs up a lifetime of shoe purchases before deciding whether to cut corners in the short run. Reputation does not work so well for one-off interactions because there is less to lose. (Do not trust your mechanic if he knows you are moving out of town!) What about the stock analysts? Their employers rely on return business from their clients, so we should expect reputation concerns to be relatively effective at discouraging shirking.

Stock analysts' conflicts of interest

If only it was always that simple. For some analysts, it is. They are the ones working at the independent research boutiques that generate revenue solely from selling equity research to clients. These analysts weigh the short-term benefit of shirking against the long-term cost of losing clients. However, many other analysts work for financial-services firms that face short-run temptations that extend beyond shirking. If these short-run temptations are tempting enough then the analysts and their employers may decide that it is not in their best interests to produce objective research at all.

For example, many analysts work for financial-services firms offering brokerage services. These firms arrange transactions on behalf of their clients—for a fee. The more transactions, the greater the revenue from the brokerage business. In the short run, brokerage firms make more revenue from their analysts' "buy" recommendations than from their "sell" recommendations.[78] Why? If an analyst issues a buy recommendation about one of the firms she follows, then any investor (even one who owns no shares in that firm) can respond by buying more shares. However, only investors who already own shares in that firm can respond to "sell" recommendations by selling shares. In the short run, at least, brokerage businesses are better off if their analysts recommend their clients buy shares in a firm even when the firm is performing poorly. This puts pressure on analysts to toe the line and favor "buy" recommendations even if the research does not support it. The pressure can be explicit, with analysts' bonuses based on brokerage revenue from trade in the firms they follow, or implicit, with overly optimistic analysts' enjoying better career prospects.[79] It looks like many analysts succumb, because their recommendations tend to be more optimistic if their employer has a large brokerage business.[80]

Other analysts' employers have significant investment banking operations that work for firms wanting to raise funds in capital markets or carry out mergers and acquisitions—again, for a fee. This generates a conflict of interest if an analyst's employer carries out such work for any of the firms being followed by its analysts, or if it wants to do so in the future. These firms are able to punish investment banks whose stock analysts give unwelcome recommendations by going to another investment bank. The threat of such punishment can motivate analysts to give positive coverage. Strict rules are in place within the large investment banks to manage this conflict. The investment banking and research departments have to be physically separated from one another. They have to be functionally separated as well: analysts are not allowed to help their employers solicit investment banking business; their pay cannot be based on the performance of the investment banking part of the firm; and investment bankers are not allowed any input into how much analysts are paid or which firms they follow.[81]

It was not always like this. Prior to the current rules being introduced in 2003, analysts' pay was closely related to the contribution they made to their employers' investment-banking business and their career prospects were closely related to how optimistic they were about firms that provided underwriting work for their employers.[82] Analysts are only human, and many succumbed to this pressure. For example, analysts tended to be more optimistic when following a firm that had given a large share of its recent underwriting business to their employer.[83] However, some analysts' concerns about their reputation might have made them less susceptible to conflicts of interest.[84] For example, individual analysts' recommendations for firms in which institutional investors had large ownership stakes tended to be less optimistic.[85] One possible explanation for this result is that analysts resisted the pressure to boost recommendations at firms where such behavior would be noticed by the institutional investors who influence the all-important *Institutional Investor* All-American rankings.

There are lessons here for shareholders: pay more attention to the all-stars' recommendations than to those of the also-rans; pay less attention to the good-news recommendations of analysts who face brokerage- or underwriting-induced conflicts of interest; and if a conflicted analyst downgrades a stock, then get out fast! It seems like this is exactly what investors did when the conflicts within investment banks were unchecked. Analysts' "buy" recommendations were associated with share price rises on average for the recommended firms, but the increases were smaller for analysts whose employers did substantial underwriting business. "Sell" recommendations were associated with price reductions, and the decreases were larger for analysts who faced a conflict of interest. Price responses were especially large for all-star analysts as defined by the *Institutional Investor* rankings.[86]

Credit rating agencies

Stock analysts are not the only outsiders to reduce the asymmetry of information between a firm and investors. The analysts who work for credit rating agencies such as Moody's and Standard & Poor's play a similar role, but they focus on a firm's ability to repay its debts. By informing bondholders and a firm's other lenders, credit rating agencies increase the discipline that is imposed by the external capital markets. Even though the information is aimed at bond investors, shareholders also get access to this information, so everyone benefits from the extra sets of eyes on a firm.

The earliest credit rating agencies sold their reports to investors. The arrival of the photocopier—and with it the ability for clients to reproduce ratings reports at low cost—changed that. Since the early 1970s, the largest credit rating agencies have generated their revenue from the firms that issue the bonds in the first place. Firms like SPX are willing to pay the largest agencies for rating their bonds because such ratings are required before large financial institutions will buy the bonds for their portfolios.[87] If SPX had not paid for the ratings, it would not have been able to borrow the money it needed to fund its expansion.

The issuer-pays funding model comes with the potential for a severe conflict of interest. If a firm's bond issue receives a low rating, the firm will probably raise less cash when it sells the bond to investors, and effectively end up borrowing at a higher interest rate. Any rating agency that assigns such a low rating risks the issuing firm going to another agency the next time it wants to raise money by issuing bonds. However, a rating agency considering boosting its ratings in response to such a threat has to consider the reputational consequences.[88] Bonds are relatively simple securities, so institutions will soon lose confidence in the agency's ratings if it responds in this way. Once this happens and the institutions start to ignore the agency's ratings, bond-issuing firms will no longer be willing to pay for the ratings.

Unfortunately for investors, agencies' concerns about their reputations do not completely eliminate the problems created by this conflict of interest. For example, researchers have found that Standard and Poor's tended to assign higher bond ratings after 1974, when the temptation to boost ratings increased after its switch to issuer-pays fees.[89] After Fitch started to challenge Moody's and Standard & Poor's, which increased the risk that the latter two agencies would lose fees if issuers switched to the new kid on the block, the quality of their ratings fell and they gave out higher ratings.[90] However, when smaller investor-pays agencies start competing with the big issuer-pays agencies, the performance of the latter improves. The arrival of agencies like these does not increase the risk of issuing firms taking their fees elsewhere, but it does make it easier for investors to identify reputation-damaging rating-inflation.[91]

Reputation can motivate managers as well

Reputation also plays an important role when a firm's executives decide what information to reveal publicly. Some of a firm's private information has to be reported. For example, data summarizing the firm's performance has to be released every three months. However, there is much more information that does not have to be reported publicly. The high management turnover at SPX during 2003 is a good example. Then there is the information that is much more subjective, such as the earnings forecasts that caused so much trouble at SPX. In this case, the firm's management has to decide *what* to say, not just whether to say it.

Bad news may be able to be kept private, temporarily at least, and if investors subsequently complain then the firm can argue that the information was not material. That was the argument that SPX used to defend its decision not to announce the management departures in 2003.[92] Profit forecasts can be made more optimistic, and if the firm's profits turn out to be lower than forecast then the firm can argue that profits were adversely affected by unpredictable events. After all, the firm cannot predict the unpredictable. SPX used the small print at the bottom of all of its profit forecasts to make sure everyone knew: "Although the company believes that the expectations reflected in its forward-looking statements are reasonable, it can give no assurance that such expectations will prove to be correct." Such disclaimers are included for a good reason: firms *cannot* predict the unpredictable, so if they were going to be hauled into court each time one of their forecasts turned out to be wrong, they would not issue any forecasts in the first place. If we want firms to issue forecasts, then we need to make it possible for them to issue overoptimistic forecasts.

Unfortunately, the ability to issue overoptimistic forecasts can lead to an outcome that is bad for everyone: firms do not tell the truth and analysts (and investors) do not believe anything that firms say. If this outcome eventuated, the whole financial system would grind to a halt, with firms unable to raise capital because investors would not be willing to buy firms' securities. The good news is that concerns about reputation can deliver a better outcome: firms tell the truth and analysts and investors believe the firms as long as the actual results are not too far away from the forecasts. The key is that, just like mechanics and their customers, firms and analysts interact repeatedly. Just like mechanics' customers, analysts can punish firms if they believe that firms have treated them badly. If we believe that a mechanic has charged us for unnecessary work on our car, then next time our car breaks down we will take it somewhere else to be repaired. If a firm's financial data shows profitability was significantly lower than the firm has previously forecast, then analysts might conclude that the firm has misled them and not believe the firm's future forecasts. This will punish executives who make overoptimistic forecasts by lowering the value of their shares and by making it harder to raise funds when the firm needs them to invest. Of course, this will also punish executives who reported their private information accurately only to be undone by unpredictable events outside their control. Unfortunately for them, punishing unlucky executives who report their private information accurately is needed to discourage executives from reporting their private information inaccurately.[93]

If the punishment is severe enough, then a firm's managers will choose to reveal their private information accurately. Sometimes, however, the likely punishment will not be severe enough to be an effective deterrent. Perhaps market conditions are so volatile that the managers think they can escape detection by blaming their forecast errors on unpredictable events outside their control. Perhaps the firm's circumstances are so complex that outsiders will find it too difficult to tell how bad the forecast errors were. Sometimes a firm's managers will not be too worried about getting caught, perhaps because they have a large number of shares to sell and want to do so before the price drops. In other cases, however, the accuracy of a firm's voluntary disclosure of its private information will be determined by the severity of the punishment that executives expect to receive if analysts decide the firm has attempted to mislead them.

SPX is punished

Only a firm's insiders will know whether forecasts that turn out to have been too optimistic were the result of bad luck or a deliberate policy to mislead outsiders. SPX is no exception. For reputational concerns to be effective, analysts need to punish the firm regardless. The analysts following SPX appeared to be in full punishment mode after the firm's February 2004 release of its financial results. In reports to their clients, analysts who were previously highly complimentary about Blystone and his team were scathing. One after another, analysts downgraded their recommendations. SPX scrambled to mend fences, hosting a dinner for the frustrated analysts, at which Blystone pledged to address the firm's communication problems. (The dinner was closed to the press, so perhaps he did not mean to address the problems straight away.) It was not an enjoyable evening out. Even SPX's spokesperson, who had spent the last year putting a positive spin on the firm's performance, described it as a "very honest session." Still, there were signs of improvement: SPX would announce all future departures of senior executives and it would resume conference calls with analysts when it released its financial results.[94]

Analysts were still skeptical six months later. One complained that the latest results showed a "marked escalation in the level of confusion" surrounding the true state of the firm. Because of the way SPX was reporting its results, he said, it was "virtually impossible" to distinguish one-off items from ongoing income and costs.[95] According to another, "people have thrown their hands up" about the quality of information being released.[96] Trust was so low that one (unsurprisingly anonymous) analyst even speculated that SPX's management was using its financial reports to drive the share price down so that they could buy the firm cheaply themselves.[97] It was going to take more than a contrite dinner to win back the analysts' trust.

Does it matter? The analysts following SPX were clearly unhappy, but that would worry the firm's managers only if analyst unhappiness translates into something that directly affects managers. Unfortunately for managers, but fortunately for shareholders, it can. Even managers who are entirely self-interested are directly affected by changes in the share price, just as long as they own shares in the firm or some of their pay is based on share-price performance. When analysts change their portfolio recommendations, investors listen. Well, they listen to some analysts. One recent study looked at over 14,000 recommendation changes made by all-star analysts and found that 15% of them triggered large share price movements.[98] Managers disappoint those analysts at their peril.

There is a darker side to the apparent costs of upsetting the analysts: managers might be so keen to avoid disappointing analysts that they fall prey to the short-termism we first met in Chapter 5. For example, they might make business decisions that are bad for shareholders in the long run but have the benefit of getting the firm "across the line" by meeting expectations in the short run. It has been suggested that SPX's executives succumbed to this pressure at the end of 2003.[99] They had spent much of the year assuring analysts that earnings would be at least $3.40 per share. With the end of the fiscal year only weeks away, SPX looked to be falling well short of that target. However, in mid-November, an opportunity presented itself when a federal jury found that Microsoft had infringed a patent owned by one of SPX's subsidiaries and awarded SPX $62m in damages. There was even better news for SPX's shareholders: as the jury found that Microsoft's infringement had been intentional, a further hearing would be held that could triple the damages to be paid. The bad news was that the hearing was scheduled for February the following year, too late for the award to appear in the current year's financial statements.[100]

Rather than wait and go back into the courtroom in February, SPX and Microsoft set about negotiating an end to their dispute. The outcome is consistent with what we know about bargaining games from Chapter 2. If the two sides could reach an agreement quickly, SPX would be able to include the damages in its 2003 financial statements and meet market expectations for the year. This gave Microsoft considerable bargaining power, because if SPX did not agree to its offer then the dispute would drag on past the end of the fiscal year—no use to any SPX executives wanting to make sure they met market expectations. Consistent with the predictions from Chapter 2, the two sides reached agreement on terms that, all things considered, were favorable to Microsoft. It would have to pay only $60m, less even than the initial damages award, and was able to license the disputed technology.[101] Perhaps this was the best possible deal for SPX's shareholders. After all, if Microsoft appealed the jury's decision then SPX might have ended up with nothing. However, SPX seemed to be keen to settle quickly: the agreement stipulated that the $60m be paid by the end of the year, just in time to be included in that year's earnings figures.[102]

The negotiated settlement was just enough to ensure that SPX's earnings for the year came in at $3.41, $0.01 above the forecast. Of course, it turned out to be a Pyrrhic victory as analysts punished the firm anyway. That punishment triggered the 21% fall in SPX's share price in February 2004. It continued throughout the year as SPX released more financial results that frustrated analysts and disappointed investors. Analysts struggled to unscramble the earnings data by taking out one-off items of good news and putting back in the ongoing items of bad news they thought should have been there all along.[103] Investors just voted with their feet: the release of SPX's financial results for the second quarter of 2004 was associated with a 9.7% decline in the firm's share price.[104]

Do analysts reduce manager–shareholder conflict?

The stock analysts who pored over SPX's results did shareholders a service when they evaluated the firm's performance and publicized what they found. A free-rider problem means that shareholders do not carry out this level of monitoring themselves, so instead this task is effectively delegated to stock analysts. The extra monitoring should reduce manager–shareholder conflict. The best way to figure out if that happens is to see if the conflict increases when fewer analysts follow a firm.

When research departments close down, analysts lose their jobs. When brokerages merge, analysts' assignments are reallocated if there are overlaps in the firms they follow. In both cases, the number of analysts following some firms will fall and shareholders lose some of their delegated monitors. If analysts help reduce manager–shareholder conflict, this conflict will increase when a reduction occurs in the number of analysts following a firm. With the increased conflict should come a lower share price. This is exactly what happens when analyst coverage falls following closures and mergers of research departments at brokerages. The average decline in share prices in the week following a closure-induced reduction in coverage during 2000–2008 was 2.6%.[105]

This suggests that reduced analyst coverage lowers the value of a firm's shares (and increased coverage increases their value), but it does not shed any light on the cause. It might be due to analysts' monitoring having the effect of reducing manager–shareholder conflict, or to something else entirely. One way to assess the role of monitoring is to look at the relationship between analyst coverage and managerial behavior. Once more, brokerage closures and mergers can shed some light. Researchers have found that after the number of analysts following a firm falls, the firm tends to pay its CEO more and to make more value-destroying acquisitions. Not only does the affected firms' performance deteriorate, but the quality of the financial information they report seems to deteriorate as well, with executives at firms with weak corporate governance taking advantage of the reduced scrutiny to obscure their performance. Based on this evidence, analysts do not just produce information themselves: their presence seems to encourage firms to produce more accurate information.[106]

The day after SPX's share price fell 21%, the activist hedge fund Relational Investors began buying a 5.7% stake in the firm.[107] Another fund, Atlantic Investment Management, built up a 6.1% stake.[108] The activist investors worked behind the scenes trying to persuade SPX's board to reform executive pay arrangements and add new independent directors. Eventually, dissatisfied with the board's progress, Relational threatened the positions of SPX's incumbent directors by nominating its own candidates for the two seats on the board that were up for election at the next annual meeting.[109] Blystone resigned just three weeks after the threat was made.[110]

It seems like an overreaction to the news that a shareholder, albeit a fairly large one, was unhappy. Even if its nominees were elected to SPX's board—and it was far from certain that this would happen—they would be just two of six directors. But something about this threat seemed to be enough to drive Blystone out. The next chapter describes the economic forces at work when activist investors stir up trouble, using the story of another General Electric alumnus who experienced something similar. The stakes, though, were very much higher than at SPX.

You can do it. We can help.

HOME DEPOT SLOGAN (2003–2009)

10 Crashing the party
DELEGATING MONITORING TO LARGE SHAREHOLDERS

FINANCIAL COMMENTATORS HAD not seen anything like it before. A podium and two large digital timers stood at the front of a basement hotel ballroom. One by one, members of the 50-strong audience stepped forward to a microphone. As each one began to speak, the timers flashed up 60 seconds and started to count down. After the minute was up, the microphone cut out and the audience member was escorted back to their seat. The master of ceremonies, who said little, declared the event finished 35 minutes after it began.[1]

This sorry spectacle was the 2006 annual meeting of Home Depot, America's 14th largest firm and its biggest home improvement retailer.[2] It was shareholders' only opportunity to directly confront the firm's CEO—master of ceremonies Bob Nardelli—and hold him to account. The thin-skinned Nardelli had been becoming increasingly unaccountable. He reportedly threatened to move Home Depot's headquarters to another city shortly after a local newspaper criticized him for a lack of community involvement.[3] When sales growth started to slip, he stopped reporting the figures and when shareholders grew restless in 2006, he suppressed discussion at the firm's annual meeting.[4] To the shareholders in the audience that day, the separation of ownership and control must have seemed very wide indeed.

In principle, shareholders can leave the monitoring role to the board of directors. However, Home Depot's shareholders knew that was not going to work for them: the board of directors did not turn up to the annual meeting! The chairwoman of the compensation committee was not even there to explain her committee's decisions. None of the directors up for election were there to be introduced to shareholders. The only director who was there, CEO Nardelli, did not allow discussion on his compensation or job performance.

Fortunately for Home Depot's shareholders, they did not need to rely on the board. They did not know it, but by the end of the year one of the growing number of activist hedge funds would buy a billion-dollar stake in Home Depot and start pressuring the board to make some changes.[5] Many hedge funds try to pick winners: they look for an undervalued firm, buy some of its shares, and wait for the price to rise.[6] In contrast, activist hedge funds invest with the specific intention of increasing the share price by actively pressuring the firm to change the way it runs its business. The fund that invested in Home Depot had a very clear idea of the change it wanted: a new CEO.

Nardelli dons an orange apron

Home Depot was struggling even before Nardelli arrived in late 2000. The culture of devolved decision-making that had previously helped it grow rapidly was holding it back; sales were growing more slowly than expected.[7] Home Depot's announcement in October 2000 that profits would fall short of the most recent forecast was associated with a 27% drop in its share price, a fall in value of $32b.[8] The board started looking for a new company president, someone who could learn the business for a few years and then succeed CEO Arthur Blank, who had founded the firm with Bernie Marcus in 1979.[9]

While this was going on, Bob Nardelli was running GE Power Systems. When Nardelli lost the race to succeed General Electric's CEO, he started fielding phone calls. Nardelli's first caller was Ken Langone, one of Home Depot's directors.[10] The other losing candidate for the GE top job was soon snapped up, and Langone knew that unless Home Depot acted quickly, it would lose Nardelli.[11] The soon to be ex-GE executive took full advantage of the bargaining power this gave him. Yes, he would come to Home Depot, but there would be no apprenticeship under Blank. He would be appointed CEO immediately and his pay would be generous. Very, very generous.

Nardelli tore up Home Depot's old operating manual, replacing the devolved operation with one much more centralized (and closer to the system he was familiar with at GE). Blank had ten of the firm's most senior managers reporting to him directly; Nardelli had 21. Blank met with his managers once every three months; Nardelli's meetings were weekly.[12] Many executives left the firm after Nardelli arrived, not all voluntarily, and the most senior replacements were close to Nardelli. Frank Blake, the new head of business development, had been Nardelli's head of business development at GE Power Systems.[13] The new head of human resources had been Nardelli's head of human resources at GE Power Systems.[14] The new general counsel had worked for Nardelli for five years, sometimes as his personal attorney and sometimes as outside counsel for GE Power Systems.[15]

Under Nardelli, Home Depot headquarters became much more involved in how stores functioned. Nardelli even proudly showed one business reporter how Home Depot's new closed-circuit television system allowed him to watch the checkout lines at any of the firm's almost 2,000 stores from the computer terminal on his desk.[16] Other changes had a more tangible effect on customers' shopping experience. Purchasing decisions started being made centrally, instead of locally as in the past: the stock of unsold ride-on lawn mowers in Arizona stores increased as a result.[17] The new centralized approach to decision-making was reinforced by hiring large numbers of ex-military personnel as trainee store managers.[18] Labor costs were cut by replacing many of the orange-aproned experts (the ex-plumbers and ex-handymen who had the knowledge to help customers) with less experienced part-timers.[19]

After several years of this, Home Depot's traditional retail business struggled. Customer satisfaction fell rapidly.[20] Lowe's Companies, the firm's smaller rival, was growing much faster than Home Depot: annual growth in sales at stores open for at least a year, a common growth measure in the retail sector, was 1.5% at Home Depot and 4.6% at Lowe's.[21] With growth in the retail business elusive, Nardelli looked for it on more familiar territory: Home Depot used the profits generated by its retail business to expand into the wholesale sector. Under Nardelli, the firm would sell supplies to professional contractors as well as its traditional do-it-yourself customers. In just three years Home Depot spent $6.8b building up this business, HD Supply.[22]

Home Depot's share price reflected investors' concerns about the firm's retail performance and skepticism that wholesaling was going to be a winner. Indeed, if a shareholder sitting in the audience at the notorious 2006 annual meeting had spent $100 on Home Depot shares the day before Nardelli joined the firm, held onto them until the day before the annual meeting, and reinvested all dividends along the way, she would have ended up with a stake worth $97. If she had invested her $100 in Lowe's, instead, her stake would have been worth $304.[23]

Despite this poor performance, Nardelli would be paid $436m during his six years as CEO.[24] It was not just the magnitude of Nardelli's pay that was notable, but also how insensitive it was to Home Depot's true performance. Some of the arrangements look just like those we saw in Chapter 6, which might have been the result of weak boards camouflaging high pay by making it look performance-based when the reality was that the pay had little to do with a firm's performance. For example, when Nardelli joined Home Depot, he had negotiated a guarantee that his annual bonus would not be less than $3m.[25] (Bonus for what? Turning up?) Even the performance-related part of his pay was notable for the wrong reasons. When the board introduced a long-term incentive pay scheme in 2002, the payout was based on Home Depot's share-price performance. However, after two years of poor share-price performance, the board quietly switched to targets based on financial ratios, according to which Home Depot's performance appeared stronger.[26] Heads, Nardelli won; tails, shareholders lost.

Shareholders are let down by the board

The 2006 annual meeting left shareholders angry and the board humiliated. After a week of bad press, "Home Despot" (as the *Wall Street Journal*'s headline writers were calling it) conceded the new format was a mistake. It assured shareholders that they could ask questions at future annual meetings and that the board would be there to hear them.[27] Nardelli even embarked on a month-long charm offensive, meeting with Home Depot's investors and granting extensive interviews to several news organizations.[28] He cannot have been charming enough, because six months later the share price was even lower.[29]

Directors' response to Home Depot's problems shows how shareholders can be let down by a weak board of directors. Shareholders were clamoring for the board to address several problems, especially Nardelli's pay, the poor performance of Home Depot's retail operations, and investor skepticism about the expansion into wholesaling. The board made almost no progress on any of these issues during the six months after the annual meeting.

The board's compensation committee began its annual review of Nardelli's pay in June, but that year the committee was under greater pressure than usual to rein in his pay. It could have reverted to basing the performance-component of Nardelli's pay on Home Depot's share price. As well as reducing the CEO's pay, this might have motivated him to reconsider the merits of some of the projects he was pushing through at Home Depot. The committee could have insisted on renegotiating Nardelli's employment agreement to bring it into line with those of CEOs at similar firms. Nardelli was reported to have offered to forego his personal use of Home Depot's corporate jets, but giving up some perks was his only concession. He apparently insisted on retaining his guaranteed bonus. In the end the committee decided not to attempt to renegotiate Nardelli's employment agreement: it was all too difficult and, besides, if the current formula was followed his pay would be lower in 2006 than it had been the year before.[30]

The board did not do much better on other fronts. The main change to the retail business was to concentrate even more power in Nardelli's hands. The executive in charge of the retail operations resigned and the division presidents who previously reported to him started reporting to Nardelli directly.[31] Plans to develop the wholesale business, now called HD Supply, continued with the board's unanimous support.[32] As the end of 2006 approached, it appeared to be business as usual at Home Depot. One exception was the appointment of the head of business development, Frank Blake, as the (non-voting) vice chairman of the board of directors.[33] The board may not have changed the firm's direction, but it had started the process of putting a successor to Nardelli in place.

Why did directors not do more? They were shareholders themselves, so they would benefit directly from changes that raised the share price. However, this incentive was weak for many directors. For example, five out of Home Depot's ten independent directors owned less than 10,000 shares each, not worth much more than the board fees they received each year.[34] Even though these directors would be better off if they could lift the share price, they would not be *much* better off.

To make matters worse, directors may have had other things on their minds—things that were important to them, but not to shareholders. Challenging Nardelli would have been personally difficult for directors, for differing reasons. The four independent directors who were on the board when it appointed Nardelli might have been reluctant to implicitly admit they had made a mistake in hiring him. They might have been motivated by a desire to stick it out and prove their critics wrong—and if the critics were right, at least delay the day of reckoning for as long as possible. The six more recent arrivals might have felt disloyal to the man who welcomed them onto the board in the first place.[35] In addition, Home Depot's board in 2006 was quite unlike the board that had built Home Depot and endorsed the decentralized culture. For example, three of the first four directors added to Home Depot's board after Nardelli's appointment had strong connections to GE, either as current directors or former executives.[36]

The board's response might have been limited because its interests were different from shareholders' and because the free-rider problem prevented shareholders from doing anything about it. As we saw in Chapter 1, the free-rider problem stops shareholders monitoring the CEO adequately, which is why the board is needed in the first place. Unfortunately, the free-rider problem also stops shareholders monitoring the board adequately: it prevented all but 50 of Home Depot's shareholders attending the firm's 2006 annual meeting. This is a problem when, as seemed to be the case at Home Depot, the board is an ineffective monitor of the CEO.

Size matters...

Before we see what happened next at Home Depot, we need to take a look at the big picture. What shareholders need is a monitor that wants the same things they do, because then shareholders can leave the delegated monitor to do its job. They will not have to monitor the monitor. Large shareholders, especially the activist hedge funds that have made their presence felt at many firms since the turn of the century, have this property.

Large shareholders want high dividends and a growing share price. If they try to influence a firm's board and CEO, we expect them to encourage actions that raise their own payoff. However, securities laws try to ensure that all shareholders are treated equally (for example, they all get the same dividends). Therefore, when large shareholders try to get the firm to increase the returns to themselves they will also be trying to get the firm to increase the returns to small shareholders.

It all sounds fine, but if small shareholders will not monitor managers, why should a large shareholder do it? When we looked at the free-rider problem in Chapter 1, we saw that shareholders who monitor management incur all the cost of doing so, but share the benefits with all of the firm's other shareholders. Whether or not the monitoring is successful often depends on other shareholders monitoring as well. Perhaps a minimum number of votes need to be cast in order for a shareholder proposal to be effective. For a small shareholder, whether or not they vote has a negligible effect on the outcome. That is, the potential benefit from monitoring is relatively small for most shareholders and incurring the costs of monitoring can have little effect on whether the benefits are actually received. Unsurprisingly, small shareholders do not put much effort into monitoring.

There are some crucial differences when the shareholder is large.[37] Monitoring is still costly, and just as costly for a large shareholder as for a small one. However, although the benefits are still shared with other shareholders, a large shareholder receives a larger proportion than a small shareholder because the large shareholder owns more shares. To further strengthen the incentive to monitor, whether or not a large shareholder monitors can have a significant effect on the outcome. For example, the way in which a large shareholder votes can determine whether or not enough votes are cast for a shareholder proposal to be effective. That is, the potential benefit from monitoring is relatively large for large shareholders and incurring the costs of monitoring can significantly increase the likelihood that the benefits are received. The larger the shareholder, the greater the potential benefit from monitoring and the greater the influence of the shareholder over whether or not the monitoring is effective. In short, large shareholders have a stronger incentive to monitor than small shareholders and the larger the shareholder, the stronger the incentive.

Home Depot had several very large shareholders as it struggled in the aftermath of the 2006 annual meeting. At the end of the year, mutual funds managed by Fidelity owned Home Depot shares worth $4.0b. Barclays Global Investors owned shares worth another $3.1b; State Street, $2.6b; Vanguard Group, $2.2b. Between them, these four investors owned 15% of Home Depot's shares.[38] According to one estimate, 89% of America's largest public corporations (that is, the firms that make up the S&P 500 stock index) have at least one shareholder that owns 5% or more of the firm's shares. At a typical firm in the index, the shareholders with large blocks of shares jointly own 12% of the firm's shares. When smaller firms are included, large shareholders jointly own 37% of the shares of a typical firm.[39]

The fund managers with big Home Depot stakes might seem like ideal delegated monitors, but there are three problems. First, they managed huge diversified portfolios of assets, so large that monitoring the management in all of these firms was impractical. In fact, at the end of 2006, Home Depot shares made up just 0.5% of the four largest shareholders' portfolios by value.[40] The empirical evidence suggests that large shareholders carry out less monitoring if a firm makes up a smaller part of their overall portfolio.[41] Second, fund managers' fees are relatively insensitive to the funds' performance due to restrictions imposed by the Investment Company Act of 1940. With the link between pay and performance broken, fund managers have little incentive to monitor.[42] Third, if a fund's manager or its representative sits on a firm's board of directors then the fund cannot buy or sell that firm's shares whenever the board has access to private information. As managed funds need to be able to trade shares at short notice, these trading restrictions discourage them from seeking board seats, which reduces the effectiveness of any monitoring that they might undertake.[43]

To cut a long story short, shareholders should not look to institutional investors to do much monitoring. Fortunately for Home Depot's shareholders, a different sort of large shareholder was about to arrive on the scene. Like the big mutual funds, this shareholder managed the portfolios of other investors. Unlike the mutual funds, it invested in just a few firms and its fee structure gave it a strong incentive to monitor the management of each and every one of them.

... but size isn't everything

This knight in shining armor was the activist hedge fund Relational Investors, run by Ralph Whitworth and David Batchelder. Relational was the activist hedge fund that worked with the pension fund CalSTRS to unseat Occidental Petroleum's Ray Irani in Chapter 2; it also helped oust John Blystone from SPX in Chapter 9. At the end of September 2006, Relational managed a portfolio of just seven stocks, worth a total of $6.0b.[44] Mutual funds, which market their products to retail investors, would not be allowed to hold a portfolio like this because the Investment Company Act of 1940 imposes restrictions ensuring that mutual funds hold diversified portfolios.[45] Hedge funds are only lightly regulated because they market their services to institutional clients and wealthy individuals. This light regulation allows them to hold portfolios that are concentrated in just a few assets.

In late 2006, Relational identified Home Depot as a firm that could increase in value with a change in strategy and, if necessary, personnel. Relational decided to follow its usual strategy of acquiring a substantial stake in the firm and approaching management with its list of suggested changes. If Home Depot's management was not receptive to Relational's suggestions, then the fund would go directly to the firm's shareholders. The battle to change its policies would then have to be fought publicly, with Relational trying to get enough shareholder support to get a seat on Home Depot's board. If it succeeded, and the new policies worked, Relational could sell its stake for a capital gain and move on, using the proceeds to buy a large stake in its next target. All shareholders—large and small—would benefit from Relational's involvement.

Relational was just one of many activist funds engaging in similar activity. Like other hedge funds that invested in shares, these ones held concentrated portfolios of shares in a relatively small number of firms. However, regular hedge funds try to pick winners. They look for undervalued firms, buy their shares, and wait for the share price to rise. The firms they target are, they believe, managed well: it is just that the market has not yet recognized it. In contrast, the activist hedge funds look for firms that are being managed poorly. The market recognizes the poor management, which is why the share price is low. The funds buy shares, but rather than sitting back and waiting for the price to rise, they actively involve themselves in improving the firms' performance and, they hope, lifting their share prices. It can take some time to implement the policy changes. On average, Relational holds shares in individual firms for 22 months, but in some cases the period is much longer (more than eight years in the case of one firm).[46] Relational's patience is quite typical: on average, activist hedge funds hold stakes for close to two years.[47] This may not seem like long, but it is long enough for boards and CEOs to know that they cannot just wait for the activist hedge funds to lose interest and move on.

Unlike mutual-fund managers, their counterparts at activist hedge funds often have a substantial part of their own wealth invested in the funds they manage. The structure of the fees generated from hedge fund clients further strengthens managers' incentives to earn high returns. For example, Relational charged its clients a two-part fee each year: 1% of the value of the assets being managed and 20% of profits in excess of the return on the S&P 500 stock index.[48] Based on Relational's stake at the end of 2006, its investment in Home Depot would generate a fixed fee of $10m per year and another $2m for each percentage point that the rate of return exceeded the market index's. This gave the decision-makers at Relational a strong incentive to improve Home Depot's performance. Other hedge funds have similar fee structures and similar incentives.[49] Portfolio concentration helps too, as it means that the funds' managers have strong incentives to make individual investments perform. There is no hiding from failure with an undiversified portfolio.

Out of all the different types of shareholders we have met, activist hedge funds have the strongest incentive to monitor management. That is why they are the ones that typically undertake one of the most expensive forms of monitoring, proxy fights. Back in Chapter 2 we saw how much control incumbent directors—and a strong CEO—exert over the board election process thanks to their right to choose the list of board candidates whose names appear on the firm's proxy statement. That list has as many names on it as there are vacancies, so it is effectively incumbent directors, not shareholders, who choose the board. However, there is nothing to stop shareholders putting together their own slate of candidates, and presenting the firm's other shareholders with a rival proxy form. Nothing, that is, except the cost. Conducting an effective proxy fight is expensive: Whitworth himself estimated the cost of carrying out a proxy fight to be more than $10m.[50] Board candidates have to be found and vetted; rival proxy forms have to be produced and then distributed to all of a firm's shareholders; and if the fight is to be successful, a lengthy and expensive public relations battle will have to be fought as well. There are only approximately 70 proxy fights at U.S. public corporations each year, but 70% of them are sponsored by activist hedge funds.[51]

However, like pieces on a chessboard, all types of shareholders have a part to play. Large shareholders with weaker incentives, such as mutual funds, may not be sufficiently motivated to launch a proxy fight, but they will probably be prepared to gather the information needed to cast informed votes if a threatened proxy fight actually goes ahead.

The hedge funds know this and tend to target firms that already have large shareholders in place.[52] Even the small shareholders, the pawns in this game of chess, have a role to play. Enough of them will need to make the effort to read the proxy statements and vote if a threatened proxy fight is to succeed.

Liquidity matters as well

Home Depot was larger than the firms usually targeted by activist hedge funds, but in many other respects it was typical. When activists select targets, they look for firms with the potential to increase in value if corporate governance improves. The firms they choose tend to be relatively profitable, but with slow sales growth and a small dividend payout to shareholders. They tend to have large amounts of cash on hand and share prices that are low relative to their economic fundamentals. In short, the typical target of an activist hedge fund is a cash cow, with the cash being kept within the firm for the benefit—directly or indirectly—of the CEO, rather than being paid out to shareholders.[53] The targets that involve actual or threatened proxy fights—that is, about 40% of them—tend to be small, undervalued firms with a recent history of poor stock returns, exactly the sort of conditions needed to attract support from small shareholders.[54]

Home Depot fit this profile closely. During the six-year period when Nardelli was CEO, the firm's total profit was $24b, but its sales were growing at one-third the rate of Lowe's.[55] Payouts to shareholders had fallen. Three years before Relational's arrival, for every $100 of cash generated by Home Depot's business operations, $43 was paid out to bondholders and shareholders, $59 was invested in the retail business, and $8 was invested in HD Supply. (The $10 shortfall came from running down Home Depot's cash reserves.) That $100 was being distributed quite differently by the time Relational turned up: $6 was being paid out to investors, $45 was being invested in the retail business, and $52 was being invested in HD Supply.[56] The undervaluation box was ticked as well. In fact, if Home Depot had been able to match the performance of Lowe's, its share price would have been 19% higher.[57]

By using criteria such as these to select targets, activist hedge funds try to identify firms with the potential to increase in value following improvements in corporate governance. If the activists are to capture some of this increase in value for themselves then they must be able to buy the shares cheaply. The cheaper the better. However, like all large shareholders, activist hedge funds face the problem of limited liquidity in the markets for target firms' shares.

To understand what market liquidity involves, we need to put the share market under a microscope. Figure 10.1 shows a very stylized view of the market for Home Depot shares at the time Relational was ready to build up its stake. The bars show the pending orders for Home Depot shares, orders to buy shares on the left of the graph and orders to sell shares on the right. If we decided to buy a few Home Depot shares, we would need a willing

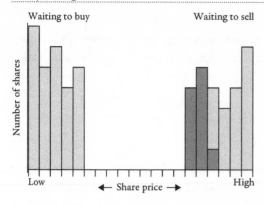

FIGURE 10.1 Illiquidity and the effects of large share purchases

seller; to find one, we would have to pay the ask price, which is the price corresponding to the first of the bars on the right of the graph. If we decided to sell some Home Depot shares instead, we would need a willing buyer: we would receive the bid price, which is the price corresponding to the last of the bars on the left of the graph.

The situation was not quite so simple for Relational when it started buying Home Depot shares because, unlike us, it wanted to buy many millions of shares. If Relational had tried to buy them all at once, it would have quickly exhausted the supply of shares offered for sale at the ask price. If it wanted to buy any more than this, it would have to start buying shares at a higher price, corresponding to the second bar on the right side of Figure 10.1. If Relational purchased the number of shares shown by the dark gray parts of the bars on the right side of the graph, it would have to pay an even higher price. Making things even worse, the price increase would have drawn investors' attention to the fact that someone—possibly an activist hedge fund—was building up a stake in the firm, which might have driven the price up even further. The only way to buy the large number of shares that Relational was seeking without driving up the price was to spread the purchases over many days and weeks and buy shares cheaply as they became available. However, in order to keep its trading secret, and stop the share price climbing on news that a large shareholder was building up a stake, Relational could not apply any pressure to Home Depot's board. A careful trading strategy was required if Relational was to build up a large stake reasonably cheaply and quickly. The more liquid the market—that is, the more shares that an investor can buy before the price increases in response—the larger the stake that activist hedge funds like Relational can acquire. This is probably why activist hedge funds tend to target firms with greater liquidity.[58]

"You can do it. We can help."

By mid-December 2006, Relational had acquired a 0.6% stake in Home Depot, worth $0.5b.[59] It was time to apply the pressure. Whitworth wrote to Nardelli, revealing his fund's ownership stake and blaming Home Depot's poor performance since Nardelli's arrival on "deficient strategy, operations, capital allocation, and governance." Once the pleasantries were out of the way, Whitworth got down to business. He wanted to meet with Nardelli and the board. He wanted a committee of independent directors—advised by lawyers and investment banks with no connection to current management—to evaluate three things: the firm's strategic direction; selling part of the company (read "HD Supply"); and "a major recomposition of the executive team." And he warned that Relational was considering nominating its own candidates for the Home Depot board at the next annual meeting.[60] While Home Depot considered its threat, Relational continued to buy Home Depot shares. By the end of the year it had doubled its stake to 1.3%, worth $1.0b.[61]

Relational's stated goals for its intervention at Home Depot were typical of what activist hedge funds try to achieve. When they target a firm, the objectives that they declare most frequently are to change the composition of the board, to sell the firm's main assets to a third party, to increase the amount of cash that the firm distributes to its shareholders, and to improve the firm's operating efficiency. Explicit objectives of replacing the CEO or board chairman are also common, as are attempts to cut executive pay or tie it more closely to performance.[62]

Relational's strategy of first approaching the target privately is one that many activists adopt. Activists do not need to apply pressure in public. They can also do so in private, at least in the early stages, with an implicit threat to go public unless they get what they want. For example, Relational had been holding private talks with Occidental Petroleum for more than a year before it went public with its demand for seats on the firm's board. At SPX, Relational was talking, or trying to talk, behind the scenes for six months before initiating a formal proxy fight.[63] Private activism often continues even after a proxy fight is underway: 25% of proxy contests are settled by the firm and the sponsor reaching an agreement in time for the sponsor to withdraw the rival slate of candidates before voting takes place.[64] One study of hedge funds' public interventions found that 48% of the funds sought to enter into talks with the firms they were targeting; just 28% of these interventions were, initially at least, "hostile."[65] Researchers with access to hedge funds' private data also report a significant role for behind-the-scenes activism.[66] When they look at institutional investors in general, there is even more activity behind the scenes: 63% have had discussions with management and 45% have met with boards without executives present.[67]

The board publicly rejected Whitworth's proposals and directors unanimously supported Nardelli and the firm's current strategy.[68] However, the threatened proxy fight changed the balance of power inside Home Depot's boardroom. Nardelli had reportedly already lost the support of some directors, including his patron Ken Langone, over his pay demands.[69] Now he faced another problem. Directors knew they were unpopular with shareholders. The large number of withheld votes in the most recent board election told them that.[70] A proxy fight would probably end the careers of some directors. Each one of them must have been wondering "Will it be me that goes?" Their best chance of surviving was to reach a deal with Nardelli that would appease Relational.

Home Depot had been telling its customers "you can do it, we can help" since it adopted the slogan in 2003. That was what Relational was telling the Home Depot board at the end of 2006. The board could do it (in this case, impose its will on Nardelli), but the pressure from the activists would help by increasing the board's bargaining power. Before Relational arrived on the scene, Nardelli and the board seemed to have resolved their latest round of bargaining over the firm's future. Each side had compared the cost of continuing bargaining with the benefit of potentially getting a bigger payoff for themselves if bargaining was prolonged and decided that the benefits did not justify the cost of continuing. The threat of a proxy fight increased the benefits to directors of prolonging bargaining in two ways. First, in the event that a proxy fight eventuated, directors' reelection prospects would be better if they had been seen to have bargained hard with Nardelli. Second, if continued bargaining improved the outcome for shareholders, the likelihood of a proxy fight eventuating would be reduced. Unfortunately for Nardelli, the threat of a proxy fight actually reduced the benefit to him of prolonging bargaining because even if extending bargaining would improve his allocation of the surplus from reaching agreement, the benefits would be short lived: the improvement in his position would make the threatened proxy fight more likely. When combined, these changes suggest the CEO would have been less inclined to continue bargaining and the board would have been more inclined to do so. As we saw in Chapter 2, this shifts the bargaining power from the CEO to the board.

The writing was on the wall. Even if Nardelli and the board had been able to reach an agreement, the shift in bargaining power meant that Nardelli would have found the outcome much less attractive than the status quo. The consequences of this prospect were felt almost immediately. Just three weeks after Relational wrote to Nardelli, Home Depot announced that he was leaving the firm. Actually, he had left the day before, replaced immediately by the recently promoted vice chairman, Frank Blake. Nardelli's departure was so sudden that Blake's employment contract had not even been agreed when the news was announced; it was not finalized until almost three weeks later. In shades of Carl Yankowski's several departures in Chapter 7, the board and Nardelli had "mutually agreed" that he would leave the firm.[71] There was little sympathy for Nardelli from the company's co-founder Bernie Marcus: "My concern is what happens in the future, and I feel very good about it."[72] Nardelli was gone and it had taken just three weeks.

Renovating Home Depot

With Nardelli out of the picture, the board now switched to directly bargaining with Relational. The outstanding matters? Board representation and the future of HD Supply. As in any bargaining game, there was a surplus to be shared if they could reach agreement: Relational would not incur the cost of carrying out its proxy fight and the directors (a few more of them, anyway) would get to keep their jobs. The two sides' bargaining power would determine how the surplus was shared.

The initial signs were discouraging. The board had just appointed another ex-GE executive, a close associate of Nardelli, as CEO. Like Nardelli, he had no prior retail experience. The board also reiterated its support for Home Depot's long-term strategy (read "HD Supply") and announced that the three directors due to retire at the next annual meeting would stay on the board.[73] Any hope the board may have had that Nardelli's departure, which was being described as a "peace offering" in the press, would satisfy Relational was quickly dispelled.[74] Whitworth complained that "[i]t's not enough to shuffle the deck chairs; they haven't changed their strategy and there isn't any fresh blood on the board."[75]

However, once the initial posturing was out of the way, the two sides quickly got down to business. The new CEO, together with two directors from the pre-Nardelli era, flew to Los Angeles to meet Relational. Whitworth reported the results of Relational's own analysis of HD Supply, which suggested the supply business was only half as profitable as Home Depot's in-house analysis indicated.[76] The meeting must have gone well because a few days later Home Depot and Relational announced they had reached an agreement. The board was in for a shake-up: David Batchelder of Relational (Whitworth's co-founder) joined the board and four of the existing directors (including the powerful Langone) would not serve past the 2008 annual meeting. In return, Relational agreed to carry out its activism at board level—it would not publicly rock the boat. The threatened proxy fight was averted without a shot being fired.[77]

Change came quickly. Even before the proxy fight was averted, two senior executives close to Nardelli had resigned.[78] One week after the end of hostilities, Home Depot announced that it was considering selling HD Supply.[79] In May, Home Depot held its 2007 annual meeting. The electronic timers were gone, all but one of the directors were back in attendance, and the new CEO even answered shareholders' questions.[80] Home Depot's founders, Marcus and Blank, attended for the first time in years, apparently as a show of support for the new CEO.[81]

At the time Nardelli left Home Depot, six out of the ten independent directors had been elected to the board while he was CEO and in a position to use his power to influence board selection.[82] Within 18 months of Relational's arrival, they were all gone. It took just three months for two of them to announce that they would not be seeking reelection to the board.[83] Two more resigned late in 2007.[84] The two survivors did not seek reelection to the board at the 2008 meeting.[85]

What just happened?

We should stop and catch our breath, which is probably what Home Depot's directors were doing at this point in the story. At first glance, events in the first few weeks following Relational's investment in Home Depot seem remarkable. The CEO had just pushed back a challenge to his pay, his strategy of expanding Home Depot's wholesale business had been endorsed by the board, and the last few directors left over from before he joined the firm would soon be retiring. He seemed untouchable. However, in the space of just a few weeks, the CEO had resigned, the wholesale business he had been building looked set to be sold off, and his nemesis had been invited into the boardroom. This all happened because one investor acquired 1.3% of the firm's shares.

Even more remarkably, this was not an isolated event. Since activist hedge funds came to prominence at the turn of the century, they have been marauding over the corporate landscape, moving from firm to firm, shaking things up as they go. In the year that Relational targeted Home Depot, there were more than 250 similar events involving activist hedge funds. Activists achieve their main stated goals in approximately 41% of cases and gain major concessions from the firms they target in another 26%. When they try to remove a CEO or board chairman, they succeed in 40% of cases; in half the cases where the CEO survives, the firm adopts the policies advocated by the activist.[86] While all this goes on, the firms' other shareholders can sit back and enjoy the benefits: on average, after filtering out the effects of any market-wide price movements, firms' share prices increase by 7.2% when activist hedge funds announce they have acquired an initial ownership stake.[87] And this all happens after activist hedge funds acquire relatively small stakes in the target firms, usually just a few percent.[88]

These ownership stakes might appear too small to be effective. However, Relational did not drive Nardelli out of Home Depot because it had 1.3% of the votes. That was never going to be enough. Relational won because if the threatened proxy fight had gone ahead, Home Depot's other shareholders would have had real choice in the next board election. That choice had been denied them in the past, when there had always been a matching number of candidates and vacancies. If the proxy fight had gone ahead, the message from Relational to the firm's disgruntled shareholders would have been the same as its message to directors: "You can do it. We can help."

For a proxy fight to succeed, enough shareholders would need to vote for Relational's board nominees. This would require some effort by shareholders, who would otherwise either not have voted or instead automatically voted for the board's own nominees. When deciding whether or not to make this effort, each shareholder would assess the personal benefit from voting. Shareholders who own only a few shares know that how they vote will have a negligible impact on the election results. Even though the benefit to them from the election of new directors may be substantial, the benefit to them *of voting* is small. We should expect the smallest shareholders to free-ride here as well. However, larger shareholders, such as the institutional investors with large Home Depot stakes, know that how they vote might affect the election outcome. They are much less likely to free-ride, so the presence of fund managers with large stakes would make it easier for Relational to get the votes needed to win a proxy fight.

Home Depot's board and CEO knew this and, just as importantly, realized that Relational's threat was credible. They will surely have conducted a thought experiment:

what happens if we call Relational's bluff? The process would have gone something like this. Relational will have to consider whether or not to carry out the threatened proxy fight. It will have to weigh up the cost and benefits of going ahead. The cost of a proxy fight is large, but for Relational there are two offsetting benefits. First, if Relational goes through with its threat then there will certainly be a proxy fight; no other shareholders have the incentive to carry one out, so if Relational decides not to carry out its threat then there will certainly *not* be a proxy fight. That is, Relational knows that it cannot free-ride on any other shareholders. Second, Relational's stake is worth $1.0b, so even a small percentage increase in Home Depot's share price will allow it to recover the cost of a proxy fight. The conclusion from this thought experiment is clear: if we call Relational's bluff, there will be a proxy fight. That is why a board that was not willing to go to its own annual meeting was suddenly flying directors across the country to meet with Relational.

The size of Relational's ownership stake was what made its threat credible. A gadfly investor—think Evelyn Davis from Chapter 1, who regularly attended Home Depot's annual meetings—could have written the letter that Whitworth sent to Home Depot at the end of 2006.[89] However, if a gadfly had threatened a proxy fight, the directors and CEO would not have been concerned. How does their thought experiment run now? The shareholder's cost of launching a proxy fight is unchanged. The shareholder's inability to free-ride is unchanged as well. However, crucially, the shareholder's small ownership stake makes the potential gains from a proxy fight so small that no gadfly in their right mind would have gone through with a threatened proxy fight. The directors and CEO can relax: only large shareholders can credibly threaten a proxy fight.

Following the activists' playbook

Relational's co-founder Batchelder now had his seat on the board and settled in to work quietly behind the scenes, in line with Relational's agreement with Home Depot. If the board did something that increased the enterprise value of Home Depot's assets by 1%, Relational's stake would have increased in value by $14m. Five of the board's outside directors would have been less than $5,000 better off if this occurred, so having a large shareholder like Batchelder on the board fundamentally altered the board's incentive to work in ways that benefited shareholders.[90]

Whichever firm they are at, once activist hedge funds get a representative onto the board they seem to work from the same playbook: reduce executive pay; sell off or shut down unwanted assets; improve operating performance by refocusing the business on its core activities; and get surplus cash out of the firm and into shareholders' pockets. Relational's time at Home Depot was no exception.

There was a significant change in executive pay at Home Depot. Although there was an uproar when Nardelli left with a severance package worth $213m, almost all of this package had been decided back in 2000 when he negotiated his employment agreement.[91]

The post-Nardelli directors could not be blamed for that. However, they could take credit for Blake's severance package: he did not get one![92] The shadow cast by Relational, which was still threatening its proxy fight when the board negotiated with Blake, boosted the board's bargaining power with the new CEO, so Relational can take some credit as well. Relational's message to the board: "You can do it. We can help." The change in executive pay did not stop with the CEO's severance package. During Nardelli's six years as CEO he was paid $436m. In contrast, during Blake's first six years as CEO he was paid $61m.[93] The magnitude of the pay reduction at Home Depot was extreme, but most activist hedge funds that target executive pay are successful. The activists achieve their main stated goals in approximately 20% of cases and achieve partial success in another 45%.[94]

Relational had been critical of Home Depot's expanding wholesale business. Sure enough, six months after Batchelder joined the board, Home Depot sold HD Supply for $8.5b. Shortly after, Home Depot announced it would buy back $11b worth of Home Depot shares from shareholders.[95] Relational had followed the activist hedge funds' playbook to the letter: sell assets that are not core to the firm's business and pay the proceeds out to shareholders. Activists that follow this strategy usually succeed: 67% of activist events that seek business restructuring and asset sell-offs achieve some measure of success, as do 64% of those seeking large cash distributions to shareholders.[96]

With Home Depot's direct involvement in the wholesaling business ended, its management was able to focus its efforts on its core retail business. For example, it reversed plans to acquire a bank, partially reversed the centralization of purchasing decisions, and closed its upmarket Expo Design Centers.[97] When activist hedge funds advocate changes related to improved operating efficiency, they are able to extract major concessions from the target firm in 64% of cases.[98] The changes at Home Depot seemed to have an effect: customer satisfaction returned to pre-Nardelli levels in 2010; same-store sales growth was higher than at Lowe's in 2010; and the relative profitability of Home Depot and Lowe's returned to pre-Nardelli levels.[99] Again, this degree of success was quite typical of activist hedge funds. Researchers who evaluated the performance of more than 2,000 separate activism events found that, on average, profits increase as a percentage of the cost of the firm's assets during the first three years after the activist's arrival. Target firms operate more efficiently during the same period. Labor productivity increases, but wages and hours worked are stable: it is shareholders who win.[100]

With executive pay cut, non-core assets sold off, and operating performance improved, the next page in the hedge funds' playbook says to ensure that the results of the improved performance are paid out to investors and not captured by the firm's insiders. Out of every $100 of cash generated by Home Depot's business operations in the first three years after getting rid of HD Supply, $79 was paid out to bondholders and shareholders; they would have received just $6 in Nardelli's last year in charge, so this was a substantial change in payout policy.[101] Changes following hedge fund activism are not usually as dramatic as this, but the statistics suggest that on average the payouts to investors increase.[102]

Selling up, moving on

We have already seen how share-market liquidity makes it easier for activist hedge funds to acquire large stakes in a firm without pushing up the share price in the process. Long-term shareholders benefit from this aspect of liquidity as well. The more shares acquired by the activist hedge fund, the stronger its incentive to monitor the firm's management, and therefore the more monitoring will occur.

Liquidity is also important once the activist has acquired its initial stake in the firm and announced its presence to investors. Sometimes an activist will decide to double down, buying an even larger stake in the firm and monitoring even more intensely. This is what Relational did, quickly increasing its stake from 0.6% to 1.6%; Relational increased it further to 2.2% in the first half of 2008.[103] Provided the market for a firm's shares is sufficiently liquid, an activist hedge fund can raise its stake before investors realize the activist will be monitoring with more intensity than expected (and before the share price goes up). Greater liquidity makes such transactions more profitable for activists, encouraging them to acquire even bigger ownership stakes.[104]

However, greater liquidity also makes it easier for an activist to cut and run. If an activist decides that a firm's problems are too difficult to solve, it can reduce its stake before investors realize it will not be doing much monitoring after all (and before the share price falls). Economists disagree about whether greater liquidity here is good or bad for shareholders. One camp argues that greater liquidity makes it more likely that activist investors will abandon monitoring and exit if the going gets tough.[105] According to this argument, a firm's shareholders would prefer its shares to be very illiquid because then an activist would have little choice other than to knuckle down and help sort out the firm's problems. The other camp argues that activists can persuade a firm's management to adopt their preferred policies by threatening to do the "Wall Street walk"—selling their shares and telling shareholders why they have done it—unless they get their own way.[106] On average, a firm's share price drops 8% when an activist hedge fund does the Wall Street walk.[107] Executives know that if an activist does walk away, the share price will probably fall, lowering the values of their ownership stakes and any components of pay linked to the share price, and possibly costing them their jobs. Greater liquidity makes the activist's threat more credible, because it allows the activist to sell more of its shares before the market gets wind of its exit and drives the share price down. According to this argument, a firm's shareholders actually prefer its shares to be very liquid because this makes it *easier* for an activist to cut and run: easier to do, and therefore less likely to be necessary.

We do not know if Relational ever threatened to do the Wall Street walk during its time at Home Depot. That is the whole point. If the threat is effective, then we will never know because the activist will not need to carry it out. Relational did eventually, and gradually, exit Home Depot. Just over three years after starting to buy Home Depot shares, Relational started to reduce its ownership stake, selling a 0.5% block of shares in March 2010 for $256m, followed by a 0.3% block in June for $168m and a 0.6% block in

November for $284m.[108] It sold its final shares after Batchelder had left the board. There was no sign that this was a protest at management actions. Rather it was business as usual for Relational, selling its stake in one firm to raise funds ready for its next activist venture.

Relational's investment in Home Depot was good for its clients, despite the toll that the American economy, and the housing market in particular, took on Home Depot's business. If Relational had invested in the S&P 500 index instead of Home Depot, and withdrawn its funds at the same time it withdrew them from Home Depot, its annual rate of return would have been 4.0% lower than the return it earned on its investment in Home Depot.[109] Relational's index-beating performance was typical for activist hedge funds, which earned annual rates of return during the period from 2001 to 2006 that beat the market by 11% on average.[110]

Home Depot's shareholders benefited as well. If an investor had spent $100 on Home Depot shares the day before Relational wrote its letter to Home Depot back in 2006, held onto them until the day after Home Depot announced Batchelder was not seeking reelection to the board, and reinvested all dividends, she would have ended up with a stake worth $111. If she had invested her $100 in Lowe's Companies, instead, her stake would have been worth just $95.[111] Again, these results are typical for shareholders of firms targeted by activist hedge funds. On average, the share price of a target firm increases significantly as soon as the market becomes aware of the activist's arrival, and these gains are not reversed in the five years that follow. Activist hedge funds are good for long-term shareholders.[112]

What can go wrong?

Activism is costly and hedge funds will intervene in a firm only if the benefits to the funds exceed these costs. Launching a proxy fight is expensive and an activist's threat to carry one out needs to be credible for its intervention to be effective. This credibility requires the gains from fighting and winning a proxy fight to be large, so the problems the activist intends to address need to be substantial enough for the rewards from fixing them to be worthwhile. The activist will wait until the severity of the firm's problems reaches a sufficiently profitable level. This leaves plenty of room for executives to misbehave without triggering activism.

Despite the high dollar value of activist hedge funds' stakes, they typically still own relatively small percentage stakes. Having an activist hedge fund as a shareholder means that more monitoring of management will be carried out, but it does not mean there will be *enough* monitoring. As long as the largest shareholder owns less than 100% of the firm's shares, there will be some monitoring activity that is not carried out even though its total benefit to shareholders exceeds its costs. That is why it is important to remember that activist hedge funds only reduce the separation of ownership and control, they do not eliminate it.

At any point in time, a typical activist hedge fund will be involved with firms in several different industries. For example, at the time Relational was threatening a proxy fight at Home Depot, its five biggest investments were in banking, life insurance, medical product manufacturing, retailing, and semiconductor manufacturing.[113] Activists holding such portfolios do not have the industry-specific knowledge to deal with industry-specific problems. Their skills, so they say, are in turning around firms with poor corporate governance. This necessitates focusing on a few fairly common problems and applying a standard set of remedial tools. Thus, activists target cash cows: firms, like Home Depot, with few profitable expansion opportunities and the cash being generated by the business kept within the firm instead of being paid out to shareholders. In order to maximize the probability of success, they tend to target firms that have already attracted institutional investors and that have liquid markets for their shares. Activist hedge funds are not the solution to manager–shareholder conflict in a firm with more industry-specific problems, or where there are few large shareholders already in place, or where the market for the firm's shares is illiquid.

Lastly, delegated monitoring works well only if the monitor—in this case, the large shareholder—does not itself need monitoring. Unfortunately, large shareholders can have interests that are different from those of other shareholders. For example, a mutual fund that owns shares in a firm might want to manage the firm's pension scheme, and so will be tempted to vote in line with the firm's management in a proxy fight.[114] An activist hedge fund might have used financial securities known as derivatives to decouple the number of shares it owns and the number of votes it can cast in a proxy fight; in extreme cases, it might even benefit from changes that *lower* the firm's share price.[115] And a large shareholder who has been a director for several years may be reluctant to reverse previous decisions. For an example of the third case we need look no further than Ken Langone. When Relational arrived on the scene, his Home Depot shares were worth $646m, which provided a strong incentive to maximize the share price.[116] However, he was the Home Depot director who had been so instrumental in hiring Nardelli and had been defending the CEO and his pay ever since. Turning against Nardelli would have imposed non-financial costs on Langone that would not be felt by the firm's other shareholders.

As we have worked through the various responses to manager–shareholder conflict, shareholders have taken an increasingly hands-off approach. At first, they tried to reduce the conflict themselves at a firm's annual meeting. Then they elected a board of directors to do the job, and watched as it monitored managers on their behalf. In turn, the board adopted its own hands-off approach, setting pay arrangements and leaving managers to work in their own best interests. In the last few chapters, the board delegated part of its monitoring role to parties outside the firm. However, in one crucial respect—ownership—shareholders have not been hands-off at all. Throughout, they have continued to own the firm. That is about to change.

4   Sell

I don't need the company to give me beer. I can buy my own beer.[1]

CARLOS BRITO (2012)

11 A new broom
THE MARKET FOR CORPORATE CONTROL

AUGUST BUSCH IV was already being groomed for the CEO's job at America's biggest brewer when he was in his early twenties.[2] When he eventually got the job, he lasted just 19 months. He was the sixth, last, and least, Busch to run Anheuser-Busch Companies Inc. One of his final tasks as CEO was to play host when his replacement, Carlos Brito, visited Anheuser-Busch's hometown of St. Louis in 2008. Before they met the press, Busch IV was struggling to decide who should sit at the head of the boardroom table, himself or his replacement.[3] It did not really matter, because just a few weeks afterwards, the table on the ninth floor of the Anheuser-Busch headquarters had gone altogether. There was no need for it anymore, because there was no board. The executive suites went as well, replaced with open-plan office space where executives worked side-by-side.[4] The ones who still had jobs, that is. Gone were the chief executive officer, the chief financial officer, and the chief information officer. Gone were the heads of the firm's international division, its Chinese operation, its brewing operations, its theme park business, and its packaging group. Gone was the head of corporate human resources.[5]

A ruthless new broom swept Anheuser-Busch's old management out of the building. It was Brito, CEO of rival brewer InBev S.A., doing the sweeping. When he had arrived in St. Louis, it was not to visit Anheuser-Busch's headquarters at 1 Busch Place. It was actually to visit InBev's new North American branch office. At 1 Busch Place.

Whassup in St Louis?

Anheuser-Busch began life in the mid-nineteenth century as a small St. Louis brewery. Busch IV's great-great-grandfather was its co-founder.[6] When Busch IV's grandfather became CEO in the mid-twentieth century, the firm's share of the U.S. beer market was just 6%, but by the time his father retired as CEO in 2002, that had grown to more than 50%.[7] The evolution of brewing technology had transformed the industry and Anheuser-Busch had emerged from that transformation as one of three national brewers, along with Miller and Coors.[8]

With a dominant position in the U.S. beer market and "Making friends is our business" as its slogan, Anheuser-Busch had grown soft.[9] Its approach appeared to be to maximize sales at almost any cost and everyone—apart from shareholders—seemed to benefit. The general public benefited from extravagant sponsorship deals such as "Grant's Farm," the animal reserve and ancestral home of the Busch family with its free admission and free beer. Revenue from merchandising and concessions did not come close to covering the cost of running the park.[10] Distributors benefited from extravagant wholesaler conventions held each year.[11] Workers benefited from Anheuser-Busch's policy of avoiding layoffs. According to one senior executive, Anheuser-Busch was "very, very successful" at it. "You don't fire your family."[12] You do, however, give every employee two free cases of beer each month.[13]

Anheuser-Busch's executives benefited more than most. The firm bought and operated a corporate retreat for them 175 miles west of its headquarters in St. Louis.[14] It paid for their $1,000 dinners. Junior executives were routinely flown first class on company business.[15] Senior executives flew by "Bud Air," Anheuser-Busch's fleet of eight executive jets, two helicopters, and a hot-air balloon.[16] The retired board chairman, a flying buff, would even fly one of them to work each day to avoid the St. Louis traffic.[17] One of the helicopters, not the hot-air balloon.

Everyone benefited, apart from shareholders. Someone who had invested $100 in Anheuser-Busch shares the day before Busch IV's father announced his retirement in 2002, and held them until the day before rumors of InBev's takeover approach surfaced in 2008, would have ended up with a stake worth $113. Investing $100 in Anheuser-Busch's two major competitors in the U.S. beer market, SABMiller and Molson Coors Brewing Company, would have returned $366 and $192, respectively, over the same period.[18] Such disappointing results are common in family firms when one family member succeeds another in the top job. Research involving firms in the U.S. and overseas suggests that firms tend to underperform after the appointment of a new CEO who is related by blood or marriage to a dominant firm insider.[19] Anheuser-Busch was no exception.

Anheuser-Busch's problems could be traced back to its past success. Thanks to that success, it had just two major competitors in the U.S. beer market. The empirical evidence suggests that the quality of corporate governance is especially important at firms operating in markets where there are just a few competitors.[20] Without the external discipline imposed by competition, firms with poor governance can get sloppy. Anheuser-Busch's shareholders needed corporate governance to be good. Unfortunately for them, governance was poor.

A failure of governance?

Busch IV's father, August Busch III, had been the driving force behind Anheuser-Busch's success since leading a boardroom coup in 1975 that toppled his own father.[21] By the end of Busch III's 27 years as CEO, the firm dominated the U.S. beer market. We have seen such transformative CEOs already, including Ray Irani at Occidental Petroleum (Chapter 2) and Michael Eisner at Disney (Chapter 5). In both those cases, the CEOs seemed able to use their success to influence the composition of their boards of directors for many years after the glow of early success had faded. Busch III was no exception. He was aided by the plurality-voting system used to elect the board at Anheuser-Busch. Each year, the board would nominate the same number of candidates as there were vacancies; all it took to be elected to the board was a single vote.[22]

Anheuser-Busch's board had 15 members when Busch III retired as CEO. With such a large board, the free-rider problem was always going to be, well, a problem. To make matters worse, the board was busy, with half the independent directors also sitting on the boards of three or more other firms. The free-rider problem was further compounded by the low ownership stakes of most independent directors. Then there was Busch III's influence. Ten directors were technically independent, but all of them had joined the board while he was CEO and chairman. On average, they had each been directors for ten years, long enough to form strong bonds.[23] Busch III sat on the same boards as four of the independent directors. For the previous 12 years, the chairmen of Anheuser-Busch, SBC Communications Inc., and Emerson Electric Co. had sat on each other's boards.[24] Before making life difficult for Busch III, the other two would want to think about the consequences for their own boardrooms. It was all very cosy.

Busch III's close ties to the independent directors help explain why he retained a very influential role when he eventually retired as CEO in 2002. He continued to hold a job as one of the firm's senior executives and continued to chair the board of directors.[25] He seemed unable or unwilling to let go. In 2005, more than three years after stepping down as CEO, Busch III was still attending meetings with advertising agencies and he was still visiting distributors.[26] He was also still being well paid: during the four and a half years that his immediate replacement was CEO, Busch III's compensation was worth the same as his replacement's: $54m.[27] Busch III may have retired as CEO, but he still dominated the firm.

This dominance continued for several years, thanks to the two-stage succession process that ultimately saw his son, Busch IV, appointed as CEO. First, Busch III's long-term understudy, Patrick Stokes, was appointed to a series of increasingly senior positions, culminating in his appointment as CEO in 2002.[28] Stokes was 59 years old when his promotion was announced, so he would not, and did not, hold the top job for long.[29] However, he held it long enough for Busch III's son to achieve enough executive experience at Anheuser-Busch for his appointment as CEO to be possible.[30] It also gave Busch IV a chance to get married. August Busch IV, oldest son of August Busch III, was married on August 5, 2006. (Look at the date again.) If the cynics are to be believed, the marriage—Busch IV leaving his wild days behind him—was the final step he needed to take to get the top job.[31] Perhaps they were right, because the firm announced eight weeks later that Busch IV would replace Stokes as CEO. Stokes replaced Busch III as board chairman, but Busch III remained on the board and remained involved.[32] He was still visiting distributors a year after his son became CEO.[33]

Busch IV's supporters could point to a successful role leading the firm's marketing operations during the late 1990s to help justify his appointment as CEO. He had been in charge of marketing when the firm hired three bullfrogs called Bud, Weis, and Er, and when it ran its famous "Whassup" campaign. However, this success had to be weighed against his checkered personal history. When he was 19, his Corvette crashed and the woman in the passenger seat, a waitress at a Tucson bar called "Dirtbag's," died at the scene. Busch IV, who was found at his home the next morning bleeding from head injuries "did not recall the accident and was not sure how he had gotten home" according to a sheriff's deputy.[34] After an eight-month investigation, prosecutors did not lay charges.[35] Just 18 months later, Busch IV was arrested after a high-speed car chase involving undercover narcotics officers, which ended in police shooting out one of his tires.[36] That time authorities pressed charges, but a jury acquitted him. His defense? He thought the undercover police officers were kidnappers.[37]

The appointment of Busch IV as CEO injected a soap opera into the heart of Anheuser-Busch. There was the awkward incident in 2005 when Busch IV walked up on the stage at one of the firm's lavish distributor conferences and knelt in homage in front of his father.[38] There was the interview with *Fortune* magazine, when Busch IV revealed that he kept letters of praise from his father in his briefcase: "Five notes of compliment from the Chief over ten years of full-time employment here. They're few and far between. But I cherish them."[39] There was the interview with *BusinessWeek*: "I love my father. Take a walk through my house, and it looks like a father museum. Every picture on the wall is of my father, or me and my father..."[40] And the one with the *Wall Street Journal*: "I never, ever had a father–son relationship."[41] This was the man Anheuser-Busch's board appointed as CEO, the man to run the business in the best interests of shareholders.

Discipline imposed by external capital markets can help in situations like this. We know from Chapter 8 that if debt levels are high, managers find it harder to use free cash flow to benefit themselves: debt creates a commitment to pay out cash to investors and that creates a need to generate the cash in the first place. Operating costs need to be kept low and it helps if the best possible CEO is in the job. If Anheuser-Busch had high debt levels, these sorts of pressures would have strengthened independent directors' bargaining position in 2002 and 2006 when first Stokes, and then Busch III's son, were appointed CEO.

Unfortunately for Anheuser-Busch's shareholders, it was not to be. Busch III's aversion to risk meant that Anheuser-Busch had been hesitant to expand internationally by acquiring overseas brewers. Funding these acquisitions would have required borrowing; without them, Anheuser-Busch's debt levels stayed low. One former Anheuser-Busch executive suggested that Busch III resisted international expansion because he would not have been able to micromanage a global firm the way that he micromanaged Anheuser-Busch.[42] Whatever the reason, the dearth of acquisitions kept debt levels low and those low debt levels meant there was too little pressure from external capital markets. It is a common problem at family firms, which are much more likely than other firms to have no debt whatsoever.[43]

It is worth pausing to marvel at the control exerted by Busch III. At times, Anheuser-Busch seemed more like a fiefdom than a public corporation. There is no better illustration of this than the succession process. Busch IV was sitting in on strategy meetings when he was in second grade, so it is hardly surprising that as he grew older, and worked his way up the ladder at Anheuser-Busch, speculation that he would eventually become CEO grew as well.[44] However, Busch IV was not the only Busch boy: at one point there was speculation that his 12-year-old half-brother might beat him to the top job.[45] One member of the extended family even claimed that Busch III encouraged sibling rivalry between his two sons.[46] According to one anonymous insider, Busch IV believed his stepmother wanted him to fail so that his half-brother would get the top job.[47] That soap opera again.

Anheuser-Busch was different from Cablevision, the family firm we met in Chapter 8, in one important respect. Cablevision had dual-class shares, so there were formal legal structures in place that gave the Dolan family control. In contrast, Anheuser-Busch had just one class of shares and Busch III owned just 0.6% of them at the time his son was appointed CEO.[48] Busch III's control of the firm was remarkable. His son's appointment as CEO illustrates—perhaps better than any other example in this book—the separation of ownership and control that plagues many modern corporations. Fortunately for shareholders, Busch III's dominance did not extend to the market for corporate control.

The market for corporate control

We have already seen two approaches to overhauling a firm's governance arrangements. First there were the leveraged buyouts that often, but not always, keep the existing management team in place. We saw one example at the hospital chain HCA in Chapter 4. There was no question of that happening at Anheuser-Busch. Who would have lent the Busches the money needed for a leveraged buyout to succeed? The second approach involved activist hedge funds threatening proxy contests and causing just enough director turnover to improve a board's effectiveness—and often to oust the existing management team. We saw this happen at Occidental Petroleum in Chapter 2, SPX in Chapter 9, and Home Depot in Chapter 10. However, during Stokes's and Busch IV's tenures as CEO, there was only one rumor of an activist hedge fund targeting Anheuser-Busch, and that came to nothing.[49] One of the factors contributing to the lack of interest from activist hedge funds was the nature of Anheuser-Busch's problems. It was not the typical target, a firm with a standard set of problems and a standard set of solutions. Its problems were small-scale, operational ones, and would require specialist management to fix. The activist investor's playbook from Chapter 10 would not help Anheuser-Busch.

There is a third approach, one we have not seen so far. In this approach, a firm offering good governance acquires all of the assets of a firm with poor governance and manages those assets itself. The poorly governed firm ceases to exist as an independent entity. This approach can work if firms that have better governance are able to get more value out of the assets, as that means they can afford to buy the assets off their current owners for a price that is both high enough for the current owners to accept and low enough for the new owners to make a profit on the deal. This is the role of the market for corporate control, the virtual marketplace where rival management teams compete for the right to manage shareholders' assets.[50] If the market for corporate control works effectively, poor management teams will be replaced by better ones and good governance will gradually expand through the financial system.

That is what happened in June 2008 when InBev launched an unsolicited takeover bid with a letter to Anheuser-Busch's board.[51] InBev had been created by the 2004 merger of large brewing companies from Belgium and Brazil. The founders of the two firms retained a 65% ownership stake in InBev and, even though the Belgians owned more shares, the merger had been arranged so that the two groups of founders jointly controlled the firm.[52] The board contained four directors nominated by the Belgians, four nominated by the Brazilians, and four directors without ties to either group—although, as these four independent directors were elected by shareholders and the founders owned 65% of the shares, the founders effectively chose the whole board.[53] These arrangements made for a much more effective board than Anheuser-Busch's shareholders had to represent them. The strong direct links between InBev's shareholders and its board were reflected in the decisions that the board made. InBev ran a tight ship. There were few perks and less sentimentality. Breweries were closed, jobs were cut, and pay was tightly tied to performance.[54]

In its letter, InBev offered to pay $65 for each Anheuser-Busch share. In total, it would pay $46b for a company worth just $38b before rumors started to push up Anheuser-Busch's share price.[55] If the deal went ahead, InBev would borrow the money it needed and buy all of Anheuser-Busch's shares. InBev shareholders would end up owning Anheuser-Busch's assets; Anheuser-Busch shareholders would get the $46b in cash. InBev needed to raise the cash used to buy Anheuser-Busch in the external capital market, so the discipline that can be generated in those markets was imposed on InBev right from the start. If the deal went ahead, InBev's management would have to perform even better in the future because of the increased debt.

Another bargaining game

Rival management teams compete in the market for corporate control, with the winner gaining the right to manage shareholders' assets. If the market works properly, then the winner will be the team that can make those assets most valuable. That team will be able to buy the assets at a price that is both high enough for the current owners (for example, Anheuser-Busch's shareholders) to benefit from the deal and low enough for the acquiring firm (for example, InBev) to find the deal profitable. The big questions: what is that price and how is it determined?

When InBev's unsolicited takeover offer arrived, Anheuser-Busch's directors found themselves in the same position as Yahoo's directors back in Chapter 3. They could accept InBev's offer, go back to InBev and try to negotiate a better one, or reject it out of hand. If an agreement was reached—either straightaway or after some negotiating—then the takeover would still have to be approved by each firm's shareholders at a special meeting called just for this purpose. Each firm has its own voting rules. At Anheuser-Busch, a takeover needed 50% support to be allowed to go ahead; at InBev, 75% support was needed.[56] If shareholders approved the deal, control of Anheuser-Busch's assets would switch to the more efficient management team under Brito. When deals are negotiated like this, the acquirer has the opportunity to take a close look at the target firm's books. With little chance of a post-takeover surprise, the target firm's board should be able to extract a high offer price from the raider.

If Anheuser-Busch's board rejected InBev's offer (or a revised offer, if InBev made one) and refused to put the offer to a shareholder vote, the ball would be in InBev's court. Perhaps InBev would walk away, leaving Anheuser-Busch's assets in the control of the inefficient management team under Busch. All the potential gains from a change in management would be lost. Alternatively, InBev might have decided to go fully hostile. That is when events can turn very nasty, very quickly. Even if InBev won a hostile takeover battle, the gains from a change in management would be offset by the costs and uncertainties of a prolonged hostile takeover battle.

When all the possibilities are taken into account, there would be more economic surplus to share around if the two boards could agree on a purchase price and avert a hostile takeover battle. If the target firm's board is weak enough—and the firm's executives have so much to lose that they want to fight—then the board is likely to reject the offer. Otherwise, the target firm's board will do what Anheuser-Busch's eventually did and negotiate with the raider to determine how this extra surplus is shared.[57]

We have seen similar problems many times before. Boards negotiated with their CEOs over projects, board composition, and post-retirement involvement in Chapter 2; they negotiated with private equity funds during management-led buyouts in Chapter 4; and they negotiated with their CEOs over pay in Chapters 5 and 6. All of these situations could be analyzed using the economists' bargaining-game framework. The negotiations between Anheuser-Busch's board and InBev can be analyzed the same way.

An important difference between this case and the bargaining games we have seen so far is that here some of the participants—some members of Anheuser-Busch's board—would be worse off if the two sides reached agreement. Their ownership stakes were small, but their annual directors' fees were not. For example, during the year before InBev launched its takeover bid, each of Anheuser-Busch's independent directors received compensation of $192,000, on average, for their duties as directors.[58] As they decided whether or not to recommend shareholders accept InBev's offer, they must have been aware that independent directors usually lose their board seats following a completed merger, although they are more likely to be appointed to the merged firm's board if they have strong social ties to the acquiring firm. There were no such ties between the directors and InBev to protect them. To make matters worse, when a director loses their job after a merger, the lost seat is not usually replaced by one at another firm.[59]

Directors in the hot seat again

At least at first, Anheuser-Busch's board did not want to sell the firm to InBev. It waited two weeks before rejecting InBev's proposal as "inadequate and not in the best interests of . . . shareholders."[60] However, Anheuser-Busch's board ultimately sought, and accepted, a revised offer from InBev. Directors' initial resistance was overcome by several factors: scrutiny from shareholders, the reputational concerns of directors with multiple board seats, and the financial concerns of directors with large ownership stakes. They all helped counteract the personal costs that a takeover would impose on the board.

Directors come under intense scrutiny during unsolicited takeover bids, perhaps much closer scrutiny than at any other time. Anheuser-Busch's directors were aware of that scrutiny. They had a fiduciary duty to the firm's shareholders, and engaged their own lawyers—independent of the firm's legal advisors—to ensure they did not breach that duty.[61] Complicating matters, hedge funds had responded to InBev's takeover bid by quickly building up sizable stakes in Anheuser-Busch. One fund manager had bought shares worth more than $1.8b in a matter of weeks.[62] Shareholders like these would scrutinize every action the board took. InBev upped the ante by nominating its own slate of candidates for Anheuser-Busch's board. If the board continued to resist InBev, directors would have to answer to their shareholders. To add to the ongoing Busch-family soap opera, one of InBev's 13 nominees was Busch III's estranged half-brother, Adolphus Busch IV.[63] The two were reported to have been feuding since Busch III toppled their father in his 1975 boardroom coup.[64]

As we found with executives' career concerns in Chapter 7, the strength of the incentives generated by a director's fate following an unsolicited takeover depends on the director's individual circumstances. Anheuser-Busch's board, typical of many, could be split into two groups. Some directors had few board memberships and would find it difficult to replace the steady income stream and prestige generated by their position at Anheuser-Busch. For these directors, resisting InBev's takeover must have been tempting. However, other directors were making a career out of sitting on boards. They were already directors of several firms and if they damaged their reputation by blocking a takeover of Anheuser-Busch, they could anticipate losing board seats at other firms. This is what typically happens to directors at poorly performing firms that succeed in blocking a takeover.[65]

There is another aspect of human nature that can potentially play a role. Directors, like the rest of us, are reluctant to admit mistakes. If directors felt they had made a mistake in hiring Busch IV as CEO, then InBev's takeover bid gave them a way to correct that mistake without having to admit making it in the first place. What were the alternatives? Reject the takeover offer and try to continue with Busch IV as CEO? The arrival of the hedge funds, and the prospect of shareholders outraged at missing out on InBev's $65 per share, would have made that difficult. Rejecting the takeover offer and replacing Busch IV as CEO would not have been much more attractive: even if it were feasible, there was the implicit admission that the board had erred in appointing Busch IV in the first place. No, InBev's takeover offer gave any directors who felt they had erred in appointing Busch IV as CEO a relatively pain-free way out of a tight spot.

What about Busch III? He had dominated the board for decades, but his influence must have weakened due to the countervailing forces directors were facing from outside the boardroom. Even if Busch III had installed his son as CEO in order to prolong his own influence over Anheuser-Busch, once InBev's takeover bid arrived, his days wielding influence were numbered. If the takeover occurred, Busch III would end up with no ownership stake and no control. However, even if the takeover did not occur, his influence was probably at an end, because the defense being considered by the board—merging with the Mexican brewer Grupo Modelo—would have weakened his grip on the firm. A merger would have brought new directors with no ties to Busch III; there was even talk that the Mexican firm's CEO might replace Busch IV in charge of the merged firm.[66] With limited prospects for continuing influence regardless of what happened, the relative financial payoffs became much more important: when the takeover eventuated, Busch III received $427m in cash for securities that had been worth $290m immediately before rumors of a takeover emerged.[67] Directors will not usually have this much at stake, but we should expect directors with larger ownership stakes to act more like shareholders when considering unsolicited takeover offers.

As InBev continued applying the pressure, Anheuser-Busch's board met twice to consider the firm's future. Busch IV pushed for a merger with the Mexican brewer in an attempt to fend off InBev, but the board decided instead to ask InBev to revise its offer to acquire the firm. According to some reports, Busch III threw his weight behind selling the firm to InBev, leading the board in abandoning his son in 2008 just like he allegedly led the board in abandoning his own father in 1975.[68]

Following board instructions, Busch IV and two independent directors approached InBev and the next day InBev raised its offer from $65 to $70 per share. Anheuser-Busch's board authorized the firm's management to enter into formal merger negotiations with InBev. After a frantic weekend bargaining, the two sides agreed to the merger terms late on Sunday afternoon.[69]

However, the agreed merger would occur only if the two firms' shareholders agreed. The close ties between InBev's shareholders and its board meant they were certain to vote in favor of the merger, but the separation of ownership and control at Anheuser-Busch meant the outcome of its shareholder vote was uncertain. However, in November 2008, the majority voted in favor of merging with InBev.[70] Dissenting shareholders—those who thought their shares would be worth more than $70 each if the merger did not occur—had to go along with the majority and sell their shares. Like all dissenting shareholders in such circumstances, they had the right to ask the courts to appraise the "fair value" of their shares, but the process is costly, time-consuming, and the outcome is uncertain.[71] Ultimately, there is not much that a dissenting shareholder can do: the majority rules.

As typically happens, the takeover was costly for the target firm's directors. When it was all over, Busch IV was the only Anheuser-Busch director to get a seat on the merged firm's board, and that seemed to be a face-saving gesture. The others all lost their jobs. On average, each of the independent directors had held a total of three directorships just before InBev launched its hostile takeover bid, compared with half that number two years later.[72]

Golden parachutes make for soft landings

So far, events at Anheuser-Busch look similar to those at HCA during the leveraged buyout we saw in Chapter 4. In each case, the firm's shareholders delegated negotiations to the board, which needed to negotiate a high purchase price if shareholders were to receive a large share of the value of any post-sale performance improvements. However, there was an important difference between the two cases. In management-led buyouts like the one involving HCA, the firm's executives want the deal to go ahead (and at a low price). In contrast, in unsolicited takeover bids like the one involving Anheuser-Busch, many executives know they will probably lose their jobs if the deal goes ahead. That is a problem for the target firm's shareholders, because—as we saw in the Microsoft–Yahoo negotiations in Chapter 3—the target firm's executives play such an important role in the takeover. In the short term, they are crucially involved in the takeover negotiations themselves. In the long term, some key personnel need to stay and others may need to go—quietly, if possible, and without defecting to competitors—if the merger is to succeed.

To understand why a target firm's executives might want to prevent a takeover going ahead, we just need to consider the costs successful takeovers impose on them. For some unfortunate executives, like Busch IV, the costs can be devastating. His marriage, which began eight weeks before his appointment as CEO was announced, ended when he filed for divorce exactly two weeks after Anheuser–Busch's shareholders voted to accept InBev's takeover offer.[73] Busch IV was plunged into depression, leading to a spell in rehab in early 2010 for treatment of that and what he described as his "other issues."[74] Although he had been appointed to the merged firm's board, he attended just one of the board's nine meetings in 2010; he did not seek reelection to the board the following year, citing "personal and health reasons."[75] A week before Christmas in 2010, Busch IV's girlfriend, an ex-Hooters waitress and aspiring art therapist, died in his bed of an accidental drug overdose. He was with her at the time.[76]

Few executives suffer falls from grace that are as spectacular as Busch IV's. However, like him, they often lose their jobs after their firm is taken over.[77] If they lose their jobs, they struggle to find similar employment for several years afterwards.[78] Anheuser-Busch's takeover was no exception. As we saw in Chapter 7, career outcomes like these can generate powerful incentives for the target firm's executives. Some know they have no future with the firm if the takeover occurs. For example, Anheuser-Busch's 61-year-old chief financial officer was filling a position that would cease to exist if the merger went ahead. His career prospects would take a dive if the takeover occurred. However, other executives will hope that they can keep their jobs, perhaps even advance further in a bigger firm, resulting in promotion tournaments like those we saw in Chapter 7. Consider the example of the 39-year-old vice president of marketing, considered by some to be Busch IV's right-hand man. He was young enough and junior enough for a merger to boost his career prospects if he could impress his new masters. He played a key role during the negotiations and led communications with employees and wholesalers during the whole period when the takeover battle was being fought. This must have impressed the InBev team, because he was appointed president of Anheuser-Busch when the takeover was completed.[79]

All sorts of incentives swirl around a target firm during an unsolicited takeover, so the firm's shareholders will benefit if its executives' interests can be better aligned with their own. For those executives looking at losing their jobs, and who might have an incentive to try to derail the takeover, the board needs to boost their payout in the event of a successful takeover. Make it worth their while. For those executives, typically younger and in positions where their career can continue, who might be tempted to curry favor with the acquiring firm at the expense of their own shareholders, the board needs to make their wealth sensitive to the takeover share price.

Boards use so-called change-in-control agreements to create these incentives. These are formal agreements between a firm and its executives that specify the payments to be made to the executives in the event that the firm is taken over. In some cases, all that is needed to trigger a payment is that the firm is acquired. In other cases, payments are made only if, in addition, the executive loses their job as a result of the takeover. Change-in-control payments come in various shapes and sizes. They can include changes in pension arrangements, as well as payments to cover the additional taxes generated by the change-in-control payouts themselves. However, the main components are payments of a fixed multiple of an executive's recent salary and annual bonuses—typically three years' worth—and accelerated vesting of unvested shares and options.[80]

The change-in-control agreements at Anheuser-Busch did not involve payouts based on salaries and bonuses, but they did ensure that unvested shares and options would vest if a change in control occurred.[81] Busch IV benefited when almost 1.5m shares and options were vested ahead of schedule; on average, Anheuser-Busch's 17 next most senior executives each had 0.2m shares and options vest the same way.[82] Anheuser-Busch was more reliant on the accelerated vesting of shares and options than most firms. At a typical large public corporation—the sort of firm that appears in the S&P 500 and S&P MidCap 400 stock market indices—only 55% of the value of the CEO's change-in-control payout comes from the accelerated vesting of unvested shares and options; the rest comes from so-called golden parachutes, compensation that the CEO would not have received without a change in control occurring. At a typical smaller firm—the sort that appears in the S&P SmallCap 600 stock market index—only 41% of the value of the CEO's change-in-control payout comes from the accelerated vesting of unvested shares and options. The total potential payout to the CEO is 0.3% of the firm's market value at a typical large firm and 0.6% at a typical small one.[83]

The proportion of firms with golden parachutes in place has increased steadily since the early 1990s: recent data shows 78% of U.S. corporations use them.[84] Golden parachutes bring executives' interests into closer alignment with shareholders' interests. They remove much of the financial incentive for executives to sabotage a takeover; the executives might even be better off if a deal goes ahead. That is one less obstacle for the acquiring firm to overcome. The empirical evidence suggests that once a takeover attempt has begun, it is more likely to succeed if the target firm's CEO has a golden parachute that is larger relative to the pay he will lose if the acquisition goes ahead. More likely to succeed, but the premium that the target firm's shareholders receive tends to be smaller.[85] One possibility is that the target firm's executives are so keen to cash in their golden parachute that they work to ensure that the takeover goes ahead, even if in doing so they do not maximize the payoff of their own shareholders. Perhaps this increased probability of success attracts potential acquirers, because firms with golden parachutes in place are more likely to be acquired.[86]

Accelerated vesting of shares and options can also motivate a target firm's executives. At the time of the takeover, Busch IV held shares and options that had been worth $46m immediately before rumors of a takeover emerged. When the takeover eventuated, he received $58m for his vested securities and $34m for his unvested ones, twice their value prior to the takeover. The firm's other senior executives each held shares and options that had been worth $12m, on average, immediately before rumors of a takeover emerged. InBev paid them each $18m, on average, for their securities that had vested by the time of the takeover and another $4.7m for securities that had not vested.[87] Payouts like these create a strong financial incentive for executives to allow a takeover to take place, a much stronger incentive than would have been generated if they had lost the unvested shares and options. These were securities that had not vested because the executives had not worked long enough since they had been granted. They had originally been granted as pay for future services rendered—and the services had not been rendered by the time the takeover occurred. Still the payouts were made.

Anheuser-Busch's executives had not been able to manage the firm in a way that the market valued at $70 per share, but the executives still benefited from the value of someone else's management. Skeptics look at such golden parachutes and shout "pay for failure." According to this view, the target firm's executives are having one final feed at the corporate trough, a feeding frenzy that is possible only because target shareholders are making such large gains that the prospect of shareholder outrage is reduced. However, there is an alternative view: golden parachutes might be a price worth paying if doing so helps complete a deal on terms favorable to the target firm's shareholders.

Accelerated vesting does not just give executives incentives to help ensure takeovers occur. It also generates incentives to make sure the takeovers occur at a share price that is high. For example, Busch IV's payouts from his vested and unvested securities increased by $13m and $7m, respectively, following the $5 increase in InBev's offer price. That gave Busch IV a strong incentive to extract a higher offer price from InBev, an incentive that benefited shareholders, who were $3.6b better off.[88] The empirical evidence suggests that a target firm's shareholders receive a takeover premium that is 16 percentage points higher, on average, if the vesting of executives' unvested shares and options is accelerated.[89]

Sometimes the acquiring firm will grant deal-sweeteners of its own to key executives in an attempt to facilitate the takeover. These are paid in addition to any change-in-control payments set by executives' employment agreements with the target firm. For example, InBev agreed that Busch IV would serve as a consultant to the merged firm's CEO until the end of 2014. This gave him an up-front payout of more than $10m and consulting fees of approximately $120,000 per month. He also received an office and secretarial support, continuation of the personal security services that had been provided by Anheuser-Busch, and the standard health and other benefits of Anheuser–Busch's salaried employees.[90] InBev agreed to pay senior executives who lost their jobs within two years of the merger occurring a lump sum equal to up to two times the sum of their annual salary and bonus. The chief financial officer would receive $2.7m. It also agreed to pay "integration bonuses" to those senior executives who remained, conditional on operating goals being met. The vice president of marketing's bonus would be $0.7m.[91]

Boards have a delicate balancing act to perform. Making golden parachutes more generous reduces executives' fear of failure, which weakens their incentive to avoid a takeover in the first place. However, this cost to shareholders will sometimes be more than offset by the reduced conflict of interest in the event that a takeover offer arrives. Even directors who work in shareholders' best interests will protect executives from *some* of the consequences of unsolicited takeovers, but they cannot afford to make golden parachutes so generous that executives are "paid to fail."

Thinking the unthinkable ... and trying to prevent it

So far in this chapter, we have looked at the incentives of directors and executives once they are confronted with an unsolicited takeover offer. Before we finish, we need to look at their incentives *before* such an offer arrives. Anheuser-Busch's "Blue Ocean" cost-cutting program provides an excellent illustration of the incentives generated by the mere threat of an unsolicited takeover offer.

Blue Ocean came to prominence when Anheuser-Busch formally rejected InBev's initial offer. In a last-ditch attempt to fend off InBev, Anheuser-Busch announced an ambitious plan to reduce its annual operating costs by more than $1b. There would be job cuts (between 10% and 15% of all salaried workers would lose their jobs), pension payouts would fall, and employee healthcare contributions would rise.[92] Unsurprisingly, given Anheuser-Busch's recent history, the plan was greeted with skepticism by many analysts. Skepticism and "Are you kidding me? This is not going to fly."[93] It looked to them like the threat of a takeover had done what the firm's board had not: prompted management to take a chainsaw to Anheuser-Busch's bloated cost structure.

This is not the first time in this book that we have seen actions taken in an attempt to avoid a bad future outcome. Previously we have seen compensation committees trying to avert shareholder outrage by hiding high pay (Chapter 6), executives making sacrifices to improve their future career prospects (Chapter 7), and executives fearing bankruptcy responding positively to the discipline of external capital markets (Chapter 8). Now we can add another one to the list: an unsolicited takeover offer can motivate a firm's directors and executives to improve their performance in an attempt to defeat the bid.

If the market for corporate control affected firms only after they received unsolicited takeover offers, then it would not do much good because such offers are relatively rare. However, some empirical evidence suggests that this type of takeover is a "court of last resort," an external source of discipline that is applied when internal ones have failed.[94] Like any effective court, if it functions well when called upon then it can have a deterrent effect. If directors and managers believe that the threat of an unfriendly takeover attempt is real then they may change their behavior before a raid is launched. There does not need to be a specific raider on the horizon. All that is needed is the prospect that someone, somewhere, will launch a takeover bid if management underperforms by a big enough margin. It may be better to avoid becoming a target in the first place, rather than waiting for a raid to occur and then trying to defeat it. If the threat of an unfriendly takeover is strong enough, then the takeover does not actually need to occur. If underperformers are targeted, then do not underperform. Shareholders benefit from the market for corporate control—and they do not even realize it.

There are signs that this is what happens. For example, after firms adopt golden parachutes—and executives' fear of a takeover falls—firm performance worsens. On a brighter note, during periods when the takeover market is more active, poorly performing CEOs are more likely to be dismissed, suggesting that directors are especially vigilant when the threat of takeover is high.[95] This might help explain Anheuser-Busch's behavior. It had actually announced the Blue Ocean cost-cutting project, which initially aimed to reduced costs by $300–$400m over the next four years, back in May 2007.[96] This was the genesis of the plan to cut costs by $1b that Anheuser-Busch hoped would save it from InBev.

Unfortunately for Busch IV, Anheuser-Busch's adoption of Blue Ocean was a case of too little, too late. It is the possibility of such misjudgments that explains why disciplinary takeovers occur at all. After all, if firms' insiders got it right every time, there would be no disciplinary takeovers. They would make just enough sacrifices to avoid triggering an unsolicited takeover bid. However, mistakes happen and misjudgments are made. Busch IV's most obvious mistake was not being aggressive enough in cutting costs, but he made other mistakes as well. The most important ones looked like naivety on his part. When he negotiated a joint venture with InBev in 2005, he did not insist on a fairly standard "standstill" provision that would have restricted InBev's ability to exploit what it learnt about Anheuser-Busch's inflated costs.[97] When he called investment bankers in to advise the firm, he did not restrict himself to a couple of advisors. Instead, he brought in several, again revealing the firm's inflated costs to outsiders.[98] He even invited Brito to one of Anheuser-Busch's lavish distributor conventions, where Brito could see the extravagance for himself.[99] At least in these cases, Busch IV's mistakes benefited Anheuser-Busch's shareholders: they facilitated the change in management team that funded the takeover premium.

Under new management

If the market for corporate control works, then changes in control should be accompanied by improvements in firm performance. InBev's cost-cutting reputation meant that Anheuser-Busch's workers awaited their new masters with trepidation.[100] They had good reason to be apprehensive. Anheuser-Busch's management had already announced plans to reduce annual costs by $1b, but InBev's management was going to do all this and more: as soon as the merger terms were agreed, they raised the target for annual cost savings by 50%.[101] And they meant it. When the Anheuser-Busch negotiating team returned from New York to St. Louis, they flew on one of the company's corporate jets; when InBev's Brito flew to St Louis, he flew on Southwest.[102] Anheuser-Busch wanted to book him a suite at the Ritz-Carlton; instead, he booked himself into the Holiday Inn.[103] Busch IV had talked the cost-cutting talk, but Brito walked the walk.

The bloated costs had developed under Busch-family management. Cutting them would involve an implicit admission that the past decisions that created that culture were mistakes. Perhaps this explains why InBev found it easier to cut costs. For example, Busch IV had managed to convert the executive dining room into a call center, but InBev removed the executive suites altogether and replaced them with open plan offices.[104] Busch IV had canceled Anheuser-Busch's order for a $40m top-of-the-line corporate jet, sparking a battle with his plane-buff father that one observer described as "World War III between the two of them." InBev put *all* of the firm's corporate jets on the market and started flying executives on commercial flights. In coach.[105] And it was InBev that stopped giving free beer to theme park employees.[106] It should not have come as a surprise because, a few months before the takeover, Brito had told Stanford MBA students "I don't have a company car. I don't care. I can buy my own car. I don't need the company to give me beer. I can buy my own beer."[107]

Switching to open plan offices and abandoning "Bud Air" were largely symbolic changes, but they set the tone for the bigger cost-cutting that followed. In December 2008, Anheuser-Busch InBev (as the merged firm was called) announced over 2,000 further job cuts.[108] As the old Anheuser-Busch headquarters in St. Louis had been reduced to a branch office of the merged firm, Anheuser-Busch management bore the brunt of the job losses. The number of company-issue Blackberries fell from 1,200 to 720.[109] In early April 2009, AB InBev announced plans to freeze company contributions to workers' pension plans and to reduce its contribution to the cost of retiree healthcare.[110] Labor costs were not the only item that AB InBev was cutting. The number of new advertisements created each year was halved.[111] The labels on bottles shrank; the glass in the bottles themselves was thinner.[112] And it worked: by March 2009, AB InBev had made such good cost-cutting progress that it raised its savings target by a further 50%.[113]

With all the borrowing InBev had undertaken in order to finance the takeover, the merged firm was under pressure to get its debt down. Cutting costs and lifting profits would help, but it would still take time. Asset sales and other restructuring would do it faster. Some asset sales were easy: the corporate retreat west of St Louis was one of the first to go.[114] Non-core assets such as the theme-park business were sold, but other sales involved brewing assets in South Korea and Central Europe. In the first year after the takeover, AB InBev's asset sales raised $6.2b.[115]

Anheuser-Busch got a complete overhaul, the likes of which its pre-takeover owners could only have dreamt about. Evidence gathered from more than a thousand similar deals shows that takeovers typically have such transformative effects. On average, acquiring firms increase the productivity of the firms they takeover. They do this by making more efficient use of the target firm's resources: on average they slash capital expenditure by 12%, cut the number of workers by 1% and managers by 6%, and reduce wages by 0.5%, all while holding output constant.[116] However, within three years, a typical acquirer sells

27% of the target firm's plants and closes another 19%. The plants that are kept increase in productivity.[117]

Sales at Anheuser-Busch fell but, much more importantly, profits increased.[118] The benefits of this increased profitability were shared around. Anheuser-Busch's shareholders got their portion of the efficiency gains up front, by selling their shares for more than what the market thought they would have been worth if Busch IV had stayed in charge. They did well, receiving $51b for shares that were worth just $38b before market rumors of a takeover started to push up the price.[119] The target firm's executives received their portion partly in the form of the premia paid for their shares and options and partly in the form of golden parachutes. Like the target's shareholders, their benefits were all received up front. In contrast, the acquiring firm's shareholders have to wait for their share of the benefits, which takes the form of higher future dividend payouts on their shares. At AB InBev the dividend-per-share grew by 51% per annum, on average, between 2008 and 2014.[120] The target firm's executives benefit from these increased dividends too, if they own their firm's shares and options.

Sometimes the pay of the acquiring firm's executives is directly tied to the performance of the takeover. It was at InBev. Shortly after the takeover was completed, approximately 40 executives were granted options in the merged firm, but these options would benefit the executives only if they could reduce AB InBev's debt to a level specified in the option contracts.[121] They achieved the targets—the asset sales helped—and when the first options vested at the start of 2014, their combined value was $2.0b. Brito's alone were worth $231m.[122]

The distribution of a takeover's efficiency gains is determined by the bargaining that goes on between the firms (to allocate the takeover's gains between the two firms) and within each firm (to allocate the firm's gains between shareholders and executives). Anheuser-Busch's board influenced the allocation by its involvement in the takeover talks, but it did not need to agree to recommend the takeover to its shareholders. It could have done what Busch IV had wanted and rejected InBev's offer. InBev's board would have done what many acquiring firms do in this situation and gone over directors' heads directly to the target firm's shareholders.[123] As we are about to see, when takeover bids go hostile like this, all hell can break loose.

We've got more money than you.[1]

BURNLEY F.C. FANS (2010)

....

12 Bypassing the board
OFFENSIVE TACTICS IN HOSTILE TAKEOVERS

WHEN MALCOLM GLAZER bought the Tampa Bay Buccaneers in 1995, the team was the laughing stock of the National Football League. Glazer's early actions—lifting ticket prices and pressuring the local county into building the team a brand-new stadium—made him a local hate-figure. Then the Bucs won the Super Bowl and he was the toast of Tampa.

After a failed attempt to buy the Los Angeles Dodgers, Glazer turned his attention to an English soccer team.[2] Manchester United was one of the most successful soccer clubs in Europe when Glazer started buying its shares. The team was on its way to winning that season's English Premier League, its fourth victory in five years.[3] Unfortunately for shareholders, the firm that owned the team—Manchester United PLC—did not have the financial performance to match. Its share price had fallen by 18% over that five-year period.[4] *Forbes* magazine estimated that the value of Glazer's Bucs operation had increased by 94% over the same period.[5] Glazer wanted to buy Manchester United and implement a similar plan to the one that turned around the Bucs. He would increase ticket prices; revenue from merchandising and sponsorship would rise; spending on recruiting new players would be capped.[6] And that was not all: there would be no more free porridge and toast at breakfast for "non-essential staff" at the team's training complex.[7] No more free porridge! The man was a monster.

Glazer's attempt to buy Manchester United started off much like InBev's successful bid for Anheuser-Busch. He approached Manchester United's board about a possible offer for the firm, just as InBev approached Anheuser-Busch's board.[8] Manchester United secretly despatched its CEO to meet Glazer's representatives in Tampa, just as Anheuser-Busch had secretly despatched its CEO to meet InBev's representatives in the same city.[9] However, that is where the similarities end, because when Manchester United rejected Glazer's initial approach, he did not come back with a higher offer, which is what InBev did when Anheuser-Busch played hard ball. Instead, Glazer launched a hostile takeover bid that lasted two bitter years.[10] It finished with three of his sons huddled in the back of a police van.[11]

A corporation or a sports club?

The soccer club known around the world as Manchester United was established in 1878 by workers at the Lancashire and Yorkshire Railway and started off playing against other railway-based teams.[12] Its ownership changed hands over the years as a succession of investors bailed it out. By the 1960s, the majority of its shares were owned by a Manchester businessman.[13] Almost three decades later, his son, Martin Edwards, was the majority owner and chairman of the board. After a failed attempt to sell Manchester United to a colorful property developer, Edwards listed Manchester United's shares on the London Stock Exchange in 1991.[14] He reduced his ownership stake with a series of share sales during the next decade.[15] By the end of May 2002, when he sold a 6.5% stake to a Scottish mining magnate, he owned just 0.07% of Manchester United.[16] When Edwards resigned from the board later that year, Manchester United's transition from a family-run firm to a fully fledged public corporation was complete.[17]

In the era of professional sports, all teams face a tension between maximizing their financial performance and maximizing their sporting performance. Some teams are little more than billionaires' playthings. There is no separation between ownership and control at those teams, so the owner is able to decide how to manage this tension. However, teams like the 1991–2005 version of Manchester United are different. Their shares are traded on public share markets, so each team has many different owners: the separation between ownership and control can be wide.

Shareholders who treat their ownership stake as an investment want the firm's profits to be high. That means high ticket prices, low player wages, and exploitation of merchandising and sponsorship opportunities. They want the team to win as well, but for these shareholders on-field success is a means to an end: a winning team will generate more ticket sales and better sponsorship deals. In contrast, the primary focus of a teams' supporters is its on-field performance. If recruiting better (and more expensive) players will make a winning season more likely, then they will want the club to hire those players. For supporters, financial performance is important as well, but again this is just a means to an end: if a team struggles financially, its chances of retaining and recruiting top players diminish.

This conflict at Manchester United burst into the open when Rupert Murdoch's British satellite television operation attempted to buy the club in 1998.[18] The bid was eventually blocked by the British government, but not before Manchester United's supporters made their displeasure known.[19] They stirred again early in 2004 following rumors of another takeover bid, this one by two Irish horse-racing tycoons.[20] However, like the anti-Murdoch protest, this one was tame compared to what happened when Glazer arrived on the scene.

If directors have small ownership stakes, the conflict between financial and sporting performance can infect the boardroom as well. Is it worth paying £100m to turn second place into first? A director with a large ownership stake might say no: first place is nice, but it is worthwhile chasing first place only if doing so leads to enough additional ticket sales and sponsorship revenue. However, a director with a small ownership stake will be insulated from the costs, but still share in the reflected glory that comes with winning on the field. Manchester United's board was small, so there was no free-rider problem to cause difficulties. However, three of the seven directors were Manchester United executives and one other director had very strong business ties with the firm. That left just three independent directors, and none were reported to have large ownership stakes.[21]

When viewed from the perspective of a shareholder, an overemphasis on winning is just another example of excessive perk consumption. We have seen examples of this before, but then it was use of a corporate jet and the funding of a private art collection. At a sports team, the perk being consumed is the enjoyment that comes from mixing with the world's best players and being part of a league-winning club. The potential for problems at Manchester United was enhanced by the club's lack of debt, which meant there was no discipline being imposed on the board from having to access external capital markets. The club was even able to spend £144m upgrading its stadium and training ground during its first ten years as a public company and still come out debt free.[22] Manchester United's small shareholders were fortunate in at least one respect: approximately 29% of the firm's shares were held by two Irish investors who were treating their investment as just that—an investment. Small shareholders could free-ride on their monitoring of the board, which in early 2004 included the Irishmen demanding that directors answer questions about corporate governance. The pair were also reported to be considering seeking a seat on the board themselves.[23]

It is clear that in early 2004, corporate governance at Manchester United was a mixed bag. Ownership stakes were too small to provide strong incentives for executives or directors, and there was no debt to discipline spending. However, there was some pressure coming on the board from outside. That pressure was about to increase enormously.

An unsolicited takeover offer

Manchester United's supporters frequently argued that a focus on maximizing the share price was inappropriate because, ultimately, it was a sports team and not a business. The problem with this argument is that as soon as a sports team lists its shares on a stock exchange, it becomes vulnerable to a takeover by investors who want to make money. These investors can wait in the wings and, once the team's management deviates far enough from policies that maximize the share price, sweep in and buy the shares of disgruntled shareholders. If the current management is bad enough, then the raider can afford to offer shareholders more for their shares than they are worth under the current management—and still make a profit on the deal. This makes the firm vulnerable to takeover. The lesson to team owners is simple: if you do not want the discipline of the market for corporate control then do not list your shares on a public share market.

Malcolm Glazer, originally from Rochester but based in Palm Beach, was one of those investors who saw an opportunity to make money. He claimed to be the quintessential self-made man, starting with just the small watch-repairing business he inherited at age 15 following his father's death. A decade later, Glazer had made enough money to branch out into real estate investment, building an empire on the back of his investments in mobile-home parks. He was, they say, a tough landlord.[24]

When Glazer added the Tampa Bay Buccaneers NFL team to his diverse portfolio of assets in 1995, it was a business deal, not a sporting one. His knowledge of football was apparently so limited that he once mistakenly cheered the opposing team at a Bucs game.[25] Glazer may not have known much about football, but he knew how to make a profit. The average ticket price at a Bucs game increased by 118% in the first four years under Glazer's control; the team went from having the 17th to the second most expensive tickets in the NFL.[26] The locals complained that Glazer bullied their community into paying for a brand-new $168m stadium by threatening to take the team elsewhere.[27] While all this was happening, the Bucs soared in value: less than five years after Glazer bought the team for $192m, *Forbes* magazine estimated it was worth $502m.[28]

Glazer targeted Manchester United for similar treatment. He wanted to buy the club off its current shareholders and then repeat the recipe that had worked at the Bucs: raise revenue and reduce costs. If he had his way, tickets to the most important matches—the European-wide Champions League—would increase in price by 25% in the first year. Overall, revenue from ticket sales would rise by 61% over the first five years he was in charge. Spending on buying new players would be tightly capped.[29] Manchester United supporters were not pleased, and that is putting it mildly. They gatecrashed a dinner being hosted by one of the investment banks working for Glazer.[30] His public relations firm was targeted by a dirty tricks campaign, with hoax callers ordering pizzas, taxis, and even a dumpster, to be delivered to their offices.[31] A director who had recently sold Manchester United shares had his home and cars vandalized.[32] An effigy of Glazer was set alight outside the team's stadium.[33]

For Glazer, one strategy would have been to acquire a moderately large ownership stake, put pressure on the board to adopt his plan, and then sit back and watch his shares increase in value. However, he wanted to buy the whole firm. His first step was to approach Manchester United's board about a possible offer for the firm, just as InBev approached Anheuser-Busch's board in Chapter 11.[34] Manchester United secretly despatched its CEO to meet Glazer's sons in Tampa, just as Anheuser-Busch had secretly despatched its CEO to meet InBev's representatives in the same city.[35] Manchester United rejected Glazer's initial approach, just as Anheuser-Busch had rejected InBev's initial one.[36] The board did not even grant Glazer's request to be allowed to inspect Manchester United's accounts.[37]

Glazer was not the type to give up quietly. This, after all, was a man who fought a 15-year battle with his four older sisters over their mother's estate.[38] Rather than going away and licking his wounds, he used the Manchester United shares he had already acquired to vote against the three directors standing for reelection at the annual meeting held three weeks after the board rejected his proposal. All were defeated. In an irony that was surely not lost on Manchester United supporters, one of the rejected directors was the one whose cars had been vandalized after selling shares to Glazer. The investment bank, law firm, and public relations firm helping Glazer with his takeover bid resigned within hours of the meeting, apparently in protest at his behavior.[39]

Another free-rider problem

In February 2005, three months after roughing up the board, Glazer returned with a formal takeover proposal.[40] This time the board granted him access to Manchester United's accounts, but it still did not recommend this proposal to shareholders.[41] As we saw in Chapter 11, after Anheuser-Busch's board rejected InBev's bid, InBev returned with a revised bid so high that the target's board had little choice other than to recommend it to shareholders. Glazer could have tried this tactic as well, but perhaps he did not want to pay that much. It would certainly have been out of character. He opted instead for a far more hostile response, bypassing the board altogether and going straight to shareholders. Glazer was trying to buy enough shares so that he could take control of the firm without the board's support. However, for such a tactic to be successful, it needed to overcome a potentially debilitating free-rider problem.

At first glance, the approach to follow seems simple enough. Firms almost always have too many shareholders for the raider to go to each one and bargain individually. (That is why the board has a role as shareholders' representative.) Instead, the raider needs to set a price and offer it to many shareholders at once. Glazer could have done this by making what is known as a tender offer to Manchester United's shareholders. This involves offering to buy all of the firm's shares that are not already owned by the raider for a fixed price. The higher the raider sets the offer price, the more likely he is to be able to buy the shares he needs to take control. If, like Glazer presumably did, the raider thinks he can run the firm more profitably than the current management, then there must be a price that is high enough to persuade shareholders to sell and low enough for the takeover to be profitable. If Glazer offered such a price and shareholders accepted it, then both sides would be better off compared to the situation where the current management stayed in place.

Unfortunately, it does not work like this. To understand how it actually works, and why it works this way, we need to step into the shoes of one of Manchester United's smaller shareholders. This shareholder owns such a small number of shares that we can behave as though our decision to accept or reject Glazer's hypothetical offer has no effect on whether the takeover bid succeeds or fails. If too few shareholders are going to tender their shares for him to win control, then our hold-or-sell decision will not change that. If enough shareholders are going to tender, then we can hold onto our shares without jeopardizing the takeover. It is this second possibility that causes the free-rider problem. As long as Glazer's offer price is less than what we think Manchester United shares will be worth if he gains control then we should hold onto our shares. Why sell them to Glazer for the offer price if we think they will be worth more than that under his management? Instead, we let everyone else sell their shares. We let Glazer take control and then we sit back and watch our shares increase in value under Glazer's more disciplined management. In short, we free-ride.

The reason the free-rider problem is a problem is that all small shareholders behave this way. Everyone is sitting back trying to free-ride off the actions of other shareholders. As a result, none of these shareholders actually sell their shares to Glazer. With nobody selling their shares, the takeover bid fails. Shareholders would be better off if they could agree to all sell their shares at the offer price. However, because each individual shareholder has an incentive to hold onto their shares as long as everyone else is selling, any agreement would unravel. The only way that a raider like Glazer could use a tender offer to buy enough shares to win control of the target firm would be to set the offer price at or above the value the shares would have under his improved management. Of course, that would mean it is the target firm's shareholders who receive the benefits of the improved management; the raider would receive nothing.[42]

Free-riding is possible during a tender offer only because shareholders who want to hold onto their shares are able to do so and still receive the benefits of any improvement in the target firm's management. This is not possible if the takeover bid goes to a shareholder vote instead. A shareholder who wants to hold onto their shares can vote against the takeover. However, if the majority of shareholders want to sell the firm to the raider, then all shareholders—even those who voted against the takeover—must sell their shares. This allows a raider to offer a lower price and keep some of the gains from the improved management for himself. It is probably why, in Chapter 11, InBev approached Anheuser-Busch's board with its unsolicited takeover offer rather than going directly to shareholders. It is also probably why Glazer approached Manchester United's board first.

Glazer did not go away when Manchester United's board turned him down. Not for long anyway. When he came back, he deployed many of the plays in the raiders' playbook, allowing Glazer to overcome the free-rider problem and ultimately take control of Manchester United—despite the board's opposition. His acquisition of Manchester United is a masterclass on how it is done.

Exploiting the anonymity of the market

Some of a raider's work is done *before* launching a tender offer, starting with under-the-radar purchases of the target firm's shares. Glazer had been able to acquire a 2.9% stake this way, paying approximately £1.20 per share, before the press reported his involvement.[43] By purchasing shares secretly—before the market realizes that a takeover bid is underway—the raider is able to buy shares from investors who are unaware that their shares could ultimately be worth much more than the current share price. If the takeover succeeds, then all the gains from shares bought secretly go to the raider. Even if the free-rider problem means that the raider makes no profit on the shares purchased by the tender offer, the raider's secret share purchases may be profitable enough for the takeover bid to be worth undertaking.[44]

The effectiveness of this approach is limited by the disclosure rules in place in most developed financial markets. For example, in the U.S., investors must reveal publicly when they have acquired a 5% ownership stake. They actually have ten days to make the announcement, which allows them to increase their stake further before the announcement is made. After that initial announcement is made, they have to report any changes of 1% or more.[45] In the United Kingdom, disclosure is required when a stake reaches 3%, and each additional 1% after that, which might explain why Glazer had stopped building his stake when it reached 2.9%.[46] If the press had not got wind of who was buying shares, his secret share purchases would have gone undetected.

As soon as investors know about a raider's initial stake, they will factor that information into the price they demand when selling their shares. Once a well-known raider acquires a stake in a firm, investors will anticipate a future takeover bid and the share price will rise in anticipation of the higher price that the raider will have to pay when he eventually launches a tender offer for the target's shares. If the price did not increase immediately, none of the target's shareholders would sell their shares. Instead they would wait to receive a higher price in the future. As the raider's stake grows, so does the market's assessment of the likelihood of a takeover, and so does the share price. This makes it more expensive for the raider to build up his stake over time.[47] Glazer may have been able to buy his initial stake for £1.20 per share, but six months later he was paying £1.96; a year after that he was paying £2.85. Paying such high prices was the only way he could build his stake, which reached 28% by the end of 2004.[48]

A raider will want to make a takeover as profitable as possible, so we should expect him to cloak his purchases in secrecy to the full extent possible. Unconfirmed press reports at the time Glazer was trying to acquire Manchester United suggested that he tried to do exactly this by using investment bank Credit Suisse First Boston to buy shares in place of his usual choice, JP Morgan.[49] That is just one way to do it. A very recent development is that a firm contemplating launching a takeover teams up with a hedge fund. The hedge fund buys a large (non-controlling) ownership stake in the target firm and then shares in the gains with the acquiring firm if the takeover is completed. This exploits the hedge fund's expertise in acquiring shares secretly and avoids tipping off investors that a full takeover bid is underway.[50]

Using large shareholders' size against them

Shareholders who sell their shares before they realize a takeover attempt is underway cannot capture any of the value gains resulting from a successful takeover. How could they? Those shareholders did not even know that there were any gains available. However, once investors know that a takeover attempt is underway, they know what is at stake. Shareholders who are able to free-ride can capture those gains for themselves. However, not all informed investors are able to free-ride. In particular, large shareholders cannot free-ride to anything like the same extent as small shareholders because a raider can use large shareholders' size against them.

Most U.S. corporations have at least one large shareholder amongst their owners. One study reports that 89% of the firms that make up the S&P 500 stock index have at least one shareholder that owns 5% or more of the firm's shares. At a typical firm in the index, the shareholders with large blocks of shares jointly own 12% of the firm's shares. When smaller firms are included in the sample, shareholders with large blocks of shares jointly own 37% of the shares of a typical firm.[51] The ownership of Manchester United was even more concentrated: when Glazer was getting ready to launch his tender offer, two Irishmen owned 29% of the firm's shares through their company Cubic Expression, a Scottish mining magnate owned 6.5%, and Glazer owned 28%.[52]

The shareholder most important to Glazer was Cubic Expression. Glazer needed to acquire 75% of Manchester United's shares because he needed that many shares to win some shareholder votes that were crucial to his plans. If Cubic did not sell its shares, his stake could not get above 71% and the bid would fail. On the other hand, if Cubic sold its shares to Glazer, he would own 57% of Manchester United; he would have to buy only another 18% to get the 75% stake that he sought. Both Glazer and Cubic knew that the takeover would definitely fail if Cubic did not sell its shares and that it would almost certainly succeed if Cubic did agree to sell.

Something similar will happen at any target firm with large shareholders. The effect of a large shareholder's decision to sell may not be as strong as it was at Manchester United. It may not convert certain failure into almost certain success. However, a hostile takeover attempt will be much more likely to succeed if the large shareholder sells its stake than if it does not. This stops a large shareholder from free-riding in the way that a small shareholder is able to free-ride once a tender offer is made. Small shareholders realize that their individual decisions have almost no effect on the outcome of the bid, allowing them to hold onto their shares and receive the full benefits from the improved management. A raider who wants their shares will have to make them a better offer than that before they will sell their shares. However, a large shareholder has a much more difficult problem to solve. It realizes that its decision whether or not to sell shares has the potential to affect the outcome. A large shareholder considering holding onto its shares needs to weigh the potential payoff following a successful takeover against the increased likelihood that the takeover attempt will fail.

The raider and large shareholder are engaged in another example of the bargaining games we met in Chapter 2. For example, if Cubic and Glazer could agree on a price, then Cubic would receive more for its shares than they would be worth if the takeover bid failed. Glazer would make a profit on the shares he bought from Cubic, as well as raising the value of the shares he had already acquired from other shareholders. The price that they negotiated would determine how this surplus would be shared by the two parties; the higher the agreed purchase price, the greater the gain to Cubic and the smaller the gain to Glazer.

Biting the bullet: Tender offers may be unavoidable

Establishing a toehold using secret share purchases and bargaining with large shareholders is common. Half of the initial bidders in hostile takeovers involving public U.S. targets during 1973–2002 had some sort of toehold at the time of the initial control bid; on average, these bidders owned 12% of the target's shares at the time they launched their takeover bids. The larger the toehold, the higher the probability of winning the takeover battle.[53]

It took Glazer two attempts, but he was able to agree terms with Cubic in May 2005.[54] This gave him a 57% stake, enough for a majority on every shareholder vote. However, Glazer actually needed a 75% majority for some crucial votes. Even after the purchase of Cubic's shares and large stakes owned by the Scottish mining magnate and other investors, Glazer was still able to acquire just 72% of Manchester United's shares. When a raider has not been able to acquire a controlling ownership stake from some combination of open-market share purchases and direct negotiations with large shareholders, he will often try to buy the remaining shares needed from shareholders via a tender offer. That is what Glazer did in May 2005 when he launched a tender offer to buy all of the Manchester United shares that he did not already own at a price of £3.00 per share.[55]

The free-rider problem we met above still applies even if the tender offer is launched after the raider has acquired a substantial, but non-controlling, stake. Unless the raider has access to the hostile-takeover playbook, it will have to set the price in its tender offer equal to the expected post-takeover value per share, or even higher. That is, it will not make any money on the shares bought as part of the tender offer. Still, the profit from the shares bought secretly and from large shareholders might make the takeover sufficiently profitable for the raider to be willing to participate. This makes the threat of a hostile takeover credible in many cases, even when there is a free-rider problem to overcome. However, if the raider cannot buy enough shares secretly, or if the large shareholders are not large enough, then these pre-tender purchases may not be profitable enough to motivate the raider to take part.

What a successful raider needs is a set of tools to make the tender-offer stage of a takeover profitable as well. The next three sections show three of them. They each reduce the benefits from free-riding by making it possible for the raider to avoid sharing (too many of) the benefits of his improved management with hold-out shareholders. We will start by considering each of the approaches and how they reduce the sharing. Then, once we have looked at all three, we will take a look at how they reduce free-riding and allow the raider to make a profit even on the shares purchased as part of the tender offer.

Threatening dilution

Raiders can extract money from a firm at the expense of hold-out shareholders using a process known as dilution. The value of the private benefits that come from controlling a firm can be substantial, especially in countries with relatively weak laws protecting minority shareholders. Even in the U.S., the private benefits of control have been estimated to be worth approximately 4% of the market value of a firm's equity. Estimates for the United Kingdom are similar.[56]

Any Manchester United shareholder who was worried about dilution had only to look at events that took place at firms that Glazer controlled in the 1990s. In 1996, Glazer owned 73% of the restaurant operator Houlihan's Restaurant Group.[57] Shortly after he acquired the Tampa Bay Buccaneers, Houlihan's agreed to pay the team $10m over a five-year period for the naming rights to the team's Tampa stadium.[58] The restaurant chain had no outlets around Tampa and just two in Florida at the time, but still its board approved the expenditure.[59] Some investors complained that the firm had overpaid for the naming rights and that Glazer was using these transactions to benefit himself at the expense of other shareholders, partly to help him raise the cash he needed to pay for the Bucs.[60] What if they were correct? For each $100 that Houlihan's overpaid for the stadium naming rights, Glazer's 73% ownership stake meant that he would be $73 worse off; non-Glazer shareholders' collective stake of 27% meant that they would be $27 worse off. However, Glazer would gain the full $100 due to his 100% ownership stake in the Bucs. The result? Glazer would have made a gain of $27 for each $100 overpaid. It would have come straight out of the pockets of the Houlihan's shareholders whose last name was not Glazer.

There was more disquiet the following year, this time at Zapata, the oil-drilling company set up by George H. W. Bush in the 1950s.[61] (Yes, *that* George H. W. Bush.) Glazer had built up a 35% stake and he used the enormous power it gave him to install himself as board chairman and one of his sons as CEO.[62] The pair set about transforming Zapata into a food-services business by acquiring firms that Glazer just happened to control.[63] For example, in May 1996, Zapata tried to buy Houlihan's for $80m. Some

Zapata shareholders sued and the firm abandoned the bid only after an unfavorable court ruling.[64] However, the transaction with perhaps the most potential for transfers in wealth occurred a few months earlier, when Zapata bought Glazer's 31% stake in Envirodyne Industries, a firm that made hot dog and sausage casings.[65]

Some Zapata shareholders alleged that the firm was overpaying for what it was buying.[66] We can ask the same question as before: what if the disgruntled shareholders were correct and Glazer was using his influence to make Zapata overpay for both acquisitions? Start with Zapata's attempted acquisition of Houlihan's. Remember, Glazer owned 73% of Houlihan's and 35% of Zapata. If Zapata had overpaid by $100, Glazer would have received $73 overpayment for his Houlihan's shares, but paid only $35 too much via his partial ownership of Zapata. The transfer from Zapata's non-Glazer shareholders to Glazer himself would have been $38 for each $100 of overpayment. The same thing would have happened if Zapata had paid too much for Glazer's stake in the sausage-casing maker. For each $100 Zapata overpaid, Glazer would have received all $100 thanks to his 100% ownership of the acquired Envirodyne shares, but he would have overpaid only $35 via his partial ownership of Zapata. That would have been a $65 transfer from Zapata's non-Glazer shareholders to Glazer himself for each $100 overpaid.

The point of mentioning these examples is not to claim that Glazer was actually transferring wealth in the way that the disgruntled shareholders alleged. Rather it is to illustrate what is possible if a shareholder owns less than 100% of a firm but effectively makes all the firm's important decisions. Even if Glazer was not doing what the shareholders alleged, and there is no hard evidence that he was, he would have been able to do it if he wanted to. Just the *ability* to do something similar can reduce the severity of the free-rider problem.

Could Glazer have done something similar at Manchester United if he had been unable to acquire all of the firm's shares? Possibly. After all, the three transactions from the 1990s illustrate the approach required: overpay from a firm where the ownership stake is relatively low and over-receive at a firm where it is relatively high. The Glazer family denied any such plans shortly after the takeover was complete.[67] However, prior to the takeover, speculation was rife that the Glazer family might sell Manchester United's main stadium, Old Trafford, or its training complex to a party affiliated with the Glazers and then rent it back.[68] If the Glazer-affiliated firms paid a knocked-down price and charged above-market rent, then Manchester United's non-Glazer shareholders would be losing out in exactly the same way the disgruntled Zapata shareholders alleged they lost out in the 1990s. The sums involved would not have been trivial either: at the time of the Manchester United takeover, Old Trafford was reported to be worth £200m.[69]

There are practical and legal constraints on a raider's ability to carry out dilution. First, the raider needs to persuade the board of the target firm to approve the transaction generating the transfer of wealth. Dilution is only ever profitable when the raider owns less than 100% of the target firm's shares, so the directors on that firm's board will have a fiduciary duty to all shareholders, not just the raider. Directors may take some persuading, either because they are not willing to dilute other shareholders' shares or because they are not willing to approve a fair transaction that might nevertheless be alleged to be part of a scheme to dilute other shareholders.

Glazer's problems in the 1990s illustrate the difficulties that uncooperative directors can cause. Press reports at the time described a dispute between Glazer and two of Zapata's independent directors, which followed the latter questioning the plan to buy Glazer's Envirodyne stake. The two directors resigned from the board a few weeks later; their replacements had close business ties to Glazer.[70] A third director—there were only four non-Glazers on the board—resigned six months later, alleging that Zapata was only interested in acquisitions that would enrich Glazer.[71] He launched legal action, reaching a confidential settlement with the firm a few months before the case was due to go to trial.[72]

Even if directors do not get in the way, a firm's shareholders can challenge transactions in the courts. However, legal action is expensive, so there is some degree of dilution that will not be challenged by shareholders. For example, despite the shareholder anger at Zapata, the legal action launched by some shareholders died out quietly before it reached court.[73] Even if legal action is pursued, the claimants need to prove that transactions involving raider-affiliated firms are at unfair prices. The problem is that nobody really knows what a fair price for these transactions is. We do not know if Houlihan's paid a fair price for the stadium naming rights, if Zapata paid a fair price for Glazer's Envirodyne stake, or if Zapata's planned acquisition of Houlihan's was fair. This uncertainty gives a raider some "wiggle room" to extract some value from the firm without sharing it with hold-out shareholders.[74]

Shifting the debt burden

If raiders structure the funding arrangements of takeovers very carefully, they can achieve the same outcome as dilution without risking a breach of their fiduciary duty to the target firms' minority shareholders. Glazer adopted such a structure when he launched his tender offer for the Manchester United shares that he did not already own.

The tender offer was a complicated transaction, involving a sequence of holding companies arranged like Russian nesting dolls, with Glazer sitting in the middle, surrounded by layer upon layer of debt. For the time being we will focus on just one of these holding companies, Red Football Ltd, which Glazer set up solely for the purpose of acquiring Manchester United. ("Red" because the Manchester United team's nickname is "The Red Devils.") Red Football was the company offering to buy Manchester United shares at a price of £3.00 each. It started with capital of £547m, but had set up a loan facility that it used to borrow an additional £265m from various investment banks.[75]

Glazer wanted to remove Manchester United from the list of firms with shares that trade on the London Stock Exchange, but such a dramatic change needed to be approved by 75% of the firm's shareholders.[76] Within a few days, Red Football had acquired enough shares to force the change through. It meant that any shareholders who did not sell their shares to Red Football during the tender offer would in the future only be able to trade them privately. By making it much more difficult for shareholders to convert their shares into cash, the change made holding onto Manchester United shares just that little bit less attractive. A few more hold-out shareholders would choose to hold out no longer.

Reaching the 75% threshold gave Glazer the option to do something else, something that would have been very effective if he had been unable to acquire all of Manchester United's shares. It gave him the option to merge Manchester United into Red Football. Like any merger in the United Kingdom, 75% of the shareholders of each affected firm would have had to approve the change for it to go ahead.[77] However, Glazer owned more than 75% of the shares at Manchester United, and he already owned 100% of the shares at Red Football, so the two votes would have been formalities.

As in any merger, the merging firms—Manchester United and Red Football in this case—would have pooled their assets and their liabilities. Manchester United would have contributed its players, sponsorship deals, stadium, and all its other assets. In return, the hold-out shareholders would have received newly printed shares in Red Football. Manchester United did not have any debt to contribute, so the merged firm would "just" have Red Football's debt to worry about. All £265m of it. After the merger had been completed, the merged firm would have had assets comprising Manchester United's players, sponsorship deals, stadium, and everything else that Manchester United owned. It would have had debt of £265m and shares owned by Glazer and any Manchester United hold-out shareholders. The merged firm would effectively have been the same old Manchester United, but with £265m of debt that was not there before the merger.

Figure 12.1 attempts to make sense of what is a complex transaction. It glosses over many of the more intricate details, but the essence of what would happen can be found in the three corporate cakes. The two cake slices on the left show what Manchester United would have looked like after the tender offer was completed and before a merger between Manchester United and Red Football. The first one shows Manchester United. There is

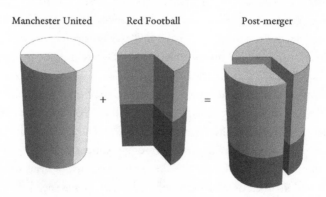

FIGURE 12.1 A debt-financed takeover

no debt slice; it is all equity, with the portion in gray belonging to hold-out shareholders and the portion in white belonging to Red Football. The second cake shows Red Football. It has a debt slice, representing the £265m that it borrowed and that it had to repay before Red Football's own shareholders (that is, Glazer) would be able to eat any of the Manchester United cake. After the merger, Manchester United would have looked like the right-hand cake. Now, thanks to that merger, the debt layer has spread to the entire cake: the debt layer attached to the Red Football portion has fallen, but one has now appeared on the non-Glazer portion. The Manchester United shareholders who held onto their shares would have ended up being responsible for repaying some of the loans Glazer had taken out to buy the rest of the shares!

It all seems unfair on the hold-out shareholders, but it is important to remember that a super-majority of the two firms' shareholders would have agreed to the merger, so it would have all been above board. However, it would have been an extremely unattractive arrangement for any Manchester United shareholders who did not sell their shares to Red Football.

The implicit threat of such a merger serves a useful purpose for a raider. It severely limits shareholders' ability to free-ride on the changes the raider plans to introduce at the target firm, and in doing so it makes the raid profitable. Before shareholders protest too much about merger-induced transfers of debt, they should remember that if the value generated by the raider's improved management of the target is large enough, then the target's shareholders may still be better off even after they allow for the increased debt burden they would have to bear.

Back-end squeeze-outs

Takeovers are complicated by the fact that nobody actually knows what the target firm will be worth under the raider's management. Target shareholders considering free-riding will each have different estimates of how much their shares would be worth if they held onto them. This means that target shareholders will each have their own price at which they are willing to sell their shares. Some will be pessimistic about the new management, and will be willing to sell cheaply. Others will be much more optimistic, and will refuse to sell unless the offer price is much higher. Then, of course, there are the stubborn shareholders who refuse to sell at practically any price. A raider may have to pay an extremely high price to persuade the last (most stubborn) shareholder to sell. Other, less stubborn, shareholders might anticipate this and hold on to receive this higher price as well. The end result is the raider having to pay a prohibitively high price to gain control of the firm.

So-called squeeze-out rights allow a raider to force hold-out shareholders to sell their shares once the raider's stake in the target firm has reached a (usually very high) threshold. They have to sell their shares at the price of the tender offer, so lose the ability to hold on for a better payout. In the United Kingdom, an acquirer can force hold-out shareholders to sell if it has been able to buy at least 90% of the shares subject to the tender offer.[78] When Red Football launched its tender offer in May 2005, it was tendering to buy the 28% of Manchester United's shares that it did not already own. It needed to buy 90% of this amount, or 25% of all of Manchester United's shares, to win the right to squeeze out stubborn shareholders. Add that to the 72% stake that Glazer already owned, and we get Glazer's target: a 97% stake.[79] He reached this target seven weeks after launching the tender offer.[80]

The mechanism in the U.S. is slightly different from the one Glazer used to squeeze out Manchester United's hold-out shareholders. However, the limitations on free-riding are similar. Here raiders frequently follow an approach with the rather unfortunate name "back-end squeeze-out." This starts with a tender offer, just like Glazer used to acquire Manchester United, but it is followed by a merger between the target firm and a new firm set up especially for the purpose by the raider. The terms of the merger will be the same as the tender offer but, unlike the tender offer that got the ball rolling, the majority rules in the back-end merger stage. This means that even shareholders who vote against the merger have to sell their shares: there is no more free-riding.[81] Of course, like any merger, the boards of both firms have to agree to the merger terms, so a back-end squeeze-out works only if the raider is able to buy enough shares through the tender offer to get control of the target firm's board.

Reducing the free-rider problem

The three approaches we have just seen deliver similar benefits to the raider, but do so in different ways. In each case, hold-out shareholders miss out on some of any increase in the target firm's value that occurs under the raider's management. With dilution, they miss out when the raider transfers some of the firm's wealth to firms with which it is affiliated. With debt-financed acquisitions, they miss out when they assume responsibility for some of the debt the raider incurred to carry out the takeover. With squeeze-outs, they miss out when they are forced to sell their shares to the raider at the tender price.

In each case, the severity of the free-rider problem is reduced.[82] We see why by stepping into the shoes of a Manchester United shareholder who was considering selling their shares to Glazer as part of the tender offer. If we had gone ahead and sold our shares to Red Football, we would have received £3.00 per share. On the other hand, if we had held onto the shares, we would have received the benefits of the more disciplined management that Glazer brought to the firm. That is how we free-ride. However, if we had thought about it, we would have realized that holding onto our shares would have some drawbacks.

First, we might be worried that Glazer would do to us what some Zapata shareholders alleged he did to them in the 1990s. Those worries would only be worsened by speculation that the Glazer family planned to sell Manchester United's main stadium to a party affiliated with the Glazers and then rent it back to the club.[83] Second, there is all the debt that we will have to share responsibility for. At the time of the tender offer, Manchester United had approximately 264m shares, so the merger with Red Football would burden Manchester United with new debt of approximately £1.00 per share. Third, if Glazer could increase his stake to 97% then we would not even get to hold onto our shares: we would have to sell them for £3.00 each like everyone else.

Should we sell our shares as part of the tender offer? If we do, we get a certain payoff equal to the offer price. Previously we have argued that if we wait then we will get the value of one share under Glazer's management, so that Glazer would have to offer to pay at least this much in order to persuade us to sell our shares. Of course, then he could not make a profit, so his motivation for the takeover would disappear. The arithmetic changes when dilution, debt-financing, and squeeze-outs are possible. Now, we should sell Glazer our shares as long as his offer price is greater than what they would be worth to us if we held on to them *and* he diluted the value of Manchester United, transferred debt onto the firm, and was able to enforce a squeeze-out. This drives a wedge between on the one hand what Glazer has to pay us in order to get hold of our shares and on the other hand what the shares will be worth to him under his management. That wedge is the source of Glazer's profit.

The three tactics we have just seen can potentially reduce the consequences of the free-rider problem, even if they cannot eliminate it altogether. Although dilution is illegal, all that is needed to reduce the severity of the free-rider problem is the *threat* of dilution. The beauty of this tactic is that it does not actually have to be carried out to reduce the free-rider problem. All that is needed is that shareholders think the raider might carry it out, so having a reputation for taking no prisoners helps. It probably helped Glazer at Manchester United. This, after all, was a man who left a trail of disgruntled shareholders, tenants, and team supporters in his wake during a business career that spanned seven decades.[84] A U.S. federal judge once described him as "a snake in sheep's clothing."[85] He was even sued by his personal attorney.[86] Many shareholders considering whether or not to sell their Manchester United shares to Glazer would have anticipated regretting a decision to hold onto them. Such anticipation would have made them willing to sell their shares at a price low enough for Glazer to make a profit from the takeover.

Debt financing is very powerful when it is available. However, many U.S. states have antitakeover laws that effectively prevent raiders merging the target firm with one of their own firms for several years after a takeover is completed, unless the target firm's board agreed to the takeover. For example, in Delaware, raiders must wait three years before they can carry out the required merger, unless the target firm's board gave its approval before the raider's stake reached 15%.[87] Squeeze-outs are perhaps the most effective way to reduce the severity of the free-rider problem, but their effectiveness is limited by the need to acquire a large stake in order to enforce the squeeze-out.

Putting the pieces together

The offensive playbook is now complete. A free-rider problem would award all the takeover gains to a target firm's current shareholders if not for the battery of offensive tactics in this playbook. What are the plays? Start with secret share purchases, the more the better. Once the market realizes that a takeover bid is underway, bargain with large shareholders. Use their size as a weapon against them and make sure they surrender some of the takeover gains. Then bite the bullet and launch a tender offer, financed by as much debt as possible. Keep an even tighter lid on the offer price needed for a successful bid by making sure shareholders are aware of the possibility of some post-takeover dilution. Mop up the stragglers with a back-end squeeze out.

It looks like the odds are stacked against a target firm's shareholders. Certainly, the target firm's shareholders lose out when these strategies are used by raiders. However, there are two things we need to be aware of before we get too critical. First, shareholders still benefit from the merger provided the amount of debt that can be shifted onto the target firm's assets is not so large that the raider can bully shareholders into selling their shares for less than they would be worth under the target firm's current management. All that is happening is that target shareholders are having to share more of the takeover benefits with the raider. What is wrong with that? The raider is the one who is taking on all the risk. It is the raider who is going to implement the changes in business strategy. Target shareholders had their chance to ensure the firm was managed well. If the takeover gain is large, it is because they failed to ensure the firm was being managed well.

There is a second, more subtle, reason why shareholders should not be too upset by the tactics described in this chapter. In fact, they should be grateful that they exist, because without them the free-rider problem would prevent raiders from profiting from hostile takeovers. If raiders could not make a profit from hostile takeovers, they would not launch them in the first place. If executives thought there was no chance of a hostile takeover being launched, then the discipline provided by the market for corporate control would disappear because the threat of a hostile takeover would be completely empty. Shareholders benefit from that discipline. Missing out on capturing all the takeover gains for themselves is the price they have to pay for that discipline to be effective.

A familiar benefit of debt

The tactics we have seen in this chapter work by allowing a raider to capture more of the benefits of a takeover, so that he does not need to share them with any of the target firm's shareholders who try to hold onto their shares. We have not said much about where these benefits come from, but we rectify that situation now.

The story so far is that the corporate decision-makers at sports teams have two conflicting interests: the team's on-field performance and the firm's financial performance.

Glazer was going to fix that at Manchester United because he viewed it as a business. However, Glazer was 76 years old when he acquired Manchester United. His sons were going to play the dominant role of overseeing the business and they claimed to be avid Manchester United fans, so any improvement in its financial performance might be temporary.[88] Would Glazer's sons be seduced by the glory of competition and start overspending? The simple answer is that they could not afford to let this happen. As we know from Chapter 8, debt ties the hands of firms' management. Firms with a lot of debt—and the new Manchester United had a great deal of debt—have no choice but to focus on maximizing their financial performance.

Manchester United fans realized this. They were so angry that when three of Glazer's sons arrived in the city to see what they had bought, they ended up barricaded in the team's stadium and had to flee hidden in the back of a police van.[89] Even after Manchester United won the English Premier League competition in three out of the next four years, Glazer was still hated in Manchester.[90] The repeated complaint from fans was that the club was burdened with too much debt.

To fully understand the role of debt at Glazer's Manchester United, we need to understand one more layer of the Russian nesting doll that had Glazer at its core. We have already seen the outer layer. That was Red Football, the company set up to hold Glazer's Manchester United shares. We have also seen how Red Football borrowed £265m to help finance its tender offer. However, we have not seen where the £547m that Glazer contributed came from. To find out, we need to take away that outer layer of the doll. Inside, we find another holding company set up by Glazer, this one called Red Football Joint Venture Limited. This was the source of the £547m contribution. It turned out that only £272m of this had come from the Glazers; the remaining £275m had been borrowed from various hedge funds, in the form of so-called payment-in-kind (PIK) loans. If Red Football Joint Venture could not repay the PIK debts, then those hedge funds could seize Red Football Joint Venture's assets. Those assets were the shares of Red Football, so that the hedge funds would ultimately have ended up owning Manchester United.[91]

The PIK loans had no effect on the free-rider problem, because they would not have been transferred to the new Manchester United if the old Manchester United merged with Red Football. Even though any shareholders who had refused to sell their shares would have been responsible for some of the £265m of Red Football's debt, they would *not* have been responsible for any of the £275m of PIK loans. Those loans would have remained Glazer's responsibility.

However, the PIK loans did affect Glazer's incentives when running Manchester United, and in exactly the way we would expect after reading Chapter 8. Manchester United had to generate enough profits to service the £265m that Red Football—the outer shell of the doll—had borrowed. However, if Glazer was going to get anything out of the takeover, Manchester United would have to generate enough profits to also service the £275m that Red Football Joint Venture—the next shell of the doll—had borrowed. That is a lot of debt to service.

In the first four years after Glazer's takeover, Manchester United paid out £167m in cash to investors in the form of interest on Red Football's loans. Would Manchester United have paid out this much cash without the commitment provided by debt? The old Manchester United probably would not have: in the last four years before the takeover, it paid out just £27m to investors, mainly in the form of dividends to shareholders. There was only one way Glazer could meet the demands of the interest payments, and that was to make sure Manchester United was making money. It seemed to be happening, because Manchester United's match-day revenue in the first four years after the takeover was 58% higher than it had been in the last four years before the takeover. Media revenue was up 48% and commercial revenue was up 68%. It received a windfall of £80m from selling a star player in 2009. Otherwise, net spending on players carried on much as usual: £106m in the first four years after the takeover, compared with £92m in the four years before the takeover.[92] Spending on porridge was down.

The elephant in the room

For any Manchester United fans who have made it this far, well done. I know it has been difficult. It might be a good idea to skip ahead to Chapter 13 now, because it is time to mention the disastrous 2013/14 season. That was the first season after the retirement of Manchester United's long-serving team manager, Sir Alex Ferguson. Manchester United finished seventh in the English Premier League competition, its worst ever result. That meant it did not qualify for the next season's prestigious, and lucrative, European-wide Champions League competition. It was a shambles.

Manchester United supporters blamed underinvestment in players, caused by the debt that the club was carrying thanks to Glazer's takeover. However, was it really a case of the Glazer chickens coming home to roost? I am going to take my life in my hands and suggest an alternative explanation, based on what we saw in Chapter 7 about the incentives generated by career concerns. Ferguson repeatedly said that he had been given enough money to spend on players, and Manchester United spent freely in the two seasons after he retired.[93] If we take Ferguson at his word, he could have invested in new players. However, Ferguson's concern would not have been the financial costs of recruiting new players. His job was to get the best on-field performance possible, and—in the short term—bringing in new players might have harmed that on-field performance. They may well have been a great long-term investment, but new, probably young and possibly inexperienced, players would need to adapt to playing at a new club. The existing players would have to adapt their game to the new arrivals. Although squad renewal may have been good in the long term, Ferguson knew that he was not going to be around in the long term. He knew he was retiring soon, so investing in the playing squad would not have been as important to him as it had been in previous years. A manager with a short-term focus will be tempted to not invest in renewal: do not worry about the future, just get the very best result possible in the current season. Go out on top. Is this a plausible explanation for what happened at Manchester United? I think it is. Before we dismiss it, we should think about this question: if Ferguson had been ten years younger, if he was hoping to work at Manchester United for another decade, would he have managed the squad differently in those final few years?

There is one other lesson to take from that disastrous season. Ferguson's (hand-picked) replacement as team manager was fired before the season was over.[94] Without the pressure generated by high debt levels, it would have been much easier for Manchester United's board to avoid admitting that it had made a mistake in hiring him. The board could have kept the new manager for a season or two and then quietly eased him out. Manchester United's board had no such luxury in 2014. All that debt meant that it had to act, and it did.

We have now seen the tactics raiders use to overcome the free-rider problem that complicates hostile tender offers. However, this is just half the story. On average, the final offer price in a hostile takeover is 61% higher than the target's share price two months before a takeover bid is launched.[95] The only way offer prices can be kept this high on average is if target firms have defensive tactics that they can use to counteract the offensive tactics we have just seen. Manchester United's board did not deploy such tactics effectively, but other firms have done so. With willpower, and the defensive playbook revealed in the next chapter, target firms can give even the most experienced hostile raiders pause for thought.

I don't think I've ever seen anything this blatant.[1]

CARL ICAHN (2010)

13 Fighting back
DEFENSIVE TACTICS IN HOSTILE TAKEOVERS

NOWADAYS LIONS GATE Entertainment Corp. is known as the maker of the hit television series *Mad Men* and the *Hunger Games* movie franchise. Back in 2009, it was a small studio trying to become a big one, racking up a run of poor financial performances in the process. Shareholders lost patience early that year when they learnt that the firm had made a loss four times larger than analysts expected: investors fled and the share price fell 27% in a single day. Waiting, ready to pounce, was the old warhorse Carl Icahn, a veteran of three decades' worth of hostile takeover attempts.

Icahn seemed to be in an extremely strong position to take control of Lions Gate. He had already built up a 9.2% toehold in the firm before declaring his intentions. Several investors owned large stakes in the firm, creating the opportunity for him to buy shares from shareholders who were too big to free-ride on his efforts. One of them was his former protégé. Even if Icahn could not acquire the whole firm, his investment in the rival film studio Metro-Goldwyn-Mayer (MGM) might offer the possibility of some profitable post-takeover dilution.

Icahn is one of the canniest, stubbornest, and best-resourced raiders the market for corporate control has ever known. Despite this reputation, Lions Gate decided to fight back. It was a dirty fight, involving almost every tactic in the defensive playbook. There were threats to slash the value of the firm if Icahn's takeover bid succeeded. All shareholders—other than Icahn—were granted rights allowing them to buy cut-price shares in the firm. Extra shares were issued to a friendly investor, making it harder for Icahn to acquire a voting majority. Everything was geared towards making completing the takeover too expensive for even Icahn's tastes. Lions Gate was playing to win. When takeovers go hostile—and boards fight back—there is no room for the faint hearted.

An attractive target

At the end of 2008, Lions Gate Entertainment Corp. operated a film studio producing and distributing films and television programs. Although the firm began life in Vancouver, it sold its Canadian assets after it acquired the California-based independent film distributor responsible for *The Blair Witch Project*.[2] After that, the firm was effectively run out of Santa Monica. Its shares were traded on the NYSE and just 8.4% of them were owned by Canadians.[3] However, partly to receive favorable tax breaks, its corporate headquarters stayed in Vancouver.[4]

Making a movie involves spending a great deal of cash up front and waiting—and hoping—for a revenue stream several years later. Raising the cash up front can be difficult for independent studios, so Lions Gate's business plan involved acquiring smaller film producers to build up a film library that would generate the cash to fund its own productions. It seemed to work, because Lions Gate owned one of the industry's largest film and television libraries.[5] It generated $100m in free cash flow each year.[6] However, as we saw in Chapter 8, all this free cash flow can create problems for a firm's shareholders. At the operational level, the firm no longer needs to go to outside capital markets to fund its day-to-day business. Money can be allocated internally, raising the possibility that executives spend the firm's cash on projects that do not benefit shareholders, instead of paying it out as dividends. Of course, even firms with lucrative cash cows may need to raise capital externally for big projects. Lions Gate did for some of its acquisitions. However, like these firms, when Lions Gate went out to borrow, it was effectively using its cash cow as collateral. External discipline was weak.

The importance of the film library to Lions Gate's business—and the way it relaxed the discipline imposed by external capital markets—meant that the quality of corporate governance was crucial to the firm's success. There were two key executives: Jon Feltheimer, who was CEO and co-chairman of the board, and Michael Burns, whose formal title was vice-chairman of the board. This team reflected Lions Gate's business model, one a seasoned television executive, the other a deal-making former investment banker. At the end of 2008, Feltheimer and Burns had effective ownership stakes of 1.7% and 1.0%. They reported to a board that had an even smaller ownership stake: the eight independent directors on the 12-member board each had effective ownership stakes of 0.06%, on average.[7] Only half of these directors were board members at another firm and only two of them had more than one other directorship.[8] This was a board that had more to lose from a successful takeover than it had to gain.

The beginning of 2009 brought news for shareholders that suggested the potential problems associated with cash cows might be eventuating. That news came in the form of the release of Lions Gate's financial results for the last three months of 2008. Stock analysts had been expecting the firm to make a loss, but the loss was four times larger than they had anticipated.[9] Costs were out of control, the studio was making too many movies, and it was making them poorly.[10] The switch from Lions Gate's traditional low-budget predictable-profit fare to big ticket movies—made possible by the film library—had not been successful. The market had noticed: the announcement of the poor financial results was associated with a 27% drop in Lions Gate's share price.[11]

Still, the cash being generated by the film library was allowing Lions Gate to continue to expand. Just a month before the bad earnings result, Lions Gate announced it was branching out into the cable television business with the $255m acquisition of the TV Guide Network cable channel.[12] The collateral served up by the film library helped raise the money for that transaction as well. That was not all. In the next few months, Lions Gate would contemplate other large acquisitions, including Disney's Miramax unit (with a price tag of more than $650m) and even MGM (with a potential price tag of $2b).[13] Lions Gate's management dreamed big dreams.

A black knight arrives

Carl Icahn was one of Lions Gate's shareholders and he was unhappy about these plans. Icahn had been baiting CEOs since he won his first proxy fight in the late 1970s, which saw him elected to an Ohio appliance manufacturer's board of directors. Six months later the company had been sold to Electrolux of Sweden and he had almost doubled his money.[14] He was still at it three decades later, managing funds worth $2.6b, when he turned his attention to Lions Gate.[15]

The first outsiders knew about Icahn's Lions Gate stake was in early 2006, when Icahn Management LP filed the Form 13F that institutional investment managers must use to report their portfolios every three months. It revealed that the funds he managed owned a 3.9% stake in Lions Gate. Icahn slowly increased this stake during the next two and a half years, before going on a buying spree in October 2008. He doubled the size of his stake in just two weeks, taking it to 9.2% of Lions Gate's outstanding shares.[16] He had passed the magical 5% threshold that meant he had to report his increased stake to the SEC, so there could be no more secret share purchases. From then on the share price reflected the news that Icahn was building up a stake. Still Icahn continued to invest: by late February 2009, his stake had grown to 14%. At this point, Icahn entered into discussions with Lions Gate's directors about gaining board representation. He wanted to appoint individuals to fill up to five of the 12 board seats. Lions Gate refused Icahn's demand, so he continued buying up the firm's shares. By February 2010, Icahn's stake had grown to 18%.[17]

It was time to launch a hostile tender offer, like the one we saw in Chapter 12. Initially Icahn offered to pay $6.00 per share and aimed to increase his stake to just under 30%.[18] The tender offer was extended again and again, with the offer price rising as high as $7.00

and the conditions of the offer varying. By the end of June, when the tender offer finally closed, Icahn had managed to increase his stake to 34%. He went out and bought more shares the day after the tender offer closed, increasing his stake to 38%.[19] Icahn seemed poised to win control of Lions Gate. He launched a second tender offer in late July.[20] Again it was extended and the offer price raised.

Unlike Manchester United in Chapter 12, this target fought back. It fought back hard. The best way to understand the various defensive tactics employed by Lions Gate's board—and by the board of any firm that attracts unwelcome attention from a raider—is to recognize that a raider will abandon a hostile takeover once it becomes clear that continuing with the raid is not in the raider's best interests. That is, the raider compares the payoff from abandoning the bid and the payoff from continuing it, and withdraws once the first payoff is bigger than the second one. Target firms' boards try to drive off a raider by increasing the raider's payoff from abandoning the bid and decreasing his payoff from continuing it.

White knights, white squires

Icahn was not Lions Gate's only large shareholder. Another was Mark Rachesky, who had worked as Icahn's chief investment advisor during the 1990s.[21] When Rachesky left to start his own fund management operation, he left on good terms: it has even been reported that the two played tennis to determine how much Icahn would invest in Rachesky's first fund.[22] By the time Icahn started buying Lions Gate shares, Rachesky—with $1.0b under management—already owned a 9.6% stake in the firm. He had been quietly building it up since 2004. He continued to increase his stake after Icahn's arrival and, by the time Icahn's discussions with Lions Gate's board had broken down, Rachesky owned just under 20% of the firm's shares.[23] With Rachesky having such a large stake and being publicly supportive of Lions Gate's management, it was no surprise when Lions Gate nominated him for a seat on the firm's board a few months later. In return, he agreed to vote for all of the board's other nominees.[24] If Icahn put up his own candidate, he would not be getting Rachesky's 20% share of the votes.

Rachesky is an example of what is known as a white squire, an investor who acquires a large ownership stake in a firm that is the target of a hostile takeover bid and who then uses that stake to support the board's defense. He made several large investments to try and defeat Icahn, including spending an estimated $106m on shares at the same time as Icahn was building up his own stake and another $106m on new securities issued by the firm in a deal that made it harder for Icahn to win a subsequent proxy fight.[25]

White squires invest in a firm, but they do not take it over completely. That is left to the so-called white knights, who enter ongoing takeover battles by making a takeover offer of their own, but one that has the support of the target firm's board. The target firm loses its independence but, at least from the board's point of view, it is better to be acquired by a firm that is broadly supportive of the current management than to be acquired by a raider who is openly hostile.

Some simple arithmetic shows how useful a white squire can be to a board. Just by holding a big stake and taking the incumbent management team's side, a white squire can make life much harder for a raider. For example, if Icahn needed to get more than 50 shares out of every 100 to win control, then Rachesky's 20% stake meant that Icahn actually needed to get more than 50 shares out of every 80. That is a much harder task.

The appearance of two investors on different sides, who both presumably wanted to make money, raises an important issue. Icahn argued that Lions Gate's managers were doing a bad job, Rachesky that they were doing a good job. They could not both be right. It is possible, of course, that white squires get involved in a dispute to help friendly management retain control, even though the white squires believe this is not in shareholders' best interests. It is possible, but it is expensive for the white squires. It seems much more likely that the two investors simply disagree about which policies would benefit shareholders more. After all, there is no guarantee that raiders always know what is best. Certainly, Icahn has a history of corporate failures to go with his successes, although his arrival on the scene has been associated with a 6.9% share-price increase on average.[26] However, we should not rule out the possibility that such contests are a strutting contest between men (yes, they are usually men) with enormous wealth and egos to match. After all, Icahn's standard response when asked about retirement—he is well into his 70s—is to ask incredulously "What else would I do? Play shuffleboard somewhere?"[27]

Ultimately, how we view takeover defenses—and how we view the particular contest described in this chapter—is influenced by our view of the participants' motivations. If raiders are shareholder-friendly activist investors trying to shake up entrenched management, then takeover defenses are bad for shareholders and a blight on the corporate landscape. On the other hand, if raiders' plans for firms would lower their value, then takeover defenses are a board's best hope of doing what it is supposed to do, which is work in shareholders' best interests. You decide.

Scorched earth policies

Remember the key idea behind takeover defenses: a raider will abandon a hostile takeover once it becomes clear that the payoff from continuing the bid is less than the payoff from abandoning it. The most effective tactics work by reducing the payoff from continuing the bid. Some work by making it more expensive to continue, others work by making the "prize" less valuable, but both approaches reduce the payoff from persevering.

One way that a target firm's management can make completing a takeover more expensive is to make changes to the way the firm is run that increase the firm's value and make shareholders demand a higher price before they tender their shares. That might explain some of the actions of Lions Gate's management. They laid off staff, reduced the number of films they were making, and sold 49% of TV Guide. According to press reports, they also dropped out of bidding for Miramax.[28]

Changes like these are not always in response to a takeover threat, but when they are, the obvious question is: why did management not make them sooner? The most obvious answer is that the defensive changes involved managers making a sacrifice—accepting unpopularity following job losses, scaling back empire-building ambitions, maybe something as simple as working a bit harder. These are defensive tactics that shareholders like, because they make the firm more valuable, whether or not the raider's takeover bid actually succeeds.

However, restructuring the firm or improving its operating performance to make buying it more expensive is just one way to reduce the raider's payoff from continuing with a raid. Another way is to reduce the post-takeover value of the target firm using a so-called scorched earth policy. The aim is not to make the firm less valuable: it is to make the firm less valuable *if the raider takes it over without the board's agreement*. The difference is crucial, because tactics that reduce the firm's value whether or not a takeover occurs lower the price that shareholders will demand before they sell their shares: they will accept a low price because their shares are less valuable if they hold onto them. This would make it cheaper for the raider to acquire the firm. However, if the value of the firm will fall only if the takeover goes ahead, then shareholders will continue to demand a relatively high price for their shares. That is how scorched earth policies allow the target firm's board to reduce the value of what the raider buys without reducing the cost of buying it. This might be enough to defeat a takeover once it is underway. The prospect of these defenses being deployed might even be enough to deter raiders from trying to take a firm over in the first place.

Of course, this works only if the board is able to actually carry out the threat. At first glance, that poses a problem. How can a pre-takeover board affect the post-takeover value of the firm, when those directors are unlikely to be around after the takeover? Easy. The pre-takeover board can enter the firm into legally binding contracts with other parties that transfer wealth from the firm to those parties—but only if a takeover occurs.

That is exactly what the software firm PeopleSoft did when it was fighting off Oracle's hostile takeover attempt in 2003. PeopleSoft introduced a program that offered customers a refund of up to five times what they paid for their software licenses if PeopleSoft was taken over in the next two years and the acquiring firm stopped supporting their software within four years. Note the key condition: the refunds would be paid only if PeopleSoft was taken over. That says it all. If *current* management dropped support for a product then customers were on their own, but if someone else did it then PeopleSoft would pay a generous refund. By the time Oracle won the takeover battle, PeopleSoft had run up a potential liability of $2.4b.[29] We can get a better appreciation of the magnitude of this scorched earth policy if we compare it to the amount that Oracle eventually paid for PeopleSoft, which was just $10b.[30]

Firms do not enter into binding contracts with just their customers. They also enter into binding contracts with their employees, which—thanks to change-in-control provisions—provide another opportunity to create a scorched earth policy. The key feature of these provisions is that they specify a transfer of wealth from shareholders to a firm's employees that occurs only if a firm is taken over, exactly what is needed for a scorched earth policy.

Back in Chapter 3 we saw how Yahoo boosted its employees' severance agreements during Microsoft's attempt to acquire the firm. One interpretation of that event was that Yahoo's board was putting a scorched earth policy in place. Lions Gate had arrangements for generous change-in-control payments of its own in place well before hostilities reached their peak. If there was a change in control—which, for this purpose, Lions Gate defined as any investor acquiring 30% or more of the firm's shares or new directors making up a majority on the board—then the senior executives' outstanding unvested shares and options would vest immediately.[31] If the CEO resigned following such a change in control, he would be entitled to a cash payout; if he was dismissed, he would be entitled to add to this payout his salary until the end of his employment agreement, which was four years away. In total, the CEO would have received $7.3m in cash if he had been dismissed following a change in control. Lions Gate's other senior executives had similar deals, although not as generous as the CEO's. All up, the top five executives were in line for a total combined payout worth $26m if they were dismissed following a change in control. That may not seem like much compared to the golden parachutes at the (much bigger) firms we have seen in previous chapters. However, it was approximately $0.22 per share at a firm that a raider was offering to buy for $7.00 per share.[32] Lions Gate's executives seemed determined to ensure their golden parachutes could be paid out if Icahn won: as the takeover battle neared its peak, Lions Gate established a $16m trust to help ensure payment of golden parachutes to the firm's senior executives if Icahn won.[33]

Not all firms have such significant defenses in place. For example, Anheuser-Busch's change-in-control arrangements did not create much of a deterrent when InBev was contemplating making an unsolicited takeover. In fact, the total value of the prospective payouts to Anheuser-Busch's five most senior executives was just $0.07 per share.[34] InBev initially offered $65 per share, so there was not much of a scorched earth policy there.

Poison puts

It is not just agreements with customers and employees that can hide scorched earth policies. Look carefully at the small print of a firm's bonds or its agreements with lenders and you will sometimes find another one. A change-in-control covenant is a clause that requires the firm to repay a loan in full immediately if there is a change in control. Approximately a quarter of investment-grade bonds (the safest ones issued by corporations) contain change-in-control covenants; the far riskier junk bonds are three times more likely to contain them.[35]

Their proponents argue that these clauses protect lenders by ensuring that they are not stuck holding bonds if the borrowers' risk increases following a change in control. Giving lenders this protection means that the firms will be allowed to pay a lower interest rate, so that shareholders are ultimately better off. However, that is just one side of the story. The other side calls these clauses poison puts: "puts" because the clause amounts to what the financial markets call a put option; "poison" because these clauses are like poison to raiders. Firms have to repay the debt early due to these clauses only if they are under attack from a raider. These firms will often be under attack at the same time that they are in a degree of financial difficulty, which is precisely the worst time to have to repay debt. This makes poison puts a strong deterrent to raiders, because if a raid succeeds then the firm that has just been acquired will suddenly be having to repay much of its outstanding debt at a time when it can least afford to do so.

Lions Gate had such a clause in its revolving credit facility. The change in control that would require immediate repayment of the outstanding loan could arise in two different ways: if any investor acquired more than 20% of the firm's shares or if new directors made up a majority of the board.[36] If any investor had acquired that many shares in mid-2010, Lions Gate would have had to repay the $199m balance of this revolving credit facility; it had $79m cash on hand, so it would have had to go out and borrow more funds to repay the balance.[37] That is why the white squire, Rachesky, stopped adding to his stake when it reached 19.999%.[38] If he had continued building up his stake, the repayments would have been triggered.

There were two added features at Lions Gate that made its poison put especially toxic. First, a change-in-management clause forced the firm to repay the outstanding balance immediately if any three of four named executives (including the CEO and vice chairman) left their jobs.[39] Second—and this really put the "scorched" in "scorched earth policy"—if Lions Gate had to repay its revolving credit facility early due to a change in control or a change in management, it might be forced to immediately repay some of its other debt as well.[40] That meant that if any investor increased his stake above 20%, it could trigger a wave of destabilizing defaults as, one by one, the firm's outstanding loans had to be repaid. The loans would fall like dominoes. Expensive dominoes. In mid-2010, Lions Gate owed $199m on its senior revolving credit facility, $236m on its senior secured second-priority notes, and $236m on its convertible senior subordinated notes. That is $671m, and the firm had just $79m cash on hand to repay it all.[41]

Stop and think about that for a minute. This is like having to repay our overdraft if we change jobs. Not if we lose our job and miss an interest payment: if we *change* jobs. And it gets worse. It is as though our mortgage contract has a clause that forces us to immediately repay the mortgage in full if we ever have to refinance our overdraft, even though we have not missed a single payment on either the overdraft or the mortgage. To make things just that little bit worse, all of this will probably happen at a time when refinancing the mortgage will result in the interest rate we have to pay on our new mortgage being higher than the one we were—successfully—paying on our old mortgage. That would create a pretty strong incentive not to change jobs.

Poison puts make effective scorched earth policies because they are written into legal contracts—bond documents or loan agreements—that will be carried out unless the lenders agree to waive the requirement. Such waivers are unlikely to happen without a target firm's approval. This arrangement also gives boards some cover—"The banker made me do it"—that increases the credibility of the threat.[42] However, the threat will not always be carried out. For example, Lions Gate's board blinked when Icahn's stake reached 20%, negotiating with its lenders to increase the level of ownership that would trigger the poison put to 50%. The board took the opportunity to change another term of the poison put: default would now be triggered if two key executives (Feltheimer and Burns) were removed from their jobs.[43] The Lions Gate board appeared to be circling the wagons around the CEO and vice chairman.

Poison pills

Scorched earth policies are tough on shareholders, because in order to punish the raider they reduce the value of a firm if a takeover is completed. Poison pills, which we look at now, also punish a raider, but they manage to do it without directly punishing the firm's other shareholders. In fact, poison pills reward the firm's other shareholders—just so long as they do not sell their shares to the raider.

Poison pills work by transferring some of the raider's wealth to shareholders who do not tender their shares, without directly affecting the firm's value. In most cases, they can be rescinded by the board of directors at trivial cost to allow mergers to be implemented. This feature pressures potential raiders to negotiate directly with the board. And they work: firms with poison pills in place are less likely to be takeover targets, but those that are targeted tend to attract higher takeover premia.[44]

The boards that implement poison pills do not call them that, of course. Instead, they use a much more innocuous name: shareholder rights plans. What could be wrong with that? It sounds harmless enough, maybe even something worth encouraging. Here is how a poison pill was going to work at Lions Gate. The firm issued one "share purchase right" to the owner of each Lions Gate share. At the time they were issued, the rights were largely worthless, but as soon as any individual investor (cough, Icahn) acquired 20% or more of the firm's shares, the rights would come to life. Shortly afterwards, the owner of every share would be able to exercise their right to pay the firm an amount equal to four times the share price and receive *eight* shares in return. Every owner, apart from the one with the large stake.[45] Every owner, that is, apart from Icahn.

Look a little more closely at how this works.[46] It helps if we use numbers, so suppose that Lions Gate's shares were selling for $9 each on the NYSE when Icahn's buying spree kicked the rights into life. Any investor could buy one Lions Gate share on the NYSE for $9. Any investor who did this—apart from Icahn—could then use the right that came with the share to pay Lions Gate $36 (that is, four times the share price) and receive eight newly issued shares in return. That is total expenditure of $45 for nine shares: the one that the investor bought on the NYSE, plus the eight additional shares bought from Lions Gate. In effect, the investor has bought nine shares for total expenditure of $45, or a price of $5 each.

So, if the effective price of a Lions Gate share is $5, why would they be selling on the NYSE for $9 each? The explanation is simple. Each share trading on the NYSE came with the right to buy eight more shares for just $36. As those eight shares were worth $40, that is a net payoff of $4. That $9 price tag is to cover the $5 value of a Lions Gate share (without the right attached) and the $4 value of the right to buy cheap shares.

Now look at it from Icahn's point of view. He was not allowed to exercise those rights, so the only way he could buy a Lions Gate share was to go out and buy one for $9. Everyone else could go out and effectively pay just $5, but he had to pay $9 and in return receive a share in the firm that was worth just $5. He had to pay the remaining $4 to compensate the shareholder for giving up the attached right, but got no value from it himself. The shareholder rights plan made it much more costly for Icahn to buy a large stake in the firm—and that is why shareholder rights plans are the most poisonous of pills for raiders to swallow.

There are two main flavors of poison pills: flip-in and flip-over. Lions Gate's were flip-ins, meaning that they gave shareholders who did not sell their Lions Gate shares to the raider the right to buy more, much cheaper, shares issued by the firm. A flip-over poison pill gives non-tendering shareholders the right to buy some of the raider's shares at a very low price. Both poison pills take some of a successful raider's wealth and transfer it to shareholders who did not sell their shares to the raider during the takeover. This forces the raider to pay a higher price in a tender offer. In many respects, it is the opposite of the dilution that we met in Chapter 12, which transferred wealth from non-tendering target shareholders to the raider. Like dilution, and unlike scorched earth policies, poison pills do not directly affect the value of the target firm: they just reslice the corporate cake.

Some firms keep poison pills in place for long periods of time. Others keep pills "on the shelf" and introduce them at very short notice in response to a specific threat. Some firms are even using poison pills to prevent activist hedge funds from buying significant stakes in firms.[47] These are not responses to threats to the target firms' existence, but threats to their executives' comfortable existence.

Poison pills can be introduced by boards without shareholder approval, unless a company's by-laws state otherwise.[48] The key issue is therefore not whether a firm has a poison pill in place, but whether the board needs shareholder approval to put one in place. If it does, then shareholders have some protection and pills that are designed solely to protect management from the threat of a hostile takeover are less likely to be adopted.

However, if shareholder approval is not required, then pills may be adopted even when doing so is not in shareholders' best interests.

Shareholders can—and do—submit non-binding proposals that seek to restrict the board's freedom. We first met these proposals, which are voted on at the annual shareholder meeting, back in Chapter 1. Some proposals advocate canceling a pill already in effect, others advocate the board putting all future poison pills to binding shareholder votes. Recent studies report that 74% of shareholder proposals to restrict poison pills attract majority support and 29% are implemented.[49] This pressure has persuaded an increasing—but still small—number of boards to seek shareholder approval for pills even though they are not legally required to do so.[50] That is what happened at Lions Gate, and there a majority of shareholders voted in favor of adopting the pill.[51]

Antitakeover laws

Lions Gate introduced two separate poison pills in its fight against Icahn, one in March 2010 when his stake was 19% and the other in July 2010 when it had grown to just short of 38%.[52] The first one would be triggered if any individual's stake reached 20%, the second one if a stake reached 38%.[53] In both cases, the triggers were set just above Icahn's holding at the time the pill was announced. On both occasions Icahn asked the British Columbia Securities Commission to throw the pill out, and on both occasions he got what he wanted. The view of the Canadian regulators was that a target firm should be able to use a poison pill to slow down a hostile takeover long enough for its board to provide shareholders with alternatives before they have to decide whether or not to tender their shares: poison pills could not be used to deny shareholders the ability to choose for themselves. The regulators decided that Lions Gate's pills were doing the latter, so they were banned.[54]

It would probably have been different in the U.S., where court decisions are driven by directors' fiduciary duty to shareholders and the business judgment rule. Boards are able to fight a hostile takeover bid provided that they can demonstrate a duty of care and a duty of loyalty. Seeking outside advice and spending board time discussing the takeover offer will probably take care of the former. Avoiding any direct conflicts of interest will take care of the latter. As we have seen each time we have met the business judgment rule, U.S. courts are reluctant to substitute their own judgment for that of the board, except when there is evidence of gross negligence by directors.[55]

Courts do not operate in a vacuum: in the last few decades, state legislatures across the U.S. have introduced a raft of laws that have made it easier for boards to resist hostile takeovers.[56] The so-called business combination laws, which impose a delay on the raider's ability to sell or spin off the target firm's assets, have attracted much of the attention of legal scholars. However, recently, researchers have widened their scope to look at the effects of directors' duties laws (which require directors to consider the interests of employees and local communities when dealing with takeover offers), control share acquisition laws (which strip raiders of their voting rights at shareholder meetings unless other shareholders vote to restore them), and fair price laws (which require the raider to pay a stipulated—and high—price for shares owned by hold-out shareholders).[57]

Perhaps the attitudes of U.S. courts and legislators explain why, just a few weeks after the February 2009 talks with Icahn broke down, Lions Gate started the process to switch from being incorporated in Canada to being incorporated in the U.S.[58] Icahn objected, claiming Lions Gate's move was so that it could defend itself using the takeover-unfriendly laws in the U.S. rather than the takeover-friendly ones in Canada.[59] According to whom you believe, Lions Gate either withdrew its application to leave Canada, or had its application rejected.[60] Whichever version is correct, Lions Gate's board had to defend itself without the help of the U.S. courts. However, if Lions Gate had moved, it would have been following a well trodden path of firms moving to jurisdictions that offered stronger takeover defenses. Indeed, some legal scholars argue that state legislatures compete to persuade firms to incorporate in their state by offering strong legal defenses against hostile takeovers, in what has been called a "race to the bottom."[61]

The wave of antitakeover laws adopted by state legislatures during the 1980s and 1990s was a boon to the researchers trying to understand how the market for corporate control affects shareholders.[62] By comparing firms' operating performance before and after the laws came into effect, they were able to see how firms responded to a weakening of the threat of a hostile takeover.[63] What they found suggested that the average CEO likes a quiet life. Once the threat of hostile takeovers was reduced, firms increased the wages of their workers and reduced plant closures. Fewer fights with labor unions will make life quieter. They also reduced construction of new plants. That is hard work too, get rid of it. Overall productivity fell.[64] However, the effects were seen only at firms that were in non-competitive industries.[65] The reduced takeover threat was followed by a reduction in firms' innovation, especially at firms without large shareholders to monitor management, or which were not exposed to the discipline that is enforced by external capital markets and competitive product markets.[66] After the takeover threat reduced, firms reduced the amount of cash that they paid out in the form of dividends, preferring to keep it within the firm where it was more easily available for managers to spend. The effect was greatest at firms with weak governance.[67]

These results suggest that the average executive will ease off once the threat of hostile takeovers is reduced, provided the board is weak enough to allow it to happen. Strong boards will try to counteract the reduced threat by strengthening executives' incentives. That seems to be what happened, because at firms with large shareholders monitoring management, the sensitivity of CEO pay to firm performance increased after the introduction of antitakeover laws. Weak boards will not be able to do this. They will probably just end up raising executive pay. Again, that is what seemed to happen: at firms with no large shareholders to monitor management, CEO pay increased following the introduction of antitakeover laws.[68]

Moving the goal posts

Fortunately for Icahn, Lions Gate was incorporated in Canada, so the antitakeover laws of many U.S. states did not come into play. By the middle of 2010, his stake had fallen slightly to 37%, but he was trying to increase it further. Lions Gate management had the support of several large investors, including Rachesky, the white squire who by this time owned a 19% stake.[69] However, the poison pills had been knocked back by the Canadian authorities, so the outcome of the takeover battle was far from certain. The scene was set for the deployment of one more antitakeover tactic, the defensive recapitalization.

The aim of a defensive recapitalization is to put more shares (and, more importantly, more votes) in the hands of friendly investors. This is achieved by printing more shares and selling them to those friendly investors, using the funds raised to reduce the firm's debt. The ingredients going into the corporate cake are unaffected; all that changes is the way it is sliced. With the equity layer being sliced into more pieces, the raider needs to buy more shares to get a voting majority. By raising the cost of successfully completing a takeover, this maneuver makes abandoning a bid appear more attractive.

There were two things stopping Lions Gate's board carrying out a defensive recapitalization in mid-2010. First, external events had forced Lions Gate and Icahn to put their battle on hold in early July. At that time, Lions Gate's management was considering buying the struggling film studio MGM.[70] The timing was largely out of Lions Gate's control: if a deal was to be done, it would have to be done quickly, before Icahn's takeover bid was resolved. Lions Gate and Icahn agreed to work together on the acquisition opportunity and, in return, Lions Gate's ability to issue new shares was severely restricted. A defensive recapitalization would have to wait, at least until this standstill agreement ended at midnight on July 19.[71] Second, the NYSE's rules prevented Lions Gate from just printing new shares and selling them to a white squire like Rachesky. The firm needed to obtain shareholder approval prior to issuing new securities to a director if the new shares exceeded 1% of the total number of shares outstanding prior to the stock issue.[72]

The Lions Gate board was able to overcome the second problem and effectively issue Rachesky with new shares amounting to 14% of the number already outstanding, far above the NYSE threshold.[73] The board found a way to do it that did not need shareholder approval. The plan involved issuing new debt, not new shares. To understand what the board planned to do, it helps to understand how the Lions Gate corporate cake was sliced. We saw the hospital chain HCA's corporate cake in Chapter 4. Lions Gate's cake could be sliced in much the same way. At the very bottom of the cake was the safest layer, the revolving credit facility with its poison put. At the end of June 2010, Lions Gate owed $199m under this facility. Above this was a layer of more risky debt, comprising so-called senior notes requiring Lions Gate to repay $236m and convertible senior subordinated notes requiring it to repay another $236m. Investors who owned the convertible notes could take them back to Lions Gate and exchange them for newly printed shares in the company. That is why they were called "convertible." The contractual terms varied, but for each new share issued under this arrangement, the amount of the outstanding borrowing was cut by between \$8.25 and \$14.28.[74] This conversion feature was not very valuable in mid-2010 because these investors could have bought shares on the NYSE for \$6.03.[75] It would have been cheaper to buy shares on the open market rather than to get them using the conversion feature.

Many of the convertible notes were owned by John Kornitzer, an investor friendly toward Lions Gate's management.[76] (How friendly? This friendly: "I wish Icahn would just go crawl under a rock.... I'm not going to sell him any [expletive] bonds.")[77] This created an opportunity for the board to carry out something similar to a defensive recapitalization without the need to get shareholder approval. Rachesky would buy Kornitzer's convertible notes and then convert them into shares, allowing him to invest in Lions Gate shares and dilute Icahn's ownership stake. As Rachesky was dealing with Kornitzer—and not Lions Gate directly—the transaction would not fall foul of the NYSE's rules about related-party transactions.

Of course, using Kornitzer's convertible notes as a means of buying newly issued shares would have been uneconomic for Rachesky due to the contractual terms of the notes themselves. This was easily fixed. Lions Gate agreed to exchange Kornitzer's notes for ones with more favorable conversion terms: the new ones could be converted into almost twice as many shares as the original notes. On average, for each share issued, the amount Lions Gate owed to the holder of the notes would fall by \$6.20 rather than \$12.37.[78]

It was an elegant solution. Lions Gate would issue the new notes to Kornitzer, not Rachesky: as far as the board was concerned, what he did with them was his business. Kornitzer would sell them to Rachesky, who would then convert the debt into enough new shares to increase his stake from 19% to 29%, and to reduce Icahn's from 37% to 33%.[79] It was a defensive recapitalization in all but name.

The standstill agreement with Icahn stopped Lions Gate's board from doing anything straightaway. However, planning took place behind the scenes as all three parties waited for the standstill agreement to expire at midnight on July 19. The machinery started up at one minute past midnight when the board met and approved the exchange of new notes for old. An hour later, Kornitzer's attorney sent payment instructions to Rachesky's attorney. By 4:00 a.m., Lions Gate and Kornitzer had signed the agreement to exchange notes; by 9:30 a.m., Rachesky had purchased the notes off Kornitzer; Rachesky converted them into 16m new Lions Gate shares that afternoon.[80] They had cost him \$6.51 each.[81]

In effect, Lions Gate printed new shares, issued them to a white squire, and reduced the amount of its borrowing. Defensive recapitalizations have some similarities to poison pills, in that they dilute the raider's stake. However, as long as the new shares are issued at a fair price—in this case, as long as they are exchanged for the right amount of debt—then they do not reduce the value of any shareholders' securities, including the raider's. This is a crucial difference from poison pills, where the value of the raider's stake is reduced when they are exercised. However, defensive recapitalizations are still effective because they force the raider to buy more shares in order to get control of the firm. This raises the cost of continuing the takeover bid, which makes abandoning the bid more attractive.

The optics of defensive recapitalizations are terrible. Perhaps that is why Lions Gate went to such lengths to present the transaction as "business as usual," going so far as to claim that the exchange of new notes for old was part of a previously announced plan to reduce debt.[82] There was just one problem: when the SEC investigated, it could not find any announcements of such a plan.[83] Icahn was quick to point out the hypocrisy of a board that had recently advised shareholders not to tender their shares to Icahn because his offer price of $7 was too low then turning around and effectively selling new shares to a director for just $6.51. He was not happy: "As much as I've been a critic of the lengths that some boards will go to entrench themselves, I don't think I've ever seen anything this blatant."[84] Ultimately the SEC agreed, finding that Lions Gate did not adequately disclose the true nature of the transactions and their intention to fend off Icahn. Lions Gate reached a settlement with the SEC, which involved paying a $7.5m penalty. However, this all happened in March 2014, more than three years afterwards, too late to have any effect on the outcome.[85]

A proxy fight of last resort

We have not quite finished yet. If the board's use of takeover defenses has stopped the raider buying a controlling stake from shareholders directly, the raider has one other option before he has to admit defeat and either go back to the board or go away altogether. If he can get control of the board, then he might be able to overturn some of the defenses. Perhaps a new board would withdraw any poison pills the previous board had introduced; it could certainly prevent any future defensive recapitalizations. The mechanism for doing this is the proxy fight we met in Chapter 10. That is why many hostile takeovers, especially those at firms with strong defenses in place, end up with a proxy fight at a meeting of the firm's shareholders.

The scene for Icahn's proxy fight was Lions Gate's 2010 annual shareholder meeting. In a concession that he was not going to be able to win total control all at once, Icahn nominated just five of his own candidates for election to the 12-member board.[86] He would have to settle for influence, and the ability to change the rules or gradually take over the board from within. However, that would happen only if he could persuade enough of Lions Gate's shareholders to elect one or more of his nominees to the board.

The way that institutional investors would vote in the proxy fight might be crucial. Since 2003, institutional investors have had to disclose how they vote and how they decide how to vote.[87] Big mutual funds can hold shares in hundreds, often thousands, of different firms. Researching each agenda item before each meeting of each firm in an institutional investor's portfolio would therefore be extremely costly, so this rule has created an industry full of so-called proxy advisory firms. They analyze corporate governance at firms and sell voting recommendations to institutional investors.[88] More than 60% of institutional investors use proxy advisory firms.[89] That is why it was so important for Lions Gate and Icahn to woo the two firms that dominate the industry, Institutional Shareholder Services (ISS) and Glass Lewis.

The major proxy advisors play a prominent role when shareholders revolt against a firm's board. For example, ISS recommended that shareholders oppose Ray Irani's reelection at the Occidental Petroleum meeting that saw him deposed as chairman. Glass Lewis recommended his reelection only after Occidental made some conciliatory changes to its plans to replace Steve Chazen as CEO.[90] ISS and Glass Lewis both recommended that shareholders oppose the reelection of Michael Eisner to Disney's board at the annual meeting that saw him stand down as Disney's chairman.[91] Recommendations issued by proxy advisory firms have a significant impact on voting outcomes.[92] One study estimated that more than 25% of mutual funds rely almost entirely on ISS when deciding how to vote.[93]

Proxy advisors are the final group of external "experts" in our governance story. We have already seen compensation consultants (Chapter 6), stock analysts (Chapter 9), and credit rating agencies (Chapter 9). Proxy advisors sell their advisory services to institutional investors. However, like the other experts we have met, proxy advisors face a potential conflict of interest.[94] For example, when Glass Lewis was being courted by Lions Gate and Icahn, it was owned by the Ontario Teachers' Pension Plan.[95] Ownership arrangements like this raise the possibility that a proxy advisory firm's recommendation will be influenced by the voting preferences of its ultimate owner, which is hardly a disinterested partner.

In the case of ISS, the conflict comes from selling services to the firms that ISS evaluates. As part of its business, ISS produces ratings that it claims measure the quality of firms' corporate governance. Researchers have found no relationship between firms' ratings and their operating performance, so the information content of these ratings is unclear.[96] Indeed, much simpler indices developed by academics do a better job of predicting firms' operating performance.[97] Nevertheless, many firms are still willing to pay ISS for advice on how they can change their governance arrangements in ways that will improve the ratings they receive. This practice has raised concerns among some observers that good ratings and firm-friendly recommendations might be used as rewards for firms that buy ISS's services.

We saw in Chapter 9 how stock analysts try to manage similar conflicts. Proxy advisors do much the same thing. For example, they are aware of the danger of acquiring a bad reputation: if institutional investors start to think that their proxy advisors are not giving independent advice, these investors may stop paying for that advice, killing the advisory business. Advisors' reputation is perhaps their most valuable asset. Another standard response is to put structures in place that are supposed to insulate the advisory business from these temptations. In the case of ISS, these are physical structures: the advisory and consulting businesses operate in separate buildings and use segregated office equipment and information databases.[98]

The proxy advisory firms produced a split decision at Lions Gate. Although Glass Lewis recommended that shareholders reject Icahn's slate, ISS supported three of his five nominees. A third, smaller, proxy advisor recommended that shareholders vote for Icahn's entire slate of candidates.[99]

In the end, it did not matter, because any possibility that Icahn would be able to win enough shareholder support disappeared when first Canadian and then U.S. courts threw out his complaints about the transaction that boosted Rachesky's ownership stake; Rachesky would be allowed to vote the 16m new shares he had just purchased.[100] Those votes turned out to be crucial, because Icahn's highest-polling nominee attracted just over 16m fewer votes than the board's lowest-polling nominee.[101] Without Rachesky's new votes in the mix, Icahn might have been able to get at least one of his nominees on the board. Instead he got none.

Icahn had needed to get seven nominees elected to the board to take control. With a little luck—and perhaps a higher offer price—Icahn could have won control of Lions Gate's board in 2010. There was nothing that the incumbent directors could have done to stop it: all directors had to stand for reelection each year, so potentially the whole board could be replaced at once. However, that is not the case at all firms. For many years, approximately 60% of U.S. corporations had staggered boards.[102] At these firms, only a fraction of directors stand for reelection each year and the successful candidates are elected for a multi-year term: typically, a third of the board stands for reelection each year and directors serve for three years. Recently, shareholder pressure has resulted in many firms—especially those with signs of better governance—de-staggering their boards.[103] We watched Evelyn Y. Davis push for this change in Chapter 1. Just 25% of the largest corporations had staggered boards in 2012.[104] If Lions Gate had a staggered voting system in place, then the very best that Icahn could have done in 2010 was to replace four of the board's 12 directors. That would not have given him control of the firm. In the very best-case scenario for Icahn, he would have had to wait until the 2011 shareholder meeting to win control of the board.

A board is more likely to reject an initial takeover bid, and target shareholders are more likely to receive a large share of the takeover gains, if the target firm has a staggered board. This observed behavior is consistent with a staggered board being an effective takeover defense and increasing the target board's bargaining power. Perhaps this is why firms with staggered boards are less likely to be the target of a takeover bid than other firms.[105] This reduced takeover threat might explain why at firms with staggered boards, the CEO is less likely to be fired, the probability of CEO turnover is less sensitive to firm performance, and shareholder-approved proposals are less likely to be implemented.[106] This all comes at a price to shareholders: firms with staggered boards tend to have low market values relative to the cost of their assets.[107]

Greenmail

Eight months after Icahn's failure at the 2010 shareholder meeting, he agreed to sell his stake in the firm. Lions Gate itself bought back 11m shares at a price of $7.00 each; Rachesky bought the same number for the same price; the remaining shares were sold to the public.[108] To rub salt into Icahn's wounds, just two weeks later, Lions Gate's board elected his nemesis Rachesky to the position of co-chairman.[109] Icahn's takeover attempt was officially defeated.

Lions Gate's share price was $6.96 immediately after the news of Icahn's retreat was announced. He did not get much of a premium over that, just 4c per share. However, Icahn owned 33% of the firm's shares. If he had tried to sell his shares on the open market, the illiquidity problems we first saw in Chapter 10 might have prevented him from selling his shares for a price of $6.96, so the premium is probably larger than it appears to be.

Whenever firms repurchase their shares from large stakeholders on terms unavailable to other shareholders, someone will mutter darkly about "greenmail" being paid.[110] It is a play on the word "blackmail," but the boards that pay it call the transaction a "targeted share repurchase." According to the critics, targeted share repurchases are essentially a bribe paid to raiders by a board, using shareholders' money, to induce them to break off the raid. This increases the raider's payoff from abandoning a bid, while leaving the payoff from continuing unchanged. If the premium is large enough, it will be in the raider's best interest to abandon the bid altogether. However, this generosity comes with strings attached. The sale is conditional on the raider abandoning his or her bid. Usually the conditions come in the form of a standstill agreement, which limits the number of the target firm's shares the ex-raider is allowed to own.

Two of the firms we met in earlier chapters paid greenmail during the hostile takeover wave of the 1980s. Occidental Petroleum paid one large shareholder 48% more than the current market value for his 4.8% stake after he fell out with CEO Armand Hammer. Shortly before the arrival of Michael Eisner, Disney paid a raider a 51% premium for the raider's 11% stake.[111] These very generous premia were not available to other shareholders, who were left owning shares that, thanks to the departure of the raider, were less valuable than before. However, the target firms' management could stay in place. Unsurprisingly, shareholders of target firms dislike greenmail: on average, target firms' share prices fall significantly when greenmail payments are announced.[112]

Firms that pay greenmail, and the raiders who receive it, come under intense scrutiny. As one of the most significant corporate raiders during the 1980s hostile takeover wave, Icahn received his share of greenmail—and of scrutiny. He was even called on to defend his tactics before Congress.[113] Partly as a consequence of such scrutiny, and partly because firms adopt the other defensive tactics we have seen, payment of greenmail peaked in the early 1980s and all but died out in the 1990s.[114] Another reason was the 50% tax on greenmail profits that the Internal Revenue Service introduced in 1987.[115]

Nevertheless, an emerging trend has activist hedge funds exiting investments by selling their shares back to firms.[116] For example, a year after retreating from Lions Gate, Icahn sold his 25% stake in MGM at a 24% premium over the price at which MGM shares were trading on private markets.[117] Another year later, Icahn sold his 13% stake in Take-Two Interactive Software (maker of the *Grand Theft Auto* video games) at a 5.7% premium.[118] The 50% premia of the 1980s have not been repeated. Yet.

A familiar story

This chapter has revealed the consistent economic rationale behind the tactics employed by Lions Gate's board. This rationale applies much more widely, whether a board is defending itself against one of the activist investors described in Chapter 10 or against investors attempting a full takeover, as in Chapters 11 and 12. The rationale is simple: corral the attacker into earning the support of the target firm's board by making it too expensive for the attacker to succeed any other way. That is why Lions Gate's board worked so hard to make it costly for Icahn to gain control. By printing more shares and issuing them to friendly investors, the board forced Icahn to acquire more shares. By improving the firm's performance, the board made each share more costly to acquire. By attaching special rights to shares that Icahn did not buy, the board tried to make them more costly still. And by implementing a scorched earth policy, the board made sure that those shares would be worth less if Icahn actually went ahead and bought them. Four different approaches, but all making it more expensive for Icahn to bypass the board. That, in a nutshell, is the board's defensive playbook.

These tactics increase the board's bargaining power, which can be good or bad for the target's shareholders. They can help the board negotiate a high price when selling the firm to one with a better management team (good) or help the board protect an entrenched, inefficient management team (bad). We need to be aware of both possibilities.

It is the same old story: tools that are good for shareholders when in the hands of a strong board can be bad news when in the hands of a weak board. Did those takeover defenses benefit or cost Lions Gate's shareholders? At one stage, Icahn was offering $7.50 for each Lions Gate share, but three years after his second tender offer closed, Lions Gate's share price had climbed above $30.[119] At first glance, it looks like the board was right to resist Icahn's takeover bid, but we need to be wary of the dangers of 20:20 hindsight. After all, perhaps the share price would have been even higher if Icahn's takeover had gone ahead. Or perhaps the rapid share-price growth happened because of changes made in response to Icahn's threat, such as the drive to get costs under control, the decision not to pursue a merger with Miramax, or the election of a large shareholder to the board, from where he could keep a close, self-interested eye on management.

A common thread

We have now made our way through 13 chapters that showcase the responses to manager–shareholder conflict. Along the way we have seen some extreme failures of corporate governance. However, it is not all bad news. There have been successes as well, and in their own way the successes reveal just as much as the failures. Activist investors eventually succeeded in driving Ray Irani out of Occidental Petroleum. Jerry Yang resigned as Yahoo's CEO after six months of pressure from more activist investors.[120] HCA boomed after a leveraged buyout narrowed the gap between ownership and control. Frank Blake, the man who replaced Bob Nardelli as Home Depot's CEO, proved to be a hit with shareholders.[121] Anheuser-Busch's shareholders gained from InBev's improved management of the firm, even though they no longer owned shares in the firm. Now, in this chapter, Lions Gate blossomed after Icahn's takeover attempt was defeated.

There is a common thread running through all of these success stories: a strong board of directors. In some cases, that strength came from activist hedge funds bolstering the board with the threat of a proxy fight. At Oxy and Home Depot, the activists had representatives inside the boardroom; at Yahoo, Carl Icahn was outside banging on the door. In other cases, large shareholders—with their strong incentive to monitor management closely—sat on the board. Tommy Frist seized the opportunity to take HCA private, even though he would lose some control in the process; August Busch III was still an influential director when Anheuser-Busch's board agreed to sell the firm and end his son's executive career; Mark Rachesky joined Lions Gate's board and eventually became co-chairman.

If a strong board is in place, directors' monitoring of management will be effective. However, there is even better news for shareholders, because a strong board will use the mechanisms we have seen in this book to complement that effective monitoring. It will adopt incentive schemes that motivate managers to work in ways that benefit shareholders and it will delegate monitoring to third parties. A weak board, however, will not monitor effectively and it will not be able to use these tools to benefit shareholders. A strong board of directors is the key to effective corporate governance.

All of these stories had happy endings for shareholders, but they had unhappy beginnings and often even unhappier middles. The problem facing shareholders is that although the tools described in this book will eventually overcome governance failures, shareholders may have to endure painful delays until this happens. It is also the problem facing the policymakers who we are about to meet as we end our journey at the furthest point from the boardroom table, in Washington, DC.

5 The rules of the game matter as well

Corporations were never designed to be democracies.[1]

PRESIDENT, BUSINESS ROUNDTABLE (2007)

14 Caught in the middle
REFORMING THE LEGAL AND REGULATORY ENVIRONMENT

THE PREVIOUS 13 chapters have featured battles between executives and shareholders at individual firms. Similar fights are taking place in congressional committee rooms, at SEC hearings, and in courtrooms and legislatures across the U.S. Lobbyists and lawyers representing shareholders' interests are busy trying to put rules in place that enhance shareholders' role in decision-making. Their counterparts representing executives' interests fight them at every turn. These skirmishes are all part of a wider battle for control of the modern corporation. The president of the Business Roundtable, the lobby group made up of large corporations' CEOs, neatly summarized the argument in congressional testimony in 2007. He told the House Financial Services Committee that "[c]orporations were never designed to be democracies," adding that "[w]hile shareholders own a corporation, they don't run it."[2] According to this corporate world-view, shareholders are more like bondholders than owners. They are entitled to receive regular dividend payouts, but only at a level chosen by the board, and they have no say in the firm's decision-making. Shareholders are to be seen and not heard. Unfortunately for the Business Roundtable, shareholders want to have a say.

At the level of individual firms, manager–shareholder conflict plays itself out as a contest to dominate the board. This should not be surprising. As we have seen in the last 13 chapters, the board of directors plays a key role in adjudicating the conflict between managers and shareholders. Some of the board's decisions affect executives and shareholders directly. Who to hire into executive jobs, who to promote, and who to fire. How much to pay them. Whether to let them use shareholders' wealth to build an empire.

Whether to allow executives to entrench themselves. Whether to give activist investors some of what they want, or force them to launch a proxy contest instead. Whether to use a poison pill to block a hostile takeover.

Some of the board's decisions affect executives and shareholders in more subtle ways, by influencing the decisions that executives make on matters that directly affect shareholders. Directors are one step removed, but they can still affect the final outcome. We took a close look at one mechanism, creating incentives by linking executive pay to firm performance, in Chapters 5 and 6. We looked at another incentive mechanism when we considered the executive labor market and the incentives generated by career concerns in Chapter 7. As we saw there, if boards make hiring and firing decisions in the best interests of shareholders then executives (especially relatively young ones) will be motivated to work in shareholders' best interests.

Performance-based pay and career concerns work by providing executives with incentives to act in shareholders' interests; external capital markets do it by restricting executives' ability to do anything else. As we saw in Chapter 8, a board can set a firm's borrowing policy so that the firm has to return to the external capital markets frequently. There is nothing quite like the discipline of having to persuade a new batch of investors to trust the firm with their savings. Even if a board is in a strong position only temporarily, borrowing to buy back shares or pay a special dividend can help to prolong the board's strength by exposing executives to the discipline of external capital markets past the time when executives start to dominate the board.

With so much potential to affect the struggle between executives and shareholders, directors' attitudes to the two sides are crucial. Their ownership stakes are typically too small to generate strong incentives to work in shareholders' interests. Performance-based pay could help motivate directors, but linking board pay closely to firm performance would inevitably result in the potential for high levels of board pay. Directors set their own pay, so using performance-based pay to generate strong incentives might solve one problem (an unmotivated board) by creating another problem (excessive board pay). However, for many directors, the pay they already receive is high enough for them to want to continue receiving it. This motivates directors to take actions that reduce the likelihood that they will lose their board seats.

As a result of directors' desire for job security, they have a strong incentive to prevent their firms becoming engaged in proxy fights. Regardless of whether the fights involve activist hedge funds wanting influence or raiders wanting full control, directors want to avoid them—and many directors will take actions to try and avoid them. However, boards that are insulated from such shareholder pressure may make different decisions from those that are not. For example, they may use the bargaining power created by devices such as poison pills to protect the firm's management. In contrast, boards influenced by shareholders may use poison pills to increase the proportion of any takeover gains received by the target firm's shareholders. Boards insulated from shareholder pressure will be tempted to filter out the effects of bad luck when setting pay, while keeping the effects of good luck in place, all to boost executive pay. Those influenced by shareholders will ensure that, as far as possible, executives are rewarded only for their own contribution to firm performance. Boards insulated from shareholder pressure may use profits to pay down debt and relax the discipline of external capital markets. Those influenced by shareholders will pay profits out to shareholders and continue to hold executives' feet to the fire.

Both sides of the battle for supremacy, executives and shareholders, know that the side that controls the board of directors controls the firm. That is why so many of the policy battles over corporate governance boil down to a fight over the extent to which boards are insulated from shareholder pressure.

Are shareholders allowed to know what is going on?

Even after what we have seen in the last 13 chapters, it still seems remarkable that a large part of the policy debate is actually about whether shareholders should be allowed to know what is going on within the firm. Within *their* firm. The answer to this question is of vital importance to both sides, because if shareholders know about governance failures then they will be more likely to support an external challenge to the managers' control of a firm. That makes activism in response to poor governance more likely to succeed, and therefore more profitable and more likely to occur. In short, a better-informed shareholder base strengthens the discipline imposed by the market for corporate control and weakens executives' influence over the board.

The SEC's disclosure rules are the main determinant of how much shareholders know about what is going on within a firm. Nowhere is this more obvious than the controversial issue of executive compensation. The history of the last quarter century shows the SEC responding to a public outraged by what it perceives as excessive pay with a series of rules requiring increasingly detailed disclosure of pay—and firms and their lobbyists responding with attempts to water down the SEC's proposals. There is an obvious voyeuristic element to the calls for pay disclosure. There is also a case to be made for the claim that, except in a few cases, any pay excesses have only a modest effect on a firm's bottom line. However, pay disclosure has the potential to show how executives' compensation is tied to a firm's performance, allowing shareholders to evaluate the extent to which executives are being motivated to undertake actions that do affect a firm's bottom line. Perhaps most importantly of all, it can also offer insight into a board's overall effectiveness. If a board is weak on pay, is it also allowing the CEO to fill the firm's management ranks with his friends and family? Is it allowing him to build an empire? Is it allowing him to duck out of confronting labor unions? Those things definitely do affect the bottom line.

Some of the SEC's disclosure rules give investors information about how much executives are actually being paid. In 1992, rule changes were developed against the backdrop of a presidential election campaign in which excessive executive pay was a hotly debated topic.[3] The SEC initially proposed that firms would have to provide shareholders with tables that summarized how much key executives were paid. CEO pay would have to be tracked against firm performance over the previous three years and shareholders would be allowed to sue if the disclosures were inaccurate.[4] The push-back from firms was so fierce that compensation consultants assisting the business press were allegedly threatened with blacklisting by corporations.[5]

For its part, the SEC was hit with a barrage of complaints. A co-chairman of the Business Roundtable complained that so much information would be released "that people are going to get lost." One firm's general counsel warned that disclosing bonus arrangements would tip off competitors about a firm's business goals. Another worried that the risk of a lawsuit would make it harder to recruit independent directors.[6] Silicon Valley firms claimed they would be ruined if they could not use stock options.[7] (Nobody was proposing to ban options, so the claim rather revealingly implied that the firms saw options as a desirable form of pay only as long as nobody could tell how much they cost shareholders.) In any event, the Business Roundtable declared, it was impossible to measure how much stock options were worth.[8] All that was missing was Helen Lovejoy: "Won't somebody please think of the children?"

In the end, the SEC backed down: the summary tables remained, but only the number of options granted would have to be reported, along with a very conservative measure of their potential payout. Shareholders would not be told their value, they would not be told the total value of the executives' pay packages, and they could not sue if the disclosures were inaccurate.[9] Still, it was progress.

Public anger at the extravagant executive pay seen in the early 2000s, driven mainly by stock options, prompted the SEC to review its disclosure rules again in 2006.[10] We have seen some of the most extreme examples of high pay in this book: Ray Irani at Occidental Petroleum, Michael Eisner at Disney, and Bob Nardelli at Home Depot. The SEC introduced new rules that required firms to include a more detailed discussion of pay in the annual proxy statement sent to shareholders. The table that summarizes compensation paid to the five top executives became more detailed and, for the first time, had to include the total pay for each of them. The rules for reporting the value of pay based on share and option grants were changed. Firms had to start providing more information about perks and golden parachutes, as well as more information about directors' pay.[11] The response from the executive lobby had much in common with 1992. Everybody seemed to agree that options were just too complicated to value for a firm to estimate their cost to shareholders.[12] The Business Roundtable wanted an even more complicated summary compensation table and no requirement for firms to disclose details of golden parachutes. It repeated the earlier claim that increased disclosure would make it even more difficult to recruit independent directors.[13] The Chamber of Commerce agreed, arguing that the "disclosures will provide information for gossips and the press, but little information that is useful to investors."[14]

The SEC also sets the rules that determine what shareholders know about *how* pay has been set. In 2006, the SEC introduced rules forcing firms to disclose the identities of compensation consultants used to help set executive pay as well as the makeup of any peer groups used for pay setting.[15] The SEC further tightened its rules in 2009 and 2012 in response to concerns about conflicts of interest that might be affecting compensation consultants. First, the SEC started forcing firms to disclose the fees paid to any compensation consultants with a potential conflict of interest.[16] Then it introduced a new rule requiring greater disclosure of the conflicts of interests themselves.[17]

Thanks to these changes, investors have access to much more information about executive pay than they did 25 years ago. However, there is a difference between disclosure and transparency, and the SEC has been complaining about the lack of transparency in firms' pay disclosure for years.[18] One study reported that the proxy statements of the largest firms grew in length by 54% between 2006 and 2011.[19] The material on executive compensation, in particular, is now full of the sort of boilerplate language that only lawyers can write—and only lawyers can understand. The irony is that many of the firms that in 1992 expressed concerns that disclosure would burden shareholders with too much information to be useful now seem to be going out of their way to drown shareholders (or, at least, shareholder dissent) under a sea of data.

When the SEC raised the issue in 2009, the Business Roundtable's suggestion was that some of the more relevant information—including the tables showing the details of executives' holdings of shares and options, their payouts from exercising options, and their pension benefits—could be dropped from the proxy statement and put on companies' websites instead.[20] If the SEC had adopted this suggestion, the information would still have been disclosed by the firm. However, it would have inevitably been put in a different place on each company's website, and the time needed to find the information—if shareholders had even bothered to look—would probably have deterred all but the most determined of shareholders. The effect would have been to undo much of the SEC's previous work on increasing pay disclosure. After all, as we saw in Chapter 6, before the 2006 changes, part of executives' pay was effectively hidden by boosting their retirement pay. Here was the Business Roundtable proposing a change that would have given weak boards that opportunity once more.

Are shareholders allowed to have a say in what is going on?

The battle over how much say shareholders have in the running of a corporation has been going on as long as the fight over information disclosure. The main mechanism for shareholder involvement in decision-making is the annual meeting and the opportunity it provides for shareholders to vote. They are able to vote on two types of proposals: ones put to them by the firm's board and, as we saw in Chapter 1, proposals sponsored by individual shareholders. The key issue when discussing shareholder involvement in decision-making is the restrictions imposed on the proposals that shareholders can sponsor.

We saw the procedure for sponsoring a proposal when we met cantankerous Evelyn Y. Davis in Chapter 1. A shareholder must submit their proposal to the firm well in advance of the annual meeting and, unless the proposal violates the rules set by the SEC, the firm is forced to put the proposal to the vote.[21] There have been skirmishes for years over what the SEC should and should not allow firms to exclude, but the SEC's policy is to allow the exclusion of proposals relating to a firm's ordinary business operations. Firms are also allowed to exclude proposals that would force them to violate state law or that have been voted on in recent years without receiving many votes.[22]

State laws typically specify that the board (alone) is responsible for carrying out a firm's ordinary business, which deprives shareholders of the power to force a board to carry out an action. The best chance of getting a proposal onto the annual meeting's agenda is therefore to make the proposal non-binding. The board will not be forced to do anything if such a proposal is passed by shareholders, but a board's refusal to implement a non-binding proposal that won majority support will soon be public information, so directors' career concerns might be enough to see a non-binding proposal implemented.

Whether or not they are non-binding, shareholder proposals cannot relate to a firm's ordinary business without falling foul of state law. However, the SEC has gradually changed the way that it applies this rule. In 1992, it stopped allowing firms to use the ordinary-business rule to exclude proposals on executive compensation plans.[23] In 2002, this was extended to stop firms excluding certain proposals relating to option-based pay for *any* workers.[24] In 2011, the SEC implemented the provision of the Dodd-Frank Act requiring that firms include a non-binding "say-on-pay" proposal seeking shareholder approval of executive compensation.[25]

What about the most important decision of all: whether or not to sell the firm to someone else? It seems ridiculous that boards dominated by entrenched executives can indefinitely prevent shareholders from making this decision, but that is the effect of a poison pill. A board's ability to do this, at least if the firm is incorporated in Delaware, was reconfirmed as recently as 2011. That is when the Delaware Chancery Court upheld the use of a poison pill by Airgas, Inc. in fighting off a hostile takeover attempt by Air Products & Chemicals, Inc. The raider had asked the court to force Airgas to cancel its poison pill, which would have had the effect of allowing shareholders to sell the firm if a majority wished to so. The judge expressed his personal view that Airgas's poison pill had served its purpose in giving directors time to let shareholders know the board's view about the proposed takeover terms, allowing shareholders to make an informed decision. However, he could not substitute his personal view for decades of legal precedent in Delaware, which meant that the Airgas board was allowed to keep its pill in place. It seems that as long as a board can argue that it believes a takeover offer is inadequate, it can effectively stop shareholders making a sale decision indefinitely. The judgment could not have been clearer: "the power to defeat an inadequate hostile tender offer ultimately lies with the board of directors."[26] Of course, it is directors, not shareholders, who decide whether an offer is adequate or not.

Shareholders' advocates have fought poison pills since their invention in the 1980s. With the courts allowing boards to use poison pills to effectively prevent shareholders deciding whether to sell a firm, most of the action takes place at the level of individual firms. The SEC's role has been largely restricted to influencing shareholders' ability to reduce the effectiveness of poison pills. The main focus has been on which shareholder proposals firms are forced to submit to a shareholder vote. For example, the SEC has allowed shareholders to sponsor non-binding proposals to repeal poison pills. Although these proposals have often succeeded at winning majority support from shareholders, they have been less successful at persuading boards to actually implement the proposals.[27] However, the SEC has allowed firms to exclude shareholder proposals to change corporations' by-laws in ways that would prohibit the maintenance or adoption of poison pills. These proposals are routinely prevented on the grounds that such by-laws would infringe boards' right to issue new securities. More sophisticated proposals have found their way onto proxy statements, however. These proposals, sponsored by Harvard professor and shareholder activist Lucien Bebchuk, seek to change a firm's by-laws so that, unless either shareholders or a super-majority of directors vote to approve a poison pill, the pill will lapse after a year.[28] Firms including Bristol-Myers Squibb, J.C. Penney, and Safeway have adopted versions of the "Bebchuk bylaw."[29]

However, the SEC's role is not limited just to setting the rules around exclusion of shareholder proposals. Its decisions can influence the effectiveness of poison pills in other, more subtle, ways. In 2011, the law firm that invented the poison pill filed a petition with the SEC asking it to tighten the disclosure rules around large shareholders. Instead of investors having to disclose their stake within ten days of reaching 5%, the lawyers wanted the SEC to force investors to report within a day of reaching the threshold.[30] This would give firms more time to introduce a poison pill and it would enable them to set a tighter limit on the stake size activist hedge funds, in particular, can acquire before they trigger the pill.[31] If this proposal is ever adopted, boards will be even more insulated from shareholder anger.

Are shareholders allowed to choose their own board?

It looks like shareholders' ability to make the decisions that affect a firm are limited, and will be so for the foreseeable future. That would not matter too much if the board was not insulated from shareholder pressure. Shareholders do not need to make decisions about how a firm is run as long as they can replace a board that is making decisions they do not like. However, Chapter 2 showed how difficult it can be to replace a board.

Congressional and SEC attempts to make board replacement easier are the focus of the final fight we will look at in this chapter. In 2003 and 2007, the SEC proposed rule changes that would have made it easier for shareholders to nominate their own candidates in board elections and get their names on the proxy statement sent to shareholders. On both occasions the SEC pulled back from the brink and allowed boards to retain their monopoly access to the proxy statement.[32] However, in 2010 the Dodd-Frank Act gave the SEC the power to prescribe rules for how firms grant access to their proxy statements. This time, the SEC decided to bite the bullet. It used the authority provided by Congress and issued Rule 14a-11, which gave shareholders of public companies the right to force a company to include in its proxy statement shareholder nominees for the board. The rule was designed in such a way that it could not be used to take full control of the board, but it still dramatically opened board elections up to competition.[33] Unsurprisingly, the executives' lobby resisted the change, with the Business Roundtable and Chamber of Commerce challenging Rule 14a-11 in the courts. Rule 14a-11 was subsequently thrown out by the DC Circuit Court of Appeals without ever coming into force.[34] Challenging incumbent directors is as difficult as it has always been.

Firms complained that the process would be hijacked by individuals and organizations with an axe to grind. However, in practice there was little to fear from the union candidates, environmental activists, and the other bogeymen used by the defenders of the status quo. Rule 14a-11 would have made it easier for such candidates to be nominated, but they would still have had to be elected by shareholders. It would have been up to the board to nominate high quality candidates and convince shareholders that they were better than the other nominees. The days of a CEO nominating his children's elementary school principal for a seat on the board would have been gone forever. Yes, firms would have spent more of shareholders' money promoting their candidates, but these costs would have been offset by the higher quality boards that would have resulted from the change. All that competition would have made boards lift their game.

The battle over access to the proxy statement continues, but now it is being fought at individual firms. Shareholder activists have begun sponsoring non-binding proposals to change companies' bylaws to open up access to the companies' proxy statements. They are trying to introduce a version of the SEC's abandoned Rule 14a-11 firm by firm. Even if the proposals pass, they are non-binding, but the activists hope that public pressure will persuade boards to adopt the proposals. Of course, games are being played here as well. Corporations have begun to introduce their own proxy access rules, but with terms so onerous that they are unlikely to be very effective. However, because the SEC allows firms to exclude shareholder-sponsored proposals if they have much in common with the board's own proposals, the ineffective proxy rules allow firms to fend off more effective ones. That is how Whole Foods Market, Inc. tried to exclude a proposal recommending proxy access be granted to groups of shareholders who had collectively owned a 3% stake for three years. The board-sponsored proposal? Access would be granted only to an *individual* shareholder who had owned a 9% stake for five years.[35] There had not been one of those for years.

The SEC initially allowed the exclusion. However, after an outcry, it reversed the decision, effectively preventing Whole Foods Market from excluding the original proposal.[36] The door that had looked like being slammed shut on shareholders suddenly burst open, just in time for the 2015 proxy season.[37] The Business Roundtable found itself in the unfamiliar position of pleading with the proxy advisory firms to "exercise restraint."[38] The Chamber of Commerce managed to contain its outrage just long enough to "respectfully request" that the SEC review its entire process for allowing firms to exclude shareholder proposals.[39]

Where will it all end?

This book is coming to an end, but the battle for control of the modern corporation looks set to continue well into the future. The battle will be fought firm by firm, as well as at the SEC. If we want to understand the battles that are fought out within individual firms, then the ideas in Chapters 1–13 will help. However, in the medium term, what happens in Washington, DC, as well as in the state legislatures, will affect what happens in the boardroom as well.

Some scholars argue that a Darwinian process ensures that optimal governance arrangements naturally evolve.[40] According to this theory, organizations with poor governance arrangements will eventually fail and those with good governance arrangements will prosper. If this has been happening in the past then the organizational forms we see today—the large corporations with their separation of ownership and control—must have the best governance arrangements. The arrangements we see today are the survivors, the ones that worked best. As circumstances change, new governance arrangements will evolve. We may be seeing that at present in the market for corporate control. The widespread adoption of poison pills and staggered boards reduced the threat of a hostile takeover in the late 1980s. Activist hedge funds filled the gap created by the demise of the corporate raider and have reinstated the threat of external intervention in a firm's affairs.

However, this might be an overly optimistic view of corporate governance. It has taken just a few pages in this chapter to illustrate some of the ways in which the evolutionary process can be interrupted by lawyers and lobbyists fighting to change the rules of the evolutionary game. It is competition like this that might be hindering the evolutionary process. Even if competition between firms with different governance arrangements eventually results in the best governance systems surviving, change might be a long time coming. In the meantime, the lessons from this book will remain valuable.

Epilogue

The insights we have acquired in this book will be useful for decades to come because the conflict between managers and shareholders shows no signs of going away.

In the space of a few months late in 2015—the period when I was finishing writing this book—more examples of the ideas described here appeared in the news. The sportswear company Under Armour, a firm with two classes of shares—one high in votes, the other low—widened the gap between ownership and control even further by issuing a third class of shares. Owners of the new shares would not get any votes at all.[41] They got ownership, but no control whatsoever. Bank of America survived a shareholder rebellion against its proposal to recombine the roles of CEO and board chairman. Despite opposition from large shareholders and the two dominant proxy advisory firms, a modest majority of shareholders supported the board's proposal.[42] Following pressure from Carl Icahn, eBay separated its (struggling) e-commerce and (booming) digital payments businesses when it spun off PayPal as a separate company, breaking up the firm's internal capital market in the process.[43] DuPont defeated an activist hedge fund's proxy fight, but the CEO resigned a few months later when the activist considered launching a second fight.[44] Pharmaceutical company Mylan launched a tender offer in the latest stage of its takeover battle with rival Perrigo.[45]

There will be many similar examples in the years to come because some of the most well-known firms to list their shares on the NYSE and NASDAQ share markets in recent years have organized their affairs in ways that portend trouble. For example, the founders of Facebook and LinkedIn have both set up their firms to have two different classes of shares. The Facebook shares owned by Mark Zuckerberg each give him ten votes whenever the firm's shareholders vote on matters affecting the firm's future. The shares that you or I might buy come with just one vote each. When the shares started trading on the NASDAQ, Zuckerberg effectively owned 21% of the company but was allowed to cast 56% of the votes.[46] Founders of other firms have used different methods to keep shareholders at bay. For example, the founders of Dunkin' Brands and Tesla have set their firms up with staggered boards, making it impossible for a raider to replace a majority of the board in a single year.[47] In all of these cases, the founders wanted outside investors' money but were not willing to give up control.

New examples, with new firms and new executives, but with the same old economic forces shaping events. Shareholders' objectives are the same; executives' incentives are the same; the challenges facing directors are the same. It is not surprising, then, that the events described in this book keep repeating themselves. If we can understand the economic forces driving the events—and my job as author has been to make sure readers can—then we can understand the conflict between managers and shareholders that drives so much corporate behavior today.

Acknowledgments

I would like to thank Scott Parris, OUP's Executive Editor of Economics and Finance, who gently coaxed revisions out of me that significantly improved this book. Most of those revisions were suggested by three anonymous reviewers, who generously took the time to read a long manuscript and put together extremely helpful and constructive comments. Glenn Boyle, Dinesh Kumareswaran, Konstantin Kvatch, and Steen Videbeck read and corrected drafts of various chapters along the way. Scott Thompson did excellent work on the Lions Gate example in Chapter 13. Finally, I would also like to thank the students in my graduate corporate governance classes at Victoria University of Wellington, who have helped me understand and develop the ideas I have finally managed to organize in this book.

Notes

1. Benoit and Kapner (2015); Damouni et al. (2015).

2. Starboard Value LP (2015).

3. Court of Chancery of the State of Delaware (2015).

4. At eBay's 2015 shareholder meeting, 59% of votes cast supported a proposal to improve proxy access, despite board opposition (eBay Inc., 2015a; 2015b, pp. 38–41). At FedEx, 54% of votes cast supported a similar proposal, again in the face of opposition from the board (FedEx Corp., 2015a; 2015b, pp. 65–67).

5. At Ford's 2015 shareholder meeting, 37% of votes cast supported a proposal that each share have one vote, despite board opposition (Ford Motor Co., 2015a; 2015b, pp. 72–74). At Google, 26% of votes cast supported a similar proposal, again in the face of opposition from the board (Google Inc., 2015a; 2015b, pp. 54–55).

6. At Starbucks's 2015 shareholder meeting, 32% of votes cast supported a proposal to prevent the CEO from chairing the board of directors, despite board opposition (Starbucks Corp., 2015a; 2015b, pp. 51–52). At Target, 38% of votes cast supported a similar proposal, again in the face of opposition from the board (Target Corp., 2015a; 2015b, pp. 79–80).

7. Tempur Sealy International, Inc (2015).

8. Michael Fries, Liberty Global (Lublin, 2015); David Zaslav, Discovery Communications (Gelles, 2015); Nick Woodman, GoPro (Egan, 2015).

9. Oracle Corp. (2012, 2013, 2014, 2015).

10. Hwang and Kim (2009, Table 2).

11. Becker and Subramanian (2013, p. 2) report that of the 16,822 candidates nominated for board seats at the 3,000 largest U.S. corporations in 2011, 99.8% were proposed by the incumbent directors and 99.9% of these were elected.

12. Berle and Means (1932).

13. For example, the average market value of the 500 largest U.S. firms increased by a factor of five between 1980 and 2011 (Gabaix et al., 2014, p. F49).

CHAPTER 1. A GADFLY IN THE OINTMENT

1. Fannie Mae's annual meeting, as reported in Hilzenrath (2007).

2. Knowlton and Klein Berlin (1989).

3. Wall Street Journal (1970); Evening Independent (1972).

4. Moin (2005); Peale (1998); Hilzenrath (2007); Morgan Stanley (2005b).

5. Morgan Stanley (2005b).

6. Bristol-Myers Squibb Company (2005).

7. Tierney (2005).

8. Davis (2005).

9. Author's calculations.

10. Hymowitz and Daurat (2013).

11. Author's analysis of ownership data.

12. For example, one recent study of 2,805 large firms over the period from 1992 to 2006 found that the median level of CEO ownership was 0.3% when stock options are excluded and 0.8% when they are included (Kim and Lu, 2011, Table 2).

13. Graham et al. (2013).

14. Philip Purcell, MBA from the University of Chicago (Wedemeyer and Sterngold, 1986); Peter Dolan, MBA from Dartmouth University (Bristol-Myers Squibb Company, 2001b; Petersen, 2001).

15. Falato et al. (2015) report that firm performance is better on average if a CEO has more positive press coverage the year before he was first appointed CEO, first became a CEO at a relatively young age, or attended a more selective college. Kaplan et al. (2012) analyzed a consulting firm's assessments of candidates for CEO positions at firms funded by private equity investors and found that subsequent firm performance tended to be best at firms with good "general ability" and "execution skills"; softer "interpersonal skills" were much less important.

16. Custódio et al. (2013) construct an index that locates a CEO on the generalist–specialist spectrum and find that generalist CEOs became more prevalent between 1993 and 2007. Custódio and Metzger (2013) find that firms expanding into different industries by acquiring other firms tend to perform better if their CEO has previous work experience in the target industry.

17. Gerald Grinstein, previously CEO of Western Air Lines Inc. and Burlington Northern Inc. (Delta Air Lines, Inc., 2005, p. 12); Peter Dolan, who joined Bristol-Myers in 1988 after eight years at General Foods, was appointed Bristol-Myers Squibb's CEO in 2001 (Bristol-Myers Squibb Company, 2001a); Philip Purcell was appointed president of the Dean Witter business unit of Sears, Roebuck & Co. in 1982, and promoted to CEO four years later (Wiener, 1986).

18. Fee et al. (2013) present evidence that is consistent with boards choosing CEOs whose individual styles and skills suggest they are a good fit for policies the board wants to adopt. In particular, policy changes tend to be substantial after a CEO is replaced, and the changes tend to be greater when the board has a larger pool of replacement CEOs to choose from.

19. Graham et al. (2013); Cain and McKeon (2016, Table 5).

20. Benmelech and Frydman (2015).

21. Graham et al. (2013, Table 5); Custódio and Metzger (2014); Cain and McKeon (2016, Table 4); Cronqvist et al. (2012).

22. Hirshleifer et al. (2012).

23. Gabaix and Landier (2008) and Terviö (2008) pioneered the use of competitive assignment models for analyzing the process by which CEOs and firms are matched. Subsequent research examines the effects of agency costs (Edmans et al., 2009), managerial risk aversion (Edmans and Gabaix, 2011), and multiple characteristics of CEO ability (Eisfeldt and Kuhnen, 2013).

24. Gabaix and Landier (2008, p. 50).

25. Coles et al. (2008, Tables 1, 3, and 4).

26. Hwang and Kim (2009, Tables 1 and 2).

27. Boston Properties Inc. (2005, p. 17); Marriott International Inc. (2005, p. 6).

28. Author's analysis of ownership data.

29. Ford Motor Co. (2005, p. 6); Comcast Corp. (2005, p. 9).

30. The minimum ownership stake is the smaller of $2,000 or 1% of the firm's market value (Securities and Exchange Commission, 1998a).

31. For example, Davis submitted 314 proposals between 1987 and 1994 (Gillan and Starks, 2000, p. 281) and 279 between 2000 and 2006 (Buchanan et al., 2012, p. 774).

32. Renneboog and Szilagyi (2011, Table 1).

33. Tierney (2005).

34. Author's analysis of voting outcomes.

35. Ten out of 341 proposals sponsored by individual shareholders during 1986–1990 won majority support (Karpoff et al., 1996, Tables 1 and 5).

36. Ertimur et al. (2010, Appendix A).

37. May Department Stores Co. (2005, p. 31); Pepco Holdings Inc. (2004, p. 28; 2005, p. 28); Morgan Stanley (2005a, p. 24).

38. Author's analysis of proxy statements.

39. Securities and Exchange Commission (1998a).

40. Author's calculations.

41. The threshold may be even tougher than this. For example, suppose there is a 10% probability that another shareholder will sponsor a similar proposal. If we sponsor one, this probability increases by 90% and, on average, we are $198 (90% of $220) better off. It is therefore worth acting ourselves only if the cost we would incur is less than $198.

42. Securities and Exchange Commission (1998a).

43. Palfrey and Rosenthal (1984).

44. Dixit and Skeath (1999, Section 11.6), which is based on Palfrey and Rosenthal (1984).

45. Piccalo (1996).

46. Wall Street Journal (1965).

47. New York Times (1977).

48. Smith (1963).

49. Washington Post (1984).

50. Doyle (1990).

51. Strauss (2003).

52. Bennetts (2002).

53. Ford Motor Co. (2003).

54. Jerome (1996).
55. Craig (2011).
56. Craig (2011).
57. Wilmington Morning Star (1980); Feldman (1998); Craig (2011).

CHAPTER 2. WHOSE SIDE ARE YOU ON?

1. Court of Chancery of the State of Delaware (1990).
2. Author's estimate using the approach described in Chapter 5. The *Wall Street Journal* reported a figure of $857m for the same period, using a different approach (Thurm, 2010).
3. Occidental Petroleum Corp. (2010d, p. 21).
4. Occidental Petroleum Corp. (2010d, p. 15).
5. Occidental Petroleum Corp. (2010d, p. 10).
6. Oxy acquired a 5.4% stake in Church & Dwight Co. in 1986 when the two companies formed a joint venture (Armand Products Co.) to produce potassium carbonate (Reckard, 1991).
7. Harris (1982). For a particularly scathing review, see Zurawik (1991).
8. For example, Hammer was reported to have spent $3.2m on 16 horses for Oxy Arabians at auctions in Arizona in 1982 (Boyer, 1982).
9. CalSTRS and Relational Investors LLC (2010c).
10. CalSTRS and Relational Investors LLC (2010b).
11. Nash (1950) suggests a list of reasonable-sounding properties that any outcome of a bargaining game should have and shows that there is only one outcome that has these properties. Roth (1979) extends his work. Rubinstein (1982) and Binmore et al. (1986) show how Nash's solution arises when the two bargaining parties make a sequence of alternating offers.
12. Supreme Court of Delaware (1991).
13. Oxy denied that these funds had been used for the foundation's art purchases (Parachini, 1990b).
14. Parachini (1990a).
15. Parachini (1989).
16. Supreme Court of Delaware (1991).
17. Court of Chancery of the State of Delaware (1990).
18. Some small shareholders challenged Oxy's museum donation, but agreed to a settlement that was regarded as a good deal for Oxy and the shareholders' lawyers. Other, much larger, shareholders challenged the proposed settlement, but the settlement was approved by the Delaware court, in part because the judge believed that the business judgment rule would protect Oxy's directors if the original challenge went to trial. See Minow (1998).
19. Follett (2010); Strine et al. (2010).
20. Temes (1990).
21. Louis Nizer (Oliver, 1998); Arthur Krim (Ostrow, 1976).
22. Albert Gore, Sr. (Occidental Petroleum Corp., 1995, p. 5).
23. George Nolley (Occidental Petroleum Corp., 1995, p. 6).
24. Erwin Piper (Baker, 1980); Aziz Syriani, president of Competrol Establishment, owned by Suliman Olayan (Lueck, 1983).
25. John Kluge (Webster, 1987).
26. Rosemary Tomich (Jacobs, 1985; Loper, 1986; Oates, 1987, 1988).

27. Krim, Kluge, and Tomich served on the special committee evaluating the museum project and also on the board of directors of the Armand Hammer United World College of the American West; the other Oxy directors on the College board were Hammer, Irani, Groman, and Moss (Minow, 1998, p. 103).

28. In 1984, Hammer removed two critical directors from the board and attempted to remove a third. Oxy repurchased the shares owned by an outside director, David Murdock, who immediately lost his seat on the board. Shortly afterwards, Hammer fired one inside director (Robert Abboud) and attempted to sell Oxy's IBP beef unit, reportedly to remove another inside director (Robert Peterson) from the board. See Williams (1984b).

29. Rose (1989).

30. Hermalin and Weisbach (1998) pioneered this approach using a theoretical model in which a board learns about a CEO's ability over time. Low-ability CEOs are fired, whereas high-ability ones keep their jobs and are able to negotiate a reduction in board independence.

31. Author's estimate using event study methodology.

32. Reckard (1991).

33. Lev (1991).

34. Peltz (1999, 2005).

35. In the years 1990, 2000, and 2010, board size was 17, 11, and 13, respectively; the percentage of directors who met the legal definition of independence was 59%, 73%, and 85%; directors' average age was 68, 61, and 68 years; and the average tenure of outside directors was 13, 7.5, and 13 years. (Source: author's analysis of Oxy's proxy statements.)

36. Rodolfo Segovia worked with Irani on an oil exploration joint venture in Colombia in the 1980s, when he was president of the Colombian national oil company and Irani was president of Occidental, before joining Oxy's board in 1994 (British Broadcasting Corporation, 1985).

37. Before he joined Oxy's board in 1996, John Chalsty was CEO of Donaldson, Lufkin & Jenrette Securities Corp., one of the underwriters of Oxy's sale of the meat-packing firm IBP in 1987 and 1991 (Arndt, 1987; Parrish, 1991).

38. Ronald Burkle had been a director of Kaufman and Broad Home Corp. alongside Irani for four years before joining Oxy's board in 1999 (Kaufman & Broad Home Corp., 1999, pp. 5–6; Occidental Petroleum Corp., 1999, p. 4). John Feick, a Canadian engineering consultant, had been a director of Canadian Occidental Petroleum Ltd, where Irani chaired the board, for two years before joining the Oxy board in 1998 (Canadian Occidental Petroleum Ltd, 1996; Reuters, 1998).

39. Chad Dreier, CEO of the homebuilder Ryland Group Inc. and former CFO of KB Home, joined Oxy's board in 2002 (Occidental Petroleum Corp., 2002).

40. Spencer Abraham shared Irani's Lebanese ancestry (Behn, 2005). He was Secretary of Energy when he appointed Irani to his advisory board (Department of Energy, 2002a) and to a task force on the future of scientific research (Department of Energy, 2002b). He was elected to Oxy's board in 2005, six months after resigning as Energy Secretary.

41. Avedick Poladian, who joined the board in 2008, was appointed a managing partner of Arthur Anderson in 1989 (Lee, 1989) and left the firm in 2002 as part of the exodus of staff in the wake of the Enron scandal (Occidental Petroleum Corp., 2010d, p. 5). Oxy changed auditors the same year (Sender, 2002).

42. Aziz Syriani and Rosemary Tomich joined Oxy's board in 1983 and 1980, respectively (Occidental Petroleum Corp., 2010d, p. 6).

43. The New York Stock Exchange requires firms to have a nominating committee made up entirely of independent directors; NASDAQ requires that either a majority of independent directors or a nominating committee made up entirely of independent directors approves all director nominations (Securities and Exchange Commission, 2003c).

44. Occidental Petroleum Corp. (2010d, p. 2).

45. Becker and Subramanian (2013, p. 2).

46. CEO ownership stake: Baker and Gompers (2003); Boone et al. (2007); Linck et al. (2008). CEO tenure: Baker and Gompers (2003); Boone et al. (2007). Director ownership: Boone et al. (2007). Takeover defenses: Fracassi and Tate (2012).

47. Palmeri (2003).

48. The returns are measured from April 30, 1999 until April 30, 2004. The benchmark is a value-weighted portfolio of all firms with SIC Code 1311, excluding Oxy.

49. Occidental Petroleum Corp. (2003, p. 2; 2004, p. A-1).

50. Occidental Petroleum Corp. (2005, p. 7).

51. Adams and Ferreira (2007) analyze the conflicting nature of the advisory and monitoring roles and show that in some circumstances shareholders benefit from having a board that is friendly to management. Schmidt (2015) reports supporting empirical evidence.

52. Author's estimates using the approach described in Chapter 5.

53. Colvin (2010); Waldman (2010).

54. Author's analysis of voting outcomes.

55. CalSTRS and Relational Investors LLC (2010b)

56. The average is calculated over the period 2000–2006 (Taylor, 2010b, Table II).

57. Board size: Yermack (1996). Insiders: Guo and Masulis (2015); Weisbach (1988). Directors' outside commitments: Fich and Shivdasani (2006). Social ties: Hwang and Kim (2009).

58. Author's calculations using information in Occidental Petroleum Corp. (2010a, p. 20). Oil and Gas News (2011) describes Irani's role.

59. Carroll (2010).

60. The board was facing pressure from two investment funds that were threatening to launch a proxy fight (CalSTRS and Relational Investors LLC, 2010b). We cover proxy fights and the role of activist hedge funds in Chapter 10.

61. Occidental Petroleum Corp. (2010b, Ex. 99.2).

62. Chalsty and Maloney, both over the board's mandatory retirement age, departed. Howard Atkins, chief financial officer of Wells Fargo & Company, and Peggy Foran, chief governance officer with Prudential Financial, joined. Foran was nominated by CalSTRS and Relational Investors (Occidental Petroleum Corp., 2010b, 2010c; CalSTRS and Relational Investors LLC, 2010a).

63. In addition, this increases the CEO's decision-making power (Adams et al., 2005).

64. Lee (1990); Pickett (1990).

65. Fahlenbrach et al. (2011, Table 1).

66. Evans et al. (2010); Fahlenbrach et al. (2011).

67. Occidental Petroleum Corp. (2012, pp. 17–18).

68. Occidental Petroleum Corp. (2013e, p. 30).

69. Krauss (2013); Olson (2013).

70. Fahlenbrach et al. (2011).

71. The returns are measured from May 31, 2011 until December 31, 2012. The benchmark is a value-weighted portfolio of all firms with SIC Code 1311, excluding Oxy.

72. Occidental Petroleum Corp. (2013a, Ex. 99.1).

73. Fahlenbrach et al. (2011).

74. Irani was reported to have proposed replacing Chazen with Dale Laurance (Lucchetti et al., 2013), who had worked with Irani at Olin Corp. (Lee, 1990).

75. Lucchetti et al. (2013).

76. Occidental Petroleum Corp. (2013a, Ex 99.1).

77. Fowler and Lublin (2013).

78. Occidental Petroleum Corp. (2013e, pp. 1–4).

79. Krauss (2013).

80. Shareholders First Pacific Advisors LLC and Matrix Asset Advisors Inc. publicly supported Chazen; the proxy advisor Institutional Shareholder Services Inc. recommended shareholders vote against Irani and Aziz Syriani in the board elections (Lublin et al., 2013).

81. Occidental Petroleum Corp. (2013b, Ex. 99.1).

82. Occidental Petroleum Corp. (2013c).

83. Reddall (2013a).

84. Occidental Petroleum Corp. (2013d).

85. Occidental Petroleum Corp. (2014).

CHAPTER 3. OVERSEEING THE UNSEEABLE

1. Delaney and Karnitschnig (2008).

2. Angel (2002, p. 15); Red Herring (1995); Squires (2008).

3. Author's calculations based on Microsoft's final offer of $33 per share.

4. Author's analysis of ownership data.

5. Author's calculations based on the May 5 opening price of $23.05.

6. Delaney (2008); Stone and Helft (2008).

7. Author's analysis of voting outcomes.

8. Gumbel (1999).

9. Maney (1995); Stross (1998).

10. Yahoo Inc. (1995); Schlender (2000).

11. Red Herring (1995).

12. Suitors included Prodigy Services Co., Compuserve, and America Online (Harmon, 1995).

13. Schlender (2000).

14. Bidders included AOL and Netscape Communications (Red Herring, 1995; Stross, 1998). Kleiner Perkins proposed to finance Yahoo if it merged with Excite, Inc., then known as Architext Software Inc. (Stross, 1998).

15. Red Herring (1995).

16. Maney (1995).

17. Levy (1998); Schlender (2000).

18. Schlender (2000).

19. The value of Yahoo's shares peaked at $132b on January 4, 2000.

20. The value of Yahoo's shares bottomed out at $4.6b on September 27, 2001.

21. Delaney and Lublin (2007).

22. The value of Yahoo's shares peaked again at $62b on January 9, 2006.

23. Delaney (2006).

24. Hansell (2006).

25. Yahoo's shares were worth $37b when the market closed on Friday, June 15, 2007. Yang's appointment as CEO was announced after markets closed on the following Monday.

26. Yahoo Inc. (2007a).

27. Yahoo Inc. (2007b, 2007c); Yang (2007).

28. Yahoo's shares were worth $25b when the market closed on January 30, 2008, the day before Microsoft made its offer to Yahoo's board.

29. Yahoo Inc. (2008a, p. 15).

30. Follett (2010); Strine et al. (2010).

31. Helft (2008b).

32. Jensen and Meckling (1976) use a theoretical model to, amongst other things, compare the behavior of a manager who owns 100% of a firm with one who owns only a portion of the firm. The manager weighs pecuniary benefits of ownership against non-pecuniary benefits of control.

33. Jenkins, Jr. (2008).

34. Yahoo Inc. (2008c, pp. 28–29).

35. Author's calculations based on Microsoft's final offer of $33 per share.

36. Author's calculations based on Yahoo's opening price of $23.05 per share.

37. Yang (1997).

38. Yahoo Inc. (2008c, pp. 28–29); Kim and Lu (2011, Table 2).

39. Yahoo Inc. (2008c, pp. 28–29).

40. Follett (2010).

41. Roy Bostock was chairman of Northwest Airlines Corp. in April 2008, when it agreed to merge with Delta Air Lines Inc. (Carey and Prada, 2008).

42. Robert Kotick, CEO of Activision, announced plans to merge with the Vivendi Games unit of Vivendi Universal in December 2007 (Richtel, 2007).

43. Vyomeshi Joshi, executive vice president of Hewlett-Packard's Imaging and Printing Group, oversaw a 5% annual drop in consumer hardware sales in the first quarter of 2008 (Hewlett Packard Co., 2008).

44. Delaney et al. (2008a).

45. Yahoo hired Goldman Sachs, Lehman Brothers, and Moelis & Company to provide financial advice, and Skadden, Arps, Slate, Meagher & Flom for legal advice. The board's outside directors hired Munger Tolles & Olson LLP as independent legal advisors (Yahoo Inc., 2008d).

46. The meeting was held by teleconference on Friday, February 8 (Delaney and Karnitschnig, 2008; Ross Sorkin and Helft, 2008).

47. Vascellaro et al. (2008).

48. Lauria and Kouwe (2008).

49. Ross Sorkin and Helft (2008).

50. Ross Sorkin and Helft (2008).

51. Delaney and Karnitschnig (2008).

52. Karnitschnig (2008a, 2008b).

53. Karnitschnig and Guth (2008).

54. Karnitschnig and Guth (2008).

55. Helft (2008a).

56. Yahoo Inc. (2008b).

57. Delaney et al. (2008b).

58. Karnitschnig and Guth (2008).

59. Karnitschnig and Guth (2008).

60. Department of Justice (2008).

61. Yahoo's share price fell to $8.94 at one point on November 20, 2008.

62. Yahoo shares traded for $33.00 at one point on September 26, 2013, the first time this had happened since Microsoft abandoned its takeover bid.

63. Karnitschnig and Guth (2008).

64. Jenkins, Jr. (2008).

65. Moore (2008).

66. Helft (2008b); Stone and Helft (2008).

67. Karnitschnig and Guth (2008).

CHAPTER 4. NARROWING THE GAP

1. Francis (2008).

2. On average, founders have ownership stakes more than four times as large as non-founders (Kim and Lu, 2011, p. 287).

3. Hospital Corporation of America (1992); HCA–The Healthcare Co. (2001b).

4. Author's analysis of proxy statements.

5. In practice, firms issue different classes of bonds, with senior bonds having a higher priority than junior bonds. This could be represented in Figure 4.1 by dividing the dark-gray slice in two, with the senior bonds represented by the bottom layer.

6. Author's estimates.

7. Strictly speaking, when we measure the increase in value of the firm as a whole we should include the increases in value of the bonds the firm has sold to investors and the stock options it has granted to employees. However, in most cases the bonds are sufficiently insensitive to the share price and the options are sufficiently few in number that we can get a good approximation using just the increase in value of the firm's shares.

8. Author's analysis of the proxy statements in 2000 for all firms with SIC code 8062.

9. Wayne Smith at Community Health Systems, Inc., and Alan Miller at Universal Health Services, Inc., respectively.

10. The market-value-weighted average CEO ownership stake at firms in Kim and Lu (2011) was 1.4% in 2006.

11. Author's estimates; HCA–The Healthcare Co. (2001a, pp. 3 and 17); LifePoint Hospitals Inc. (2001, pp. 1 and 8).

12. Edmans et al. (2009) make this assumption in their analysis of ownership-generated incentives.

13. Author's analysis of the firms' balance sheets.

14. Edmans et al. (2009) develop a theoretical model that assumes managerial effort has a multiplicative (upward) effect on firm value and a multiplicative (downward) effect on the enjoyment an executive derives from his income. They show that this implies the dollar change in wealth for a percentage change in firm value, divided by annual pay, is independent of firm size, which motivates its use as an incentive measure.

15. Author's estimates using the approach described in Chapter 5. Bovender's pay relates to FY 2001. LifePoint's CEO died after a year in the job, in June 2001; his pay relates to this 12-month period.

16. At the time, Bovender owned more than twice the minimum required number of shares (HCA Inc., 2006a, pp. 6 and 31).

17. Core and Guay (1999).

18. Bovender retired from HCA in 1994 and rejoined as president and chief operating officer in August 1997 (Columbia/HCA Healthcare Corp., 1997).

19. Author's analysis of HCA's proxy statements.

20. Author's analysis of HCA's proxy statements.

21. Author's analysis of HCA's annual cash flow statements.

22. Author's estimates.

23. Himmelberg et al. (1999, Table 4B) provide empirical evidence of these predictions for share-price volatility, growth opportunities (proxied by investment and R&D expenditure), and discretionary spending (proxied by advertising spending, soft capital, and the ratio of operating income to sales). However, the dependent variable is percentage equity ownership, with no allowance for stock options.

24. The vesting of shares and options is discussed in Chapter 5.

25. Ofek and Yermack (2000).

26. Author's estimates.

27. Author's analysis of HCA's proxy statements and the Form 4s filed by Richard Bracken, Samuel Hazen, and Milton Johnson during 2005.

28. HCA Inc. (2005, Ex. 99-1). The share price fell from $54.91 to $50.05 on July 13.

29. Sasseen (2010).

30. Ross Sorkin (2006).

31. HCA Inc. (2007, p. F-14).

32. HCA Inc. (2006c, Ex. 99(a)(4); 2007).

33. Guo et al. (2011, Table II).

34. HCA Inc. (2007, p. F-14).

35. Bovender's effective ownership stake increased from 0.54% to 0.73%. The post-buyout result refers to his ownership stake as at March 31, 2007 in order to include options granted to him shortly after the buyout was completed. Some of these options had performance-based vesting criteria, but the effect of these is ignored for the purposes of calculating Bovender's ownership stake. These calculations assume that all of an increase in enterprise value benefits shareholders. Given HCA's high post-buyout debt levels, some of any gain would benefit bondholders, leaving a smaller gain for shareholders, and therefore a smaller gain for Bovender. In general, the effective ownership stake described in this chapter overestimates a CEO's incentives for firms with very high debt levels.

36. Author's estimates.

37. Author's analysis of ownership data in HCA Inc. (2006b).

38. HCA Inc. (2007, p. F-14).

39. Management contributed equity to 62% of buyouts during the period 1990–2006. The median management equity stake was 6.5% and percentage of board seats taken by private equity sponsors was 50% (Guo et al., 2011, Table VII).

40. McCue and Thompson (2012).

41. Author's analysis of HCA's financial statements.

42. Bharath et al. (2014, Table 9).

43. Davis et al. (2014).

44. Author's analysis of HCA's cash flow statements.

45. HCA Holdings, Inc. (2011, p. 32).

46. HCA announced the buyout offer on July 24, 2006 (HCA Inc., 2006b, p. 26). Its closing share price on Friday, June 23 was $42.75.

47. Guo et al. (2011, Table I).

48. HCA Inc. (2006b, p. 89).

49. Myerson (1997).

50. HCA Inc. (2006b, pp. 34 and 36).

51. Golden (2008).

52. HCA Inc. (2006b, pp. B-2 and C-2).

53. HCA Inc. (2006b, pp. 21–22).

54. French (2006).

55. HCA Holdings, Inc. (2011, p. 32).

56. Author's calculations using information from HCA Holdings, Inc. (2011, 2012).

CHAPTER 5. A PRIMER ON PAY

1. Arango (2008).

2. Jeffrey Katzenberg, DreamWorks Studios (Parkes, 1999); Steve Jobs, Pixar (Orwall and Wingfield, 2004); Michael Ovitz (Orwall, 2004); and Roy Disney (Orwall, 2003).

3. Reingold and Grover (1999).

4. Disney's profit in 1998 was 5.9% lower than in the previous year; the value of Disney shares fell by 5.0% over the course of the year, while the S&P 500 index increased by 7.4% (author's calculations).

5. Author's calculations assuming that the total return earned by Disney shareholders equaled the total return on the S&P 500 index over the same period.

6. Crystal (1991); Flanigan (1992).

7. Orwall (1997).

8. Andersen (1991); Rockwell (1992).

9. Models of the trade-off between risk and incentives in managerial compensation schemes with this feature include Milgrom and Roberts (1992, Chapter 7).

10. Stewart (2005, pp. 46–51).

11. Press reports named Eisner, Alan Hirschfield (current chairman and CEO of 20th Century-Fox Film Corp.), Dennis Stanfill (past chairman and CEO of 20th Century-Fox Film Corp.), and Frank Wells (current Vice Chairman of Warner Bros.) as candidates for the job (Sansweet, 1984).

12. Landro (1984).

13. Cieply (1985).

14. Kaplan and Minton (2012, p. 58).

15. Stein (1989) shows that managers have this incentive even when stock markets are fully rational. Managers attempt to increase share prices by boosting short-run performance, but the

stock market anticipates this and factors it into prices. Managers are nevertheless trapped into boosting profits because investors anticipate such behavior.

16. Narayanan (1985) shows that this behavior can occur when managers' decisions affect market perceptions of their ability. Artificially boosting short-term perceived ability boosts short-term pay without necessarily lowering long-term pay.

17. Laux (2012) shows that managers can face these incentives when their decisions affect market perceptions of their ability.

18. Buchan (1989).

19. Stewart (2005, p. 96).

20. Author's analysis of Disney's income statements.

21. The return is measured from September 21, 1984 to January 11, 1989.

22. Author's estimate using the approach described later in this chapter.

23. Stern designed a Manhattan apartment for Eisner's parents in the 1970s and Eisner's "Rust Trust" house in the Encinal Bluffs neighborhood of Malibu in the late 1990s (Brown, 1990; Iovine, 1999; Weiss, 2007).

24. In their competitive assignment model of executive compensation, Edmans and Gabaix (2011) examine the implications of wealthy CEOs requiring higher pay to compensate them for making sacrifices and stronger incentives to induce them to make the sacrifices in the first place.

25. Arrow (1965); Pratt (1964).

26. The capital charge used to calculate economic profit would rise from 9% to 11% of the book value of Disney's equity (Walt Disney Co., 1995, p. 9).

27. Author's analysis of Disney's proxy statements.

28. Arango (2008).

29. From the cover of the April 25, 1988 issue: "Why is this mouse smiling? Because Michael Eisner's magic has transformed Disney into a \$3 billion kingdom."

30. Author's analysis of Disney's balance sheets.

31. Gabaix and Landier (2008) and Gabaix et al. (2014) analyze the implications of increasing firm size for CEO pay using a competitive assignment model.

32. Gabaix et al. (2014, p. F49).

33. For example, Frydman and Saks (2010) report evidence challenging the proposed link between firm size and CEO pay.

34. Harris (1994).

35. Court of Chancery of the State of Delaware (2005).

36. Fabrikant (1996).

37. Walt Disney Co. (1997, pp. 4–6).

38. Brown (1990); Iovine (1999).

39. Prior to joining the Disney board, Stern designed the Casting Center at Walt Disney World in Florida (1989); the Yacht and Beach Club Resorts at Walt Disney World (1991); and Hotel Cheyenne and Newport Bay Club Hotel at Euro Disney (1992). After joining the board, he designed the Feature Animation Building in Burbank; the Disney Boardwalk at Walt Disney World (1996); the Ambassador Hotel at Tokyo Disney (1996); and worked on the master plan of the new community, Celebration, established near Walt Disney World (1997).

40. Walt Disney Co. (1993); Court of Chancery of the State of Delaware (2005, p. 136).

41. Associated Press (1996).

42. Rice (2000).

43. Court of Chancery of the State of Delaware (1998).

44. Orwall and Lublin (1997).

45. In addition, 8% of votes opposed Eisner's new bonus scheme, and another 3% abstained (Orwall, 1997). Shareholder approval was needed if Eisner's bonus was to qualify as performance-based compensation under Section 162(m) of the tax code, and therefore be a deductible expense. The board could still pay a bonus even if shareholders voted against the scheme, incurring the extra tax burden, so shareholders did not have the ability to prevent Eisner from being paid a bonus (Walt Disney Co., 1997, pp. 22–23).

46. Byrne et al. (1997).

47. Walt Disney Co. (1997, pp. 12–13).

48. Author's analysis of Eisner's employment agreements.

49. Vacations and heart surgery: Burroughs and Masters (1996); sharing control: Court of Chancery of the State of Delaware (2005, p. 15).

50. Court of Chancery of the State of Delaware (2005, pp. 14 and 29).

51. Ovitz and Eisner signed the letter agreement, and Disney announced the news, on August 14; the board and compensation committee met on September 26 (Court of Chancery of the State of Delaware, 2005, pp. 24–30).

52. Court of Chancery of the State of Delaware (2005, pp. 36–37 and 54–58).

53. Burroughs and Masters (1996).

54. Court of Chancery of the State of Delaware (2005, pp. 59–62).

55. Court of Chancery of the State of Delaware (2005, pp. 65–66 and 76–80).

56. Reuters (1996).

57. Author's valuation of the accelerated vesting of stock options on December 12, 1996, when Disney announced Ovitz's termination.

58. Court of Chancery of the State of Delaware (2005).

59. Supreme Court of Delaware (2006, pp. 1–2).

60. Court of Chancery of the State of Delaware (2005, p. 135).

61. Court of Chancery of the State of Delaware (2005, p. 2).

62. Byrne et al. (1994).

63. Author's analysis of Disney's proxy statements.

64. Bulow and Shoven (2005); Hancock et al. (2005).

65. Author's estimate.

66. Author's estimates.

67. Author's analysis of Disney's proxy statements.

68. The returns are measured from January 11, 1989 until September 30, 1998. The film and television portfolio comprised Capital Cities/ABC Inc., King World Productions Inc., Paramount Communications Inc., Time Inc., Turner Broadcasting System Inc., Viacom Inc., and Warner Communications. The hotel-operator portfolio comprised Club Med Inc., Gaylord Entertainment Co., Hilton Hotels Corp., Marriott Corp., and Starwood Hotels & Resorts World. The toy-manufacturers portfolio comprised Hasbro Inc. and Mattel Inc.

69. Holmström (1979) and Shavell (1979) establish the "informativeness principle," which states that all informative signals about an agent's performance should be included in a contract.

70. Author's analysis of the two firms' balance sheets.

71. Gillan et al. (2009, Table III).

72. Occidental Petroleum Corp. (1995, p. 14).

73. Gillan et al. (2009, p. 1637).

74. Walt Disney Co. (2000, Ex. 10(a), Section 10).

75. Holmström and Ricart i Costa (1986) show that manager–shareholder conflict involving attitudes to risk can be reduced using employment agreements that give managers protection against downward revisions in the level of their pay.

76. Gillan et al. (2009, Table V).

77. Rau and Xu (2013).

78. Carr (1989); Harmetz (1988).

79. Brown (1999).

80. Stewart (2005, pp. 321–328).

81. Shiller (2005).

82. Go.com internet portal (Hansell, 2001), Fox Family cable channel (James and Hofmeister, 2004), and Capital Cities/ABC (Orwall, 2002).

83. Verrier and Eller (2004).

84. Brown (2002).

85. Investors in Disney and the S&P 500 index earned 2.3% and 6.1% p.a., respectively, over the period from January 8, 1997 until January 8, 2004.

86. Orwall et al. (2004).

87. Walt Disney Co. (2006, p. 29).

88. Author's estimate.

CHAPTER 6. HIDING HIGH PAY

1. Kristof and Haddad (2006).

2. Bruce Karatz was appointed CEO of Kaufman & Broad in 1986; Larry Mizel founded Mizel Development Corporation, predecessor of MDC Holdings, in 1972 (KB Home, 2006d, p. 12; MDC Holdings Inc., 2006, p. 9).

3. Reuters (2005).

4. Greenspan (2005).

5. The changes in revenue are measured from fiscal year 2005 to fiscal year 2010; the changes in share price are measured from July 20, 2005 until July 20, 2010.

6. Author's estimates using the approach described in Chapter 5.

7. The annual rates of return, measured from July 20, 2000 until July 20, 2005, of the ten firms with the largest sales during the 2000 financial year, were: Lennar, 46%; Centex, 51%; MDC Holdings, 51%; KB Home, 55%; Pulte, 55%; Toll Brothers, 57%; Beazer Homes USA, 59%; DR Horton, 61%; NVR, 69%; and Ryland Group, 73%. (Del Webb Corp., the eighth largest by sales, is excluded as it was acquired by Pulte in 2001.)

8. KB Home (2008c, pp. 29–30).

9. For example: "The Committee sought to provide an appropriate level of compensation in light of these challenging market conditions and the accomplishments of the executive officers with respect to their foresight in strengthening the financial condition of the Company and mitigating losses in shareowner value compared to the other publicly-held homebuilders as a whole." (MDC Holdings Inc., 2008, p. 27).

10. MDC Holdings Inc. (2008, pp. 15–19).

11. Bebchuk and Fried (2004).

12. KB Home (2004, 2005c).

13. Gisquet (2005); Levenson (2006).

14. Gisquet (2005); Berry (2004); KB Home (2005b).

15. Malmendier and Tate (2009).

16. Furlong (2002, 2004, 2006).

17. KB Home (2005a, p. 37; 2006d, p. 44; 2007, p. 48).

18. KB Home (2001, Ex. 10.1).

19. KB Home (2005a).

20. Helman (2005); Los Angeles Times (2005); Franklin (2005).

21. MGM Mirage (2005; 2006, Ex. 99).

22. Gannett Co. Inc. (2005); Goldman Sachs Group, Inc. (2005); Target Corp. (2005); Temple-Inland Inc. (2005); UnitedHealth Group Inc. (2005).

23. Hirschberg (2005).

24. Author's estimates using the approach described in Chapter 5.

25. State of California (2006).

26. Bebchuk and Fried (2004).

27. Ertimur et al. (2011).

28. Author's analysis of voting outcomes.

29. Kristof and Haddad (2006).

30. For example, there were more than 200 pay-related shareholder proposals at S&P 1500 firms in 2003 alone, many of them sponsored by pension funds (Ertimur et al., 2011, Figure 1).

31. Author's analysis of voting outcomes.

32. A firm's senior executives must file a so-called Form 4 with the SEC before the end of the second business day after they are granted securities in the firm (Securities and Exchange Commission, 2002c).

33. Author's estimates using information in KB Home (2006d).

34. Murphy (2013, Figure 2.4 and 2.5).

35. Core et al. (1999, Table 2); Cyert et al. (2002, Table 3A); Hwang and Kim (2009, Table 5); Hartzell and Starks (2003, Table V).

36. Since the end of 2006, the aggregate value of perks has to be reported unless their value is less than $10,000; individual perks worth at least $25,000 and contributing at least 10% of the total must be itemized (Securities and Exchange Commission, 2006a, p. 72).

37. KB Home (2007, p. 48).

38. Securities and Exchange Commission (2006a, p. 74).

39. This assumes that the committee meeting was held on the first Thursday in October, consistent with KB Home's practice in 2003–2005.

40. United States District Court, Central District of California (2009).

41. Author's estimates.

42. Author's estimates.

43. Option grants had to be disclosed on Form 4 within ten days of the end of the month in which they were granted, or on Form 5 within 45 days of the end of the fiscal year (Collins et al., 2009, Note 22).

44. Author's estimates.

45. Stannard and Guthrie (2013).

46. Bizjak et al. (2009, p. 4822).

47. Forelle and Bandler (2006).

48. Choi et al. (2013, Table 1).

49. Bebchuk et al. (2010); Collins et al. (2009).

50. KB Home (2006b; 2006c, Ex. 99.2).

51. KB Home (2006c, Ex. 99.1).

52. Fried (2008, Section II.B.2).

53. Emshwiller (2010).

54. Securities and Exchange Commission (2009b).

55. Author's calculations using information in KB Home (2006d).

56. KB Home (2008b, Ex. 99.1).

57. Ryland's CEO also received lump-sum cash payments totaling $25m from the firm's retirement program, which he had built up during his time in the job (Ryland Group Inc., 2009, Ex. 10.39).

58. Author's estimate using information in Standard Pacific Corp. (2008, Ex. 10.1).

59. Pulte Homes Inc. (2010, Ex. 10.1).

60. Beazer Homes USA Inc. (2011, p. 45); Securities and Exchange Commission (2011b).

61. Kaufman & Broad Home Corp. (1996, Ex. 10.20); KB Home (2001, Ex. 10.1).

62. KB Home (2001, Ex. 10.1, paragraph 6).

63. Kaufman & Broad Home Corp. (1996, Ex. 10.20, paragraph 4(b)(iii)); KB Home (2001, Ex. 10.1, paragraph 4(f)).

64. Kaufman & Broad Home Corp. (1996, Ex. 10.20, paragraph 6(b)); KB Home (2001, Ex. 10.1, paragraph 5(c)).

65. Author's analysis of Karatz's employment agreements.

66. Firms must also disclose the post-employment payments that the top five executives are entitled to, but in a part of the proxy statement with a lower profile than the summary compensation table.

67. KB Home (2006a, 2008a).

68. KB Home's shares were worth $8.1b on July 20, 2005.

69. KB Home (2008c, pp. 29–30).

70. The new bonus formula was first used in the 2008 fiscal year. It implied a bonus of $6.5m, but the compensation committee used its discretion and reduced Mezger's bonus to $2.75m (KB Home, 2009, pp. 40–42).

71. MDC Holdings Inc. (2008, pp. 35–36).

72. MDC Holdings Inc. (2008, p. 28).

73. MDC Holdings Inc. (2008, pp. 15–19).

74. MDC Holdings Inc. (2009, pp. 24 and 36).

75. MDC Holdings Inc. (2008, p. 16).

76. MDC Holdings Inc. (1994, pp. 17–19).

77. Author's analysis of MDC's annual reports.

78. MDC Holdings Inc. (2008, p. 15).

79. Graybow (2008).

80. Toll Brothers Inc. (2005, pp. 11–14; 2008, pp. 10–12).

81. Morse et al. (2011).

82. Garvey and Milbourn (2006).

83. Faulkender and Yang (2013, Table 1).

84. Core et al. (1999, Table 2).

85. Securities and Exchange Commission (2006a, p. 333).

86. MDC Holdings Inc. (2011, p. 34).

87. Author's analysis of firms' annual reports.

88. Ferracone and Harris (2011, p. 22).

89. Bizjak et al. (2011); Faulkender and Yang (2010, 2013).

90. Bizjak et al. (2011, Tables 4 and 7).

91. Cadman et al. (2010, p. 266).

92. Cadman et al. (2010, Table 1).

93. Securities and Exchange Commission (2009a, pp. 45–58).

94. Cadman et al. (2010); Murphy and Sandino (2010); Armstrong et al. (2012).

95. Author's estimates using the approach described in Chapter 5.

96. Gabaix and Landier (2008, pp. 87–88).

97. Bereskin and Cicero (2013).

98. Author's estimates using end-of-year shares outstanding.

CHAPTER 7. SEPARATING THE WHEAT FROM THE CHAFF

1. Palm Inc. (2001a, Ex. 99.1).

2. Gaither (2003).

3. Kirsner (2009).

4. Author's calculations.

5. Butter and Pogue (2002, p. 289).

6. The returns are measured from immediately before Palm's IPO until November 8, 2001.

7. Palm Inc. (2001a, Ex. 99.1); Wong (2001).

8. Author's calculations.

9. Majesco Holdings Inc. (2004a); Majesco Entertainment Co. (2005b).

10. Ambient Devices (2007); Kirsner (2009).

11. 3Com Corp. (1999).

12. Palm Inc. (2002a, p. 17).

13. Wong (2001).

14. Edwards (2001); Lohr (2000).

15. Tam (2001a).

16. Palm's share price fell from $19.375 on March 6, 2001 (the day before the agreement with Extended Systems was signed) to $7.11 on May 16, 2001 (the day before the agreement was terminated).

17. Palm Inc. (2001b).

18. Paul (2001); Tam (2001d).

19. Tam (2000a, 2000b).

20. Tam (2000c, 2001d).

21. Tam (2001c).

22. Tam (2001c); Weisman (2001).

23. Tam (2001b).

24. Yankowski was executive vice president of Reebok International Ltd and CEO of the Reebok Division, widely regarded as the number-two position in the firm (Reebok International Ltd., 1999, p. 22). Investor concerns about Yankowski's industry experience are described in Tam (2001c).

25. Oppel (1999).

26. Hermalin and Weisbach (1998) and Holmström (1999) present formal models along these lines.

27. Dikolli et al. (2014).

28. Palm Inc. (2001e, 2001f).

29. Tam (2001b).

30. Tam (2001b).

31. Palm Inc. (2001a, Ex. 99.1).

32. Palm Inc. (2001c) describes Yankowski's employment agreement; Palm Inc. (2002b) describes his severance agreement.

33. Wong (2001).

34. For example, Yankowski's severance agreement when he left Majesco in 2005 states that "the Company will adhere to its internal policy of limiting any Company response to inquiries . . . about the circumstances of [Yankowski's] employment and resignation to statements that [Yankowski] served as Chairman and Chief Executive Officer from August 24, 2004 through July 8, 2005 until his resignation by mutual agreement and that it is Company policy to only provide this information." (Majesco Entertainment Co., 2005a, Ex. 10.2)

35. Wilde (1895, Act 1).

36. Hermalin and Weisbach (1998) use a theoretical model to demonstrate that when boards evaluate executives with more uncertain *actual* ability they should tolerate lower levels of *perceived* ability.

37. Allgood and Farrell (2003, Fig. 1); Kim (1996).

38. Palm Inc. (2001d; 2002a, p. 16; 2002b, p. 9; 2003, p. 219).

39. Fee and Hadlock (2004); Hayes et al. (2006).

40. Palm Inc. (2002b, pp. 5 and 6).

41. PalmOne Inc. (2003).

42. Mitra (2007).

43. Author's estimate using the approach described in Chapter 5.

44. PalmOne Inc. (2005).

45. Fee et al. (2012, p. 11).

46. Fee and Hadlock (2004, p. 5).

47. Gaither (2003).

48. Garlo (2002, 2003).

49. Majesco Holdings Inc. (2004a).

50. Majesco Holdings Inc. (2005a).

51. Author's analysis of the two firms' annual reports for the fiscal years ending during 2004.

52. Majesco Holdings Inc. (2005a); Majesco Entertainment Co. (2005c, 2005e).

53. Majesco Holdings Inc. (2004b, 2005b); Saltzman (2005); Majesco Entertainment Co. (2005d).

54. Majesco Entertainment Co. (2005a, Ex. 10.2).

55. Majesco Entertainment Co. (2005b).

56. Majesco Entertainment Co. (2006, p. 20).

57. Author's estimates using the approach described in Chapter 5.

58. PalmOne Inc. (2005, Ex. 99.1); Majesco Entertainment Co. (2005a, Ex. 10.2).

59. Author's calculations.

60. Lawton (2007).

61. Burrows (2005).

62. Palm Inc. (2005, p. 51); Hewlett Packard Co. (2005, p. 34).

63. Author's estimate using the approach described in Chapter 5.

64. Yankowski was appointed CEO of Ambient Devices in January 2008 and left in September 2009 (Ambient Devices, 2008; Kirsner, 2009).

65. Fee et al. (2012, Tables 2 and 3); Fee and Hadlock (2003).

66. Palm Inc. (2002b, p. 6).

67. Palm Inc. (2003, p. 214).

68. Huson et al. (2001, Table VI); Mobbs and Raheja (2012, Table 8).

69. The return is measured from October 28, 2002 to October 28, 2003.

70. Lazear and Rosen (1981); Rosen (1986); Prendergast (1993).

71. Bradley, EVP Personal Systems Group; Vyomesh Joshi, EVP Imaging and Printing Group; and Ann Livermore, EVP HP Enterprise Business (Hewlett Packard Co., 2010, p. 55).

72. Cichello et al. (2009).

73. Lawton (2007); Hempel and Kowitt (2010).

74. Palm Inc. (2010); Worthen and Sherr (2011); Sherr (2011); Hewlett Packard Co. (2011b).

75. Hewlett Packard Co. (2012).

76. Author's calculations using information in Hewlett Packard Co. (2005, 2011a).

77. Ricadela (2013); TIBCO Software Inc. (2014).

78. PalmSource Inc. (2005a, 2005b).

79. Linck et al. (2009, Table 9.A).

80. Linck et al. (2009, Table 9).

81. Safeguard Scientifics Inc. (1999); Novell Inc. (2001).

82. Safeguard Scientifics Inc. (2002, p. 7); Novell Inc. (2003, p. 6); Informatica Corp. (2003); Chase Corp. (2004, p. 25).

83. Chase Corp. (2005, p. 3); Uni-Pixel Inc. (2007).

84. Tessera Technologies Inc. (2005); Leapfrog Enterprises Inc. (2005).

85. Wipro Ltd (2012); Harris Corp. (2013).

86. Brickley et al. (1999, Table 3).

87. Ferris et al. (2003, Table IV); Brickley et al. (1999, Table 7).

88. Author's estimate using the approach described in Chapter 4.

89. Kirsner (2009).

90. Fama (1980) shows how executives' concerns about their reputations reduce manager–shareholder conflict. Holmström (1999) develops a formal mathematical model of the link between an executive's incentives and the labor market learning about his ability.

91. Seinfeld (1995).

92. Kale et al. (2009).

93. Palm Inc. (2001e, 2001f).

94. Retirements are concentrated among CEOs who are 64–66 years old (Brickley et al., 1999, footnote 3).

95. Holmström (1999) develops a theoretical model explaining the role of age in determining the strength of career-based incentives.

96. Gateway 2000 Inc.(2000, p. 11; 2001, p. 12).

97. Apple Computer Inc. (1992, 1996); AT&T Corp. (2001); Palm Inc. (2001f).

98. Narayanan (1985).

99. Li et al. (2014).

100. Barker and Mueller (2002); Dechow and Sloan (1991); Serfling (2014).

101. Yim (2013).

102. Core et al. (2005) discuss the importance of considering all sources of pay–performance sensitivity.

103. Gibbons and Murphy (1992).

104. Mobbs and Raheja (2012).

CHAPTER 8. WITH ONE HAND TIED BEHIND THEIR BACK

1. Grant and Berman (2005).

2. Gould (1965).

3. Schwartz (1981).

4. Schwartz (1981).

5. Cablevision Systems Corp. (2009a, pp. 1–2 and 45).

6. Miller et al. (2007, Tables 3 and 4).

7. More than one class of share is issued at 21% of family firms and the family is over-represented on the board at 60% of family firms (Villalonga and Amit, 2009, Table 5).

8. Author's calculations, based on information in Cablevision Systems Corp. (2009d).

9. Cablevision Systems Corp. (2009d, pp. 4–6); Grant (2005c).

10. Cablevision Systems Corp. (2009c, Ex. 99.2).

11. Madison Square Garden Co. (2011b, pp. 7–9).

12. Author's estimate using event study methodology.

13. Cablevision Systems Corp. (2010, Ex. 99.1).

14. AMC Networks Inc. (2012, pp. 8–10).

15. Author's estimate using event study methodology.

16. Jim Dolan would continue as CEO of the cable system; Hank Ratner, Cablevision's Vice Chairman, became CEO of Madison Square Garden (Cablevision Systems Corp., 2009c, Ex. 99.2); Josh Sapan, CEO of Cablevision's Rainbow Media division, become AMC Network's CEO (Cablevision Systems Corp., 2011, Ex. 99.1).

17. Author's analysis of Cablevision's annual reports.

18. Cablevision Systems Corp. (2009a, p. 33).

19. Grant (2005c); Siegel (2005).

20. Author's estimates using the approach described in Chapter 5.

21. Pulley (2003).

22. Grant (2005c).

23. Associated Press (2003).

24. Berkowitz (2003); Moss and Farrell (2003).

25. Cablevision Systems Corp. (2004, p. I-27).

26. Grant (2004).

27. Cablevision Systems Corp. (2005a, pp. 58–59).

28. Somayaji (2005).

29. Baumann (2005).

30. Cablevision Systems Corp. (2005b).

31. Grant (2005b).

32. Grant (2005a); Li (2005).

33. Cablevision Systems Corp. (2005c, Ex. 99.1).

34. Cablevision Systems Corp. (2005d).

35. Grant and Berman (2005).

36. Cablevision Systems Corp. (2005e).

37. Somayaji (2004, 2005).

38. Author's calculations.

39. Author's calculations using information in Cablevision Systems Corp. (2005f, pp. 36–44).

40. Jensen (1986).

41. Jensen (1986) develops this theory in the context of his free cash flow concept; Stulz (1990) develops a formal mathematical model.

42. Cablevision Systems Corp. (2006c).

43. Cablevision Systems Corp. (2006b, p. 17).

44. Miller and Modigliani (1961); Modigliani and Miller (1958).

45. Gunther and Kim (2004).

46. Cablevision Systems Corp. (2006d, p. 53).

47. Horne (1917, pp. 241–242).

48. Caney (2002).

49. The share price fell from $48.01 at the start of the year to $4.95 on August 13.

50. Cablevision Systems Corp. (2002a, 2002b).

51. Author's calculations using information in Cablevision Systems Corp. (2006a).

52. Bolton and Scharfstein (1990) use a theoretical model to show how, by issuing short-term debt, a firm can commit not to divert resources to insiders. Lenders threaten to cut off funding in the future if the current short-term debt is not repaid in full, which gives management an incentive to not waste free cash flow.

53. Steinhauer (2004).

54. Soshnick (2004); Madison Square Garden Co. (2014, p. 39).

55. Berger and Ofek (1995); Hoechle et al. (2012, Table 3); Lang and Stulz (1994, Table 6).

56. Kumar (2008).

57. Author's calculations. Some of the $3b increase in enterprise value would have been absorbed by bond prices, so the share price increase reported here overestimates the true value.

58. Ahn and Denis (2004); Gertner et al. (2002).

59. Chemmanur et al. (2014).

60. Ahn and Denis (2004); Burch and Nanda (2003).

61. Cablevision Systems Corp. (2009b, p. 72); Madison Square Garden Inc. (2010, p. 27); Madison Square Garden Co. (2011a, p. 28; 2014, p. 39).

62. Author's estimates using the approach described in Chapter 4.

63. Securities and Exchange Commission (2006a).

64. Author's analysis of Cablevision's proxy statements.

65. Author's analysis of Madison Square Garden's and AMC Networks' proxy statements.

66. Author's analysis of Cablevision's proxy statements.

67. Wruck and Wruck (2002, Table 3).

68. The share price fell from $38.52 on July 18, 2007 to $19.48 on July 14, 2008.

69. Mullaney and Miller (2008); Adegoke (2008).

70. Cablevision Systems Corp. (2008, p. 77; 2009d, p. 77).

71. Kumar and Worden (2009).

CHAPTER 9. NO SKIN IN THE GAME

1. Associated Press (2004b).

2. Alexander (2010).

3. Alexander (2008).

4. Author's analysis of SPX's balance sheets.

5. Author's estimate using the approach described in Chapter 5.

6. SPX Corp. (2004b, Ex. 99.1).

7. Reuters (2004b).

8. Author's estimate using event study methodology.

9. SPX Corp. (1995b).

10. The return is measured from April 27, 1988, when the firm's name changed, to April 27, 1995.

11. SPX Corp. (1995a); Wall Street Journal (1995).

12. SPX Corp. (1995c).

13. Haar (1998).

14. SPX Corp. (1998a; 2001a; 2003a, pp. 2–6).

15. Author's analysis of SPX's 1995 and 2003 income statements.

16. Author's analysis of the firms' annual reports.

17. SPX Corp. (1999, Ex. 99.1).

18. SPX Corp. (1998b, p. 49).

19. The CEO was appointed CEO of another manufacturing firm (Armstrong Holdings, Inc., 2000); the CFO was appointed CFO of a food marketer (Quaker Oats Co., 1998); the EVP Operations became president of a manufacturing firm (Terex Corp., 1999); the general counsel was appointed general counsel at an insurance firm (Chubb Corp., 1999); and the SVP Human Resources took a similar position at another insurance firm (SHRM Foundation, 2010, p. 31).

20. SPX Corp. (1998b, pp. 48–49).

21. Charlotte Business Journal (2003), United Dominion Industries Ltd. (2000a, 2000b).

22. Ehrbar (1998).

23. SPX Corp. (1996b).

24. SPX Corp. (2004a, pp. 3–7).

25. Dielectric acquired Central Tower Inc. and TCI International in 2001 and Flash Technology and Brookstone Telecom in February 2003; V&C acquired Daniel Valve Company in 2002 and Hankison International in 2003; Life Science Solutions acquired Kendro Laboratory Products in 2001 (SPX Corp., 2004a, pp. 73–75).

26. SPX Corp. (2002c); Fairfax Group (2013).

27. Ehrbar (1998); Lang (2001).

28. SPX Corp. (1996a, 2004a).

29. Lipin (1998).

30. Lublin (2002).

31. SPX Corp. (2002b).

32. Author's estimates of Blystone's pay in 1997 and 2002 using the approach described in Chapter 5.

33. Harford and Li (2007, Table VIII).

34. SPX Corp. (1998b; 2001b, Ex. 99.2, p. 6).

35. If these deals were anticipated by investors then the market response to the news reveals information only about how investors viewed the merger terms relative to their previous expectations.

36. Author's estimates using event study methodology.

37. Securities and Exchange Commission (2002b).

38. SPX Corp. (2003a, p. 23).

39. SPX Corp. (1996a, p. 29).

40. SPX Corp. (2003b).

41. SPX Corp. (2003d, 2004c).

42. United States District Court, Western District of North Carolina, Charlotte Division (2004, p. 18).

43. Dielectric's president was appointed in October 2001 and left in June 2003 (Dielectric Communications, 2001; United States District Court, Western District of North Carolina, Charlotte Division, 2004, p. 19).

44. SPX Corp. (2004e, p. 26).

45. SPX Corp. (2004a, p. 35).

46. V&C's president was appointed in November 2002 and left in November 2003 (SPX Corp., 2002a; United States District Court, Western District of North Carolina, Charlotte Division, 2004, p. 19).

47. Securities and Exchange Commission (2000).

48. SPX Corp. (2004f)

49. Author's analysis of ownership data.

50. SPX Corp. (2004a, 2004b).

51. Author's estimate using event study methodology.

52. Author's analysis of ownership data.

53. Jagolinzer (2009).

54. United States District Court, Western District of North Carolina, Charlotte Division (2004, 2007).

55. Pulliam and Barry (2012); Pulliam et al. (2012); Pulliam (2013).

56. Lloyd (2004a); Lerner (2003).

57. Padley (2003).

58. Lerner (2003).

59. Dow Jones News Service (2004); Lerner (2003).

60. Agrawal and Chen (2008, Table 2).

61. Fernando et al. (2012, Table 2).

62. Agrawal and Chen (2008, Table 2).

63. SPX Corp. (2004a).

64. Associated Press (2004b).

65. Reuters (2004b).

66. Author's calculations.

67. Wiersema and Zhang (2011, p. 1174).

68. Agrawal and Chen (2008, p. 507).

69. Groysberg et al. (2011).

70. Wall Street Journal (2013).

71. Groysberg et al. (2011).

72. Peltz (2011).

73. Groysberg et al. (2011).

74. Lloyd (2004a); Radio World (2004).

75. Scharfstein and Stein (1990) show how individuals concerned about their reputation can exhibit herd behavior. Trueman (1994) develops a similar theory, but tailored specifically to security analysts.

76. Welch (2000).

77. Hong et al. (2000).

78. Irvine (2004); Jackson (2005).

79. Cowen et al. (2006, p. 125); Hong and Kubik (2003).

80. Ljungqvist et al. (2007, Table 2).

81. Securities and Exchange Commission (2003e).

82. Groysberg et al. (2011); Hong and Kubik (2003).

83. Agrawal and Chen (2008); Ljungqvist et al. (2007, Table 2).

84. Clarke et al. (2007); Fang and Yasuda (2009).

85. Ljungqvist et al. (2007, Table 2).

86. Agrawal and Chen (2008, Table 6).

87. White (2010).

88. Mathis et al. (2009) show that, provided a rating agency generates a sufficiently large fraction of its business from other sources, reputational concerns will motivate it to produce accurate bond ratings. Bolton et al. (2012) show that competition amongst rating agencies weakens the power of reputational concerns.

89. Jiang et al. (2012).

90. Becker and Milbourn (2011).

91. Xia (2014).

92. Lloyd (2004a).

93. Stocken (2000) develops a formal model of this possibility and shows that the threat of future difficulties raising capital can persuade managers to report their private information accurately.

94. Lloyd (2004a).

95. Laing (2004).

96. Lloyd (2004b).

97. Laing (2004).

98. Only 11% of recommendation changes made by non-all-star analysts triggered a large share price movement (Loh and Stulz, 2011, Table 3).

99. Laing (2004).

100. Veverka (2003).

101. SPX Corp. (2004b, Ex. 99.1).

102. SPX Corp. (2003c).

103. Laing (2004).

104. Author's estimate using event study methodology.

105. Kelly and Ljungqvist (2012).

106. Chen et al. (2015); Irani and Oesch (2013).

107. Relational Investors LLC (2004a, 2004b).

108. Atlantic Investment Management Inc. (2004).

109. Relational Investors LLC (2004a).

110. SPX Corp. (2004d).

CHAPTER 10. CRASHING THE PARTY

1. Nocera (2006); Ward (2006b).

2. Cacace and Tucksmith (2006).

3. Kempner (2005); Saporta (2005, 2007).

4. Terhune (2006).

5. Relational Investors LLC (2007).

6. Ordower (2007).

7. Brooks (2000).

8. Author's estimate using event study methodology.

9. Lublin et al. (2000); Sellers (2001).

10. Sellers (2001, 2002).

11. Lublin et al. (2000).

12. Sellers (2002).

13. Home Depot Inc. (2002).

14. Home Depot Inc. (2001c).

15. Aman (2002); Furfaro (2001).

16. Reingold (2005).

17. Zimmerman (2008).

18. Grow et al. (2006).

19. Lublin et al. (2007).

20. In 2005, Home Depot had the largest annual decline of any firm in the University of Michigan's American Customer Satisfaction Index (Degross, 2006).

21. Author's analysis of the firms' annual reports for 2001–2006.

22. Home Depot Inc. (2007a, p. 58).

23. The returns are measured from December 4, 2000 until May 24, 2006.

24. Author's estimate using the approach described in Chapter 5.

25. Home Depot Inc. (2001a, Ex. 10.17, paragraph 4.3).

26. Home Depot's Long-Term Incentive Plans for the 2002–2004 and 2003–2005 periods based pay on the firm's share-price performance relative to other retail firms (Home Depot Inc., 2003, p. 26; 2004, p. 26). However, this was changed for the 2004–2006 period to base pay on growth in the firm's earnings per share (Home Depot Inc., 2005, p. 36).

27. Dobrzynski (2006); Peters (2006).

28. Bond (2006); Ward (2006a).

29. Home Depot's share price fell from $38.40 when the market closed on May 25, the day of the meeting, to $37.72 on November 24.

30. Lublin et al. (2007).

31. Home Depot Inc. (2006b).

32. Home Depot Inc. (2006c).

33. Home Depot Inc. (2006b).

34. Home Depot Inc. (2006d, pp. 4 and 47).

35. Home Depot Inc. (2007j, pp. 3 and 9–10).

36. Two GE directors joined Home Depot's board in 2001 and an ex-CEO of GE Appliances joined in 2004 (Home Depot Inc., 2001b, 2005).

37. Shleifer and Vishny (1986) develop a theoretical model of the role that a large shareholder can play in reducing manager–shareholder conflict.

38. Author's calculations using information in FMR Corp. (2007), Barclays Global Investors UK Holdings Limited (2007), State Street Corp. (2007), and Vanguard Group Inc. (2007).

39. Holderness (2009).

40. Author's calculations using information in FMR Corp. (2007), Barclays Global Investors UK Holdings Limited (2007), State Street Corp. (2007), and Vanguard Group Inc. (2007).

41. Fich et al. (2015).

42. Ordower (2007, pp. 345–352).

43. Coffee (1991, Section IV.B.3).

44. Relational Investors LLC (2006).

45. Section 5(b) of the Investment Company Act prevents a "diversified" mutual fund from investing more than 25% of its portfolios (by value) in securities in any individual firm that comprise more than 5% of the fund's value or more than 10% of the issuing firm's voting rights.

46. Author's calculations using information in Relational's quarterly Form 13F filings.

47. Brav et al. (2009, p. 205).

48. Laing (2007).

49. Ordower (2007, pp. 345–352).

50. Relational Investors LLC (2009).

51. Fos (2015).

52. Brav et al. (2009); Fos (2015).

53. Brav et al. (2009, Table 5.1); Klein and Zur (2009, Table III).

54. Klein and Zur (2009, Table VI.B); Fos (2015).

55. Author's calculations using information in the two firm's annual reports for 2001–2006.

56. Author's calculations using information in Home Depot Inc. (2007a).

57. Author's estimate assuming Home Depot could match Lowe's ratio of enterprise value to sales.

58. Brav et al. (2009, Table 5.1).

59. Author's calculations using information in Home Depot Inc. (2006e).

60. Home Depot Inc. (2006e).

61. Author's calculations using information in Relational Investors LLC (2007).

62. Brav et al. (2008a, Table I.A); Klein and Zur (2009, Table I.E).

63. CalSTRS and Relational Investors LLC (2010b); Relational Investors LLC (2004a).

64. Fos (2015).

65. Brav et al. (2008a, Table I).

66. Becht et al. (2009).

67. McCahery et al. (2016).

68. Home Depot Inc. (2006e).

69. Lublin et al. (2007); Thomas (2007).

70. Home Depot Inc. (2006a, p. 25).

71. Home Depot Inc. (2007b, 2007c).

72. Weber (2007).

73. Home Depot Inc. (2007b, Ex. 99.1).

74. Zimmerman and Lublin (2007b).

75. Creswell and Barbaro (2007).

76. Zimmerman and Lublin (2007a).

77. Home Depot Inc. (2007d).

78. Home Depot Inc. (2007e).

79. Home Depot Inc. (2007m).

80. Home Depot Inc. (2007l).

81. Barbaro (2007).

82. Home Depot Inc. (2007j, pp. 3 and 9–10).

83. Home Depot Inc. (2007f).

84. Home Depot Inc. (2007g, 2007h).

85. Home Depot Inc. (2007d, 2008).

86. Brav et al. (2008a).

87. Brav et al. (2008a); Klein and Zur (2009).

88. Brav et al. (2009).

89. Reuters News (2003, 2005); Home Depot Inc. (2007l).

90. Author's calculations.

91. Author's estimate using the approach described in Chapter 5.

92. Home Depot Inc. (2007j, p. 56).

93. Author's estimates using the approach described in Chapter 5.

94. Brav et al. (2008a, Table I).

95. Home Depot Inc. (2007i, 2007k).

96. Brav et al. (2008a, Table I).

97. Adler (2008); Zimmerman (2008, 2009).

98. Brav et al. (2008a, Table I).

99. Author's calculations using information in Reingold (2008), ACSI (2011), and the two firms' annual reports for 2009 and 2010.

100. Bebchuk et al. (2015, Tables 3 and 4); Brav et al. (2015).

101. Author's analysis of Home Depot's annual cash flow statements.

102. On average, the annual payout to shareholders increases by between 0.3% and 0.5% of the market value of the targeted firm's equity (Brav et al., 2008a).

103. Author's analysis of ownership data.

104. Maug (1998) develops a formal theoretical model of this mechanism.

105. Coffee (1991); Bhide (1993).

106. Admati and Pfleiderer (2009); Edmans (2009).

107. Brav et al. (2008a, pp. 1764–1766).

108. Author's analysis of ownership data.

109. Author's analysis of the trading strategy that matches Relational's dollar-value injections of funds and its percentage withdrawals of funds.

110. Author's calculations using information in Brav et al. (2008b, Table 6).

111. The returns are measured from December 12, 2006 until March 25, 2011.

112. Brav et al. (2008b); Bebchuk et al. (2015, Section IV.B).

113. Prudential Financial Inc., $1.8b; Baxter International Inc., $1.2b; Home Depot Inc., $1.0b; Sovereign Bancorp Inc., $0.8b; and National Semiconductor Corp., $0.8b (Relational Investors LLC, 2007).

114. Davis and Kim (2007).

115. Hu and Black (2006, 2008).

116. Author's calculations using information in Home Depot Inc. (2006d, p. 47).

CHAPTER 11. A NEW BROOM

1. Leonard (2012).

2. Thomson (1990).

3. McWilliams (2008b).

4. Kesmodel and Vranica (2009); McWilliams (2009b).

5. McWilliams (2008c); St. Louis Post-Dispatch (2009).

6. New York Times (1913).

7. Tremblay and Tremblay (2005, Figure 3.15).

8. Adams (2006).

9. Krebs and Orthwein (1953).

10. Stange (2000).

11. MacIntosh (2011, pp. 64–66).

12. McWilliams (2009b).

13. Tomich and McWilliams (2008).

14. Flynn (1992); MacIntosh (2011, p. 67).

15. MacIntosh (2011, pp. 10–11).

16. Davies (2008b).

17. Arndorfer (2005).

18. The returns are measured from April 23, 2002 until May 22, 2008.

19. Pérez-González (2006); Villalonga and Amit (2006).

20. Giroud and Mueller (2010, 2011).

21. Berfield (2011).

22. Anheuser-Busch Companies Inc. (2007, p. 4).

23. Author's calculations using information in Anheuser-Busch Companies Inc. (2002a).

24. Busch III, chairman of Anheuser-Busch from 1977, joined the boards of Anheuser-Busch, Southwestern Bell, and Emerson Electric in 1963, 1980, and 1985, respectively; Edward Whitacre Jr., CEO and chairman of SBC Communications Inc. from 1990, joined the three boards in 1988, 1986, and 1990, respectively; Charles Knight, chairman of Emerson Electric since 1974, joined the three boards in 1987, 1974, and 1972, respectively (Anheuser-Busch Companies Inc., 2002a; Emerson Electric Co., 2002; SBC Communications Inc., 2002).

25. Anheuser-Busch Companies Inc. (2005, p. 9).

26. Arndorfer (2005).

27. Author's estimates using the approach described in Chapter 5.

28. At the end of 1999, Stokes, the head of Anheuser-Busch's U.S. beer subsidiary, was promoted to head the firm's international operations, a promotion that was perceived by some as a sign that he was being groomed to succeed Busch III as CEO (Stamborski, 1999). Stokes was promoted again the next year, when he was appointed Senior EVP of Anheuser-Busch (Stamborski, 2000). Stokes was appointed CEO in 2002 (Anheuser-Busch Companies Inc., 2002b).

29. Anheuser-Busch Companies Inc. (2002b).

30. In 2000, Busch IV was promoted and joined the committee of senior executives who made all major decisions at Anheuser-Busch (Stamborski, 2000). When Busch III retired as CEO, Busch IV succeeded Stokes as president of the U.S. beer subsidiary (Anheuser-Busch Companies Inc., 2002b).

31. Kratz (2006).

32. Anheuser-Busch Companies Inc. (2006a).

33. MacIntosh (2011, p. 127).

34. Courier (1983).

35. Berfield (2011).

36. Associated Press (1985).

37. Berfield (2011).

38. Beirne (2005).

39. Sellers (1997).

40. Khermouch and Forster (2002).

41. Kesmodel (2008).

42. Berfield (2011).

43. Strebulaev and Yang (2013).

44. Flynn (1992); Sellers (1997); Khermouch and Forster (2002).

45. Ludington (1991).

46. Berfield (2011).

47. Khermouch and Forster (2002).

48. Author's calculations using information in Anheuser-Busch Companies Inc. (2006b).

49. Dorfman (2007).

50. Jensen and Ruback (1983) interpret the principal actors in the market for corporate control as managerial teams that compete for the right to manage firms. Manne (1965) sparked interest in the market for corporate control by arguing that many mergers were motivated by the profits to be made by replacing inferior management teams.

51. Strictly speaking, InBev's letter contained a "non-binding proposal" to buy Anheuser-Busch, rather than an offer (InBev S.A., 2008c).

52. InBev S.A. (2008a, pp. 121–122).

53. Anheuser-Busch InBev S.A. (2009, p. 131).

54. Bianconi (2005); Henson (2006); Meller (2005); Moffett (2008).

55. Rumors that the brewer InBev was planning to try and acquire Anheuser-Busch surfaced almost three weeks earlier in a story on the *Financial Times'* "Alphaville" website (Hume, 2008).

56. Anheuser-Busch Companies Inc. (2008f, p. 68).

57. Betton et al. (2009).

58. Author's calculations using information in Anheuser-Busch Companies Inc. (2008d, pp. 12–13).

59. Harford (2003); Ishii and Xuan (2014).

60. Anheuser-Busch Companies Inc. (2008a).

61. Anheuser-Busch Companies Inc. (2008f, pp. 21–22).

62. Paulson & Co. Inc. (2008a, 2008b).

63. InBev S.A. (2008b).

64. Bryant (2008).

65. Harford (2003).

66. MacIntosh (2011, pp. 195–198).

67. Author's estimates using information in Busch III (2008).

68. MacIntosh (2011, pp. 260–262).

69. Anheuser-Busch Companies Inc. (2008f, pp. 22–25).

70. Anheuser-Busch Companies Inc. (2008b).

71. Wertheimer (1998).

72. Author's calculations.

73. Peterson (2009).

74. Peterson (2011).

75. Anheuser-Busch InBev S.A. (2011, pp. 154 and 166); Kesmodel (2011).

76. Berfield (2011).

77. Hartzell et al. (2004); Kini et al. (2004).

78. Agrawal and Walkling (1994); Hartzell et al. (2004).

79. MacIntosh (2011, pp. 299–301); McWilliams (2008d).

80. Fich et al. (2013, Table 1.D).

81. Anheuser-Busch Companies Inc. (2008d, pp. 50–51).

82. Author's calculations using information in the executives' Form 4s filed on November 19, 2008.

83. Offenberg and Officer (2014, Tables 3 and 6).

84. Bebchuk et al. (2014, Table 1).

85. Bebchuk et al. (2014, Table 5); Fich et al. (2013, Tables 4 and 5).

86. Bebchuk et al. (2014, Table 4); Sokolyk (2011, Table 5).

87. Author's estimates using information in the executives' Form 4s filed on November 19, 2008.

88. Author's calculations.

89. Elkinawy and Offenberg (2013, Table VI), based on data from takeovers completed during the period 2005–2009. Sokolyk (2011, Table 7) reports a smaller effect, nine percentage points, during the earlier period 1990–2004.

90. Anheuser-Busch InBev S.A. (2009, p. 167).

91. Anheuser-Busch Companies Inc. (2008f, pp. 46–47).

92. Anheuser-Busch Companies Inc. (2008c); Davies (2008a).

93. McWilliams (2008a).

94. Kini et al. (2004).

95. Bebchuk et al. (2014); Mikkelson and Partch (1997).

96. McWilliams (2007).

97. MacIntosh (2011, pp. 143–144).

98. MacIntosh (2011, pp. 129–134).

99. MacIntosh (2011, p. 146).

100. Tomich and McWilliams (2008).

101. Anheuser-Busch Companies Inc. (2008e).

102. Frankel (2010); MacIntosh (2011, p. 312).

103. MacIntosh (2011, p. 324).

104. Kesmodel and Vranica (2009); MacIntosh (2011, p. 105–106).

105. Frankel (2010); Kesmodel and Vranica (2009); Roberts (2013).

106. Albright and Thrash (2009).

107. Leonard (2012).

108. Anheuser-Busch InBev S.A. (2008).

109. Kesmodel and Vranica (2009).

110. McWilliams (2009a).

111. Kesmodel and Vranica (2009).

112. Leonard (2012).

113. Wiggins (2009).

114. Hugo Real Property, LP (2011).

115. Anheuser-Busch InBev S.A. (2011, pp. 87–88).

116. Li (2013, Table 3).

117. Maksimovic et al. (2011).

118. Anheuser-Busch InBev S.A. (2011).

119. Author's calculations.

120. Author's analysis of AB InBev's annual reports.

121. Anheuser-Busch InBev S.A. (2009, pp. 146–147).

122. Author's estimates.

123. Anheuser-Busch Companies Inc. (2008f, p. 24).

CHAPTER 12. BYPASSING THE BOARD

1. Taylor (2010a).

2. Winkley and Fatsis (2004).

3. MU Finance PLC (2010, p. 53).

4. The return is measured from March 3, 1998 until March 3, 2003.

5. Burke (2003); Ozanian (1998).

6. Mansell and O'Connor (2005).

7. Marlow and Goodman (2010).

8. Winkley and Fatsis (2004).

9. Garrahan (2004d); Ross Sorkin and de la Merced (2008).

10. Garrahan (2004e).

11. Rich (2005).

12. Kay and Power (2010).

13. Weir (1999).

14. Donkin (1989); Financial Times (1991).

15. Weir (1999).

16. Citywire (2002).

17. Manchester United PLC (2002).

18. Voyle et al. (1998).

19. Reuters (1999).

20. Express (2004).

21. At the time of the 2004 annual meeting, when Glazer succeeded in blocking the elections of three directors, the board comprised the CEO, commercial director, finance director, Manchester United's solicitor, and three independent directors (Jones and Kennedy, 2004).

22. Manchester United PLC (2000).

23. Garrahan (2004a, 2004b, 2004c).

24. Keefe and Ballingrud (1995).

25. Lyall (2005); Ruth (2005).

26. Team Marketing Report (1994, 1998).

27. Testerman (2001).

28. Fisher and Ozanian (1999).

29. Mansell and O'Connor (2005).

30. Harris (2005).

31. Hall and Watts (2004).

32. Bose (2004).

33. Rushe (2005).

34. Winkley and Fatsis (2004).

35. Garrahan (2004d); Ross Sorkin and de la Merced (2008).

36. Garrahan (2004e).

37. Garrahan (2004d).

38. Keefe and Ballingrud (1995).

39. Jones and Kennedy (2004); Rushe (2004).

40. Garrahan (2005c).

41. Garrahan (2005a, 2005b).

42. Grossman and Hart (1980) identify the free-rider problem present in tender offers.

43. Author's calculations using information in Johnson (2003).

44. Shleifer and Vishny (1986) develop a formal model of how a raider benefits from acquiring an initial ownership stake in a firm.

45. Securities and Exchange Commission (1998b, Section III).

46. At the time of the Manchester United takeover, this was required by Section 199 of the Companies Act 1985. The same rules still apply, but now according to rules imposed by the Financial Conduct Authority (Financial Conduct Authority, 2015a, Section 5.1.2).

47. Shleifer and Vishny (1986) prove formally that the target firm's share price is higher if the raider's initial ownership stake is larger.

48. Reuters (2003, 2004a).

49. Garrahan and Thal Larsen (2004).

50. Barusch (2014).

51. Holderness (2009).

52. Citywire (2005).

53. Betton et al. (2009, Tables 2 and 7).

54. Davies and Garrahan (2005); Garrahan (2004d).

55. Red Football Ltd (2005b).

56. Albuquerque and Schroth (2010); Barclay and Holderness (1989); Dyck and Zingales (2004).

57. Zapata Corp. (1996b, p. 77).

58. Zapata Corp. (1996b, p. 350).

59. DeGeorge (1996); Dougherty (1996).

60. Testerman (1996).

61. Myerson (1995).

62. Zapata Corp. (1996b, pp. 78–79 and 86).

63. Zapata Corp. (1996a, pp. 1–2).

64. Keefe (1996); St. Petersburg Times (1996).

65. Zapata Corp. (1996a, pp. 1–2).

66. Zapata Corp. (1996a, pp. 10–11).

67. Rich (2005).

68. Power (2004); Quinn (2005).

69. Osborne (2005).

70. DeGeorge (1996).

71. Zapata Corp. (1995).

72. Zapata Corp. (1999, p. 10).

73. Zapata Corp. (1999, pp. 9–10).

74. Yarrow (1985) presents a formal model of the freedom to dilute that is created by the costs of legal action.

75. Red Football Ltd (2005b).

76. At the time of the Manchester United takeover, a 75% majority was needed to pass a special resolution, according to Section 378 of the Companies Act 1985. Currently, a 75% majority is needed to cancel a "Premium" listing according to rules imposed by the Financial Conduct Authority (Financial Conduct Authority, 2015b, Section 5.2.5).

77. At the time of the Manchester United takeover, a 75% majority was needed to pass a special resolution, according to Section 378 of the Companies Act 1985.

78. Section 979 of the Companies Act 2006.

79. Red Football Ltd (2005b).

80. Red Football Ltd (2005a).

81. In Delaware, if the raider owns enough of the target's shares to win a merger vote, then it is now allowed to use a so-called short-form merger that avoids the need for a shareholder vote and leads to a quick, relatively low-cost, completion of the takeover (Delaware General Corporation Law, §251(h)). Previously, the raider needed to own at least 90% of the target's shares in order to use a short-form merger (§253).

82. The result that the free-rider problem is reduced is proved formally by Grossman and Hart (1980) for dilution, by Müller and Panunzi (2004) for debt-financing, and by Amihud et al. (2004) and Yarrow (1985) for squeeze-outs.

83. Power (2004); Quinn (2005).

84. Testerman (1996); Dolan (1995); Carlton (2000).

85. Associated Press (1990).

86. Rushe (2005).

87. Delaware Code, Title 8, §203.

88. Red Football Ltd (2005b).

89. Rich (2005).

90. Kay and Power (2010); MU Finance PLC (2010, p. 53).

91. Red Football Ltd (2005b).

92. Author's calculations using information in Manchester United PLC's annual reports and MU Finance PLC (2010).

93. Ducker (2010, 2014b).

94. Ducker (2014a).

95. Betton et al. (2009, Table 1).

CHAPTER 13. FIGHTING BACK

1. Worden (2010b).

2. Lions Gate Entertainment Corp. (2003, 2006).

3. Lions Gate Entertainment Corp. (2009d).

4. Lions Gate Entertainment Corp. (2010a, p. 33).

5. Gimbel (2006).

6. Lions Gate Entertainment Corp. (2009f).

7. Author's analysis of ownership data.

8. Lions Gate Entertainment Corp. (2008b, pp. 7–9).

9. Associated Press (2009).

10. Lions Gate's management presented a blunt assessment of the firm's performance in the earnings conference call (Lions Gate Entertainment Corp., 2009e).

11. Author's estimate using event study methodology.

12. Lions Gate Entertainment Corp. (2009a).

13. Zeidler (2010c); McCracken and Spector (2010).

14. Dow Jones News Service (1979); Williams (1984a).

15. Icahn (2009).

16. Author's calculations using information in Icahn Management LP (2006) and Icahn (2008).

17. Securities and Exchange Commission (2014a, pp. 3–4).

18. Icahn (2010c).

19. Icahn (2010d).

20. Icahn (2010e).

21. Supreme Court, New York County (2011).

22. Vardi (2013).

23. Author's calculations using information in Seemore Advisors LLC (2004), MHR Fund Management LLC (2006), and Rachesky (2009).

24. Lions Gate Entertainment Corp. (2009b).

25. Author's analysis of ownership data.

26. Venkiteshwaran et al. (2010, Table 4).

27. Morrissey (2011).

28. Eller (2009a); Lions Gate Entertainment Corp. (2009e); Nakashima (2009); Zeidler (2010a).

29. PeopleSoft Inc. (2004, pp. 14–15).

30. Oracle Corp. (2004).

31. Lions Gate Entertainment Corp. (2004, pp. B.10–B.11).

32. Author's analysis of the change-in-control payments reported in Lions Gate Entertainment Corp. (2010j, pp. 45 and 48).

33. Lions Gate Entertainment Corp. (2010k).

34. Author's calculations using information in Anheuser-Busch Companies Inc. (2008d).

35. Chava et al. (2010, Table 2).

36. Lions Gate Entertainment Corp. (2008a, Ex. 10.51, pp. 12 and 109–111).

37. Lions Gate Entertainment Corp. (2010b).

38. Rachesky (2009).

39. Lions Gate Entertainment Corp. (2008a, Ex. 10.51, pp. 12 and 109–111).

40. This was a standard feature of Lions Gate's convertible senior subordinated notes (Lions Gate Entertainment Corp., 2005, p. 28). The senior secured second-priority notes appear to have had a similar feature (Lions Gate Entertainment Corp., 2009c).

41. Lions Gate Entertainment Corp. (2010b, pp. 16 and 19–24).

42. Grover (2009).

43. Lions Gate Entertainment Corp. (2010c, Ex. 10.77).

44. Sokolyk (2011).

45. Lions Gate Entertainment Corp. (2010d).

46. Lions Gate's shareholder rights plan was not quite this simple in practice. The amount that the owners of one share would have to pay if they exercised their purchase right was equal to four times the share price at the "separation time." In return, they would receive shares worth twice that amount, where the value was calculated using the share price at the time of the "flip-in event" (Lions Gate Entertainment Corp., 2010d, p. 3).

47. For example, Hertz Global Holdings, Inc. (2013); Safeway Inc. (2013); Sotheby's (2013).

48. Cremers and Ferrell (2014).

49. Ertimur et al. (2010, Appendix A).

50. Laide (2009).

51. Lions Gate Entertainment Corp. (2010e).

52. Icahn (2010b, 2010d).

53. Lions Gate Entertainment Corp. (2010d, 2010f).

54. British Columbia Securities Commission (2010a, 2010b).

55. Betton et al. (2008, Section 3.5.1).

56. Karpoff and Wittry (2015).

57. Cain et al. (2014).

58. Lions Gate Entertainment Corp. (2009d).

59. Icahn (2010f, Ex. 99(a)(1)(i), p. 39).

60. Lions Gate Entertainment Corp. (2010l, p. 11); Icahn (2010f, Ex. 99(a)(1)(i), p. 39).

61. Bebchuk and Cohen (2003).

62. Bertrand and Mullainathan (2003, Table 1) and Karpoff and Wittry (2015, Table 2) report details of the passage of state antitakeover legislation.

63. Academic researchers have also investigated the statistical relationship between crude measures of firms' takeover defenses and their operating performance and found that firms with stronger defenses tend to be less profitable and less valuable (Bebchuk et al., 2009; Core et al., 2006).

64. Bertrand and Mullainathan (1999, 2003).

65. Giroud and Mueller (2010).

66. Atanassov (2013).

67. Francis et al. (2011).

68. Bertrand and Mullainathan (2000).

69. Author's calculations using information in Icahn (2010e) and Rachesky (2010).

70. Worden (2010a).

71. Lions Gate Entertainment Corp. (2010g).

72. Section 312.03(b) of the NYSE Listed Company Manual.

73. Author's calculations using information in Rachesky (2010).

74. Lions Gate Entertainment Corp. (2010b, pp. 16 and 19–24).

75. This was Lions Gate's closing share price on July 19, 2010, the last day of Icahn's standstill agreement with Lions Gate.

76. Lions Gate Entertainment Corp. (2010h).

77. Eller (2009b).

78. Author's calculations, using information in Lions Gate Entertainment Corp. (2010b, pp. 19–24).

79. Author's calculations using information in Icahn (2010e) and Rachesky (2010).

80. Securities and Exchange Commission (2014a, para. 28–32).

81. Author's calculations using information in Rachesky (2010).

82. Lions Gate Entertainment Corp. (2010h, Ex. 99.1).

83. Securities and Exchange Commission (2014a, para. 36).

84. Worden (2010b).

85. Securities and Exchange Commission (2014a).

86. Icahn (2010a).

87. Securities and Exchange Commission (2003a, 2003b).

88. Two SEC no-action letters clarified that relying on proxy advisory firms to effectively make voting decisions meets the requirements of the new rule (Securities and Exchange Commission, 2004a, 2004b).

89. McCahery et al. (2016).

90. Reddall (2013b).

91. Associated Press (2004a).

92. Examples include uncontested board elections (Cai et al., 2009), proxy fights (Alexander et al., 2010), shareholder proposals (Morgan et al., 2011), and say-on-pay votes (Ertimur et al., 2013; Larcker et al., 2015).

93. Iliev and Lowry (2015).

94. Government Accountability Office (2007).

95. Ontario Teachers' Pension Plan (2013).

96. Daines et al. (2010).

97. Bebchuk et al. (2009); Core et al. (2006); Gompers et al. (2003).

98. Government Accountability Office (2007, p. 10).

99. Zeidler (2010b).

100. Lions Gate Entertainment Corp. (2011a, pp. 30–31).

101. Lions Gate Entertainment Corp. (2010i).

102. Bates et al. (2008); Bebchuk and Cohen (2005).

103. Guo et al. (2008).

104. Bebchuk et al. (2013, p. 165).

105. Bates et al. (2008); Kadyrzhanova and Rhodes-Kropf (2011).

106. Faleye (2007).

107. Bates et al. (2008); Bebchuk and Cohen (2005); Bebchuk et al. (2009); Cohen and Wang (2013); Faleye (2007).

108. Lions Gate Entertainment Corp. (2011b).

109. MHR Fund Management LLC (2011).

110. Davidoff (2013); Hoffman and Benoit (2014); Kim and Oran (2013).

111. Author's calculations using information in Cole (1984) and Hayes (1984).

112. Bradley and Wakeman (1983); Dann and DeAngelo (1983); Mikkelson and Ruback (1991); Peyer and Vermaelen (2005).

113. Ross (1984).

114. Manry and Nathan (1999); Peyer and Vermaelen (2005).

115. Section 5881 of the Internal Revenue Code (Langley, 1987).

116. Davidoff (2013); Hoffman and Benoit (2014); Kim and Oran (2013).

117. Grover (2012); Spector and Kung (2012).

118. Carew and Nayak (2013).

119. Lions Gate's average closing share price in December 2013 was $30.12.

120. Aktas et al. (2013, Table 1).

121. Reingold (2014).

CHAPTER 14. CAUGHT IN THE MIDDLE

1. Westbrook (2007).

2. Westbrook (2007).

3. Gigot (1992); Salwen (1992a).

4. Salwen (1992c).

5. Cowan (1992).

6. Lublin (1992).

7. McCartney (1992a).

8. McCartney (1992b).

9. Salwen (1992b).

10. Scannell (2006).

11. The SEC's final rule for reporting the value of share and option grants was announced in the middle of 2006, amended in December the same year, and amended again in 2009 (Securities and Exchange Commission, 2006a, 2006b, 2009a).

12. Schroeder (2006).

13. Business Roundtable (2006).

14. Chamber of Commerce (2006).

15. Securities and Exchange Commission (2006a).

16. Securities and Exchange Commission (2009a).

17. Securities and Exchange Commission (2012).

18. Westbrook (2007); Younglai (2009).

19. Gregory (2012).

20. Business Roundtable (2009).

21. Strictly speaking, the SEC does not rule on whether firms can exclude proposals. Instead, staff issue "no-action letters" to indicate that they would not recommend SEC enforcement action if a proposal is excluded. Only a court can decide whether a firm is obligated to include a proposal in its proxy statement (Securities and Exchange Commission, 2001).

22. Securities and Exchange Commission (2001).

23. Labaton (1992).

24. Securities and Exchange Commission (2002a).

25. Securities and Exchange Commission (2011a).

26. Court of Chancery of the State of Delaware (2011).

27. Ertimur et al. (2010, Appendix A).

28. M&A Journal (2006).

29. Bristol-Myers Squibb Company (2006); J. C. Penney Company, Inc. (2008); Safeway Inc. (2008).

30. Wachtell, Lipton, Rosen, and Katz (2011).

31. Bebchuk and Jackson (2012).

32. Securities and Exchange Commission (2003d, 2007).

33. The nominating shareholders needed to have owned at least 3% of the firm's shares for at least the last three years, and the total number of shareholder nominees could not exceed 25% of the size of the board (Securities and Exchange Commission, 2010).

34. United States Court of Appeals for the District of Columbia Circuit (2011).

35. Securities and Exchange Commission (2014b).

36. Securities and Exchange Commission (2015).

37. Ackerman and Lublin (2015); Morgenson (2015).

38. Business Roundtable (2015).

39. Chamber of Commerce (2015).

40. Kole and Lehn (1997).

EPILOGUE

1. Under Armour Inc. (2015).

2. Lublin and Rexrode (2015a, 2015b); Rexrode and Lublin (2015); Rexrode (2015).

3. Jakab (2015).

4. Herbst-Bayliss and Flaherty (2015).

5. Beilfuss (2015).

6. Facebook Inc. (2012); LinkedIn Corp. (2011).

7. Dunkin' Brands Group Inc. (2011); Tesla Motors Inc. (2010).

Bibliography

3Com Corp. (1999). 3Com names former Sony executive Carl Yankowski chief executive officer for its Palm Computing subsidiary. December 2. Press release.

Ackerman, A. and Lublin, J. S. (2015). Whole Foods dispute prompts SEC review of corporate ballots. *Wall Street Journal (Online)*, January 19.

ACSI (2011). Customer satisfaction weakens; biggest slump since 2008 means economic recovery remains fragile. February 15. Press Release.

Adams, R., Almeida, H., and Ferreira, D. (2005). Powerful CEOs and their impact on corporate performance. *Review of Financial Studies*, 18(4):1403–1432.

Adams, R. B. and Ferreira, D. (2007). A theory of friendly boards. *Journal of Finance*, 62(1):217–250.

Adams, W. J. (2006). Markets: Beer in Germany and the United States. *Journal of Economic Perspectives*, 20(1):189–205.

Adegoke, Y. (2008). Harbinger hoping to meet Cablevision about options. *Reuters*, August 22.

Adler, J. (2008). ILC debate's new twist: Home Depot drops its bid. *American Banker*, 173(17):1.

Admati, A. R. and Pfleiderer, P. (2009). The "Wall Street walk" and shareholder activism: Exit as a form of voice. *Review of Financial Studies*, 22(7):2645–2685.

Agrawal, A. and Chen, M. A. (2008). Do analyst conflicts matter? Evidence from stock recommendations. *Journal of Law and Economics*, 51(3):503–537.

Agrawal, A. and Walkling, R. A. (1994). Executive careers and compensation surrounding takeover bids. *Journal of Finance*, 49(3):985–1014.

Ahn, S. and Denis, D. J. (2004). Internal capital markets and investment policy: Evidence from corporate spinoffs. *Journal of Financial Economics*, 71(3):489–516.

Aktas, N., de Bodt, E., and Roll, R. (2013). MicroHoo: Deal failure, industry rivalry, and sources of overbidding. *Journal of Corporate Finance*, 19:20–35.

Albright, M. and Thrash, R. (2009). It's last call for free beer. *St. Petersburg Times*, January 6:1A.

Albuquerque, R. and Schroth, E. (2010). Quantifying private benefits of control from a structural model of block trades. *Journal of Financial Economics*, 96(1):33–55.

Alexander, C. R., Chen, M. A., Seppi, D. J., and Spatt, C. S. (2010). Interim news and the role of proxy voting advice. *Review of Financial Studies*, 23(12):4419–4454.

Alexander, D. (2008). Major piece of Muskegon's history joining scrapheap. *MLive.com*, December 6.

Alexander, D. (2010). Terrace Point, former SPX Corp. headquarters, readied for new tenant. *MLive.com*, July 28.

Allgood, S. and Farrell, K. A. (2003). The match between CEO and firm. *Journal of Business*, 76(2):317–341.

Aman, C. (2002). The 2002 GC compensation survey: Frank Fernandez. *Corporate Counsel*, 9(7):78.

Ambient Devices (2007). Ambient Devices launches the world's first weather-forecasting umbrella. July 30. Press release.

Ambient Devices (2008). Ambient Devices taps Carl Yankowski to help drive next growth phase. January 2. Press release.

AMC Networks Inc. (2012). Form DEF 14A. Filed on April 24.

Amihud, Y., Kahan, M., and Sundaram, R. K. (2004). The foundations of freezeout laws in takeovers. *Journal of Finance*, 59(3):1325–1344.

Andersen, K. (1991). Look, Mickey, no kitsch! *Time*, 138(4):66.

Angel, K. (2002). *Inside Yahoo! Reinvention and the Road Ahead*. John Wiley & Sons, Inc., New York.

Anheuser-Busch Companies Inc. (2002a). Form DEF 14A. Filed on March 12.

Anheuser-Busch Companies Inc. (2002b). Patrick T. Stokes named president and chief executive officer of Anheuser-Busch Companies, Inc.; August A. Busch IV succeeds Stokes as president of brewing subsidiary. April 24. Press release.

Anheuser-Busch Companies Inc. (2005). Form 10-K for the period ended December 31, 2004. Filed on March 10.

Anheuser-Busch Companies Inc. (2006a). Form 8-K. Filed on September 27.

Anheuser-Busch Companies Inc. (2006b). Form DEF 14A. Filed on March 9.

Anheuser-Busch Companies Inc. (2007). Form DEF 14A. Filed on March 12.

Anheuser-Busch Companies Inc. (2008a). Form 8-K. Filed on June 26.

Anheuser-Busch Companies Inc. (2008b). Form 8-K. Filed on November 12.

Anheuser-Busch Companies Inc. (2008c). Form 8-K. Filed on June 30.

Anheuser-Busch Companies Inc. (2008d). Form DEF 14A. Filed on March 10.

Anheuser-Busch Companies Inc. (2008e). Form DEFA14A. Filed on July 15.

Anheuser-Busch Companies Inc. (2008f). Form DEFM14A. Filed on October 6.

Anheuser-Busch InBev S.A. (2008). Anheuser-Busch InBev announces workforce reductions in the U.S. December 8. Press release.

Anheuser-Busch InBev S.A. (2009). Form 20FR12B. Filed on September 14.

Anheuser-Busch InBev S.A. (2011). Annual report for the period ended December 31, 2010.

Apple Computer Inc. (1992). Nagel appointed to Apple executive management team. January 28. Press release.

Apple Computer Inc. (1996). Nagel leaves Apple to head AT&T labs worldwide. April 15. Press release.

Arango, T. (2008). Far from Disney's fold, but at home on the web. *New York Times*, November 23:BU1.

Armstrong, C. S., Ittner, C. D., and Larcker, D. F. (2012). Corporate governance, compensation consultants, and CEO pay levels. *Review of Accounting Studies*, 17(2):322–351.

Armstrong Holdings, Inc. (2000). Armstrong elects former GE, General Signal exec to lead next phase of growth. August 8. Press release.

Arndorfer, J. B. (2005). Third act: A-B's struggles bring back The Chief. *Advertising Age*, 76(4):1.

Arndt, M. (1987). Occidental's IBP will offer stock. *Chicago Tribune*, August 20:1.

Arrow, K. J. (1965). *Aspects of the Theory of Risk Bearing*. Academic Publishers, Helsinki.

Associated Press (1985). Brewery heir arrested after two police chases. *Associated Press*, May 31.

Associated Press (1990). Judge refuses to block Harley investor's actions. *Associated Press*, March 1.

Associated Press (1996). Head of Georgetown University joins Disney board. *Associated Press*, June 25.

Associated Press (2003). Most powerful Atlas rocket carries Cablevision satellite into space. *Associated Press Newswires*, July 18.

Associated Press (2004a). Second proxy firm says Disney shareholders should vote against Eisner. *Associated Press Newswires*, February 26.

Associated Press (2004b). SPX ratings cut after earnings report. *Associated Press Newswires*, February 28.

Associated Press (2009). Lionsgate moves to 3rd-quarter loss as feature films underperform, costs rise. *Associated Press Newswires*, February 10.

Atanassov, J. (2013). Do hostile takeovers stifle innovation? Evidence from antitakeover legislation and corporate patenting. *Journal of Finance*, 68(3):1097–1131.

Atlantic Investment Management Inc. (2004). Form SC 13D. Filed on August 9.

AT&T Corp. (2001). Form 10-K405 for the period ended December 31, 2000. Filed on April 2.

Baker, E. (1980). Postscript: No rocking chair for L.A.'s retired administrative officer. *Los Angeles Times*, September 12:C1.

Baker, M. and Gompers, P. A. (2003). The determinants of board structure at the initial public offering. *Journal of Law and Economics*, 46:569–598.

Barbaro, M. (2007). Apologetic, Home Depot tries to move beyond Nardelli's shadow. *New York Times*, May 25:C3.

Barclay, M. J. and Holderness, C. G. (1989). Private benefits from control of public corporations. *Journal of Financial Economics*, 25(2):371–395.

Barclays Global Investors UK Holdings Limited (2007). Form 13F-NT for the period ended December 31, 2006. Filed on February 14.

Barker, V. L. and Mueller, G. C. (2002). CEO characteristics and firm R&D spending. *Management Science*, 48(6):782–801.

Barusch, R. (2014). DealPolitik: Ruling puts crimp in takeover alliances. *Wall Street Journal*, November 10:C4.

Bates, T. W., Becher, D. A., and Lemmon, M. L. (2008). Board classification and managerial entrenchment: Evidence from the market for corporate control. *Journal of Financial Economics*, 87(3):656–677.

Baumann, G. (2005). EchoStar to purchase satellite from Cablevision's Rainbow unit. *Bloomberg*, January 20.

Beazer Homes USA Inc. (2011). Form DEF 14A. Filed on December 22.

Bebchuk, L. and Fried, J. (2004). *Pay Without Performance*. Harvard University Press, Cambridge, Massachusetts.

Bebchuk, L., Hirst, S., and Rhe, J. (2013). Towards the declassification of S&P 500 boards. *Harvard Business Law Review*, 3(1):157–184.

Bebchuk, L. A., Brav, A., and Jiang, W. (2015). The long-term effects of hedge fund activism. *Columbia Law Review*, 115(5):1085–1155.

Bebchuk, L. A. and Cohen, A. (2003). Firms' decisions where to incorporate. *Journal of Law and Economics*, 46(2):383–425.

Bebchuk, L. A. and Cohen, A. (2005). The costs of entrenched boards. *Journal of Financial Economics*, 78(2):409–433.

Bebchuk, L. A., Cohen, A., and Ferrell, A. (2009). What matters in corporate governance? *Review of Financial Studies*, 22(2):783–827.

Bebchuk, L. A., Cohen, A., and Wang, C. C. Y. (2014). Golden parachutes and the wealth of shareholders. *Journal of Corporate Finance*, 25:140–154.

Bebchuk, L. A., Grinstein, Y., and Peyer, U. (2010). Lucky CEOs and lucky directors. *Journal of Finance*, 65(6):2363–2401.

Bebchuk, L. A. and Jackson, R. J. (2012). The law and economics of blockholder disclosure. *Harvard Business Law Review*, 2:39–60.

Becht, M., Franks, J., Mayer, C., and Rossi, S. (2009). Returns to shareholder activism: Evidence from a clinical study of the Hermes UK Focus Fund. *Review of Financial Studies*, 22(8):3093–3129.

Becker, B. and Milbourn, T. (2011). How did increased competition affect credit ratings? *Journal of Financial Economics*, 101(3):493–514.

Becker, B. and Subramanian, G. (2013). Improving director elections. *Harvard Business Law Review*, 3(1):1–34.

Behn, S. (2005). "Lebanese-Americans" honor progress, kin. *Washington Times*, April 8.

Beilfuss, L. (2015). Perrigo asks shareholders to reject Mylan's latest bid. *Wall Street Journal (Online)*, September 17.

Beirne, M. (2005). A-B pits Americana against "foreign beers". *Adweek*, March 28.

Benmelech, E. and Frydman, C. (2015). Military CEOs. *Journal of Financial Economics*, 117(1):43–59.

Bennetts, L. (2002). The C.E.O.'s worst nightmare. *Vanity Fair*, 503:74.

Benoit, D. and Kapner, S. (2015). Activist knocks on Macy's doors. *Wall Street Journal*, July 16:B1.

Bereskin, F. L. and Cicero, D. C. (2013). CEO compensation contagion: Evidence from an exogenous shock. *Journal of Financial Economics*, 107(2):477–493.

Berfield, S. (2011). Fall of the house of Busch. *Bloomberg Businessweek*, July 4(4236):64–70.

Berger, P. G. and Ofek, E. (1995). Diversification's effect on firm value. *Journal of Financial Economics*, 37(1):39–65.

Berkowitz, H. (2003). Which ones to hold? Cablevision is shuffling its properties in an attempt to transform itself, but few know which cards will be dealt. *Newsday*, June 2:A25.

Berle, A. A. and Means, G. C. (1932). *The Modern Corporation and Private Property*. Macmillan, New York.

Berry, K. (2004). Coming home. *Los Angeles Business Journal*, September 6:24.

Bertrand, M. and Mullainathan, S. (1999). Is there discretion in wage setting? A test using takeover legislation. *RAND Journal of Economics*, 30(3):535–554.

Bertrand, M. and Mullainathan, S. (2000). Agents with and without principals. *American Economic Review*, 90(2):203–208.

Bertrand, M. and Mullainathan, S. (2003). Enjoying the quiet life? Corporate governance and managerial preferences. *Journal of Political Economy*, 111(5):1043–1075.

Betton, S., Eckbo, B. E., and Thorburn, K. S. (2008). Corporate takeovers. In Eckbo, B. E., editor, *Handbook of Corporate Finance: Empirical Corporate Finance*, volume 2, chapter 15, pages 289–427. North Holland, Amsterdam.

Betton, S., Eckbo, B. E., and Thorburn, K. S. (2009). Merger negotiations and the toehold puzzle. *Journal of Financial Economics*, 91(2):158–178.

Bharath, S., Dittmar, A., and Sivadasan, J. (2014). Do going-private transactions affect plant efficiency and investment? *Review of Financial Studies*, 27(7):1929–1976.

Bhide, A. (1993). The hidden costs of stock market liquidity. *Journal of Financial Economics*, 34(1):31–51.

Bianconi, C. (2005). Brazilian executives spell change for InBev. *Reuters News*, March 24.

Binmore, K., Rubinstein, A., and Wolinsky, A. (1986). The Nash bargaining solution in economic modelling. *RAND Journal of Economics*, 17(2):176–188.

Bizjak, J., Lemmon, M., and Nguyen, T. (2011). Are all CEOs above average? An empirical analysis of compensation peer groups and pay design. *Journal of Financial Economics*, 100(3):538–555.

Bizjak, J., Lemmon, M., and Whitby, R. (2009). Option backdating and board interlocks. *Review of Financial Studies*, 22(11):4821–4847.

Bolton, P., Freixas, X., and Shapiro, J. (2012). The credit ratings game. *Journal of Finance*, 67(1):85–111.

Bolton, P. and Scharfstein, D. S. (1990). A theory of predation based on agency problems in financial contracting. *American Economic Review*, 80(1):93–106.

Bond, P. (2006). Q&A Bob Nardelli. *Atlanta Journal–Constitution*, July 9:E1.

Boone, A. L., Field, L. C., Karpoff, J. M., and Raheja, C. G. (2007). The determinants of corporate board size and composition: An empirical analysis. *Journal of Financial Economics*, 85(1):66–101.

Bose, M. (2004). Fans turn nasty in opposition to Glazer. *Daily Telegraph*, October 6:1.

Boston Properties Inc. (2005). Form DEF 14A. Filed on April 8.

Boyer, E. J. (1982). Hopeful investors gallop into breeding Arabian horses. *Los Angeles Times*, November 29:A1.

Bradley, M. and Wakeman, L. M. (1983). The wealth effects of targeted share repurchases. *Journal of Financial Economics*, 11(1–4):301–328.

Brav, A., Jiang, W., and Kim, H. (2009). Hedge fund activism: A review. *Foundations and Trends in Finance*, 4(3):185–246.

Brav, A., Jiang, W., and Kim, H. (2015). The real effects of hedge fund activism: Productivity, asset allocation, and labor outcomes. *Review of Financial Studies*, 28(10):2723–2769.

Brav, A., Jiang, W., Partnoy, F., and Thomas, R. (2008a). Hedge fund activism, corporate governance, and firm performance. *Journal of Finance*, 53(4):1729–1775.

Brav, A., Jiang, W., Partnoy, F., and Thomas, R. (2008b). The returns to hedge fund activism. *Financial Analysts Journal*, 64(6):45–61.

Brickley, J. A., Linck, J. S., and Coles, J. L. (1999). What happens to CEOs after they retire? New evidence on career concerns, horizon problems, and CEO incentives. *Journal of Financial Economics*, 52(3):341–377.

Bristol-Myers Squibb Company (2001a). Peter R. Dolan named next CEO of Bristol-Myers Squibb. February 7. Press release.

Bristol-Myers Squibb Company (2001b). Peter R. Dolan succeeds Charles A. Heimbold, Jr. as chief executive officer of Bristol-Myers Squibb. May 1. Press release.

Bristol-Myers Squibb Company (2005). Bristol-Myers Squibb annual meeting of stockholders–Final. *FD (Fair Disclosure) Wire*, May 3.

Bristol-Myers Squibb Company (2006). Form 8-K. Filed on March 13.

British Broadcasting Corporation (1985). "Important" new oil field discovered in Arauca. *BBC Monitoring Service: Latin America*, February 19.

British Columbia Securities Commission (2010a). Majority reasons for decision. *2010 BCSEC-COM 432*.

British Columbia Securities Commission (2010b). Reasons for decision. *2010 BCSECCOM 629*.

Brooks, R. (2000). Home Depot warns of a profit shortfall. *Wall Street Journal*, October 13:A3.

Brown, C. (1999). Katz bites the mouse. *Newsweek*, 133(20):51.

Brown, C. (2002). Disney fills the gap. *Los Angeles Times*, September 27:C1.

Brown, P. L. (1990). Disney deco. *New York Times*, April 8:A18–A21.

Bryant, T. (2008). The Busch who embraces InBev. *St. Louis Post–Dispatch*, July 9:A1.

Buchan, J. (1989). Film successes produce a record quarter for Disney. *Financial Times*, January 26:33.

Buchanan, B., Netter, J. M., Poulsen, A. B., and Yang, T. (2012). Shareholder proposal rules and practice: Evidence from a comparison of the United States and United Kingdom. *American Business Law Journal*, 49(4):739–803.

Bulow, J. and Shoven, J. B. (2005). Accounting for stock options. *Journal of Economic Perspectives*, 19(4):115–134.

Burch, T. R. and Nanda, V. (2003). Divisional diversity and the conglomerate discount: Evidence from spinoffs. *Journal of Financial Economics*, 70(1):69–98.

Burke, M. (2003). Like father, unlike son. *Fortune*, September 15:81–84.

Burroughs, B. and Masters, K. (1996). The mouse trap. *Vanity Fair*, 436:266–272.

Burrows, P. (2005). HP says goodbye to drama. *BusinessWeek*, 3950:83–86.

Busch III, A. A. (2008). Form 4. Filed on November 19.

Business Roundtable (2006). Letter to the Securities and Exchange Commission. April 10.

Business Roundtable (2009). Letter to the Securities and Exchange Commission. September 15.

Business Roundtable (2015). Letter to Institutional Shareholder Services Inc. and Glass, Lewis & Co. January 23.

Butter, A. and Pogue, D. (2002). *Piloting Palm: The Inside Story of Palm, Handspring, and the Birth of the Billion-Dollar Handheld Industry*. John Wiley & Sons, New York.

Byrne, J. A., Bongiorno, L., and Grover, R. (1994). That eye popping executive pay. *Business Week*, 3368:52.

Byrne, J. A., Grover, R., and Melcher, R. A. (1997). The best and worst boards. *Business Week*, 3556:90–98.

Cablevision Systems Corp. (2002a). Cablevision Systems Corporation announces fully-funded growth plan. August 8. Press release.

Cablevision Systems Corp. (2002b). Form 8-K. Filed on November 8.

Cablevision Systems Corp. (2004). Form 10-Q for the period ended September 30, 2004. Filed on November 9.

Cablevision Systems Corp. (2005a). Form 10-K for the period ended December 31, 2004. Filed on March 16.

Cablevision Systems Corp. (2005b). Form 8-K. Filed on February 11.

Cablevision Systems Corp. (2005c). Form 8-K. Filed on March 3.

Cablevision Systems Corp. (2005d). Form 8-K. Filed on March 11.

Cablevision Systems Corp. (2005e). Form 8-K. Filed on April 8.

Cablevision Systems Corp. (2005f). Form DEF 14A. Filed on April 29.

Cablevision Systems Corp. (2006a). Form 10-K for the period ended December 31, 2006. Filed on March 2.

Cablevision Systems Corp. (2006b). Form 10-Q for the period ended March 31, 2006. Filed on May 10.

Cablevision Systems Corp. (2006c). Form 8-K. Filed on April 10.

Cablevision Systems Corp. (2006d). Form DEF 14A. Filed on April 28.

Cablevision Systems Corp. (2008). Form DEF 14A. Filed on April 9.

Cablevision Systems Corp. (2009a). Form 10-K for the period ended December 31, 2008. Filed on February 26.

Cablevision Systems Corp. (2009b). Form 10-Q for the period ended March 31, 2009. Filed on May 7.

Cablevision Systems Corp. (2009c). Form 8-K. Filed on July 31.

Cablevision Systems Corp. (2009d). Form DEF 14A. Filed on April 8.

Cablevision Systems Corp. (2010). Form 8-K. Filed on November 18.

Cablevision Systems Corp. (2011). Form 8-K. Filed on March 11.

Cacace, L. M. and Tucksmith, R. K. (2006). Largest U.S. corporations. *Fortune*, 153(7):F1–F20.

Cadman, B., Carter, M. E., and Hillegeist, S. (2010). The incentives of compensation consultants and CEO pay. *Journal of Accounting and Economics*, 49(3):263–280.

Cai, J., Garner, J. L., and Walkling, R. A. (2009). Electing directors. *Journal of Finance*, 64(5):2389–2421.

Cain, M. D. and McKeon, S. B. (2016). CEO personal risk-taking and corporate policies. *Journal of Financial and Quantitative Analysis*, 51(1):1–26.

Cain, M. D., McKeon, S. B., and Davidoff Solomon, S. (2014). Do takeover laws matter? Evidence from five decades of hostile takeovers. DERA Working Paper Series, Securities and Exchange Commission.

CalSTRS and Relational Investors LLC (2010a). CalSTRS and Relational commend Occidental Petroleum's election of board nominee, Margaret "Peggy" Foran. December 9. Press release.

CalSTRS and Relational Investors LLC (2010b). Letter to Occidental Petroleum's board of directors. July 30.

CalSTRS and Relational Investors LLC (2010c). Letter to Occidental Petroleum's lead independent director and the executive compensation and human resources committee chairman. May 4.

Canadian Occidental Petroleum Ltd (1996). Canadian Occidental quarterly results. May 9. Regulatory News Service.

Caney, D. (2002). Cablevision sees subs decline, to address fund gap. *Reuters News*, July 27.

Carew, S. and Nayak, M. (2013). Take-Two to buy back all of Icahn shares; directors leave. *Reuters*, November 27.

Carey, S. and Prada, P. (2008). Delta, Northwest agree to merge; may start trend. *Wall Street Journal*, April 15:B1.

Carlton, S. (2000). Bucs fans win in ticket settlement. *St. Petersburg Times*, June 22:1A.

Carr, J. (1989). Katzenberg reanimates Disney. *Boston Globe*, November 12:B1.

Carroll, J. (2010). Occidental's Irani, highest-paid oil chief executive, to step down in May. *Bloomberg*, October 14.

Chamber of Commerce (2006). Letter to the Securities and Exchange Commission. April 7.

Chamber of Commerce (2015). Letter to the Securities and Exchange Commission. February 4.

Charlotte Business Journal (2003). Former United Dominion chief sues SPX. *Charlotte Business Journal*, December 24.

Chase Corp. (2004). Form DEF 14A. Filed on December 21.

Chase Corp. (2005). Form DEF 14A. Filed on December 21.

Chava, S., Kumar, P., and Warga, A. (2010). Managerial agency and bond covenants. *Review of Financial Studies*, 23(3):1120–1148.

Chemmanur, T. J., Krishnan, K., and Nandy, D. K. (2014). The effects of corporate spin-offs on productivity. *Journal of Corporate Finance*, 27:72–98.

Chen, T., Harford, J., and Lin, C. (2015). Do analysts matter for governance? Evidence from natural experiments. *Journal of Financial Economics*, 115(2):383–410.

Choi, S. J., Wiechman, A. C., and Pritchard, A. C. (2013). Scandal enforcement at the SEC: The arc of the option backdating investigations. *American Law and Economics Review*, 15(2):542–577.

Chubb Corp. (1999). Chubb board declares regular quarterly dividend and elects new officers. June 11. Press release.

Cichello, M. S., Fee, C. E., Hadlock, C. J., and Sonti, R. (2009). Promotions, turnover, and performance evaluation: Evidence from the careers of division managers. *Accounting Review*, 84(4):1119–1143.

Cieply, M. (1985). Two Disney directors who helped lead takeover defense are stepping down. *Wall Street Journal*, January 16:8.

Citywire (2002). Edwards cashes in United shares. *Citywire*, May 28.

Citywire (2005). Glazer launches £790 million bid for Manchester United. *Citywire*, May 12.

Clarke, J., Khorana, A., Patel, A., and Rau, P. R. (2007). The impact of all-star analyst job changes on their coverage choices and investment banking deal flow. *Journal of Financial Economics*, 84(3):713–737.

Coffee, J. C. (1991). Liquidity versus control: The institutional investor as corporate monitor. *Columbia Law Review*, 91(6):1277–1368.

Cohen, A. and Wang, C. C. Y. (2013). How do staggered boards affect shareholder value? Evidence from a natural experiment. *Journal of Financial Economics*, 110(3):627–641.

Cole, R. J. (1984). Occidental buys back 5% stake. *New York Times*, July 20:D1.

Coles, J. L., Daniel, N. D., and Naveen, L. (2008). Boards: Does one size fit all? *Journal of Financial Economics*, 87(2):329–356.

Collins, D. W., Gong, G., and Li, H. (2009). Corporate governance and backdating of executive stock options. *Contemporary Accounting Research*, 26(2):403–445.

Columbia/HCA Healthcare Corp. (1997). Jack O. Bovender, Jr. named president and chief operating officer of Columbia/HCA. August 4. Press release.

Colvin, G. (2010). As executive compensation becomes topic A (again), the real outrage is how CEOs are paid, not how much. *Fortune*, 161(6):86.

Comcast Corp. (2005). Form DEF 14A. Filed on April 8.

Core, J. E. and Guay, W. (1999). The use of equity grants to manage optimal equity incentive levels. *Journal of Financial Economics*, 28(2):151–184.

Core, J. E., Guay, W. R., and Rusticus, T. O. (2006). Does weak governance cause weak stock returns? An examination of firm operating performance and investors' expectations. *Journal of Finance*, 61(2):655–687.

Core, J. E., Guay, W. R., and Thomas, R. S. (2005). Is U.S. CEO compensation broken? *Journal of Applied Corporate Finance*, 17(4):97–104.

Core, J. E., Holthausen, R. W., and Larcker, D. F. (1999). Corporate governance, chief executive officer compensation, and firm performance. *Journal of Financial Economics*, 51(3):371–406.

Courier (1983). Brewing heir can't recall fatal accident. *Courier*, November 15:11A.

Court of Chancery of the State of Delaware (1990). Sullivan v. Hammer: Opinion. *Civil Action No. 10823*.

Court of Chancery of the State of Delaware (1998). In Re Walt Disney Company Derivative Litigation: Opinion. *Civil Action No. 15452*.

Court of Chancery of the State of Delaware (2005). In Re The Walt Disney Company Derivative Litigation: Opinion and Order. *Civil Action No. 15452*.

Court of Chancery of the State of Delaware (2011). In Re Airgas Inc. Shareholder Litigation: Opinion. *Civil Action No. 5256-CC*.

Court of Chancery of the State of Delaware (2015). In Re Dole Food Co., Inc. Stockholder Litigation: Memorandum Opinion. *Civil Action Nos. 8703-VCL*.

Cowan, A. L. (1992). Executives are fuming over data on their pay. *New York Times*, August 25:D1.

Cowen, A., Groysberg, B., and Healy, P. (2006). Which types of analyst firms are more optimistic? *Journal of Accounting and Economics*, 41(1):119–146.

Craig, S. (2011). Goldman brushes off the gadfly. *DealBook*, May 4.

Cremers, M. and Ferrell, A. (2014). Thirty years of shareholder rights and firm value. *Journal of Finance*, 69(3):1167–1196.

Creswell, J. and Barbaro, M. (2007). Home Depot board ousts chief, saying goodbye with big check. *New York Times*, January 4:A1.

Cronqvist, H., Makhija, A. K., and Yonker, S. E. (2012). Behavioral consistency in corporate finance: CEO personal and corporate leverage. *Journal of Financial Economics*, 103(1):20–40.

Crystal, G. S. (1991). *In Search of Excess: The Overcompensation of American Executives*. W. W. Norton & Company, New York.

Custódio, C., Ferreira, M. A., and Matos, P. (2013). Generalists versus specialists: Lifetime work experience and chief executive officer pay. *Journal of Financial Economics*, 108(2):471–492.

Custódio, C. and Metzger, D. (2013). How do CEOs matter? The effect of industry expertise on acquisition returns. *Review of Financial Studies*, 26(8):2008–2047.

Custódio, C. and Metzger, D. (2014). Financial expert CEOs: CEO's work experience and firm's financial policies. *Journal of Financial Economics*, 114(1):125–154.

Cyert, R. M., Kang, S.-H., and Kumar, P. (2002). Corporate governance, takeovers, and top-management compensation: Theory and evidence. *Management Science*, 48(4):453–469.

Daines, R. M., Gow, I. D., and Larcker, D. F. (2010). Rating the ratings: How good are commercial governance ratings? *Journal of Financial Economics*, 98:439–461.

Damouni, N., Stone, M., and Oran, O. (2015). Hedge funds propose Macy's unlocks real estate value—Sources. *Reuters News*, June 3.

Dann, L. Y. and DeAngelo, H. (1983). Standstill agreements, privately negotiated stock repurchases, and the market for corporate control. *Journal of Financial Economics*, 11(1–4):275–300.

Davidoff, S. M. (2013). Yahoo's share buyback is legal, but timing is suspect. *New York Times*, July 24:B4.

Davies, M. (2008a). Anheuser details staff benefit, pension reductions: Memo. *Reuters News*, June 29.

Davies, M. (2008b). A tale of jet-setting and cost cutting. *Reuters DealZone*, July 1.

Davies, P. J. and Garrahan, M. (2005). Glazer claims his United prize after Irish tycoons sell their 29% stake. *Financial Times*, May 13:1.

Davis, E. Y. (2005). Shareholders resolutions submitted by Evelyn Y. Davis, famous shareholder activist, editor of Highlights and Lowlights, for 2005 proxy statements. March 1. Press release.

Davis, G. F. and Kim, H. (2007). Business ties and proxy voting by mutual funds. *Journal of Financial Economics*, 85(2):552–570.

Davis, S. J., Haltiwanger, J., Handley, K., Jarmin, R., Lerner, J., and Miranda, J. (2014). Private equity, jobs, and productivity. *American Economic Review*, 104(12):3956–3990.

Dechow, P. M. and Sloan, R. G. (1991). Executive incentives and the horizon problem: An empirical investigation. *Journal of Accounting and Economics*, 14(1):51–89.

DeGeorge, G. (1996). Is Zapata the Glazers' toy? *BusinessWeek*, 3496:116.

Degross, R. (2006). Big push, few results on service. *Atlanta Journal–Constitution*, February 21:C1.

Delaney, K. J. (2006). Spreading change: As Yahoo falters, executive's memo calls for overhaul. *Wall Street Journal*, November 18:A1.

Delaney, K. J. (2008). Yahoo holders turn up heat after Microsoft deal talks fail. *Wall Street Journal*, May 6:B1.

Delaney, K. J., Guth, R. A., and Karnitschnig, M. (2008a). Microsoft makes grab for Yahoo—software giant's bid is aimed at Google. *Wall Street Journal*, February 2:A1.

Delaney, K. J. and Karnitschnig, M. (2008). Yahoo considers playing a Google defense. *Wall Street Journal*, February 9:A3.

Delaney, K. J., Karnitschnig, M., and Guth, R. A. (2008b). Microsoft, Yahoo try to make nice. *Wall Street Journal*, May 3:A3.

Delaney, K. J. and Lublin, J. S. (2007). Amid missteps, Yahoo's Semel resigns as CEO: Company faces heat from Google, investors. *Wall Street Journal*, June 19:A1.

Delta Air Lines, Inc. (2005). Form DEF 14A. Filed on April 18.

Department of Energy (2002a). New members named to Secretary of Energy Advisory Board. May 7. Press release

Department of Energy (2002b). Secretary Abraham establishes task force on the future of science programs at DOE. December 16. Press release

Department of Justice (2008). Yahoo! Inc. and Google Inc. abandon their advertising agreement. November 5. Press release 08-981.

Dielectric Communications (2001). Dielectric names new president. October 17. Press release.

Dikolli, S. S., Mayew, W. J., and Nanda, D. (2014). CEO tenure and the performance–turnover relation. *Review of Accounting Studies*, 19(1):281–327.

Dixit, A. K. and Skeath, S. (1999). *Games of Strategy*. W. W. Norton & Company, New York.

Dobrzynski, J. H. (2006). Home Despot. *Wall Street Journal*, May 31:A12.

Dolan, C. (1995). Dogged controversy: A millionaire's fees for mutts and kids. *Wall Street Journal*, August 18:A1.

Donkin, R. (1989). Manchester Utd bid abandoned. *Financial Times*, October 12:28.

Dorfman, B. (2007). Anheuser-Busch at all-time high on Pershing story. *Reuters News*, June 5.

Dougherty, L. (1996). Stadium name: Old news, fresh anger. *St. Petersburg Times*, June 12:3B.

Dow Jones News Service (1979). Tappan agrees to be acquired by Swedish firm for $55.8 mill. *Dow Jones News Service*, October 11.

Dow Jones News Service (2004). SPX puts 4Q rev boost at 10%. *Dow Jones News Service*, January 20.

Doyle, J. M. (1990). To corporate biggies, the lady is a pest. *Associated Press*, April 11.

Ducker, J. (2010). Ferguson backs the Glazers and calls an end to big spending. *Times*, July 29:77.

Ducker, J. (2014a). Ferguson backed move to sack Moyes: Support for United's "Chosen One" had waned considerably. *Times*, April 23:60.

Ducker, J. (2014b). Van Gaal given green light to keep spending. *Times*, September 5:80.

Dunkin' Brands Group Inc. (2011). Form 424B4. Filed on July 27.

Dyck, A. and Zingales, L. (2004). Private benefits of control: An international comparison. *Journal of Finance*, 59(2):537–600.

eBay Inc. (2015a). Form 8-K. Filed on May 5.

eBay Inc. (2015b). Form DEF 14A. Filed on March 23.

Edmans, A. (2009). Blockholder trading, market efficiency, and managerial myopia. *Journal of Finance*, 64(6):2481–2513.

Edmans, A. and Gabaix, X. (2011). The effect of risk on the CEO market. *Review of Financial Studies*, 24(8):2822–2863.

Edmans, A., Gabaix, X., and Landier, A. (2009). A multiplicative model of optimal CEO incentives in market equilibrium. *Review of Financial Studies*, 22(12):4881–4917.

Edwards, C. (2001). Palm's market starts to melt in its hands. *BusinessWeek*, 3735:42.

Egan, M. (2015). America's highest paid CEO earns $285 million. *CNN Wire*, April 18.

Ehrbar, A. (1998). Case study of a CEO "thinking quantum". *Directors & Boards*, 23(1):37–42.

Eisfeldt, A. L. and Kuhnen, C. M. (2013). CEO turnover in a competitive assignment framework. *Journal of Financial Economics*, 109(2):351–372.

Elkinawy, S. and Offenberg, D. (2013). Accelerated vesting in takeovers: The impact on shareholder wealth. *Financial Management*, 42(1):101–126.

Eller, C. (2009a). Lions Gate cutting jobs again. *Los Angeles Times*, March 28:B3.

Eller, C. (2009b). Lions Gate's own drama. *Los Angeles Times*, March 20:B1.

Emerson Electric Co. (2002). Form DEF 14A. Filed on December 16.

Emshwiller, J. R. (2010). KB Home ex-CEO gets detention. *Wall Street Journal*, November 11:B3.

Ertimur, Y., Ferri, F., and Muslu, V. (2011). Shareholder activism and CEO pay. *Review of Financial Studies*, 24(2):535–592.

Ertimur, Y., Ferri, F., and Oesch, D. (2013). Shareholder votes and proxy advisors: Evidence from say on pay. *Journal of Accounting Research*, 51(5):951–996.

Ertimur, Y., Ferri, F., and Stubben, S. R. (2010). Board of directors' responsiveness to shareholders: Evidence from shareholder proposals. *Journal of Corporate Finance*, 16(1):53–72.

Evans, J. H., Nagarajan, N. J., and Schloetzer, J. D. (2010). CEO turnover and retention light: Retaining former CEOs on the board. *Journal of Accounting Research*, 48(5):1015–1047.

Evening Independent (1972). Hard hat Evelyn. *Evening Independent*, April 20.

Express (2004). Fans fight takeover threat. *Express*, January 20:71.

Fabrikant, G. (1996). Finance chief quits Disney to take top executive job at Hilton. *New York Times*, February 3:35–36.

Facebook Inc. (2012). Form 424B4. Filed on May 18.

Fahlenbrach, R., Minton, B. A., and Pan, C. H. (2011). Former CEO directors: Lingering CEOs or valuable resources? *Review of Financial Studies*, 24(10):3486–3518.

Fairfax Group (2013). History of Fairfax. www.fairfaxco.us/about.php.

Falato, A., Li, D., and Milbourn, T. (2015). Which skills matter in the market for CEOs? Evidence from pay for CEO credentials. *Management Science*, 61(12):2845–2869.

Faleye, O. (2007). Classified boards, firm value, and managerial entrenchment. *Journal of Financial Economics*, 83(2):501–529.

Fama, E. F. (1980). Agency problems and the theory of the firm. *Journal of Political Economy*, 88(2):288–307.

Fang, L. and Yasuda, A. (2009). The effectiveness of reputation as a disciplinary mechanism in sell-side research. *Review of Financial Studies*, 22(9):3735–3777.

Faulkender, M. and Yang, J. (2010). Inside the black box: The role and composition of compensation peer groups. *Journal of Financial Economics*, 96(2):257–270.

Faulkender, M. and Yang, J. (2013). Is disclosure an effective cleansing mechanism? The dynamics of compensation peer benchmarking. *Review of Financial Studies*, 26(3):806–839.

FedEx Corp. (2015a). Form 8-K. Filed on September 28.

FedEx Corp. (2015b). Form DEF 14A. Filed on August 17.

Fee, C. E. and Hadlock, C. J. (2003). Raids, rewards, and reputations in the market for managerial talent. *Review of Financial Studies*, 16(4):1315–1357.

Fee, C. E. and Hadlock, C. J. (2004). Management turnover across the corporate hierarchy. *Journal of Accounting and Economics*, 37(1):3–38.

Fee, C. E., Hadlock, C. J., Huang, J., and Pierce, J. R. (2012). Industry conditions and CEO labor markets. Michigan State University.

Fee, C. E., Hadlock, C. J., and Pierce, J. R. (2013). Managers with and without style: Evidence using exogenous variation. *Review of Financial Studies*, 26(3):567–601.

Feldman, A. (1998). Fighting the fat cats for decades, Evelyn Davis has grilled biz bigwigs in outrageous fashion. *New York Daily News*, May 24.

Fernando, C. S., Gatchev, V. A., and Spindt, P. A. (2012). Institutional ownership, analyst following, and share prices. *Journal of Banking and Finance*, 36(8):2175–2189.

Ferracone, R. and Harris, D. (2011). Say on pay: Identifying investor concerns. Council of Institutional Investors.

Ferris, S. P., Jagannathan, M., and Pritchard, A. C. (2003). Too busy to mind the business? Monitoring by directors with multiple board appointments. *Journal of Finance*, 58(3):1087–1111.

Fich, E. M., Harford, J., and Tran, A. L. (2015). Motivated monitors: The importance of institutional investors' portfolio weights. *Journal of Financial Economics*, 118(1):21–48.

Fich, E. M. and Shivdasani, A. (2006). Are busy boards effective monitors? *Journal of Finance*, 61(2):689–724.

Fich, E. M., Tran, A. L., and Walkling, R. A. (2013). On the importance of golden parachutes. *Journal of Financial and Quantitative Analysis*, 48(6):1717–1753.

Financial Conduct Authority (2015a). Disclosure rules and transparency rules. Release 157. FCA Handbook.

Financial Conduct Authority (2015b). Listing rules. Release 157. FCA Handbook.

Financial Times (1991). Manchester United shares start trading at discount. *Financial Times*, June 11:21.

Fisher, D. and Ozanian, M. K. (1999). Cowboy capitalism. *Forbes*, 164(7):170–177.

Flanigan, J. (1992). Who cheers Eisner's payout? Disney shareholders. *Los Angeles Times*, December 6:D1.

Flynn, J. (1992). A tall order for the prince of beers. *Business Week*, 3257:66–68.

FMR Corp. (2007). Form 13F-HR for the period ended December 31, 2006. Filed on February 14.

Follett, M. (2010). Gantler v. Stephens: Big epiphany or big failure—a look at the current state of officers' fiduciary duties and advice for potential protection. *Delaware Journal of Corporate Law*, 35(2):563–582.

Ford Motor Co. (2003). Bill Ford delivers new Jaguar X-Type sedan to Evelyn Y. Davis, stockholder activist. December 15. Press release.

Ford Motor Co. (2005). Form DEF 14A. Filed on April 6.

Ford Motor Co. (2015a). Form 8-K. Filed on May 19.

Ford Motor Co. (2015b). Form DEF 14A. Filed on March 27.

Forelle, C. and Bandler, J. (2006). The perfect payday. *Wall Street Journal*, March 18:A1.

Fos, V. (2015). The disciplinary effects of proxy contests. *Management Science*, forthcoming.

Fowler, T. and Lublin, J. S. (2013). Occidental reassures on leadership. *Wall Street Journal (Online)*, April 8.

Fracassi, C. and Tate, G. (2012). External networking and internal firm governance. *Journal of Finance*, 67(1):153–194.

Francis, B. B., Hasan, I., John, K., and Song, L. (2011). Corporate governance and dividend payout policy: A test using antitakeover legislation. *Financial Management*, 40(1):83–112.

Francis, T. (2008). Boss talk: HCA chief enjoying the private life. *Wall Street Journal*, January 7:B1.

Frankel, T. C. (2010). A-B jets linger as clipped wings: 2007 rift between Busches over plane may have cleared runway for InBev takeover. *St. Louis Post-Dispatch*, January 10:A1.

Franklin, S. (2005). Occidental agrees to buy Vintage for $3.5 bln in cash and stock. *Bloomberg*, October 14.

French, R. (2006). Shareholders sue challenging HCA buyout; CEO says suits were expected. *Associated Press Newswires*, July 29.

Fried, J. M. (2008). Option backdating and its implications. *Washington and Lee Law Review*, 65(3):853–886.

Frydman, C. and Saks, R. E. (2010). Executive compensation: A new view from a long-term perspective, 1936–2005. *Review of Financial Studies*, 23(5):2099–2138.

Furfaro, D. T. (2001). Albany, N.Y.–area attorney named to executive post of Home Depot. *Knight Ridder Tribune Business News*, February 28.

Furlong, L. (2002). Taking care of business. *Golf Digest*, 53(9):172.

Furlong, L. (2004). In good company. *Golf Digest*, 55(10):132.

Furlong, L. (2006). Executive order. *Golf Digest*, 57(10):166.

Gabaix, X. and Landier, A. (2008). Why has CEO pay increased so much? *Quarterly Journal of Economics*, 123(1):49–100.

Gabaix, X., Landier, A., and Sauvagnat, J. (2014). CEO pay and firm size: An update after the crisis. *Economic Journal*, 124(574):F40–F49.

Gaither, C. (2003). On the sidelines. *Boston Globe*, June 2:C1.

Gannett Co. Inc. (2005). Form DEF 14A. Filed on March 11.

Garlo, N. (2002). Interview: Finnish CRF Box sees strong growth, Nasdaq listing. *Reuters News*, August 23.

Garlo, N. (2003). Interview: Finland's CRF Box says bucking industry downturn. *Reuters News*, September 10.

Garrahan, M. (2004a). Irish team eyes seat on board of Man U. *Financial Times*, February 12:21.

Garrahan, M. (2004b). Key shareholders query Man Utd accounts. *Financial Times*, January 30:1.

Garrahan, M. (2004c). Man United tycoons tackle board. *Financial Times*, January 26:19.

Garrahan, M. (2004d). Man Utd backed Glazer move. *Financial Times*, November 17:21.

Garrahan, M. (2004e). Man Utd ends talks with Glazer over share offer. *Financial Times*, October 26:22.

Garrahan, M. (2005a). Man United board to allow Glazer to study its finances. *Financial Times*, February 11:19.

Garrahan, M. (2005b). Man Utd board spurns Glazer bid. *Financial Times*, April 22:22.

Garrahan, M. (2005c). US tycoon makes new move for Man Utd. *Financial Times*, February 7:19.

Garrahan, M. and Thal Larsen, P. (2004). Glazer lifts his stake in Man United to 25.5%. *Financial Times*, October 16:1.

Garvey, G. T. and Milbourn, T. T. (2006). Asymmetric benchmarking in compensation: Executives are rewarded for good luck but not penalized for bad. *Journal of Financial Economics*, 82(1):197–225.

Gateway 2000 Inc. (2000). Form DEF 14A. Filed on April 7.

Gateway Inc. (2001). Form DEF 14A. Filed on April 4.

Gelles, D. (2015). It's (still) their party. *New York Times*, May 17:1.

Gertner, R., Powers, E., and Scharfstein, D. (2002). Learning about internal capital markets from corporate spin-offs. *Journal of Finance*, 57(6):2479–2506.

Gibbons, R. and Murphy, K. J. (1992). Optimal incentive contracts in the presence of career concerns: Theory and evidence. *Journal of Political Economy*, 100(3):468–505.

Gigot, P. A. (1992). Executive pay: An embarrassment to free marketers. *Wall Street Journal*, January 10:A8.

Gillan, S. L., Hartzell, J. C., and Parrino, R. (2009). Explicit versus implicit contracts: Evidence from CEO employment agreements. *Journal of Finance*, 64(4):1629–1655.

Gillan, S. L. and Starks, L. T. (2000). Corporate governance proposals and shareholder activism: The role of institutional investors. *Journal of Financial Economics*, 57(2):275–305.

Gimbel, B. (2006). Last of the indies. *Fortune*, 154(2):130–138.

Giroud, X. and Mueller, H. M. (2010). Does corporate governance matter in competitive industries? *Journal of Financial Economics*, 95(3):312–331.

Giroud, X. and Mueller, H. M. (2011). Corporate governance, product market competition, and equity prices. *Journal of Finance*, 66(2):563–600.

Gisquet, V. (2005). The biking builder. *Forbes.com*, March 18.

Golden, D. (2008). School of hard knocks. *Conde Nast Portfolio*, 2(11):132.

Goldman Sachs Group, Inc. (2005). Form DEF 14A. Filed on February 24.

Gompers, P., Ishii, J., and Metrick, A. (2003). Corporate governance and equity prices. *Quarterly Journal of Economics*, 118(1):107–155.

Google Inc. (2015a). Form 8-K. Filed on June 4.

Google Inc. (2015b). Form DEF 14A. Filed on April 23.

Gould, J. (1965). Community-antenna TV: Picture of vast potential. *New York Times*, December 6:75.

Government Accountability Office (2007). Corporate shareholder meetings: Issues relating to firms that advise institutional investors on proxy voting. *Report to Congressional Requesters*, GAO-07-765.

Graham, J. R., Harvey, C. R., and Puri, M. (2013). Managerial attitudes and corporate actions. *Journal of Financial Economics*, 109(1):103–121.

Grant, P. (2004). Cablevision's spinoff is for the dreamers. *Wall Street Journal*, September 7:C1.

Grant, P. (2005a). Chairman's board purge alters Cablevision picture. *Wall Street Journal*, March 4:A1.

Grant, P. (2005b). Dolans' memos stir up confusion over fate of Voom. *Wall Street Journal*, March 2:A10.

Grant, P. (2005c). Family divide: At Cablevision, father-son split looms over future. *Wall Street Journal*, January 24:A1.

Grant, P. and Berman, D. K. (2005). Dolan pledges $400 million to Voom. *Wall Street Journal*, March 30:C5.

Graybow, M. (2008). Toll Brothers chief defends his pay packages. *Reuters News*, February 21.

Greenspan, A. (2005). Testimony of Chairman Alan Greenspan, Federal Reserve Board's semi-annual Monetary Policy Report to the Congress before the Committee on Financial Services, U.S. House of Representatives July 20, 2005. Federal Reserve Board.

Gregory, H. J. (2012). Innovations in proxy statements. *PracticalLaw.com*, July–August:28–32.

Grossman, S. J. and Hart, O. D. (1980). Takeover bids, the free-rider problem, and the theory of the corporation. *Bell Journal of Economics*, 11(1):42–64.

Grover, R. (2009). Fighting takeovers by playing the debt card. *BusinessWeek*, April 8.

Grover, R. (2012). Icahn to sell back MGM shares for $590 million, studio prepares IPO. *Reuters News*, July 31.

Grow, B., Brady, D., and Arndt, M. (2006). Renovating Home Depot. *BusinessWeek*, 3974:50–58.

Groysberg, B., Healy, P. M., and Maber, D. A. (2011). What drives sell-side analyst compensation at high-status investment banks? *Journal of Accounting Research*, 49(4):969–1000.

Gumbel, A. (1999). Analysis: The cyberpunks. *Independent (London)*, March 24:5.

Gunther, M. and Kim, H. (2004). Cablevision's new frontier. *Fortune*, 149(12):144–150.

Guo, L. and Masulis, R. W. (2015). Board structure and monitoring: New evidence from CEO turnovers. *Review of Financial Studies*, 28(10):2770–2811.

Guo, R.-J., Kruse, T. A., and Nohel, T. (2008). Undoing the powerful anti-takeover force of staggered boards. *Journal of Corporate Finance*, 14(3):274–288.

Guo, S., Hotchkiss, E. S., and Song, W. (2011). Do buyouts (still) create value? *Journal of Finance*, 66(2):479–517.

Haar, D. (1998). SPX's Blystone puts his mettle to acquisition pedal. *Hartford Courant*, March 24:D1.

Hall, J. and Watts, R. (2004). Glazer secures financing for Man Utd offer. *Sunday Telegraph*, October 10:1.

Hancock, P., Mendoza, R. G., and Merton, R. C. (2005). A proposal for expensing employee compensatory stock options for financial reporting purposes. *Journal of Applied Corporate Finance*, 17(3):95–101.

Hansell, S. (2001). Disney, in retreat from internet, to abandon Go.com portal site. *New York Times*, January 30:C1.

Hansell, S. (2006). These days, No. 1 portal seems to be a step behind. *New York Times*, October 11:C1.

Harford, J. (2003). Takeover bids and target directors' incentives: The impact of a bid on directors' wealth and board seats. *Journal of Financial Economics*, 69(1):51–83.

Harford, J. and Li, K. (2007). Decoupling CEO wealth and firm performance: The case of acquiring CEOs. *Journal of Finance*, 62(2):917–949.

Harmetz, A. (1988). Film: Raising the odds. *New York Times*, September 11:A74.

Harmon, A. (1995). The oracle of Yahoo has internet surfers going gaga. *Los Angeles Times*, April 10:1.

Harris, C. (2005). Mudlark: Man Utd fans who came to dinner. *Financial Times*, May 14:24.

Harris, K. (1982). Hammer plans film exports to China, USSR. *Los Angeles Times*, September 15:E1.

Harris, K. (1994). Studio chief Katzenberg to leave Disney. *Los Angeles Times*, August 25:A1.

Harris Corp. (2013). Vyomesh Joshi (VJ) elected to Harris Corporation board of directors. August 27. Press release.

Hartzell, J. C., Ofek, E., and Yermack, D. (2004). What's in it for me? CEOs whose firms are acquired. *Review of Financial Studies*, 17(1):37–61.

Hartzell, J. C. and Starks, L. T. (2003). Institutional investors and executive compensation. *Journal of Finance*, 58(6):2351–2374.

Hayes, R. M., Oyer, P., and Schaefer, S. (2006). Coworker complementarity of the stability of top-management teams. *Journal of Law, Economics and Organization*, 22(1):184–212.

Hayes, T. C. (1984). Steinberg sells stake to Disney. *New York Times*, June 12:D1.

HCA–The Healthcare Co. (2001a). Form 10-K for the period ended December 31, 2000. Filed on March 30.

HCA–The Healthcare Co. (2001b). Jack O. Bovender, Jr. named HCA president & chief executive officer; HCA co-founder Dr. Thomas F. Frist, Jr. remains as chairman. January 8. Press release.

HCA Holdings, Inc. (2011). Form 424B4. Filed on March 11.

HCA Holdings, Inc. (2012). Form DEF 14A. Filed on March 16.

HCA Inc. (2005). Form 8-K. Filed on July 13.

HCA Inc. (2006a). Form DEF 14A. Filed on April 13.

HCA Inc. (2006b). Form DEFM14A. Filed on October 17.

HCA Inc. (2006c). Form SC 13E3. Filed on November 17.

HCA Inc. (2007). Form 10-K for the period ended December 31, 2006. Filed on March 27.

Helft, M. (2008a). Lawsuit criticizes Yahoo retention plan. *New York Times*, June 3:10.

Helft, M. (2008b). Yahoo celebrates (for now). *New York Times*, May 5:1.

Helman, C. (2005). Oxy moron? Qaddafi cuts a deal—for himself. *Forbes*, 175(4):46a.

Hempel, J. and Kowitt, B. (2010). 10 smartest people in tech. *Fortune*, 162(2):82–94.

Henson, C. (2006). InBev beer cutbacks brew discontent. *Wall Street Journal*, September 27:B5B.

Herbst-Bayliss, S. and Flaherty, M. (2015). DuPont CEO departure buys time to appease Peltz. *Reuters News*, October 6.

Hermalin, B. E. and Weisbach, M. S. (1998). Endogenously chosen boards of directors and their monitoring of the CEO. *American Economic Review*, 88(1):96–118.

Hertz Global Holdings, Inc. (2013). Form 8-K. Filed on December 30.

Hewlett Packard Co. (2005). Form 10-K for the period ended October 31, 2005. Filed on December 21.

Hewlett Packard Co. (2008). Q1 2008 Hewlett-Packard earnings conference call. *FD (Fair Disclosure) Wire*, February 19.

Hewlett Packard Co. (2010). Form DEF 14A. Filed on January 27.

Hewlett Packard Co. (2011a). Form 10-K for the period ended October 31, 2011. Filed on December 14.

Hewlett Packard Co. (2011b). Form 8-K. Filed on August 18.

Hewlett Packard Co. (2012). Form 8-K. Filed on March 23.

Hilzenrath, D. S. (2007). There's always Mrs. Davis to look out for shareholders. *Washington Post*, December 17:D02.

Himmelberg, C. P., Hubbard, R. G., and Palia, D. (1999). Understanding the determinants of managerial ownership and the link between ownership and performance. *Journal of Financial Economics*, 53(3):353–384.

Hirschberg, L. (2005). Giving them what they want. *New York Times Magazine*, September 4:30–35, 50, 54–55.

Hirshleifer, D., Low, A., and Teoh, S. H. (2012). Are overconfident CEOs better innovators? *Journal of Finance*, 67(4):1457–1498.

Hoechle, D., Schmid, M., Walter, I., and Yermack, D. (2012). How much of the diversification discount can be explained by poor corporate governance? *Journal of Financial Economics*, 103(1):41–60.

Hoffman, L. and Benoit, D. (2014). Activist funds dust off "greenmail" playbook. *Wall Street Journal*, June 12:C1.

Holderness, C. G. (2009). The myth of diffuse ownership in the United States. *Review of Financial Studies*, 22(4):1377–1408.

Holmström, B. (1979). Moral hazard and observability. *Bell Journal of Economics*, 10(1):74–91.

Holmström, B. (1999). Managerial incentive problems: A dynamic perspective. *Review of Economic Studies*, 66(1):169–182.

Holmström, B. and Ricart i Costa, J. (1986). Managerial incentives and capital management. *Quarterly Journal of Economics*, 101(4):835–860.

Home Depot Inc. (2001a). Form 10-K for the period ended January 28, 2001. Filed on April 23.

Home Depot Inc. (2001b). Form DEF 14A. Filed on April 23.

Home Depot Inc. (2001c). The Home Depot appoints Donovan executive vice president–human resources. March 26. Press release.

Home Depot Inc. (2002). The Home Depot names Francis S. Blake as executive vice president–strategy, business development & corporate operations. March 18. Press release.

Home Depot Inc. (2003). Form DEF 14A. Filed on April 18.

Home Depot Inc. (2004). Form DEF 14A. Filed on April 12.

Home Depot Inc. (2005). Form DEF 14A. Filed on April 11.

Home Depot Inc. (2006a). Form 10-Q for the period ended April 30, 2006. Filed on June 1.

Home Depot Inc. (2006b). Form 8-K. Filed on October 12.

Home Depot Inc. (2006c). Form 8-K. Filed on December 1.

Home Depot Inc. (2006d). Form DEF 14A. Filed on April 14.

Home Depot Inc. (2006e). Form DEFA14A. Filed on December 18.

Home Depot Inc. (2007a). Form 10-K for the period ended January 29, 2007. Filed on March 29.

Home Depot Inc. (2007b). Form 8-K. Filed on January 4.

Home Depot Inc. (2007c). Form 8-K. Filed on January 24.

Home Depot Inc. (2007d). Form 8-K. Filed on February 6.

Home Depot Inc. (2007e). Form 8-K. Filed on February 1.

Home Depot Inc. (2007f). Form 8-K. Filed on March 19.

Home Depot Inc. (2007g). Form 8-K. Filed on November 15.

Home Depot Inc. (2007h). Form 8-K. Filed on December 17.

Home Depot Inc. (2007i). Form 8-K. Filed on August 28.

Home Depot Inc. (2007j). Form DEF 14A. Filed on April 13.

Home Depot Inc. (2007k). Form SC TO-I. Filed on September 4.

Home Depot Inc. (2007l). Home Depot Inc. shareholders meeting–Final. *FD (Fair Disclosure) Wire*, May 24.

Home Depot Inc. (2007m). The Home Depot announces strategic evaluation of HD Supply. February 12. Press release.

Home Depot Inc. (2008). Form 8-K. Filed on March 3.

Hong, H. and Kubik, J. D. (2003). Analyzing the analysts: Career concerns and biased earnings forecasts. *Journal of Finance*, 58(1):313–351.

Hong, H., Kubik, J. D., and Solomon, A. (2000). Security analysts' career concerns and herding of earnings forecasts. *RAND Journal of Economics*, 31(1):121–144.

Horne, C. F. (1917). *The Sacred Books and Early Literature of the East*, volume VI: Medieval Arabic, Moorish, and Turkish. Parke, Austin, and Lipscomb, New York.

Hospital Corporation of America (1992). Bovender named HCA chief operating officer; elected to board of directors. November 16. Press release.

Hu, H. T. C. and Black, B. (2006). The new vote buying: Empty voting and hidden (morphable) ownership. *Southern California Law Review*, 79(4):811–908.

Hu, H. T. C. and Black, B. (2008). Equity and debt decoupling and empty voting II: Importance and extensions. *University of Pennsylvania Law Review*, 156(3):625–739.

Hugo Real Property, LP (2011). Premier Lake of Ozarks retreat: History. http://privatelakeretreat.com/history.html.

Hume, N. (2008). InBev targets takeover of Anheuser-Busch. *FT Alphaville*, May 23.

Huson, M. B., Parrino, R., and Starks, L. T. (2001). Internal monitoring mechanisms and CEO turnover: A long-term perspective. *Journal of Finance*, 56(6):2265–2297.

Hwang, B.-H. and Kim, S. (2009). It pays to have friends. *Journal of Financial Economics*, 93(1):138–158.

Hymowitz, C. and Daurat, C. (2013). Best-paid women in S&P 500 settle for less remuneration. *Bloomberg*, August 13.

Icahn, C. C. (2008). Form SC 13D. Filed on October 20.

Icahn, C. C. (2009). Form 13F-HR for the period ended December 31, 2008. Filed on February 13.

Icahn, C. C. (2010a). Form PREC14A. Filed on November 26.

Icahn, C. C. (2010b). Form SC 13D. Filed on February 16.

Icahn, C. C. (2010c). Form SC TO-C. Filed on February 16.

Icahn, C. C. (2010d). Form SC TO-T. Filed on July 1.

Icahn, C. C. (2010e). Form SC TO-T. Filed on July 20.

Icahn, C. C. (2010f). Form SC TO-T. Filed on March 1.

Icahn Management LP (2006). Form 13F-HR for the period ended March 31, 2006. Filed on May 15.

Iliev, P. and Lowry, M. (2015). Are mutual funds active voters? *Review of Financial Studies*, 28(2):446–485.

InBev S.A. (2008a). Annual report for the period ended December 31, 2007.

InBev S.A. (2008b). Form PREC14A. Filed on July 7.

InBev S.A. (2008c). Form SUPPL. Filed on June 16.

Informatica Corp. (2003). Informatica names Carl J. Yankowski to board of directors; former CEO of Palm brings extensive brand-building expertise to Informatica. July 17. Press release.

Iovine, J. V. (1999). A Dean's remodeling job: Himself. *New York Times*, July 1:F1.

Irani, R. M. and Oesch, D. (2013). Monitoring and corporate disclosure: Evidence from a natural experiment. *Journal of Financial Economics*, 109(2):398–418.

Irvine, P. J. (2004). Analysts' forecasts and brokerage-firm trading. *Accounting Review*, 79(1):125–149.

Ishii, J. and Xuan, Y. (2014). Acquirer-target social ties and merger outcomes. *Journal of Financial Economics*, 112(3):344–363.

J. C. Penney Company, Inc. (2008). Form 8-K. Filed on April 2.

Jackson, A. R. (2005). Trade generation, reputation, and sell-side analysts. *Journal of Finance*, 60(2):673–717.

Jacobs, J. (1985). Connoisseurs await "bash of the year". *Los Angeles Times*, November 1:F4.

Jagolinzer, A. D. (2009). SEC Rule 10b5-1 and insiders' strategic trade. *Management Science*, 55(2):224–239.

Jakab, S. (2015). Ahead of the tape. *Wall Street Journal*, July 16:C1.

James, M. and Hofmeister, S. (2004). This family was really messed up. *Los Angeles Times*, June 15:A1.

Jenkins, Jr., H. W. (2008). Jerry Yang's scorched earth. *Wall Street Journal*, May 7:A17.

Jensen, M. C. (1986). Agency costs of free cash flow, corporate finance, and takeovers. *American Economic Review, Papers and Proceedings*, 76(2):323–329.

Jensen, M. C. and Meckling, W. H. (1976). Theory of the firm: Managerial behavior, agency costs and ownership structure. *Journal of Financial Economics*, 3(4):305–360.

Jensen, M. C. and Ruback, R. S. (1983). The market for corporate control: The scientific evidence. *Journal of Financial Economics*, 11(1–4):5–50.

Jerome, R. (1996). Evelyn Y. Davis. *People*, 45(20):69–72.

Jiang, X., Harris Stanford, M., and Xie, Y. (2012). Does it matter who pays for bond ratings? Historical evidence. *Journal of Financial Economics*, 105(3):607–621.

Johnson, S. (2003). US sports investor buys Man Utd stake. *Financial Times*, March 3:26.

Jones, D. and Kennedy, S. (2004). Advisers desert Glazer over Man Utd vote. *Reuters News*, November 13.

Kadyrzhanova, D. and Rhodes-Kropf, M. (2011). Concentrating on governance. *Journal of Finance*, 66(5):1649–1685.

Kale, J. R., Reis, E., and Venkateswaran, A. (2009). Rank-order tournaments and incentive alignment: The effect on firm performance. *Journal of Finance*, 64(3):1479–1512.

Kaplan, S. N., Klebanov, M. M., and Sorensen, M. (2012). Which CEO characteristics and abilities matter? *Journal of Finance*, 67(3):973–1007.

Kaplan, S. N. and Minton, B. A. (2012). How has CEO turnover changed? *International Review of Finance*, 12(1):57–87.

Karnitschnig, M. (2008a). Corporate news: Microsoft, Yahoo hold meetings. *Wall Street Journal*, April 4:B3.

Karnitschnig, M. (2008b). Microsoft pitches merger vision to Yahoo at meeting. *Wall Street Journal*, March 14:A3.

Karnitschnig, M. and Guth, R. A. (2008). Microsoft seeks partners for a new run at Yahoo. *Wall Street Journal*, July 2:A1.

Karpoff, J. M., Malatesta, P. H., and Walkling, R. A. (1996). Corporate governance and shareholder initiatives: Empirical evidence. *Journal of Financial Economics*, 42(3):365–395.

Karpoff, J. M. and Wittry, M. D. (2015). Institutional and political economy considerations in natural experiments: The case of state antitakeover laws. Working paper, University of Washington.

Kaufman & Broad Home Corp. (1996). Form 10-K for the period ended November 30, 1995. Filed on February 23.

Kaufman & Broad Home Corp. (1999). Form DEF 14A. Filed on March 1.

Kay, O. and Power, H. (2010). Bittersweet affair as Red Devil returns to a sea of green and gold. *Times*, March 10:2.

KB Home (2001). Form 10-Q for the period ended August 31, 2001. Filed on October 12.

KB Home (2004). KB Home wins American Business Award for Best Overall Company. May 12. Press release.

KB Home (2005a). Form DEF 14A. Filed on February 24.

KB Home (2005b). KB Home chairman and CEO Bruce Karatz mentors on CNN's *The TurnAround*. April 29. Press release.

KB Home (2005c). KB Home's Bruce Karatz named Best Chairman by American Business Awards. June 7. Press release.

KB Home (2006a). Form 10-K for the period ended November 30, 2005. Filed on February 10.

KB Home (2006b). Form 8-K. Filed on August 25.

KB Home (2006c). Form 8-K. Filed on November 13.

KB Home (2006d). Form DEF 14A. Filed on March 6.

KB Home (2007). Form DEF 14A. Filed on March 5.

KB Home (2008a). Form 10-K for the period ended November 30, 2007. Filed on January 29.

KB Home (2008b). Form 8-K. Filed on December 24.

KB Home (2008c). Form DEF 14A. Filed on March 5.

KB Home (2009). Form DEF 14A. Filed on March 9.

Keefe, R. (1996). Shareholder wins ruling on Glazer merger plans. *St. Petersburg Times*, September 25:1E.

Keefe, R. and Ballingrud, D. (1995). The making of Malcolm Glazer. *St. Petersburg Times*, January 22:1A.

Kelly, B. and Ljungqvist, A. (2012). Testing asymmetric-information asset pricing models. *Review of Financial Studies*, 25(5):1366–1413.

Kempner, M. (2005). Home Depot skimps on philanthropy: Other companies more generous. *Atlanta Journal–Constitution*, October 16:A1.

Kesmodel, D. (2008). Beer clan: Anheuser CEO fights for his legacy. *Wall Street Journal*, May 27:A1.

Kesmodel, D. (2011). Busch to step down from Anheuser board. *Wall Street Journal (Online)*, March 28.

Kesmodel, D. and Vranica, S. (2009). Unease brewing at Anheuser as new owners slash costs. *Wall Street Journal*, April 29:A1.

Khermouch, G. and Forster, J. (2002). Is this Bud for you, August IV? *Businessweek*, 3807:72–78.

Kim, E. H. and Lu, Y. (2011). CEO ownership, external governance, and risk-taking. *Journal of Financial Economics*, 102(2):272–292.

Kim, S. and Oran, O. (2013). Companies, investors eye amicable divorce in share buybacks. *Reuters News*, December 13.

Kim, Y. (1996). Long-term firm performance and chief executive turnover: An empirical study of the dynamics. *Journal of Law, Economics, and Organization*, 12(2):480–496.

Kini, O., Kracaw, W., and Mian, S. (2004). The nature of discipline by corporate takeovers. *Journal of Finance*, 59(4):1511–1552.

Kirsner, S. (2009). Ex-Palm CEO Carl Yankowski out at Ambient Devices. *Boston.com*, October 19.

Klein, A. and Zur, E. (2009). Entrepreneurial shareholder activism: Hedge funds and other private investors. *Journal of Finance*, 64(1):187–228.

Knowlton, C. and Klein Berlin, R. (1989). Ready for your annual meeting? *Fortune*, 119(9):137–140.

Kole, S. and Lehn, K. (1997). Deregulation, the evolution of corporate governance structure, and survival. *American Economic Review*, 87(2):421–425.

Kratz, E. F. (2006). A beer scion passes the marriage test. *Fortune*, 154(6):36.

Krauss, C. (2013). Occidental Petroleum chief to stay until end of 2014. *New York Times*, April 30:B4.

Krebs, R. and Orthwein, P. J. (1953). *Making Friends Is Our Business: 100 Years of Anheuser-Busch*. Cuneo Press, Inc.

Kristof, K. M. and Haddad, A. (2006). How KB Home CEO's pay went through the roof. *Los Angeles Times*, December 17:C1.

Kumar, V. (2008). "Dolan discount" affliction. *Wall Street Journal*, May 2:C1.

Kumar, V. and Worden, N. (2009). Dolans explore splitting Cablevision. *Wall Street Journal*, May 8:B1.

Labaton, S. (1992). Companies told to let holders vote on pay. *New York Times*, February 14:D5.

Laide, J. (2009). Research spotlight: Shareholder input on poison pills. *FactSet SharkRepellent*, June 15.

Laing, J. R. (2004). Numbers game. *Barron's*, 84(37):20–24.

Laing, J. R. (2007). Insiders, look out! *Barron's*, 87(8):27–30.

Landro, L. (1984). Very successful Paramount facing major restructuring. *Wall Street Journal*, September 12:35.

Lang, A. (2001). Interview with Joel Stern, partner, Stern, Stewart & Co. *CNNfn Business Unusual*, May 15.

Lang, L. H. P. and Stulz, R. M. (1994). Tobin's *q*, corporate diversification, and firm performance. *Journal of Political Economy*, 102(6):1248–1280.

Langley, M. (1987). Bill to increase taxes by $23 billion hits companies, the wealthy hardest. *Wall Street Journal*, December 21:1.

Larcker, D. F., McCall, A. L., and Ormazabal, G. (2015). Outsourcing shareholder voting to proxy advisory firms. *Journal of Law and Economics*, 58(1):173–204.

Lauria, P. and Kouwe, Z. (2008). SOS @Yahoo! Desperate Yang tries to stave off Microsoft. *New York Post*, February 9:25.

Laux, V. (2012). Stock option vesting conditions, CEO turnover, and myopic investment. *Journal of Financial Economics*, 106(3):513–526.

Lawton, C. (2007). Hard drive: How H-P reclaimed its PC lead over Dell. *Wall Street Journal*, June 4:A1.

Lazear, E. P. and Rosen, S. (1981). Rank-order tournaments as optimum labor contracts. *Journal of Political Economy*, 89(5):841–864.

Leapfrog Enterprises Inc. (2005). LeapFrog Enterprises appoints David Nagel to its board of directors. September 7. Press release.

Lee, P. (1989). Arthur Andersen names head of western operation. *Los Angeles Times*, November 3:3.

Lee, P. (1990). The heir, apparently. *Los Angeles Times*, March 18:1.

Leonard, D. (2012). The plot to destroy America's beer. *Bloomberg Businessweek*, 4302:64–71.

Lerner, S. (2003). Merrill puts out "sell" on SPX Corp. *CBS.MarketWatch.com*, July 1.

Lev, M. (1991). Occidental reports loss of $2 billion. *New York Times*, January 31:4.

Levenson, E. (2006). My idea of fun. *Fortune*, 154(5):111.

Levy, S. (1998). Surfers, step right up! *Newsweek*, 131(21):74.

Li, K. (2005). Cablevision future hinges on deadline for Voom. *Reuters News*, March 4.

Li, X. (2013). Productivity, restructuring, and the gains from takeovers. *Journal of Financial Economics*, 109(1):250–271.

Li, X., Low, A., and Makhija, A. K. (2014). Career concerns and the busy life of the young CEO. Working paper, Ohio State University.

LifePoint Hospitals Inc. (2001). Form 10-K for the period ended December 31, 2000. Filed on March 13.

Linck, J. S., Netter, J. M., and Yang, T. (2008). The determinants of board structure. *Journal of Financial Economics*, 87(2):308–328.

Linck, J. S., Netter, J. M., and Yang, T. (2009). The effects and unintended consequences of the Sarbanes-Oxley Act on the supply and demand for directors. *Review of Financial Studies*, 22(8):3287–3328.

LinkedIn Corp. (2011). Form 424B4. Filed on May 19.

Lions Gate Entertainment Corp. (2003). Form 8-K. Filed on October 27.

Lions Gate Entertainment Corp. (2004). Form DEF 14A. Filed on July 29.

Lions Gate Entertainment Corp. (2005). Form 424B3. Filed on June 23.

Lions Gate Entertainment Corp. (2006). Form 8-K. Filed on January 25.

Lions Gate Entertainment Corp. (2008a). Form 10-Q for the period ended June 30, 2008. Filed on August 8.

Lions Gate Entertainment Corp. (2008b). Form DEF 14A. Filed on July 24.

Lions Gate Entertainment Corp. (2009a). Form 8-K. Filed on January 9.

Lions Gate Entertainment Corp. (2009b). Form 8-K. Filed on July 10.

Lions Gate Entertainment Corp. (2009c). Form 8-K. Filed on October 27.

Lions Gate Entertainment Corp. (2009d). Letter to the British Columbia Securities Commission re: Lions Gate Entertainment Corp. (the "filer")–application for a decision under the securities legislation of British Columbia, Alberta, Ontario, Quebec and Manitoba (the "jurisdictions") that the filer is not a reporting issuer. April 24.

Lions Gate Entertainment Corp. (2009e). Q3 2009 Lions Gate Entertainment earnings conference call. *Voxant FD Wire*, February 10.

Lions Gate Entertainment Corp. (2009f). Q4 2009 Lions Gate Entertainment earnings conference call. *CQ FD Disclosure*, June 2.

Lions Gate Entertainment Corp. (2010a). Form 10-K for the period ended March 31, 2010. Filed on June 1.

Lions Gate Entertainment Corp. (2010b). Form 10-Q for the period ended June 30, 2010. Filed on August 9.

Lions Gate Entertainment Corp. (2010c). Form 8-K. Filed on June 25.

Lions Gate Entertainment Corp. (2010d). Form 8-K. Filed on March 12.

Lions Gate Entertainment Corp. (2010e). Form 8-K. Filed on May 14.

Lions Gate Entertainment Corp. (2010f). Form 8-K. Filed on July 2.

Lions Gate Entertainment Corp. (2010g). Form 8-K. Filed on July 9.

Lions Gate Entertainment Corp. (2010h). Form 8-K. Filed on July 21.

Lions Gate Entertainment Corp. (2010i). Form 8-K. Filed on December 17.

Lions Gate Entertainment Corp. (2010j). Form DEF 14A. Filed on November 19.

Lions Gate Entertainment Corp. (2010k). Form SC 14D9. Filed on May 17.

Lions Gate Entertainment Corp. (2010l). Form SC 14D9. Filed on March 12.

Lions Gate Entertainment Corp. (2011a). Form 10-Q for the period ended December 31, 2010. Filed on February 9.

Lions Gate Entertainment Corp. (2011b). Form 8-K. Filed on August 30.

Lipin, S. (1998). SPX is buying General Signal for $2 billion. *Wall Street Journal*, July 20:A3.

Ljungqvist, A., Marston, F., Starks, L. T., Wei, K. D., and Yan, H. (2007). Conflicts of interest in sell-side research and the moderating role of institutional investors. *Journal of Financial Economics*, 85(2):420–456.

Lloyd, M. E. (2004a). SPX Corp. takes steps to boost credibility on Street. *Dow Jones News Service*, March 5.

Lloyd, M. E. (2004b). Tales of the tape: SPX Corp's stumbles attract activists. *Dow Jones News Service*, August 31.

Loh, R. K. and Stulz, R. M. (2011). When are analyst recommendation changes influential? *Review of Financial Studies*, 24(2):593–627.

Lohr, S. (2000). Microsoft will challenge Palm's hand-held computer dominance. *New York Times*, April 18:C1.

Loper, M. L. (1986). "Impressionist": An impressive gala preview. *Los Angeles Times*, June 27:H1.

Los Angeles Times (2005). Ecuador oil chief steps down. *Los Angeles Times*, August 5:C2.

Lublin, J. S. (1992). Executives grumble about SEC plan to require more pay data. *Wall Street Journal*, September 21:B1.

Lublin, J. S. (2002). Tyco CEO search will raise bar. *Wall Street Journal*, June 11:B8.

Lublin, J. S. (2015). Parsing the pay and performance of top CEOs. *Wall Street Journal*, June 25:B1.

Lublin, J. S., Lucchetti, A., and Fowler, T. (2013). Proxy adviser advises against re-election of Occidental chairman. *Wall Street Journal (Online)*, April 11.

Lublin, J. S., Murray, M., and Brooks, R. (2000). Home Depot nabs GE's Nardelli as CEO. *Wall Street Journal*, December 6:A3.

Lublin, J. S. and Rexrode, C. (2015a). ISS opposes Bank of America proposal allowing board to combine chairman, CEO. *Wall Street Journal (Online)*, September 5.

Lublin, J. S. and Rexrode, C. (2015b). Proxy advisor Glass Lewis opposes Bank of America board proposal. *Wall Street Journal (Online)*, September 3.

Lublin, J. S., Zimmerman, A., and Terhune, C. (2007). Moving out: Behind Nardelli's abrupt exit. *Wall Street Journal*, January 4:A1.

Lucchetti, A., Lublin, J. S., and Fowler, T. (2013). Occidental faces a new fight at the top. *Wall Street Journal*, March 30:B1.

Ludington, C. (1991). Bud man: Prince of beers August Busch IV pours a little dash into the family business. *Chicago Tribune*, June 14:1.

Lueck, T. L. (1983). Saudi investor buys stake in Occidental. *New York Times*, July 22:D2.

Lyall, S. (2005). English are hostile after a U.S. soccer takeover. *New York Times*, May 19:A1.

M&A Journal (2006). The Bebchuk bylaw: Devilish . . . but brilliant. *M&A Journal*, 6(10):1–14.

MacIntosh, J. (2011). *Dethroning the King: The Hostile Takeover of Anheuser-Busch, an American Icon*. John Wiley & Sons, Inc., Hoboken, New Jersey.

Madison Square Garden Co. (2011a). Form 10-Q for the period ended March 31, 2011. Filed on May 6.

Madison Square Garden Co. (2011b). Form DEF 14A. Filed on October 13.

Madison Square Garden Co. (2014). Form 10-Q for the period ended December 31, 2013. Filed on February 7.

Madison Square Garden Inc. (2010). Form 10-Q for the period ended March 31, 2010. Filed on May 7.

Majesco Entertainment Co. (2005a). Form 10-Q for the period ended July 31, 2005. Filed on September 14.

Majesco Entertainment Co. (2005b). Form 8-K. Filed on July 12.

Majesco Entertainment Co. (2005c). Majesco Entertainment launches intergalactic adventure of a lifetime as "Advent Rising" ships today for Xbox(R). May 31. Press release.

Majesco Entertainment Co. (2005d). Majesco Entertainment reduces fiscal 2005 financial outlook. July 12. Press release.

Majesco Entertainment Co. (2005e). Majesco reports record second quarter 2005 financial results. June 7. Press release.

Majesco Entertainment Co. (2006). Form 10-K for the period ended October 31, 2005. Filed on February 1.

Majesco Holdings Inc. (2004a). Form 8-K. Filed on August 27.

Majesco Holdings Inc. (2004b). Form 8-K. Filed on October 7.

Majesco Holdings Inc. (2005a). Form 424B1. Filed on January 26.

Majesco Holdings Inc. (2005b). Form 8-K. Filed on March 2.

Maksimovic, V., Phillips, G., and Prabhala, N. (2011). Post-merger restructuring and the boundaries of the firm. *Journal of Financial Economics*, 102(2):317–343.

Malmendier, U. and Tate, G. (2009). Superstar CEOs. *Quarterly Journal of Economics*, 124(4):1593–1638.

Manchester United PLC (2000). Manchester United PLC: Final results. October 2. Regulatory News Service.

Manchester United PLC (2002). Directorate. November 30. Regulatory News Service 4910E.

Maney, K. (1995). A big Yahoo! On-line guide surges on internet. *USA Today*, October 13:02B.

Manne, H. G. (1965). Mergers and the market for corporate control. *Journal of Political Economy*, 73(2):110–120.

Manry, D. and Nathan, K. (1999). Greenmail premia, board composition and management shareholdings. *Journal of Corporate Finance*, 5(4):369–382.

Mansell, I. and O'Connor, A. (2005). Revealed: Glazer's plan for Manchester United. *Times*, June 10:1.

Marlow, B. and Goodman, M. (2010). Devils in the red: How Manchester United became a piggy bank for its American owners. *Sunday Times*, January 17:1.

Marriott International Inc. (2005). Form DEF 14A. Filed on March 31.

Mathis, J., McAndrews, J., and Rochet, J.-C. (2009). Rating the raters: Are reputation concerns powerful enough to discipline rating agencies? *Journal of Monetary Economics*, 56(5):657–674.

Maug, E. (1998). Large shareholders as monitors: Is there a trade-off between liquidity and control? *Journal of Finance*, 53(1):65–98.

May Department Stores Co. (2005). Form DEF 14A. Filed on May 27.

McCahery, J. A., Sautner, Z., and Starks, L. T. (2016). Behind the scenes: The corporate governance preferences of institutional investors. *Journal of Finance*, 71(6):2905–2932.

McCartney, R. J. (1992a). Business seems to get boost on pay issue. *Washington Post*, June 5:B9.

McCartney, R. J. (1992b). Executives quietly defend top-dollar pay packages. *Washington Post*, February 21:A1.

McCracken, J. and Spector, M. (2010). Low bids for MGM cloud fate of studio. *Wall Street Journal*, January 12:B1.

McCue, M. J. and Thompson, J. M. (2012). The impact of HCA's 2006 leveraged buyout on hospital performance. *Journal of Healthcare Management*, 57(5):342–357.

McWilliams, J. (2007). Despite expansion in China and experimental drinks, Anheuser-Busch assures analysts that it is committed to the core. *St. Louis Post-Dispatch*, May 23:C1.

McWilliams, J. (2008a). A-B prepared to reject InBev bid, report says plan to boost stock price. *St. Louis Post-Dispatch*, June 26:A1.

McWilliams, J. (2008b). Brito begins to brew new company. *St. Louis Post-Dispatch*, July 16:A1.

McWilliams, J. (2008c). InBev plans big changes at the top. *St. Louis Post-Dispatch*, November 7:B1.

McWilliams, J. (2008d). Point man for A-B is brewer of consensus. *St. Louis Post-Dispatch*, October 27:A1.

McWilliams, J. (2009a). A-B reins in benefits. *St. Louis Post-Dispatch*, April 9:A11.

McWilliams, J. (2009b). Drastic changes, no apologies. *St. Louis Post-Dispatch*, November 15:A1.

MDC Holdings Inc. (1994). Form DEF 14A. Filed on May 25.

MDC Holdings Inc. (2006). Form DEF 14A. Filed on February 28.

MDC Holdings Inc. (2008). Form DEF 14A. Filed on March 13.

MDC Holdings Inc. (2009). Form DEF 14A. Filed on March 2.

MDC Holdings Inc. (2011). Form DEF 14A. Filed on March 1.

Meller, P. (2005). Belgian brewer acquires a taste for Brazilian frugality. *New York Times*, September 27:C7.

MGM Mirage (2005). Form 8-K. Filed on April 28.

MGM Mirage (2006). Form 8-K. Filed on February 10.

MHR Fund Management LLC (2006). Form 13F-HR for the period ended March 31, 2006. Filed on May 15.

MHR Fund Management LLC (2011). Form SC 13D. Filed on September 15.

Mikkelson, W. H. and Partch, M. M. (1997). The decline of takeovers and disciplinary managerial turnover. *Journal of Financial Economics*, 44(2):205–228.

Mikkelson, W. H. and Ruback, R. S. (1991). Targeted repurchases and common stock returns. *RAND Journal of Economics*, 22(4):544–561.

Milgrom, P. and Roberts, J. (1992). *Economics, Organization and Management*. Prentice Hall, Englewood Cliffs, New Jersey.

Miller, D., Breton-Miller, I. L., Lester, R. H., and Cannella Jr., A. A. (2007). Are family firms really superior performers? *Journal of Corporate Finance*, 13(5):829–858.

Miller, M. H. and Modigliani, F. (1961). Dividend policy, growth, and the valuation of shares. *Journal of Business*, 34(4):411–433.

Minow, N. (1998). What's wrong with these pictures? The story of the Hammer Museum litigation. In Bellow, G. and Minow, M., editors, *Law Stories*, chapter 5, pages 101–129. University of Michigan Press, Ann Arbor, Michigan.

Mitra, S. (2007). Eric Benhamou: The saga of Palm (part 6). http://www.sramanamitra.com/2007/09/17/eric-benhamou-the-saga-of-palm-part-6/.

Mobbs, S. and Raheja, C. G. (2012). Internal managerial promotions: Insider incentives and CEO succession. *Journal of Corporate Finance*, 18(5):1337–1353.

Modigliani, F. and Miller, M. H. (1958). The cost of capital, corporation finance and the theory of investment. *American Economic Review*, 48(3):261–297.

Moffett, M. (2008). At InBev, a gung-ho culture rules. *Wall Street Journal*, May 28:B1.

Moin, D. (2005). Pumping up to $30b: Federated's new era begins as May fades. *Women's Wear Daily*, July 14:1.

Moore, H. N. (2008). Jerry Yang's failure to communicate. *Wall Street Journal's Deal Journal blog*, May 7.

Morgan, A., Poulsen, A., Wolf, J., and Yang, T. (2011). Mutual funds as monitors: Evidence from mutual fund voting. *Journal of Corporate Finance*, 17(4):914–928.

Morgan Stanley (2005a). Form DEF 14A. Filed on February 15.

Morgan Stanley (2005b). Morgan Stanley annual meeting of shareholders–Final. *FD (Fair Disclosure) Wire*, March 15.

Morgenson, G. (2015). S.E.C. reversal may clear way for shareholders to challenge companies. *New York Times*, January 20:B3.

Morrissey, J. (2011). The raider in winter. *New York Times*, April 17:BU1.

Morse, A., Nanda, V., and Seru, A. (2011). Are incentive contracts rigged by powerful CEOs? *Journal of Finance*, 66(5):1779–1821.

Moss, L. and Farrell, M. (2003). Who's running Voom. *Multichannel News*, 24(40):3, 42.

MU Finance PLC (2010). Preliminary offering memorandum. January 11.

Mullaney, T. and Miller, M. (2008). Gabelli calls on Dolan family to break up Cablevision. *Bloomberg*, 7 August.

Müller, H. and Panunzi, F. (2004). Tender offers and leverage. *Quarterly Journal of Economics*, 119(4):1217–1248.

Murphy, K. J. (2013). Executive compensation: Where we are, and how we got there. In Constantinides, G., Harris, M., and Stulz, R., editors, *Handbook of the Economics of Finance: Volume 2A Corporate Finance*, chapter 4, pages 211–356. Elsevier Science North Holland, Amsterdam.

Murphy, K. J. and Sandino, T. (2010). Executive pay and "independent" compensation consultants. *Journal of Accounting and Economics*, 49(3):247–262.

Myerson, A. R. (1995). George Bush's old company is quitting oil patch. *New York Times*, April 7:D1.

Myerson, A. R. (1997). A gentler hand at Columbia's helm. *New York Times*, July 26:34.

Nakashima, R. (2009). Lions Gate sells 49 percent stake in TV Guide for $123m to One Equity Partners, Allen Shapiro. *Associated Press Newswires*, May 29.

Narayanan, M. P. (1985). Managerial incentives for short-term results. *Journal of Finance*, 40(5):1469–1484.

Nash, J. F. (1950). The bargaining problem. *Econometrica*, 18(2):155–162.

New York Times (1913). Adolphus Busch dies in Prussia. *New York Times*, October 11:15.

New York Times (1977). Gag order in G.M. nepotism suit. *New York Times*, September 14:82.

Nocera, J. (2006). The board wore chicken suits. *New York Times*, May 27:C1.

Novell Inc. (2001). Novell names Carl Yankowski to Novell board of directors. June 26. Press release.

Novell Inc. (2003). Form DEF 14A. Filed on March 17.

Oates, M. (1987). The presence of power leaves fame standing at benefit door. *Los Angeles Times*, November 23:F1.

Oates, M. (1988). Broadway at the Bowl: Bet on a sequel. *Los Angeles Times*, August 31:1.

Occidental Petroleum Corp. (1995). Form DEF 14A. Filed on March 14.

Occidental Petroleum Corp. (1999). Form DEF 14A. Filed on March 16.

Occidental Petroleum Corp. (2002). R. Chad Dreier elected to Occidental board of directors. December 10. Press release.

Occidental Petroleum Corp. (2003). Form DEF 14A. Filed on March 12.

Occidental Petroleum Corp. (2004). Form DEF 14A. Filed on March 15.

Occidental Petroleum Corp. (2005). Form DEF 14A. Filed on March 15.

Occidental Petroleum Corp. (2010a). Form 10-K for the period ended December 31, 2009. Filed on February 25.

Occidental Petroleum Corp. (2010b). Form 8-K. Filed on October 14.

Occidental Petroleum Corp. (2010c). Form 8-K. Filed on December 13.

Occidental Petroleum Corp. (2010d). Form DEF 14A. Filed on March 23.

Occidental Petroleum Corp. (2012). Form DEF 14A. Filed on March 20.

Occidental Petroleum Corp. (2013a). Form 8-K. Filed on April 8.

Occidental Petroleum Corp. (2013b). Form 8-K. Filed on April 29.

Occidental Petroleum Corp. (2013c). Form 8-K. Filed on May 3.

Occidental Petroleum Corp. (2013d). Form 8-K. Filed on October 18.

Occidental Petroleum Corp. (2013e). Form DEF 14A. Filed on March 22.

Occidental Petroleum Corp. (2014). Form 8-K. Filed on February 14.

Ofek, E. and Yermack, D. (2000). Taking stock: Equity-based compensation and the evolution of managerial ownership. *Journal of Finance*, 55(3):1367–1384.

Offenberg, D. and Officer, M. S. (2014). The totality of change-in-control payments. *Journal of Corporate Finance*, 29:75–87.

Oil and Gas News (2011). Irani may re-energise Oxy Middle East strategy. *Oil and Gas News*, February 28.

Oliver, M. (1998). Arthur Groman: Lawyer for rich, famous. *Los Angeles Times*, December 3:A30.

Olson, B. (2013). Occidental's Irani out as investor revolt ends rule. *Bloomberg*, May 3.

Ontario Teachers' Pension Plan (2013). Teachers' sells 20% stake in Glass Lewis to AIMCo. August 28. Press release.

Oppel, R. A. (1999). Reebok head quits his post unexpectedly. *New York Times*, December 2:C5.

Oracle Corp. (2004). Form SC TO-T. Filed on December 13.

Oracle Corp. (2012). Form 8-K. Filed on November 7.

Oracle Corp. (2013). Form 8-K. Filed on November 1.

Oracle Corp. (2014). Form 8-K. Filed on November 7.

Oracle Corp. (2015). Form 8-K. Filed on November 20.

Ordower, H. M. (2007). Demystifying hedge funds: A design primer. *UC Davis Business Law Journal*, 7:323–372.

Orwall, B. (1997). Disney holders decry payouts at meeting. *Wall Street Journal*, February 26:A3.

Orwall, B. (2002). Disney shake-up leaves Lyne in charge of lifting ABC out of ratings doldrums. *Wall Street Journal*, January 8:B8.

Orwall, B. (2003). Roy Disney quits company board and calls on Eisner to resign. *Wall Street Journal*, December 1:A1.

Orwall, B. (2004). The mousetrap: In court case, a vivid portrayal of Eisner's boardroom tactics. *Wall Street Journal*, November 23:A1.

Orwall, B. and Lublin, J. S. (1997). The plutocracy: If a company prospers, should its directors behave by the book? *Wall Street Journal*, February 24:A1.

Orwall, B., Steinberg, B., and Lublin, J. S. (2004). Disney's Eisner steps down from chairman post after protest garners 43% of voted shares. *Wall Street Journal*, March 4:A1.

Orwall, B. and Wingfield, N. (2004). The end: Pixar breaks up with distribution partner Disney. *Wall Street Journal*, January 30:B1.

Osborne, A. (2005). Glazer saves himself £22m at United. *Daily Telegraph*, May 28:26.

Ostrow, R. J. (1976). Prosecutor to seek felony charges against Hammer. *Los Angeles Times*, January 20:B3.

Ozanian, M. K. (1998). Selective accounting. *Forbes*, 162(13):124–134.

Padley, K. (2003). SPX net for quarter falls, stock declines. *Reuters News*, October 29.

Palfrey, T. R. and Rosenthal, H. (1984). Participation and the provision of discrete public goods: A strategic analysis. *Journal of Public Economics*, 24(2):171–193.

Palm Inc. (2001a). Form 8-K. Filed on November 9.

Palm Inc. (2001b). Form 8-K. Filed on May 24.

Palm Inc. (2001c). Form DEF 14A. Filed on September 4.

Palm Inc. (2001d). Palm acquires assets and hires key talent from Be. August 16. Press release.

Palm Inc. (2001e). Palm hires chief operating officer; sees signs of improvement; share strong. June 4. Press release.

Palm Inc. (2001f). Palm names David C. Nagel president, CEO of Platform Solutions. August 27. Press release.

Palm Inc. (2002a). Form 10-K for the period ended May 31, 2002. Filed on July 30.

Palm Inc. (2002b). Form DEF 14A. Filed on August 26.

Palm Inc. (2003). Form 424B3. Filed on September 29.

Palm Inc. (2005). Form 10-K for the period ended June 3, 2005. Filed on July 29.

Palm Inc. (2010). Form 8-K. Filed on July 2.

Palmeri, C. (2003). Occidental: From excess to success. *Business Week*, April 7:65–66.

PalmOne Inc. (2003). Form 425. Filed on October 29.

PalmOne Inc. (2005). Form 8-K. Filed on January 25.

PalmSource Inc. (2005a). Form 8-K. Filed on May 24.

PalmSource Inc. (2005b). Form 8-K. Filed on September 9.

Parachini, A. (1989). Occidental, not Hammer's foundation, purchased art. *Los Angeles Times*, August 18:3.

Parachini, A. (1990a). Occidental discloses ownership of $1.4 million in artworks. *Los Angeles Times*, April 3:F4.

Parachini, A. (1990b). Oxy denies using any more funds for Hammer's art. *Los Angeles Times*, March 13:D2.

Parkes, C. (1999). Walt Disney settles legal fight with Katzenberg. *Financial Times*, July 8:7.

Parrish, M. (1991). Occidental will sell its stake in Iowa beef unit. *Los Angeles Times*, September 5:49.

Paul, F. (2001). Palm cuts PDA price—analysts cite glut. *Reuters News*, May 15.

Paulson & Co. Inc. (2008a). Form 13F-HR. Filed on August 13.

Paulson & Co. Inc. (2008b). Form 13F-HR. Filed on November 14.

Peale, C. (1998). Corporate gadfly enlivens annual meeting. *Cincinnati Post*, May 16.

Peltz, J. F. (1999). A new, truly improved Occidental Petroleum? *Los Angeles Times*, August 29:1.

Peltz, J. F. (2005). Well-oiled turnaround. *Los Angeles Times*, June 5:C1.

Peltz, M. (2011). All-America Research Team—Four decades of excellence. *Institutional Investor*, October.

PeopleSoft Inc. (2004). Form 10-Q for the period ended September 30, 2004. Filed on November 9.

Pepco Holdings Inc. (2004). Form DEF 14A. Filed on April 1.

Pepco Holdings Inc. (2005). Form DEF 14A. Filed on March 31.

Pérez-González, F. (2006). Inherited control and firm performance. *American Economic Review*, 96(5):1559–1588.

Peters, J. W. (2006). Home Depot alters rules for electing its directors. *New York Times*, June 2:C3.

Petersen, M. (2001). Bristol-Myers Squibb names marketing official as chief executive. *New York Times*, February 8:1.

Peterson, D. (2009). After marriage of A-B and InBev, Busch IV filed for divorce. *St. Louis Post-Dispatch*, January 30:D3.

Peterson, D. (2011). Busch IV talks about death of girlfriend, his depression. *St. Louis Post-Dispatch*, January 4:A1.

Peyer, U. C. and Vermaelen, T. (2005). The many facets of privately negotiated stock repurchases. *Journal of Financial Economics*, 75(2):361–395.

Piccalo, G. (1996). Annual meeting marked by face-off between Turner and gadfly Davis. *Associated Press*, June 7.

Pickett, M. (1990). Turmoil at the top: Oxy's procession of presidents. *Los Angeles Times*, March 18:6.

Power, H. (2004). Glazer frustrated as Man Utd board tries nipping bid in bud. *The Lawyer*, November 22:11.

Pratt, J. W. (1964). Risk aversion in the small and in the large. *Econometrica*, 32(1/2):122–136.

Prendergast, C. (1993). The role of promotion in inducing specific human capital acquisition. *Quarterly Journal of Economics*, 108(2):523–534.

Pulley, B. (2003). Family ties. *Forbes*, 171(11):68–72.

Pulliam, S. (2013). SEC expands probe on executive trades. *Wall Street Journal*, February 5:C3.

Pulliam, S. and Barry, R. (2012). Dark markets: Executives' good luck in trading own stock. *Wall Street Journal*, November 28:A1.

Pulliam, S., Eaglesham, J., and Barry, R. (2012). Insider-trading probe widens: U.S. launches criminal investigation into stock sales by company executives. *Wall Street Journal*, December 11:A1.

Pulte Homes Inc. (2010). Form 8-K. Filed on February 16.

Quaker Oats Co. (1998). Quaker names new chief financial officer—Terence D. Martin. November 11. Press release.

Quinn, J. (2005). Irish tycoons "will refuse to sell to Glazer at 300p". *Daily Mail*, February 8:73.

Rachesky, M. H. (2009). Form SC 13D. Filed on March 18.

Rachesky, M. H. (2010). Form SC 13D. Filed on July 21.

Radio World (2004). Dielectric names new president; Kling retires. *Radio World*, January 22.

Rau, P. R. and Xu, J. (2013). How do ex ante severance pay contracts fit into optimal executive incentive schemes? *Journal of Accounting Research*, 51(3):631–671.

Reckard, E. S. (1991). Occidental dumps Arm & Hammer stake, 7 weeks after death of Armand Hammer. *Associated Press*, January 28.

Red Football Ltd (2005a). Red Football Limited for Manchester United PLC: Offer update. June 28. Regulatory News Service 13070.

Red Football Ltd (2005b). Unconditional mandatory cash offer by Rothschild on behalf of Red Football Limited for Manchester United PLC. May 13. Regulatory News Service 2970M.

Red Herring (1995). Yahoo!'s founders talk technology, money, and trends. *Red Herring*, October 1:24.

Reddall, B. (2013a). Occidental shareholders vote out long-time chairman Irani. *Reuters*, May 3.

Reddall, B. (2013b). Oxy's Irani gets Glass Lewis nod after recent changes. *Reuters News*, May 1.

Reebok International Ltd. (1999). Form 10-K405 for the period ended December 31, 1998. Filed on March 24.

Reingold, J. (2005). Bob Nardelli is watching. *Fast Company*, 101:76–83.

Reingold, J. (2008). Home Depot's total rehab. *Fortune*, 158(6):159–166.

Reingold, J. (2014). When your legacy gets hacked. *Fortune*, 170(7):90–98.

Reingold, J. and Grover, R. (1999). Special report: Executive pay. *BusinessWeek*, April 19:72.

Relational Investors LLC (2004a). Form PREC14A. Filed on November 15.

Relational Investors LLC (2004b). Form SC 13D. Filed on November 15.

Relational Investors LLC (2006). Form 13F-HR for the period ended September 30, 2006. Filed on November 14.

Relational Investors LLC (2007). Form 13F-HR for the period ended December 31, 2006. Filed on February 14.

Relational Investors LLC (2009). Letter to the Securities and Exchange Commission re: Facilitating shareholder director nominations. August 14.

Renneboog, L. and Szilagyi, P. G. (2011). The role of shareholder proposals in corporate governance. *Journal of Corporate Finance*, 17(1):167–188.

Reuters (1996). Disney says president Michael Ovitz resigns. *Reuters News*, December 13.

Reuters (1998). Occidental appoints Canadian exec. to board. *Reuters News*, July 16.

Reuters (1999). UK blocks BSkyB/Man Utd deal. *Reuters News*, April 10.

Reuters (2003). Soccer: American football tycoon increases stake in Man Utd. *Reuters News*, October 2.

Reuters (2004a). Man Utd confirms Glazer raises stake to 27.6 pct. *Reuters News*, October 19.

Reuters (2004b). SPX shares tumble on weak 2004 outlook, downgrades. *Reuters News*, February 28.

Reuters (2005). California real estate panel says the market is still hot, downplays concerns about a bust. *Reuters News*, April 20.

Reuters News (2003). Home Depot directors re-elected, but critics heard. *Reuters News*, May 30.

Reuters News (2005). Home Depot holders OK vote on severance pacts. *Reuters News*, May 26.

Rexrode, C. (2015). BofA's Moynihan backed as chairman. *Wall Street Journal*, September 23:C1.

Rexrode, C. and Lublin, J. S. (2015). Bank of America vote brings out broader complaints. *Wall Street Journal (Online)*, September 14.

Ricadela, A. (2013). HP's Whitman reassigns Bradley in revamp amid PC-industry slump. *Bloomberg News*, June 19.

Rice, L. (2000). Declaration of independence. *Harvard Law Bulletin*, Summer:Article 2.

Rich, T. (2005). Judge us on the long haul, pleads Glazer. *Daily Telegraph*, July 2:1.

Richtel, M. (2007). Guitar Hero gets an accompanist. *New York Times*, December 5:1.

Roberts, D. (2013). Carlos Brito: (Brew)master of the universe. *Fortune*, 68(4):74–79.

Rockwell, J. (1992). Hotels as well as amusements use fantasy at Euro Disneyland. *New York Times*, April 14:C13.

Rose, F. (1989). Head of Occidental's art museum panel was confused on project, filings show. *Wall Street Journal*, August 3:B3.

Rosen, S. (1986). Prizes and incentives in elimination tournaments. *American Economic Review*, 76(4):701–715.

Ross, N. L. (1984). Panel hears debate over mergers. *Washington Post*, March 29:B1.

Ross Sorkin, A. (2006). Huge buyout of hospital group highlights era of going private. *New York Times*, July 25:A1.

Ross Sorkin, A. and de la Merced, M. J. (2008). Brewer bids $46 billion for Busch. *New York Times*, June 12:C1.

Ross Sorkin, A. and Helft, M. (2008). Yahoo's directors discuss how to face Microsoft bid. *New York Times*, February 9:2.

Roth, A. E. (1979). *Axiomatic Models of Bargaining*. Lecture Notes in Economics and Mathematical Systems 170. Springer-Verlag, Berlin Heidelberg.

Rubinstein, A. (1982). Perfect equilibrium in a bargaining model. *Econometrica*, 50(1):97–109.

Rushe, D. (2004). War is declared on Manchester United. *Sunday Times*, November 14: Business 11.

Rushe, D. (2005). Chequered past of Man Utd bidders. *Sunday Times*, February 13:Business 9.

Ruth, D. (2005). The man don't give a Buc. *Guardian*, July 12.

Ryland Group Inc. (2009). Form 8-K. Filed on February 26.

Safeguard Scientifics Inc. (1999). Safeguard Scientifics announces election of Carl J. Yankowski, president and CEO of Reebok Unlimited, to its board of directors. June 7. Press release.

Safeguard Scientifics Inc. (2002). Form DEF 14A. Filed on April 19.

Safeway Inc. (2008). Form 8-K. Filed on March 11.

Safeway Inc. (2013). Form 8-K. Filed on September 18.

Saltzman, M. (2005). Ambitious "Advent" launched before its time. *Gannett News Service*, June 16.

Salwen, K. G. (1992a). Clinton backs executive pay set by holders. *Wall Street Journal*, October 9:C1.

Salwen, K. G. (1992b). SEC to allow investors more room to talk. *Wall Street Journal*, October 15:C1.

Salwen, K. G. (1992c). SEC unveils new rules on disclosures of corporate executives' pay packages. *Wall Street Journal*, February 14:A4.

Sansweet, S. J. (1984). Disney's chief is ousted: Board studies "short list" to determine his successor. *Wall Street Journal*, September 10:3.

Saporta, M. (2005). Atlanta's quiet company: Home Depot's civic presence minimal. *Atlanta Journal–Constitution*, October 16:D1.

Saporta, M. (2007). Nardelli out at Home Depot: Nardelli barely registered on civic meter. *Atlanta Journal–Constitution*, January 4:C6.

Sasseen, J. (2010). Hiding behind their hedges. *BusinessWeek*, March 8(4169):44–50.

SBC Communications Inc. (2002). Form DEF 14A. Filed on March 11.

Scannell, K. (2006). SEC to propose overhaul of rules on executive pay. *Wall Street Journal*, January 10:A1.

Scharfstein, D. S. and Stein, J. C. (1990). Herd behavior and investment. *American Economic Review*, 80(3):465–479.

Schlender, B. (2000). How a virtuoso plays the web. *Fortune*, 141(5):F79–F83.

Schmidt, B. (2015). Costs and benefits of friendly boards during mergers and acquisitions. *Journal of Financial Economics*, 117(2):424–447.

Schroeder, R. (2006). SEC to vote on executive-pay rules Tuesday. *Dow Jones Business News*, January 17.

Schwartz, T. (1981). Cablevision's brash maverick. *New York Times*, August 3:D1.

Securities and Exchange Commission (1998a). Final rule: Amendments to rules on shareholder proposals. *Release No. 34-40018; IC-23200; File No. S7-25-97.*

Securities and Exchange Commission (1998b). Final rules: Amendments to beneficial ownership reporting requirements. *Release No. 34-39538; File No. S7-16-96.*

Securities and Exchange Commission (2000). Final rule: Selective disclosure and insider trading. *Release Nos. 33-7881, 34-43154, IC-24599, File No. S7-31-99.*

Securities and Exchange Commission (2001). Division of Corporation Finance, Staff Legal Bulletin No. 14 (CF). *Shareholder Proposals.*

Securities and Exchange Commission (2002a). Division of Corporation Finance, Staff Legal Bulletin No. 14A. *Shareholder Proposals.*

Securities and Exchange Commission (2002b). Final rule: Certification of disclosure in companies' quarterly and annual reports. *Release Nos. 33-8124, 34-46427, IC-25722; File No. S7-21-02.*

Securities and Exchange Commission (2002c). Final rule: Ownership reports and trading by officers, directors and principal security holders. *Release Nos. 34-46421; 35-27563; IC-25720; File No. S7-31-02.*

Securities and Exchange Commission (2003a). Final rule: Disclosure of proxy voting policies and proxy voting records by registered management investment companies. *Release Nos. 33-8188, 34-47304, IC-25922; File No. S7-36-02.*

Securities and Exchange Commission (2003b). Final rule: Proxy voting by investment advisers. *Release No. IA-2106; File No. S7-38-02.*

Securities and Exchange Commission (2003c). NASD and NYSE rulemaking: Relating to corporate governance. *Release No. 34-48745; File Nos. SR-NYSE-2002-33, SR-NASD-2002-77, SR-NASD-2002-80, SR-NASD-2002-138, SR-NASD-2002-139, and SR-NASD-2002-141.*

Securities and Exchange Commission (2003d). Proposed rule: Security holder director nominations. *Release Nos. 34-48626; IC-26206; File No. S7-19-03.*

Securities and Exchange Commission (2003e). Ten of nation's top investment firms settle enforcement actions involving conflicts of interest between research and investment banking. Press release 2003-54.

Securities and Exchange Commission (2004a). Investment Advisers Act of 1940, Rule 206(4)-6, Egan-Jones Proxy Services. *No-Action Letter to Kent S. Hughes.*

Securities and Exchange Commission (2004b). Investment Advisers Act of 1940, Rule 206(4)-6, Institutional Shareholder Services, Inc. *No-Action Letter to Mari Anne Pisarri.*

Securities and Exchange Commission (2006a). Final rule: Executive compensation and related person disclosure. *Release Nos. 33-8732A; 34-54302A; IC-27444A; File No. S7-03-06.*

Securities and Exchange Commission (2006b). Interim final rules: Executive compensation disclosure. *Release Nos. 33-8765; 34-55009; File No. S7-03-06.*

Securities and Exchange Commission (2007). Proposed rule: Shareholder proposals. *Release No. 34-56160; IC-27913; File No. S7-16-07.*

Securities and Exchange Commission (2009a). Final rule: Proxy disclosure enhancements. *Release Nos. 33-9089; 34-61175; IC-29092; File No. S7-13-09.*

Securities and Exchange Commission (2009b). SEC charges home builder's former human resources executive with stock options backdating. *Litigation Release No. 21039; Accounting and Auditing Enforcement Release No. 2969.*

Securities and Exchange Commission (2010). Final rule: Facilitating shareholder director nominations. *Release Nos. 33-9136; 34-62764; IC-29384; File No. S7-10-09.*

Securities and Exchange Commission (2011a). Final rule: Shareholder approval of executive compensation and golden parachute compensation. *Release Nos. 33-9178; 34-63768; File No. S7-31-10.*

Securities and Exchange Commission (2011b). SEC obtains settlement with CEO to recover compensation and stock profits he received during company's fraud. Press release 2011-61.

Securities and Exchange Commission (2012). Final rule: Listing standards for compensation committees. *Release Nos. 33-9330; 34-67220; File No. S7-13-11.*

Securities and Exchange Commission (2014a). Administrative proceeding. *Release No. 71717; File No. 3–15791.*

Securities and Exchange Commission (2014b). Division of Corporation Finance, shareholder proposal no-action letter issued under Exchange Act Rule 14a-8. *No-Action Letter to Whole Foods Market, Inc.*

Securities and Exchange Commission (2015). Division of Corporation Finance, review of shareholder proposal no-action letter issued under Exchange Act Rule 14a-8. *No-Action Letter to Whole Foods Market, Inc.*

Seemore Advisors LLC (2004). Form 13F-HR for the period ended June 30, 2004. Filed on August 16.

Seinfeld (1995). The hot tub. Series 7, Episode 5. First broadcast October 19.

Sellers, P. (1997). Bud-Weis-Heir. *Fortune*, 135(1):90–93.

Sellers, P. (2001). Exit the builder, enter the repairman. *Fortune*, 143(6):86–88.

Sellers, P. (2002). Something to prove. *Fortune*, 145(13):88–98.

Sender, H. (2002). Andersen's audit-client defections come at perfect time for its overstaffed rivals. *Wall Street Journal*, April 4:C1.

Serfling, M. A. (2014). CEO age and the riskiness of corporate policies. *Journal of Corporate Finance*, 25:251–273.

Shavell, S. (1979). Risk sharing and incentives in the principal and agent relationship. *Bell Journal of Economics*, 10(1):55–73.

Sherr, I. (2011). Tablet war is an Apple rout. *Wall Street Journal*, August 12:B1.

Shiller, R. J. (2005). *Irrational Exuberance*. Princeton University Press, Princeton, second edition.

Shleifer, A. and Vishny, R. W. (1986). Large shareholders and corporate control. *Journal of Political Economy*, 94(3):461–488.

SHRM Foundation (2010). Rebuilding the talent value proposition for what's next: Executive summaries. *12th Annual SHRM Foundation Thought Leaders Retreat*, October 5–6.

Siegel, J. (2005). Oedipus at the Garden. *New York Magazine*, 38(10):22, 24–27, 114–115.

Smith, G. (1963). Wit and ire mark meeting of I.B.M. *New York Times*, May 1:50.

Sokolyk, T. (2011). The effects of antitakeover provisions on acquisition targets. *Journal of Corporate Finance*, 17(3):612–627.

Somayaji, C. (2004). Cablevision scraps spinoff of satellite business. *Bloomberg.com*, December 21.

Somayaji, C. (2005). Cablevision's Dolan family may buy satellite-TV unit. *Bloomberg.com*, January 20.

Soshnick, S. (2004). Madison Square Garden picks architect for renovation. *Bloomberg*, November 11.

Sotheby's (2013). Form 8-K. Filed on October 4.

Spector, M. and Kung, M. (2012). MGM reaches deal with Icahn. *Wall Street Journal*, August 1:B3.

SPX Corp. (1995a). Form 8-K. Filed on July 5.

SPX Corp. (1995b). SPX Corporation passes $1 billion revenue mark. February 17. Press release.

SPX Corp. (1995c). SPX Corporation selects John B. Blystone as chairman, president and chief executive officer. November 30. Press release.

SPX Corp. (1996a). Form 10-K405 for the period ended December 31, 1995. Filed on March 27.

SPX Corp. (1996b). SPX Corporation to sell Sealed Power Division. August 29. Press release.

SPX Corp. (1998a). Form 8-K. Filed on October 9.

SPX Corp. (1998b). Form S-4. Filed on August 7.

SPX Corp. (1999). Form 8-K. Filed on January 6.

SPX Corp. (2001a). Form 8-K. Filed on June 7.

SPX Corp. (2001b). Form 8-K. Filed on March 12.

SPX Corp. (2002a). Howard D. Wynn named president SPX Valves & Controls. November 4. Press release.

SPX Corp. (2002b). SPX board of directors amends Blystone contract. July 8. Press release.

SPX Corp. (2002c). SPX Corporation acquires Vance International. October 15. Press release.

SPX Corp. (2003a). Form 10-K for the period ended December 31, 2002. Filed on March 17.

SPX Corp. (2003b). Form 8-K. Filed on October 28.

SPX Corp. (2003c). SPX Corporation and Microsoft reach settlement in patent infringement suit. December 24. Press release.

SPX Corp. (2003d). SPX updates 2003 free cash flow target. December 12. Press release.

SPX Corp. (2004a). Form 10-K for the period ended December 31, 2003. Filed on February 26.

SPX Corp. (2004b). Form 8-K. Filed on February 27.

SPX Corp. (2004c). Form 8-K. Filed on January 20.

SPX Corp. (2004d). Form 8-K. Filed on December 9.

SPX Corp. (2004e). Form DEF 14A. Filed on March 17.

SPX Corp. (2004f). SPX chairman adopts 10b5-1 plan. January 2. Press release.

Squires, P. (2008). Steve Case searches for another iconic brand. *Virginia Business*, June 1.

St. Louis Post-Dispatch (2009). A-B executives: Where are they now? *St. Louis Post-Dispatch*, November 15:A9.

St. Petersburg Times (1996). Glazer's Houlihan's deal called off. *St. Petersburg Times*, October 6:1E.

Stamborski, A. (1999). A-B replaces international division chief with Stokes. *St. Louis Post-Dispatch*, November 30:C6.

Stamborski, A. (2000). Busch III yields brewery operations to Stokes; Busch IV is promoted. *St. Louis Post-Dispatch*, July 29:1.

Standard Pacific Corp. (2008). Form 8-K. Filed on March 26.

Stange, J. (2000). An almost-free getaway at Grant's Farm. *Associated Press Newswires*, September 2.

Stannard, T. and Guthrie, G. (2013). Easy money: Managerial power and the option backdating game revisited. Working paper, Victoria University of Wellington.

Starboard Value LP (2015). Letter to Marissa A. Mayer, President and CEO, Yahoo! Inc. March 9.

Starbucks Corp. (2015a). Form 8-K. Filed on March 23.

Starbucks Corp. (2015b). Form DEF 14A. Filed on January 23.

State of California (2006). Report of the Office of the Attorney General's investigation of the J. Paul Getty Trust. October 2. Office of the Attorney General.

State Street Corp. (2007). Form 13F-HR for the period ended December 31, 2006. Filed on February 14.

Stein, J. C. (1989). Efficient capital markets, inefficient firms: A model of myopic corporate behavior. *Quarterly Journal of Economics*, 104(4):655–669.

Steinhauer, J. (2004). Seeking ideas, Garden plans a renovation. *New York Times*, June 18:B1.

Stewart, J. B. (2005). *DisneyWar*. Simon & Schuster, New York.

Stocken, P. C. (2000). Credibility of voluntary disclosure. *RAND Journal of Economics*, 31(2):359–374.

Stone, B. and Helft, M. (2008). Yahoo chief says he was open to deal. *New York Times*, May 6:1.

Strauss, G. (2003). "Queen of the corporate jungle" stalks annual meetings. *USA Today*, April 28:B.04.

Strebulaev, I. A. and Yang, B. (2013). The mystery of zero-leverage firms. *Journal of Financial Economics*, 109(1):1–23.

Strine, L. E., Hamermesh, L. A., Balotti, R. F., and Gorris, J. (2010). Loyalty's core demand: The defining role of good faith in corporation law. *Georgetown Law Journal*, 98(3):629–696.

Stross, R. E. (1998). How Yahoo! won the search wars. *Fortune*, 137(4):148–154.

Stulz, R. M. (1990). Managerial discretion and optimal financing policies. *Journal of Financial Economics*, 26(1):3–27.

Supreme Court, New York County (2011). Carl C. Icahn, Plaintiffs v. Lions Gate Entertainment Corp., Defendants: Decision. *651076/2010*.

Supreme Court of Delaware (1991). Kahn v. Sullivan: Opinion. *594 A.2d 48*.

Supreme Court of Delaware (2006). In Re The Walt Disney Company Derivative Litigation. *Civil Action No. 15452*.

Tam, P.-W. (2000a). As Christmas approaches, parts shortages plague electronics makers. *Wall Street Journal*, October 10:B1.

Tam, P.-W. (2000b). Palm earnings beat expectations as revenue more than doubles. *Wall Street Journal*, September 26:B6.

Tam, P.-W. (2000c). Palm's sales miss upside hopes and stock falls 14% after hours. *Wall Street Journal*, December 21:B9.

Tam, P.-W. (2001a). Palm agrees to buy Extended Systems to widen its reach. *Wall Street Journal*, March 7:B5.

Tam, P.-W. (2001b). Palm's CEO quits amid slowing sales, mounting losses. *Wall Street Journal*, November 9:B3.

Tam, P.-W. (2001c). Palm's fortunes take a tumble, pressuring CEO. *Wall Street Journal*, June 4:B1.

Tam, P.-W. (2001d). Pilot error: How Palm tumbled from star of tech to target of Microsoft. *Wall Street Journal*, September 7:A1.

Target Corp. (2005). Form DEF 14A. Filed on April 11.

Target Corp. (2015a). Form 8-K. Filed on June 12.

Target Corp. (2015b). Form DEF 14A. Filed on April 27.

Taylor, D. (2010a). Rebellion whips up Old Trafford but Ferguson opts out. *Guardian*, January 18:7.

Taylor, L. A. (2010b). Why are CEOs rarely fired? Evidence from structural estimation. *Journal of Finance*, 65(6):2051–2087.

Team Marketing Report (1994). Average NFL ticket prices. *Team Marketing Report*, September.

Team Marketing Report (1998). Average NFL ticket prices. *Team Marketing Report*, September.

Temes, J. (1990). Nizer at 88, still nimble: Firm he founded in stellar comeback. *Crain's New York Business*, 6(17):1.

Temple-Inland Inc. (2005). Form DEF 14A. Filed on March 25.

Tempur Sealy International, Inc (2015). Form 8-K. Filed on May 13.

Terex Corp. (1999). Form DEF 14A. Filed on April 5.

Terhune, C. (2006). Home Depot says it won't report key sales measure. *Wall Street Journal*, May 17:B2.

Terviö, M. (2008). The difference that CEOs make: An assignment model approach. *American Economic Review*, 98(3):642–668.

Tesla Motors Inc. (2010). Form 424B4. Filed on June 29.

Tessera Technologies Inc. (2005). David Nagel joins Tessera Technologies' board of directors. September 7. Press release.

Testerman, J. (1996). Shareholders file suit to block deal by Glazer. *St. Petersburg Times*, May 10:1E.

Testerman, J. (2001). We paid for it: It paid off. *St. Petersburg Times*, January 25:1A.

Thomas, L. (2007). A director decides to override a friendship. *New York Times*, January 5:C1.

Thomson, S. (1990). Beer company needs strong leadership. *St. Louis Post-Dispatch*, February 25:E1.

Thurm, S. (2010). Oracle's Ellison: Pay king. *Wall Street Journal*, July 27:A1.

TIBCO Software Inc. (2014). Form 8-K. Filed on June 24.

Tierney, M. (2005). Buzz off? Not this gadfly. *Atlanta Journal–Constitution*, May 22:F1.

Toll Brothers Inc. (2005). Form DEF 14A. Filed on February 18.

Toll Brothers Inc. (2008). Form DEF 14A. Filed on February 8.

Tomich, J. and McWilliams, J. (2008). If Carlos Brito takes over A-B . . . "He's going to come in swinging". *St. Louis Post-Dispatch*, July 13:A1.

Tremblay, V. J. and Tremblay, C. H. (2005). *The U.S. Brewing Industry: Data and Economic Analysis*. MIT Press, Cambridge, Massachusetts.

Trueman, B. (1994). Analyst forecasts and herding behavior. *Review of Financial Studies*, 7(1):97–124.

Under Armour Inc. (2015). Form 8-K. Filed on June 15.

Uni-Pixel Inc. (2007). Uni-Pixel expands its board of directors with the addition of five new members providing specific relevant expertise to its leadership. March 20. Press release.

United Dominion Industries Ltd. (2000a). Holland retires as CEO of United Dominion. December 22. Press release.

United Dominion Industries Ltd. (2000b). United Dominion terminates sale discussions. December 13. Press release.

United States Court of Appeals for the District of Columbia Circuit (2011). Business Roundtable and Chamber of Commerce of the United States of America, petitioners v. Securities and Exchange Commission, respondent. *No. 10-1305.*

United States District Court, Central District of California (2009). Securities and Exchange Commission vs. Gary A. Ray, complaint. *CV09-3430.*

United States District Court, Western District of North Carolina, Charlotte Division (2004). In Re SPX Corp. securities litigation, consolidated amended complaint. *3:04CV99.*

United States District Court, Western District of North Carolina, Charlotte Division (2007). In Re SPX Corp. securities litigation, order and final judgment. *3:04CV99.*

UnitedHealth Group Inc. (2005). Form DEF 14A. Filed on April 7.

Vanguard Group Inc. (2007). Form 13F-HR for the period ended December 31, 2006. Filed on February 13.

Vardi, N. (2013). The smart money behind "The Hunger Games". *Forbes*, 192(7):48.

Vascellaro, J. E., Karnitschnig, M., and Guth, R. A. (2008). Yahoo, News Corp. in talks amid Microsoft bid. *Wall Street Journal*, February 14:B1.

Venkiteshwaran, V., Iyer, S. R., and Rao, R. P. (2010). Is Carl Icahn good for long-term shareholders? A case study in shareholder activism. *Journal of Applied Corporate Finance*, 22(4):45–57.

Verrier, R. and Eller, C. (2004). A clash of CEO egos gets blame in Disney–Pixar split. *Los Angeles Times*, February 2:A1.

Veverka, M. (2003). PeopleSoft: A wolf in sheep's clothing? *Barron's*, 83(47):T2.

Villalonga, B. and Amit, R. (2006). How do family ownership, control and management affect firm value? *Journal of Financial Economics*, 80(2):385–417.

Villalonga, B. and Amit, R. (2009). How are U.S. family firms controlled? *Review of Financial Studies*, 22(8):3047–3091.

Voyle, S., Newman, C., Wighton, D., and Jones, S. (1998). Opposition mounts to BSkyB–Man Utd deal. *Financial Times*, September 10:1.

Wachtell, Lipton, Rosen & Katz (2011). Petition for rulemaking under Section 13 of the Securities Exchange Act of 1934. March 7. Letter to the Securities and Exchange Commission.

Waldman, P. (2010). Ray Irani making $59 million as Americans deplore executive pay. *Bloomberg*, March 25.

Wall Street Journal (1965). Con Edison's holders approve 2-for-1 split: Firm says '64 net rose. *Wall Street Journal*, January 26:8.

Wall Street Journal (1970). GM easily turns back the first assault from within by liberal reform activists. *Wall Street Journal*, May 25:4.

Wall Street Journal (1995). SPX chief executive quits post at request of company's board. *Wall Street Journal*, July 3:B4.

Wall Street Journal (2013). How the survey was conducted. *Wall Street Journal (Online)*, April 16.

Walt Disney Co. (1993). Los Angeles educator Reveta Franklin Bowers elected to Walt Disney board of directors. April 26. Press release.

Walt Disney Co. (1995). Form DEF 14A. Filed on January 6.

Walt Disney Co. (1997). Form DEF 14A. Filed on January 9.

Walt Disney Co. (2000). Form 10-Q for the period ended June 30, 2000. Filed on August 14.

Walt Disney Co. (2006). Form DEF 14A. Filed on January 11.

Ward, A. (2006a). Home Depot pins hopes on charm. *Financial Times*, July 12:15.

Ward, A. (2006b). Investors feel locked out at Home Depot. *Financial Times*, June 2:28.

Washington Post (1984). Post to remain public, chairman tells meeting. *Washington Post*, May 12.

Weber, H. R. (2007). Home Depot CEO Nardelli abruptly resigns. *Associated Press Newswires*, January 4.

Webster, B. (1987). John Kluge starts over—at the top. *Washington Post*, May 3:H9.

Wedemeyer, D. and Sterngold, J. (1986). Dean Witter executive adds title of chairman. *New York Times*, August 13.

Weir, K. (1999). Edwards nets 41 mln stg from Man Utd deal. *Reuters News*, October 7.

Weisbach, M. S. (1988). Outside directors and CEO turnover. *Journal of Financial Economics*, 20:431–460.

Weisman, R. (2001). Talking commuting: Carl Yankowski chief executive officer, Palm Inc. *Boston Globe*, June 4:C.4.

Weiss, K. R. (2007). Public sand, but a private playground. *Los Angeles Times*, September 2:A1.

Welch, I. (2000). Herding among security analysts. *Journal of Financial Economics*, 58(3):369–396.

Wertheimer, B. M. (1998). The shareholders' appraisal remedy and how courts determine fair value. *Duke Law Journal*, 47(4):613–712.

Westbrook, J. (2007). SEC's Cox wants "plain English" in pay disclosures. *Washington Post*, March 9:D3.

White, L. J. (2010). Markets: The credit rating agencies. *Journal of Economic Perspectives*, 24(2):211–226.

Wiener, S. (1986). Sears chooses Purcell as head of Dean Witter. *Wall Street Journal*, August 13.

Wiersema, M. F. and Zhang, Y. (2011). CEO dismissal: The role of investment analysts. *Strategic Management Journal*, 32(11):1161–1182.

Wiggins, J. (2009). AB InBev to speed asset sales to cut debt. *Financial Times*, March 6:14.

Wilde, O. (1895). The importance of being earnest: A trivial comedy for serious people.

Williams, J. D. (1984a). Carl Icahn testifies on charges stemming from 1980 stock sale. *Wall Street Journal*, March 15:1.

Williams, W. (1984b). The uneasy peace at Occidental. *New York Times*, September 9:A1.

Wilmington Morning Star (1980). Companies complain of harrassment. *Wilmington Morning Star*, February 16:4–A.

Winkley, B. and Fatsis, S. (2004). Soccer club gets buyout approach from NFL owner. *Wall Street Journal*, October 5:A18.

Wipro Ltd (2012). Wipro Limited appoints Vyomesh Joshi to its board. October 1. Press release.

Wong, M. (2001). Palm CEO Carl Yankowski resigns. *Associated Press Newswires*, November 9.

Worden, N. (2010a). Lions Gate, MGM hold deal talks. *Wall Street Journal*, June 25:B5.

Worden, N. (2010b). Lions Gate moves to thwart Icahn. *Wall Street Journal*, July 22:B10.

Worthen, B. and Sherr, I. (2011). H-P girds for iPad battle. *Wall Street Journal*, July 1:B1.

Wruck, E. G. and Wruck, K. H. (2002). Restructuring top management: Evidence from corporate spinoffs. *Journal of Labor Economics*, 20(S2):S176–S218.

Xia, H. (2014). Can investor-paid credit rating agencies improve the information quality of issuer-paid rating agencies? *Journal of Financial Economics*, 111(2):450–468.

Yahoo Inc. (1995). Yahoo, the popular guide to the Internet, obtains financing from Sequoia Capital and celebrates its one-year anniversary at Internet World; Founders plan to run Yahoo Inc. full time—Yahoo will stay free for users. April 11. Press release.

Yahoo Inc. (2007a). Form 8-K. Filed on June 18.

Yahoo Inc. (2007b). Q2 2007 Yahoo, Inc. earnings conference call. *FD (Fair Disclosure) Wire*, July 17.

Yahoo Inc. (2007c). Q3 2007 Yahoo, Inc. earnings conference call. *FD (Fair Disclosure) Wire*, October 16.

Yahoo Inc. (2008a). Form 10-K for the period ended December 31, 2007. Filed on February 27.

Yahoo Inc. (2008b). Form 8-K. Filed on February 19.

Yahoo Inc. (2008c). Form DEFC14A. Filed on June 9.

Yahoo Inc. (2008d). Yahoo! board of directors says Microsoft's proposal substantially undervalues Yahoo! February 12. Press release.

Yang, J. (1997). Living the cyberlife: Turn on, type in and drop out. *Forbes ASAP*, 160:50–51.

Yang, J. (2007). Where does Yahoo! head next? October 16. Yahoo! Yodel blog post.

Yarrow, G. K. (1985). Shareholder protection, compulsory acquisition and the efficiency of the takeover process. *Journal of Industrial Economics*, 34(1):3–16.

Yermack, D. (1996). Higher market valuation of companies with a small board of directors. *Journal of Financial Economics*, 40:185–211.

Yim, S. (2013). The acquisitiveness of youth: CEO age and acquisition behavior. *Journal of Financial Economics*, 108(1):250–273.

Younglai, R. (2009). US SEC to firms: Cut the mind numbing disclosures. *Reuters News*, November 5.

Zapata Corp. (1995). Form 8-K. Filed on November 21.

Zapata Corp. (1996a). Form 10-K405 for the period ended September 30, 1996. Filed on December 30.

Zapata Corp. (1996b). Form S-4. Filed on June 25.

Zapata Corp. (1999). Form 10-Q for the period ended June 30, 1999. Filed on August 16.

Zeidler, S. (2010a). Disney Miramax deadline delayed, parties mull bids. *Reuters News*, March 31.

Zeidler, S. (2010b). Icahn says Lions Gate win "virtually impossible". *Reuters News*, December 14.

Zeidler, S. (2010c). Lions Gate, Weinsteins eye Disney's Miramax: Sources. *Reuters News*, February 8.

Zimmerman, A. (2008). Home Depot learns to go local. *Wall Street Journal*, October 7:B1.

Zimmerman, A. (2009). Home Depot shutters Expo. *Wall Street Journal*, January 27:B3.

Zimmerman, A. and Lublin, J. S. (2007a). Home Depot bows to Whitworth again. *Wall Street Journal*, February 13:A3.

Zimmerman, A. and Lublin, J. S. (2007b). Home Depot directors to visit activist investor. *Wall Street Journal*, January 20:A3.

Zurawik, D. (1991). "Chernobyl" fails to enlighten. *Baltimore Sun*, April 22:1D.

Index